ASSEMBLY LANGUAGE FOR THE APPLESOFT PROGRAMMER

C. W. FINLEY, JR.,
Chemistry Department

and

ROY E. MYERS
Mathematics Department

The Pennsylvania State University
New Kensington Campus

ADDISON-WESLEY PUBLISHING COMPANY

Reading, Massachusetts • Menlo Park, California
Don Mills, Ontario • Wokingham, England • Amsterdam
Sydney • Singapore • Tokyo • Mexico City • Bogota
Santiago • San Juan

Many of the designations used by manufacturers and sellers to distinguish their products are claimed as trademarks. Where these designations appear in the book and the authors are aware of a trademark claim, the designations have been printed with initial capital letters—for example, Applesoft or Mini assembler.

Appendix E reprinted from the *Apple II Reference Manual* with permission from Apple Computer Inc.

Library of Congress Cataloging in Publication Data

Finley, Clarence W.
Assembly language for the Applesoft programmer.

Includes index.
1. Assembler language (Computer program language)
I. Myers, Roy E. II. Title.
QA76.73.A8F56 1984 001.64'24 84-16816
ISBN 0-201-05209-1

ABCDEFGHIJ-HA-8987654
First printing, December 1984

PREFACE

Applesoft BASIC is a good programming language. It is versatile and easy to learn. Its power and simplicity have made it (and the Apple II) extremely popular with both amateur and professional computer users.

While some might argue that BASIC is not a "state of the art" language, most Applesoft programmers find it quite satisfactory. The primary limitation is speed: when manipulating large collections of data or when working with high resolution graphics, Applesoft may be too slow for comfort. Tone routines and music generating programs require rapid access of the Apple speaker; something that is not really possible with Applesoft. Similarly, communication with external devices (printers, disk drives, etc.) cannot be handled by BASIC programs.

In those instances in which Applesoft falls short, users can turn to machine language subroutines. Many are already in the Apple, accessible through a CALL. Many others have been published in computer magazines. The programmer who is familiar with assembly language can access these routines, modify them to suit individual preferences, or develop new machine language routines.

It is the purpose of this book to introduce the Applesoft programmer to assembly language programming. We assume familiarity with Applesoft and focus on the means of developing machine language routines that can be accessed from Applesoft, although such routines can certainly be linked and used independently. Each topic is introduced in a sufficiently elementary fashion to meet the needs of the novice. The pace is necessarily rapid, as techniques are presented that should be of value to the more sophisticated reader.

In the process of learning assembly language programming, it is necessary to become familiar with the inner workings of the computer. As a consequence, assembly language programmers typically become much better Applesoft programmers because a deeper understanding of the computer is developed and an appreciation for the limits of Applesoft is acquired.

We prefer to introduce topics through example programs, and do so when we can. Often, however, a meaningful demonstration of a new command or concept cannot be given in a brief program. In most of these cases, reference is made to program examples that appear elsewhere in the book. Each of the later chapters develops a sequence of example programs that leads to a significant application program.

As you increase in proficiency you may see ways of improving the example programs. We hope that this will be the case. We have tried to make the examples readable and reasonably clear. As a consequence, some may not be quite as efficient or versatile as possible. Our guiding principles in developing examples have been:

1. Make it work.
2. Make it clear.
3. Make it run as fast as possible.

When 2 and 3 were in conflict, we chose to have 2 dominate.

As you read through this book, remember that assembly language programming is not a spectator sport. You must participate if you are to learn. Try the examples. Modify them. Develop similar programs. Experiment!

CONTENTS

SECTION

I

QUICK AND EASY

CHAPTER 1

INTRODUCTION

Before starting to write machine language programs, we will look at one of the many machine language programs that already reside in the computer. To do so, from Applesoft BASIC, type CALL -151 and press RETURN. The familiar prompt symbol] will be replaced with the symbol *. You have entered the "Monitor."

The Monitor is itself a machine language program that is present in every Apple II. There are three Monitors corresponding to different versions of the Apple, but for the purposes of this book the differences are transparent. That is to say, you should not notice any difference between the Monitor in your machine and what we mean by the "Monitor." Apple Computer Inc. has been very careful to make the Apple IIe Monitor perfectly compatible with the Apple II PLUS Monitor. The differences between these Monitors and the older version are well documented in your *Apple Reference Manual.* In each case the Monitor is a supervisory program, which oversees the operation of all programs.

We are able to access the Monitor subroutines from programs written in other languages. You may have done this in an Applesoft program (have you ever used CALL -936 ?). The CALL -151 used above was accessing a Monitor subroutine.

LOOKING AT A MACHINE LANGUAGE PROGRAM

We can also use Monitor commands directly, without the intervention of Applesoft commands. That is what we will do now. Type FBE2.FBEF and press RETURN. The following is what you should see on your screen.

```
*FBE2.FBEF
FBE2- A0 C0 A9 0C 20 A8
FBE8- FC AD 30 C0 88 D0 F5 60*
```

The screen display is a "memory dump" of a portion of the Apple memory. It shows the numbers, in hexadecimal ($) notation, that are stored in memory locations $FBE2 through $FBEF. The $ sign preceding FBE2 (or FBEF) means that this is the hexadecimal (base sixteen) representation of a number. All numbers in this book that have a $ preceding them are hexadecimal ($) numbers. If you are not familiar with base sixteen representations, help is available in Appendix B.

In this case the numbers (A0 C0 A9, etc.) are the machine language instructions (machine codes) that provide the "bell" for the Apple. It is a part of the Monitor. If you use the command PRINT CHR$(7) you are accessing this machine language program. You are also using it if you press CONTROL-G. Apple syntax and error messages are accompanied by a "beep." Again, this program is used.

To run this program directly, type FBE2G and press RETURN. The "bell" should sound. To use the program from Applesoft, first return to Applesoft. Press CONTROL-C then RETURN; or press CONTROL-RESET; or type 3D0G and press return. (The process you use depends on which Monitor you have. Try one, then another, until one of them returns you to Applesoft.)

From Applesoft BASIC, type CALL 64482 ($FBE2 → 15*4096 + 11*256 + 14*16 + 2*1 → 64482). After the CALL 64482 you will be running the machine language program that sounds the "beep."

Return to the Monitor (type CALL -151 and press RETURN). (CALL -151 runs another machine language Monitor program, located at 65536 − 151 = 65385 [decimal], or $FF69 [$FF69 → 15*4096 + 15*256 + 6*16 + 9*1 → 65385]. This program turns off Applesoft and puts you in direct control of the

Monitor.) Again type FBE2.FBEF (note that these are hexadecimal numbers, but the Apple Monitor does not need the $) and press RETURN to get the memory dump shown above.

While the numbers contained in memory locations $FBE2 through $FBEF are the machine language instructions for the "bell," and are easily recognized as such by the 6502 computer, the codes are not very meaningful to us. To be able to read the program it is necessary to translate the code into a form that is easier to understand. Fortunately, the Apple Monitor will do a lot of the work for us. Type FBE2L (no $, because you are using the Monitor) and press RETURN.

The screen display shows the same information as our earlier memory dump, along with some additional information. The first seven lines of this listing are shown in Program 1.1.

PROGRAM 1.1 The Apple bell

```
Loc.      M. C.        A. L.
FBE2-  A0  C0          LDY  #$C0
FBE4-  A9  0C          LDA  #$0C
FBE6-  20  A8  FC      JSR  $FCA8
FBE9-  AD  30  C0      LDA  $C030
FBEC-  88              DEY
FBED-  D0  F5          BNE  $FBE4
FBEF-  60              RTS#
```

The left column (underneath the heading Loc.) contains memory addresses (Locations) in the range from $FBE2 to $FBEF. The middle part of the display (underneath the heading M. C.) contains the hexadecimal numbers we obtained in the earlier memory dump, and is the Machine Code "bell" program. At the right (underneath the heading A. L.) is an interpretation of the hexadecimal code as "Assembly Language" instructions. (The term "assembly language" will be more fully defined in Chapter 2.) While the hexadecimal memory dump may not be very intelligible to us, our goal is to understand the assembly language instructions, and to develop skill in writing programs in assembly language.

The assembly language instructions are not actually executed by the computer. The hexadecimal codes in the column labeled M. C. in Program 1.1 represent the machine language instructions that are an intelligible program (to the 6502 microprocessor) and can be executed. The assembly language instructions (mnemonics) are an attempt to represent the machine language instructions in a form that is more readable by programmers.

We will postpone further discussion of the "bell" program until Chapter 2. It uses more instructions than we want to consider at this time.

A Graphic Example

We will now use the Monitor to enter a machine language program. First enter the Monitor (CALL -151), then type

```
300:A9 20 85 E6 A9 7F 85 1C 20 F6 F3 8D 57
    C0 8D 50 C0 20 1B FD 8D 51 C0 60
```

and press RETURN.

We have just entered a machine language program beginning at memory location $300. To be certain you were successful, type 300.317 (no $) and press RETURN. You should get the memory dump shown below.

```
300- A9 20 85 E6 A9 7F 85 1C
308- 20 F6 F3 8D 57 C0 8D 50
310- C0 20 1B FD 8D 51 C0 60
```

To see what the program does, execute it. Type 300G and press RETURN.

The program should clear high-resolution graphics page 1 to white, then display it. But that's not all. As you look at the white graphics screen, considering that it would be convenient to return to the text screen, the program is waiting for you to press a key. When you do, the text page will be displayed, and the program will end.

Now let's look more carefully at this program. Type 300L and press RETURN. The screen will fill with a listing. The first ten lines are the program we entered, and are shown in Program 1.2.

PROGRAM 1.2

```
Loc.    M. C.       A. L.
300-  A9 20       LDA #$20
302-  85 E6       STA $E6
304-  A9 7F       LDA #$7F
306-  85 1C       STA $1C
308-  20 F6 F3    JSR $F3F6
30B-  8D 57 C0    STA $C057
30E-  8D 50 C0    STA $C050
311-  20 1B FD    JSR $FD1B
314-  8D 51 C0    STA $C051
317-  60          RTS
```

The numbers along the left side of Program 1.2 do not appear on your screen.. We will use them as references as we discuss the program. In our discussion we will be studying the right column, which contains the assembly language instructions.

Line 1: `LDA #$20`

This can be read as "LoaD the Accumulator with the hexadecimal number 20." The accumulator (or A-register) is a register in the 6502 computer. It is a data storage location, similar to a memory location. We will be using the accumulator for many purposes. At present it is being used for temporary data storage. The # symbol means that we are going to load the accumulator with the NUMBER that follows. The $ has its usual meaning: The number that follows is in hexadecimal notation. After this command is executed the accumulator will contain the number $20 (2*16 + 0*1 → 32). The previous contents of the accumulator are LOST.

Line 2: `STA $E6`

This is read as "STore the Accumulator in location $E6." Since we know the accumulator had the number $20 in it, we can now be sure that location $E6 (14*16 + 6*1 → 230) contains the number $20. The contents of the accumulator are not changed. It still contains $20. Lines 1 and 2 in combination have the effect of the Applesoft statement POKE 230,32 (230 → $E6; 32 → $20).

Line 3: `LDA #$7F`

We now change the contents of the accumulator to $7F (7*16 + 15*1 → 127). Again the accumulator is being used for temporary storage.

Line 4: `STA $1C`

The contents of the accumulator are placed in memory location $1C (1*16 + 12*1 → 28). Lines 3 and 4 have the effect of POKE 28, 127.

Line 5: `JSR $F3F6`

Read this as "Jump to the SubRoutine that begins at memory location $F3F6." This program line transfers control to another machine language program, a subroutine that begins at $F3F6. The command is very much like the GOSUB available in Applesoft. When the subroutine has done its deed it will return control to Program 1.2, which will continue with the command of line 6.

The subroutine at $F3F6 is available as CALL 62454 ($15*4096 + 3*256 + 15*16 + 6*1 \rightarrow 62454$). It determines which high-resolution graphics screen should be used for plotting, and which HCOLOR has been most recently used for plotting. It then clears the graphics screen, using the identified HCOLOR to paint the entire screen.

Applesoft uses memory location $E6 (decimal 230) to remember which Hi-Res screen is being used. When location $E6 contains a $20 the plotting screen is page 1; when location $E6 contains a $40 the plotting screen is page 2. Since we have arranged for location $E6 to contain $20, the subroutine at $F3F6 will clear page 1 of graphics.

Applesoft uses memory location $1C to remember which HCOLOR should be used for plotting. The code for HCOLOR = 3 is $7F (decimal 127); so lines 4 and 5 assure us that the graphics screen will be cleared to HCOLOR = 3 (white) by the subroutine of $F3F6.

For more information on graphics commands and locations, see Chapters 10, 11, 12.

Line 6: `STA $C057`

While this appears to store the contents of the accumulator in location $C057, the effect is very different. Location $C057 is a "soft switch." Any attempt to save information at this location will result in "toggling" the switch. There are eight soft switches in the Apple (discussed in Chapters 10 and 11; summarized in Table 11.1). The effect of this one is to set the graphics display to hi-res graphics, rather than lo-res graphics. The soft switch does not cause a graphics page to be displayed; that is done by the command of line 7.

Line 7: `STA $C050`

This command does not actually store the contents of the accumulator in memory location $C050. $C050 is another soft switch. Toggling this switch causes the screen display to change from text to graphics (again, refer to Chapters 10 and 11 for more information on soft switches).

Line 8: `JSR $FD1B`

This command transfers control to a machine language subroutine that begins at memory location $FD1B. This subroutine is part of the Monitor. The subroutine behaves somewhat like the GET command of Applesoft. Its function is to wait until a key is pressed, load the keycode into the accumulator, then return from the subroutine. In this case, we are not interested in knowing which key has been pressed. We use the keypress simply as a signal to continue with the execution of the next line of the program.

Line 9: `STA $C051`

As in lines 6 and 7, we are toggling another soft switch. It causes the screen display to be taken from text rather than graphics.

Line 10: `RTS`

Read this as ReTurn from Subroutine. Remember, the Monitor is a machine language program that controls the execution of all other programs. When we run the program listed above by typing 300G, we have essentially caused the Monitor to execute a JSR $300. The Monitor passes control to our program (in effect a subroutine). When our program executes RTS, control is returned to the Monitor. If we execute our program from Applesoft, using CALL 768, then the RTS will cause a return to Applesoft. In general, RTS causes a return of control to the program (or language) that called the subroutine.

NOTES AND SUGGESTIONS

1. Try some modifications of the program given above. Instead of clearing the high-res screen to white, clear it to HCOLOR = 2. In order to do this, we must store the proper color code in memory location $1C. Since the code for HCOLOR = 2 is $55 (5*16 + 5*1 → 85), we will change line 3 of the program to read

```
LDA #$55
```

If the program has been entered as above, we can make this change by typing (from the Monitor)

```
305:55
```

Then type 300L to list the program. It should look like the listing shown in Program 1.3 (below), except that line 3 should now read

```
304-  A9 55        LDA #$55
```

Type 300G to run the program.

Other color codes can be used. The color codes used for the standard HCOLORs are given in Table 1.1.

TABLE 1.1 COLOR Codes

	COLOR CODE	
HCOLOR	*HEX*	*DEC*
0	$00	0
1	$2A	42
2	$55	85
3	$7F	127
4	$80	128
5	$AA	170
6	$D5	213
7	$FF	255

You might also try color codes that are not associated with the standard HCOLORs. They give interesting results.

2. The program given above can be used from within an Applesoft program (use the command CALL 768). However, it is at present rather useless since it performs no valuable function. We could turn it into an alternate to the HGR command by modifying it to read as follows:

PROGRAM 1.3

Memory Locations	Machine Codes	Assembler Instructions	Remarks
300–	A9 20	LDA #$20	IDENTIFY PAGE 1
302–	85 E6	STA $E6	OF GRAPHICS
304–	A9 7F	LDA #$7F	CHOOSE COLOR

```
306-      85 1C       STA $1C      FOR BACKGROUND
308-      20 F6 F3    JSR $F3F6    CLEAR SCREEN TO COLOR CHOSEN
30B-      8D 54 C0    STA $C054    DISPLAY PAGE 1
30E-      8D 57 C0    STA $C057    SET HIGH RES MODE
311-      8d 53 C0    STA $C053    SET MIXED TEXT-GRAPHICS MODE
314-      8D 50 C0    STA $C050    DISPLAY GRAPHICS
317-      60          RTS          RETURN FROM SUBROUTINE
```

Enter this program from the Monitor by typing

```
300:A9 20 85 E6 A9 7F 85 1C 20 F6 F3 8D 54 C0 8D 57 C0 8D 53
    C0 8D 50 C0 60
```

Then press RETURN. To check your typing, list the program by typing 300L. Compare with the listing shown above.

Now try the program. Return to Applesoft and call the subroutine (CALL 768). If you would prefer to clear the screen to a color other than white, change line 3 of the program to provide a different color code.

3. If you want to save the above program to disk, use the BSAVE command. The program begins at $300 and is $18 bytes long. We can save it with

```
BSAVE PROGRAM,A$300,L$18
```

The program can then be used within an Applesoft program by providing the line

```
1  PRINT CHR$(4);"BLOAD PROGRAM"
```

Any later program line can access this subroutine by using CALL 768.

4. Try another modification. Change the program of Program 1.3 so that the "bell" will sound just before the program waits for a keypress (line 8). The assembly language instruction JSR $FBE2 will call the bell subroutine. Add the code 20 E2 FB before the code for line 8 of the program.

Some Advice

So far we have entered machine language programs by typing (from the Monitor) the hexadecimal codes of the program operations. This procedure is satisfactory only for very short and simple programs. It is not a method we can endorse for anyone wishing to learn how to write machine language programs.

THE MINIASSEMBLER

If you do not wish to purchase an assembler, an alternative is available in most Apples. If you have an Apple that has Integer Applesoft available, or if you have a DOS 3.3 System Master diskette, you already have an assembler: the Apple Miniassembler. Appendix A explains how you can gain access to this assembler. The Miniassembler is better than no assembler at all, but it is very limited. The Miniassembler requires that you do most of the bookkeeping related to your program. It does not permit you to define variables, provide labels, edit, or insert remarks. In fact, the Miniassembler does not produce a source file, but provides line-by-line assembly of the source program as you type it. While these limitations make it a very poor substitute for a fully implemented assembler, there are times when it can be acceptable (if you are broke!).

The Miniassembler is useful for entering short programs, or for editing, testing, and debugging programs. In general, it is useful in those cases in which a small amount of program code is to be entered, tested, and modified again on an interactive basis.

CHAPTER 2

ELEMENTARY PROGRAMMING

The purpose of this chapter is to begin the description of: 1) "assembly language," (2) "machine language," and (3) the function of an "assembler." These descriptions will not be nearly complete until after Chapter 6. We also intend to provide a bit of entertainment by investigating the solution to a word game.

A palindrome is a word, sentence, or verse that reads the same backward as it does forward. One of the more well known palindromes is the one attributed to Napoleon regarding his imprisonment on the island of Elba.

"ABLE WAS I ERE I SAW ELBA"

If you are not as careful with punctuation marks nor embedded blanks as was Napoleon, you will accept another well known palindrome, concerning Ferdinand de Lesseps.

"A MAN, A PLAN, A CANAL, PANAMA"

Some other possibilities you may wish to consider while doing this part of the chapter are:

1. PULL UP IF I PULL UP
2. NAME NO ONE MAN
3. MADAM, I'M ADAM
4. WAS IT ELIOT'S TOILET I SAW
5. NO EVIL RED RUM MURDER LIVES ON
6. SUMS ARE NOT SET AS A TEST ON ERASMUS

It should be clear that a computer program is not needed to solve the word game proposed above. However, by developing a solution we shall be able to illustrate the development of an assembly language program. The solution is simple enough that we need not spend much time on it, and can focus full attention on the program.

We will use the program for another purpose: to illustrate the use of an assembler. You will see that an assembler is a valuable tool in the development of the program, and that it will also provide a documented version of the program that is relatively easy to read and understand. This can be valuable to another person who tries to use your program, and to you as you develop later modifications.

A SOLUTION

Our problem is this: we want to print a string, then print it backwards to see whether the two agree. The following BASIC program will do the job.

PROGRAM 2.1

```
10  REM  PROGRAM 2.1
20  TEXT : HOME
30  INPUT "ENTER STRING "; ST$
40  HOME
50  PRINT ST$
60  FOR I =  LEN (ST$) TO 1 STEP - 1
70  PRINT  MID$ (ST$,I,1);
80  NEXT I
```

The program prints the string, then its reversed form directly below. As long as the string will fit on a single screen line, it is easy to compare the two in order to see whether the string is a palindrome.

The above program prints the reversed form of a string by reading backwards through the characters of the string. Our objective is to develop a machine language program that will do this. At this time we do not want to be concerned with the way strings are stored and accessed, so we will not model our assembly language program after the Applesoft program above.

Instead of reversing the characters of the stored string, we shall print the string on the text screen, then copy and reverse the contents of the entire screen line. This process requires that we be familiar with the way the Apple II text screen is arranged. What follows is a short description of text screen addressing. See Chapter 10 for a more complete explanation.

The Apple II text screen display is a reflection of the contents of memory locations 1024 through 2047. We can control the text screen display by controlling the contents of these memory locations. For example, the sequence of commands

```
HOME : POKE 1030,193
```

will display a letter "A" in the seventh position of the first text screen line. This is because that screen's position is controlled by memory location 1030, and the ASCII screen code for the letter "A" is 193. An asterisk will be displayed in the same screen position by the command

```
HOME : POKE 1030,170
```

and an underline by

```
HOME : POKE 1030,223
```

(For a complete list of ASCII screen codes, see Table 7 of the *Apple II Reference Manual*, or Tables 2-4 and 2-6 of the *Apple IIe Reference Manual*.)

Although memory locations 1024 through 2047 are used to control the text display, the mapping of these locations is not done in the manner that you might expect. Figure 2.1 gives a memory map for the text screen.

From this figure you can see that the uppermost screen line is controlled by memory locations 1152 through 1191. Note that any screen location can be identified by its corresponding memory location. For example, the tenth posi-

FIGURE 2.1 Text addressing

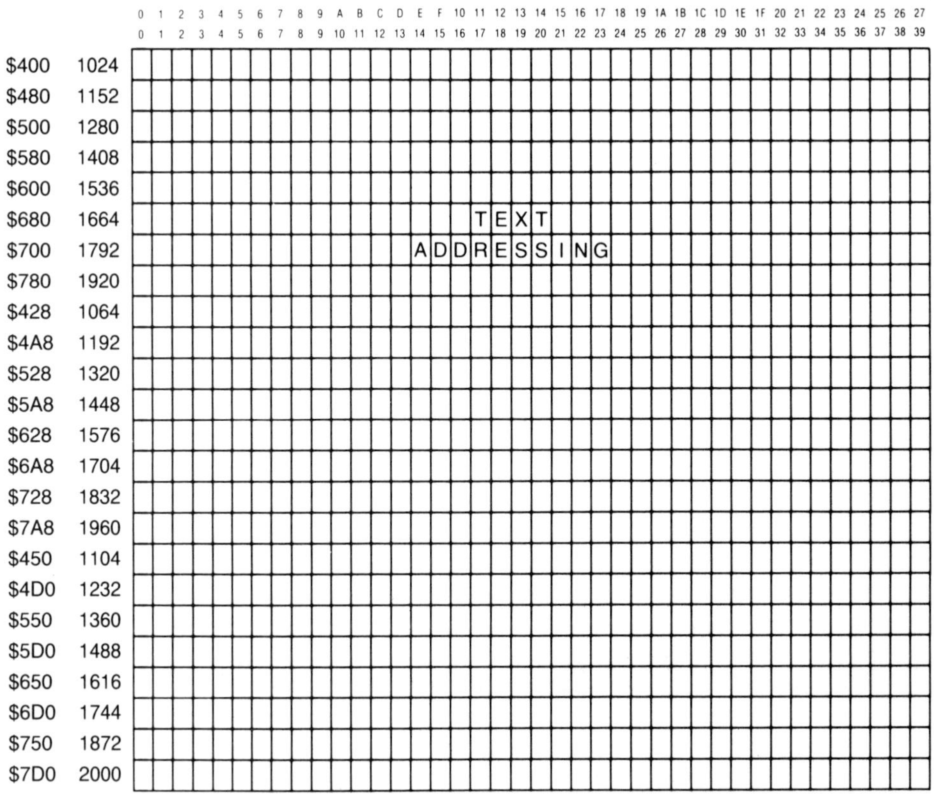

tion of the 7th screen line is associated with memory location 1801, and a "P" will be displayed there by

```
HOME : POKE 1801,208
```

since the ASCII screen code for "P" is 208.

All PRINT statements function by storing appropriate ASCII codes in memory locations that control the screen display. The ASCII screen code for a space is 160. The HOME command clears the screen by storing this value in each TEXT SCREEN memory location.

AN ALTERNATE SOLUTION

The following Applesoft program prints a string on the top line of the text screen; it is then copied in reverse form on the second screen line.

PROGRAM 2.2

```
10  REM PROGRAM 2.2
20  TEXT : HOME
30  INPUT "ENTER STRING ";ST$
40  HOME
50  PRINT ST$
60  VTAB 20
70  GOSUB 100
80  END
90  REM  * SUBROUTINE *
100 Y = 39
110 X = 0
120 A =  PEEK (1024 + Y)
130  POKE 1152 + X,A
140 X = X + 1
150 Y = Y - 1
160  IF Y = > 0 THEN 120
170  RETURN
```

The above program does not serve as well as we might like, since it reverses an entire screen line. As a result, if only five characters are printed at the left of the first screen line, those five characters will appear in reverse order at the right of the second screen line. That is easily cured (do you see how?), and we will provide a solution later. For now, we shall consider an assembly language program that performs the same function as the subroutine (lines 100 through 170) of Program 2.2.

AN ASSEMBLY LANGUAGE SOLUTION

You may see that Program 2.2 is not as efficient as possible. This is intentional. The subroutine (lines 100 through 170) was written so that it could be translated, line-by-line, to a corresponding assembly language program. Table 2.1 shows the two programs. We shall discuss each line in detail.

TABLE 2.1 Program comparison

Applesoft Program	*Assembly Language Program*
110 Y = 39	300- A0 27 LDY #$27
120 X = 0	302- A2 00 LDX #$00
130 A = PEEK (1024 + Y)	304- B9 00 04 LDA $0400,Y
140 POKE 1152 + X,A	307- 9D 80 04 STA $0480,Y
150 X = X + 1	30A- E8 INX
160 Y = Y - 1	30B- 88 DEY
170 IF Y => 0 THEN 130	30C- 10 F6 BPL $0304
180 RETURN	30E- 60 RTS

Consider the first line in Table 2.1.

```
110 Y = 39                    |  300- A0 27      LDY #$27
```

The 6502 microprocessor has three registers, called the X-register, the Y-register, and the A-register (Accumulator). (A more nearly complete description of what these registers do is given in Chapter 3.) Each of these registers can hold a single eight-bit number (one byte), and thus can accept numbers between 0 and 255. In the Applesoft program, Y is a real variable, but in this program it takes on only integer values between 0 and 39 so, the Y-register can be used for the same purpose. The assembly language statement LDY #$27 means "LoaD the Y-register with the number whose hexadecimal ($) form is 27." Note that the hexadecimal form $27 represents the number whose decimal form is 39 (2*16 + 7 → 39). (For a review of hexadecimal representation of numbers consult Appendix B.)

The notation to the immediate left of the assembly language statement (300- A0 27) displays the location (300) and the machine language translation (A0 27) of the assembly language statement (LDY #$27). The computer will execute the machine language instruction; the assembly language form is for us to use.

In summary, an "assembler" translates mnemonics (LDY #$27), which are easy for people to read, into "machine language" (A0 27), which is executable by the machine (the 6502). On the other hand, a "disassembler" translates machine language (A0 27) into the mnemonics (LDA #$27) that are easy for us to understand. More about this later, especially in Chapters 3 and 4.

You are not expected to know the codes for the mnemonics. A complete list of the assembler mnemonics and their machine language translations for the 6502 microprocessor is given in Appendix E. More importantly, your assembler will provide the codes when it assembles your program—that is part of its function!

The selection of $300 as the location for the beginning of the machine language instructions is somewhat arbitrary. It was necessary to choose a location that would not be disturbed by the Applesoft program. Other locations could have been used. Chapter 7 discusses the overall memory usage of the Apple II.

Consider the next line of Table 2.1.

```
120 X = 0                    | 302- A2 00      LDX #$00
```

The assembly language program uses the X-register in the manner that the real variable X is used by the Applesoft program. Again, this is possible since X will only take on the integer values between 0 and 39. Since the machine language instructions A0 27 (mnemonics LDY #$27) occupied memory locations $300 and $301, the next machine language instructions (A2 00) are stored in the next available locations ($302 and $303). A2 is the machine code for LDX #, which translates to "LoaD the X-register with the hexadecimal ($) number that immediately follows (00)."

The next line to consider is:

```
130 A = PEEK (1024 + Y)      | 304- B9 00 04  LDA $0400,Y
```

Here we load the A-register (Accumulator) with the contents of the memory location whose address is given as the sum of $0400 (which translates from hex as 0∗4096 + 4∗256 + 0∗16 + 0∗1 → 1024) and the contents of the Y-register. As a result, the Accumulator receives the ASCII screen code of the character stored at the end of the text line 1 (when the Y-register contains $27). Notice that the instruction LDA $0400,Y requires a three-byte machine code (B9 00 04). The address part, 00 04, represents $0400, and is in the standard Low Byte–High Byte (LBHB) form required by the 6502.

```
140 POKE 1152 + X,A          | 307- 9D 80 04  STA $0480,Y
```

Here is another three-byte instruction, which is quite similar to the previous one. This time the contents of the Accumulator are stored in the memory location whose address is the sum of $0480 (0∗4096 + 4∗256 + 8∗16 + 0∗1 → 152) and the contents of the X-register. When the X-register contains a zero the memory location identifies the leftmost position of the second line of the text screen. This entire text screen line is accessible as the X-register contents vary from 0 to $27.

```
150 X = X + 1                | 30A- E8         INX
```

Having copied one character from the first to the second line of the text screen, we now increment the contents of the the X-register so that the next character that is copied will be further to the right. Note that the code for the instruction INX requires a single byte.

```
160 Y =Y - 1                 | 30B-88          DEY
```

This one-byte code decrements the contents of the Y-register so that the character to be copied will be to the left of the previous one. (Note that we are reading the first screen line in a right-to-left manner.) We will read the entire line of text by having the contents of the Y-register vary between $27 and $00.

```
170 IF Y => 0 THEN 130       | 30C- 10 F6      BPL $0304
```

We would like to interpret BPL $0304 as "If the most recent result [of decrementing the Y-register] is positive or zero, then branch to the instruction at memory location $0304." Actually, BPL is often read as "Branch if PLus," or "Branch if Positive." That is all right, but only if you are willing to admit that zero is a positive number. Notice that BPL $0304 has a two-byte representation. Further note that the destination address ($0304) does not appear as part of the code. This instruction is discussed in detail in Chapter 3—for now we shall note that $10 is the code for BPL. The number $F6 (15∗16 + 6∗1 → 246) can also be interpreted as −10 (see Appendix B). With this interpretation, the machine code 10 F6 directs a branch backward ten bytes. If you imagine a pointer aimed at the byte beyond the $F6 (thus pointing at location $030E), and then move the pointer back ten bytes, you will be pointing at location $0304. There is such a pointer, called the Program Counter. It is discussed further in Chapter 3. Thus the BPL functions as a relative branch, identifying the number (positive or negative) of bytes from the current instruction to the next instruction.

Finally we have a ReTurn-from-Subroutine instruction.

```
180 RETURN                   | 30E- 60         RTS
```

If we call this machine language program *from* an Applesoft program, we might do so with CALL 768. The program begins at location \$300 (3*256 + 0*16 + 0*1 → 768). When the RTS instruction is executed, program control is returned to the calling program.

TESTING

Enter the machine language program and test it. For the present, the simplest way to do that may be from the Monitor as follows:

```
CALL -151

*300: AD 27 A2 00 B9 00 04 9D 80 04 E8 88 10 F6 60
```

When the machine code is entered, list it (actually this is a disassembly) to confirm that it looks like this:

```
*300L

300-  A0 27      LDY #$27
302-  A2 00      LDX #$00
304-  B9 00 04   LDA $0400,Y
307-  9D 80 04   STA $0480,Y
30A-  E8         INX
30B-  88         DEY
30C-  10 F6      BPL $0304
30E-  60
```

Correct any errors, then return to Applesoft. You can test the program by entering some characters on the uppermost line of the text screen, then calling the machine language program with CALL 768. The line of text should be copied, in reverse order, onto the second line of text.

To use the machine language program for the palindrome example, try the following.

```
10 TEXT : HOME
20 INPUT "ENTER STRING ";ST$
30 HOME
40 PRINT ST$
50 VTAB 20
60 CALL 768
70 END
```

As mentioned earlier the program has a fault: It does not position the reversed message directly under the original (unless the original was a full forty characters long). We shall correct this situation later. First, we shall consider the merits of using an assembler for writing assembly language programs.

ASSEMBLERS

An assembler is a program that translates assembly language mnemonics, such as

```
LDY #$27
LDX #$00
LDA $0400,Y
  .
  .
  .
```

into machine language (code), such as

```
A0 27
A2 00
B9 00 04
     .
     .
     .
```

Several assemblers are commercially available for use with the Apple II. We have used several, including the S-C Assembler (S-C Software Corp., Box 280300, Dallas, TX 75228), BIG MAC (available from A.P.P.L.E., 21246 68th Ave. S., Kent, WA 98032), and LISA (available from your local software house). We endorse them all. We used the S-C Assembler to write the programs in this book, and the program listings shown in the book are S-C Assembler listings. The programs in the book are written so as to be easily modified for use by any of these assemblers. The modifications are usually no more than changing the S-C directives to the appropriate directives for your assembler. The assembler thus relieves the programmer of the onerous tasks of looking up the codes for assembly language mnemonics, of keeping track of the length of each instruction, and of organizing the machine code in memory.

Most assemblers do not stop at this point. They also permit the programmer to define constants, variables, and labels, and to add comments that make the assembly language program more readable. If we first define the constants WIDTH, ZERO, LINE1, and LINE2 to be $27, $00, $0480 respectively, the program can be rewritten as follows:

```
1000 * EXAMPLE PAL1
1010 WIDTH  .EQ $27
1020 ZERO   .EQ $00
1030 LINE1  .EQ $0400
1040 LINE2  .EQ $0480
1050        .OR $0300
1060 BEGIN  LDY #WIDTH   WIDTH OF SCREEN
1070        LDX #ZERO    INITIALIZE X
1080 LOOP   LDA LINE1,Y  GET CHAR FROM LINE
1009        STA LINE2,X  STORE IT IN LINE 2
1100        INX          INC. LINE2 INDEX
1110        DEY          DEC. LINE1 INDEX
1120        BPL LOOP     CONTINUE ACROSS SCREEN
1130        RTS          DONE; RETURN TO MAIN PGM.
```

A program in a form like that shown above is called source code. Assemblers use varying formats for their source code. We have adopted the form used by the S-C Assembler, but you should find it similar to others.

The first column on the left contains the line numbers. They are used for editing (inserting lines, deleting lines, etc.), but have NOTHING to do with program control or flow. That is, there is no GOTO (line number), nor is there a GOSUB (line number) as there is in Applesoft. Some assemblers do not use line numbers, but provide other means of identifying and editing lines of source code.

The second column contains the labels. They are used to control program flow in a fashion somewhat similar to line numbers in Applesoft.

The third column contains the assembly language instruction mnemonics. The mnemonics were assigned (invented) by the manufacturer of the 6502 and are intended to jog your memory as to the function the 6502 is performing.

The fourth column contains the operand(s) for the instruction. The instruction (when assembled into machine code by the assembler) tells the 6502 what to do with the operand.

The fifth column contains the comments. The S-C Assembler does not require a special character to denote the beginning of a comment. Some assemblers do require that a comment begin with a special character (usually the * or the ;).

The notation used by assemblers also varies. In lines 1010 through 1040, we have defined several constants by using the .EQ directive. A common alternate to .EQ is EQU; your assembler may use this.

Line 1050 of our source code identifies the ORigin of the program. That is the memory location at that the assembler begins to store the machine code for the program. (This code is called the object code.) ORG is often used instead of .OR, and some assemblers have a default destination for the object code if no origin is specified. The S-C Assembler's default origin is $0800. This default causes a CRASH when an Applesoft program is used to CALL machine code that was assembled at $0800. When the Applesoft program is subsequently loaded it is also loaded at $0800, which destroys the machine code. (CRASH AND BURN—probably an on/off cycle will be required. If this happens to you, check the origin of the machine code. Move it to safety.)

Note that the label LOOP was not explicitly defined along with the variables WIDTH, ZERO, LINE1, and LINE2, but was implicitly defined within the program. Other labels can be defined in a similar way, and are convenient ways of identifying locations of subroutines, branch destinations, tables of numbers, exit points, etc.

Your assembler may allow you to keep the use of hexadecimal notation to a minimum, but you will find it difficult to program in assembly language without it. You may be able to specify numbers in decimal form. For example, line 1010 might have been written as

```
1010  WIDTH .EQ 39
```

The presence or absence of the $ is a signal to the assembler that the number that follows is in hexadecimal or decimal form.

Assemblers provide other features as well. We shall point out some of these as we proceed. However, since the features vary with the assembler, we shall not attempt a thorough discussion of such features. Consult the manual for your assembler.

ASSEMBLING THE CODE

The assembly language source code can be stored in a disk file for later use, and the assembler can be directed to assemble the code. The results of assembling the above program should be something like this:

```
                  1000 * EXAMPLE PAL1
0027-             1010 WIDTH  .EQ $27
0000-             1020 ZERO   .EQ $00
```

```
0400-           1030 LINE1   .EQ $0400
0480-           1040 LINE2   .EQ $0480
                1050         .OR $0300
0300- A0 27     1060 BEGIN   LDY #WIDTH    WIDTH OF SCREEN
0302- A2 00     1070         LDX #ZERO     INITIALIZE X
0304- B9 00 04  1080 LOOP    LDA LINE1,Y   GET CHAR FROM LINE 1
0307- 9D 80 04  1090         STA LINE2,X   STORE IT IN LINE 2
030A- E8        1100         INX           INC. LINE2 INDEX
030B- 88        1110         DEY           DEC. LINE1 INDEX
030C- 10 F6     1120         BPL LOOP      CONTINUE ACROSS SCREEN
030E- 60        1130         RTS           DONE; RETURN TO MAIN PGM.

SYMBOL TABLE

0300- BEGIN
0400- LINE1
0480- LINE2
0304- LOOP
0027- WIDTH
0000- ZERO
```

Note that the hexadecimal machine code is listed alongside the assembly language code. It has also been entered into the designated memory locations. The symbol table provided at the end of the source listing shows the identity and location of all labels.

AN IMPROVEMENT

It was pointed out earlier that the palindrome program would be more useful if the reversed string were displayed on the screen directly below the original. We can easily arrange for this: As the characters are copied from the first line of text, they are read from right-to-left. If we avoid copying the blank (space) characters at the right of the line of characters, we can achieve the goal. That is possible by modifying the beginning of the program.

```
                1000 * EXAMPLE PAL2
0028-           1010 WIDTH   .EQ $28
0000-           1020 ZERO    .EQ $00
0400-           1030 LINE1   .EQ $0400
0480-           1040 LINE2   .EQ $0480
                1050         .OR $0300
```

```
0300- A0 28     1060 BEGIN  LDY #WIDTH    WIDTH OF SCREEN
0302- 88        1070 LOOP1  DEY           DEC. LINE1 INDEX
0303- B9 00 04  1080        LDA LINE1,Y   GET CHAR FROM LINE 1
0306- C9 A0     1090        CMP #$A0      IS IT A SPACE?
0308- F0 F8     1100        BEQ LOOP1     IF SO, SKIP IT
030A- A2 00     1110        LDX #ZERO     INIT. X
030C- B9 00 04  1120 LOOP   LDA LINE1,Y   GET CHAR FROM LINE 1
030F- 9D 80 04  1130        STA LINE2,X   STORE IN LINE 2
0312- E8        1140        INX           INC. LINE2 INDEX
0313- 10 F7     1150        BPL LOOP      CONTINUE ACROSS
                                          SCREEN
0315- 60        1160        RTS           DONE; RETURN TO MAIN PGM.

SYMBOL TABLE

0300- BEGIN
0400- LINE1
0480- LINE2
030C- LOOP
0302- LOOP1
0028- WIDTH
0000- ZERO
```

The example presented in this chapter illustrates some similarities between Applesoft programs and assembly language programs. Both use branches, loops, and subroutines, along with simple arithmetic.

You should not expect that assembly language programs can be developed by translating a corresponding Applesoft program. There are occasions when that can be done, but such a process generally leads to inefficient programs. In this example we first wrote the assembly language program, then translated it into Applesoft. The resulting Applesoft program does work, but it is not as efficient as it might have been. Generally, an equivalent assembly language program will have more lines of coding than the Applesoft program, but the assembly language program will run much faster. In fact, in Chapter 13 where searching and sorting are discussed, we are able to show a speed increasing by a factor of 45 over an equivalent Applesoft program. An Applesoft sort requires more than sixteen minutes to run; the equivalent program in assembly language requires less than twenty-two seconds to run! On the other side of the ledger, the Applesoft program is 44 lines long and the equivalent assembly language program is 103 lines long. A trade-off of slightly more than twice as many lines of code for a forty-five times faster execution speed is not bad!

NOTES AND SUGGESTIONS

1. Modify PAL2 so that the reversed string is printed on the third line of the text screen.
2. Modify PAL2 so that the reversed string is compared with the original (it will not be necessary to print the reversed string). Have the program "beep" (see the programs that control the Apple's speaker later in this chapter) if the reversed string differs from the original. Have it end silently if the two agree.

THE SPEAKER

The speaker is one of the nice features built into the Apple II/IIe. If you have encountered it as a "beep" associated with ?SYNTAX ERROR, you may not associate the speaker with fond memories. If so, perhaps the music we develop here will improve its image. The music, however, is incidental to our main purpose, which is to introduce the assembler commands BEQ, BNE, DEC, DEX, INY, JMP, NOP.

The speaker can be accessed through the Applesoft command PEEK(-16336). Each time Applesoft encounters this command, it will make an attempt to read the contents of memory location -16336. This memory location is wired to the speaker, and an attempt to read the contents will result in "tweaking" the speaker. The cardboard cone of the speaker can occupy one of two positions (in or out). Each time the speaker is tweaked, the cone changes position. If the position changes rapidly, the vibration generates sound with a tone controlled by the frequency of the vibration.

We can vibrate the speaker with Applesoft programs like

```
10  X = PEEK(-16336)
20  GOTO 10
```

or with assembly language programs like Program 2.3.

PROGRAM 2.3 Speaker tweaker

```
                1000 * PROGRAM 2.3 SPEAKER TWEAKER
                1010 * TOO FAST TO HEAR
C030-           1020 SPKR   .EQ $C030
                1030        .OR $300
0300- AD 30 C0  1040 TWEAK  LDA SPKR
```

```
0303- 4C 00 03 1050        JMP TWEAK

SYMBOL TABLE

C030- SPKR
0300- TWEAK
```

Program line 1020 identifies the variable SPKR with memory location $C030; line 1030 locates the program at memory location $300. The attempt to read the contents of SPKR, in line 1040, will tweak the speaker, causing it to change positions. The JMP (JuMP) in line 1050 has the effect of a GOTO 1040, tweaking the speaker again. Lines 1040 and 1050 make up a two line infinite loop. To interrupt the loop, press CONTROL-RESET.

You will probably be disappointed if you enter Program 2.3 and run it. This is because of a problem that is rarely, if ever, encountered in Applesoft programs: Program 2.3 runs too fast. Not enough time elapses between successive tweaks. Program 2.4 wastes a little time between successive tweaks, through the use of the NOP (No OPeration) command. While the NOP statements cause no action, they do take a small amount of time. Try some adaptations of Program 2.4 by adding more NOP statements between successive tweaks.

PROGRAM 2.4 Audible tweaker

```
               1000 * PROGRAM 2.4 AUDIBLE TWEAKER
C030-          1010 SPKR   .EQ $C030
               1020        .OR $300
0300- AD 30 C0 1030 TWEAK  LDA SPKR
0303- EA       1040        NOP          DELAY
0304- EA       1050        NOP          BETWEEN
0305- EA       1060        NOP          SUCCESSIVE
0306- EA       1070        NOP          TWEAKS
0307- 4C 00 03 1080        JMP TWEAK

SYMBOL TABLE

C030- SPKR
0300- TWEAK
```

We can generate a wide range of tones by varying the number of NOP statements placed between successive tweaks. This leads to very lengthy and cumbersome programs, however. Since the present intent of the NOP is to waste time, it will be worthwhile seeking a more convenient way of wasting a controlled amount of time. We will return to the Apple's BELL subroutine to find out how to do this. The program was listed in Chapter 1 as Program 1.1. Program 2.5 repeats the subroutine, in commented form, set to run at $300.

PROGRAM 2.5 Apple bell subroutine

```
               1000 * PROGRAM 2.5 APPLE BELL SUBROUTINE
C030-          1010 SPKR   .EQ $C030
FCA8-          1020 WAIT   .EQ $FCA8
               1030        .OR $300
0300- A0 C0    1040 BELL   LDY #$C0     NUMBER OF TWEAKS
0302- A9 0C    1050 BELL2  LDA #$0C     DURATION OF DELAY
0304- 20 A8 FC 1060        JSR WAIT     BETWEEN SUCCESSIVE TWEAKS
0307- AD 30 C0 1070        LDA SPKR
030A- 88       1080        DEY          COUNT NUMBER OF TWEAKS
030B- D0 F5    1090        BNE BELL2    DONE YET?
030D- 60       1100        RTS          DONE

SYMBOL TABLE

0300- BELL
0302- BELL2
C030- SPKR
FCA8- WAIT
```

In Program 2.5, the Y-register is used to control the number of times the speaker is tweaked. In line 1040 it is loaded with the number $C0 (C*16 + 0*1 → 192). Then each time the speaker is tweaked (line 1070) the number contained in the Y-register is decreased by one. This is done by the DEY (DEcrement Y-register) in line 1080.

Program 2.5 uses an assembly language command we have not encountered earlier, BNE. BNE (Branch if most recent result is Not Equal to zero) is a command we have not used previously. In this case it causes the program to cycle back to line 1050 repeatedly until the Y-register is decremented all the way to zero. Then the BNE does not cause a branch, but allows program execution to fall through to line 1100, which ends the subroutine.

Lines 1050 and 1060 provide our sought-for controllable pause between successive tweaks. WAIT is another subroutine built into the Apple II/IIe. It causes a pause for a period of time that is a function of the contents of the A-register.

Suggestion: Modify line 1050 of the above program to control the WAIT subroutine. Run the modified program with the A-register receiving values such as $10, $20, $30, etc. Note the resulting variation in tone.

Notice that while the Y-register controls the number of tweaks, and thus influences the length of time the bell is sounded, the length of the delay in WAIT also affects the duration of the tone. As a result, high pitched notes (enter WAIT with small numbers in the A-register) will not last as long as low tones (enter WAIT with large numbers in the A-register).

To correct this situation, we will develop a TONE subroutine (Program 2.6) with a controllable tone and a controllable tone length. As a first attempt, consider Program 2.6.

PROGRAM 2.6 Variable tone

```
                   1000 * PROGRAM 2.6 VARIABLE TONE
C030-              1010 SPKR    .EQ $C030
                   1020         .OR $300
0300- AD 30 C0     1030 TWEAK   LDA SPKR     TWEAK SPEAKER
0303- A2 FF        1040         LDX #$FF     DELAY BETWEEN TWEAKS
0305- CA           1050 PAUSE   DEX          COUNT DOWN
0306- D0 FD        1060         BNE PAUSE    DONE?
0308- F0 F6        1070         BEQ TWEAK    START OVER
030A- 60           1080         RTS          DONE

SYMBOL TABLE

0305- PAUSE
C030- SPKR
0300- TWEAK
```

By now you should be able to decipher parts of this program by yourself. We will point out the new commands DEX (line 1050) and BEQ (line 1070).

DEX (DEcrement X-register) behaves like DEY. The X-register is used here to control the frequency of tweaks. When the X-register is decremented all the way to zero, line 1060 does not cause a branch back to PAUSE, but allows program control to fall through to line 1070. The BEQ (Branch if most recent result [of decrementing the X-register] is EQual to zero) returns to TWEAK to begin a new cycle.

Program 2.6 establishes an infinite loop. The program (and tone) can be terminated by pressing CONTROL-RESET.

Suggestion: Modify line 1040 in order to obtain different tones.

Controlling Note Length

PROGRAM 2.7

```
                   1000 * PROGRAM 2.7 INTERMEDIATE
                   1010 * NOT AUDIBLE
0006-              1020 COUNTR .EQ $06
C030-              1030 SPKR   .EQ $C030
                   1040        .OR $300
0300- A9 FF        1050        LDA #$FF      INIT COUNTR FOR
0302- 85 06        1060        STA COUNTR    DURATION OF TONE
0304- AD 30 C0     1070 TWEAK  LDA SPKR
0307- A2 20        1080        LDX #$20      SET PITCH
0309- C6 06        1090 COUNT  DEC COUNTR
030B- F0 05        1100        BEQ DONE
030D- CA           1110        DEX
030E- D0 F9        1120        BNE COUNT
0310- F0 F2        1130        BEQ TWEAK
0312- 60           1140 DONE   RTS

SYMBOL TABLE

0309- COUNT
0006- COUNTR
0312- DONE
C030- SPKR
0304- TWEAK
```

This is an intermediate program, leading to Program 2.8. The main feature we wish to point out here is COUNTR, identified as memory location $06. When COUNTR is initialized to $FF (lines 1050, 1060) the duration of the tone is established. Each time the X-register is decremented, COUNTR is also decremented. If the X-register is decremented to zero, the speaker is tweaked and the X-register is restored to its initial value. When COUNTR is decremented to zero, line 1080 causes a branch to the end of the program.

Program 2.7 is ineffective because the tone is too short. $FF (decimal 255 or binary 11111111) is the largest number we can put into COUNTR (or any eight-bit register or memory location—more on this in Chapters 3 and 4). Only 255 decrements bring us to zero and the end of the tone. That is far too short. Program 2.8 uses COUNTR as the second stage in a two-stage counter.

PROGRAM 2.8

```
                  1000 * PROGRAM 2.8 TONE SUBROUTINE
0006-             1010 COUNTR .EQ $06
0007-             1020 PITCH  .EQ $07
C030-             1030 SPKR   .EQ $C030
                  1040        .OR $300
0300- AD 30 C0    1050 TWEAK  LDA SPKR
0303- A6 07       1060        LDX PITCH
0305- 88          1070 COUNT  DEY          ANOTHER COUNTER
0306- D0 04       1080        BNE FREQ     256 DEY'S?
0308- C6 06       1090        DEC COUNTR
030A- F0 05       1100        BEQ DONE
030C- CA          1110 FREQ   DEX
030D- D0 F6       1120        BNE COUNT
030F- F0 EF       1130        BEQ TWEAK
0311- 60          1140 DONE   RTS

SYMBOL TABLE

0305- COUNT
0006- COUNTR
0311- DONE
030C- FREQ
0007- PITCH
C030- SPKR
0300- TWEAK
```

Now the Y-register protects COUNTR from being decremented as frequently as it had been before (lines 1070, 1080). Only when the Y-register reads zero (every 256 DEYs) will COUNTR be decremented by 1. Otherwise Program 2.8 functions very much like Program 2.7.

Controlling Tone

Program 2.8 provides a very usable TONE subroutine. With it loaded at $300 we can access it from Applesoft to play simple tones.

Neither of the authors is musically inclined. Piano lessons in the early years did not have long lasting effects. Thus it was with great effort that the following Applesoft program was developed. Undoubtedly any musically inclined programmer can do better.

PROGRAM 2.9

```
1  REM PROGRAM 2.9
2  REM MELODY
3  REM ASSUMES THAT PROGRAM 2.8
4  REM IS LOADED AT $300
10 FOR I = 1 TO 6
20 READ DUR: POKE 6,DUR: REM DURATION OF NOTE
30 READ PITCH: POKE 7,PITCH
40 CALL 768
50 NEXT I
60 DATA 64,203,64,171,64,128,128,102,64,128,255,102
```

Program 2.10 uses the Apple game paddle to identify notes to be played. Line 1040 of the program identifies the variable PDL with memory location $FB1E. This is the location of the beginning of a Monitor subroutine that reads the game paddles. If the subroutine is entered with the X-register containing 0, the subroutine will read game paddle 0 {lines 1090, 1100}. On return from the subroutine, the A-register will contain a number between 0 and 255 {the number that would be returned by the Applesoft command PDL(0)}. If the subroutine is entered with the X-register containing a 1, 2, or 3, the subroutine will read game paddle 1, 2, or 3, respectively.

PROGRAM 2.10

```
                1000 * PROGRAM 2.10 PADDLE TONE
0006-           1010 COUNTR .EQ $06
0007-           1020 PITCH  .EQ $07
C030-           1030 SPKR   .EQ $C030
FB1E-           1040 PDL    .EQ $FB1E
                1050        .OR $300
                1060 *** MAIN PROGRAM
0300- A9 20     1070 START  LDA #$20
0302- 85 06     1080        STA COUNTR
0304- A2 00     1090        LDX #$00      READ
0306- 20 1E FB  1100        JSR PDL       PADDLE 0
0309- 85 07     1110        STA PITCH
030B- 20 11 03  1120        JSR TWEAK
030E- 4C 00 03  1130        JMP START
                1140 *** TONE SUBROUTINE
0311- AD 30 C0  1150 TWEAK  LDA SPKR
```

```
0314- A6 07     1160        LDX PITCH
0316- 88        1170 COUNT  DEY
0317- D0 04     1180        BNE FREQ
0319- C6 06     1190        DEC COUNTR
031B- F0 05     1200        BEQ DONE
031D- CA        1210 FREQ   DEX
031E- D0 F6     1220        BNE COUNT
0320- F0 EF     1230        BEQ TWEAK
0322- 60        1240 DONE   RTS

SYMBOL TABLE

0316- COUNT
0006- COUNTR
0322- DONE
031D- FREQ
FB1E- PDL
0007- PITCH
C030- SPKR
0300- START
0311- TWEAK
```

In Program 2.10, as soon as the game paddle reading has been stored as PITCH, control is transferred to the subroutine TONE, which is the same (except for a change of label: TWEAK → TONE) as Program 2.8. Upon return from the TONE subroutine, JMP START (line 1130) starts the program over again.

This program is an infinite loop. Press CONTROL-RESET to stop it.

Suggestion: Rewrite the MAIN part of Program 2.10 so that game paddle 1 identifies the number stored in COUNTR, and thus controls the duration of the note that is played.

In this and the previous chapter, we have provided examples of some of the most frequently used assembly language instructions. There are variations of several of these instructions, and there are many other instructions to consider. In the next chapter we shall introduce additional assembly language instructions as we look at the architecture of the 6502 processor and the memory organization of the Apple II/IIe.

SECTION

II

FUNDAMENTALS OF 6502 PROGRAMMING

CHAPTER 3

THE ARCHITECTURE AND THE INSTRUCTION SET

We are leaving the area of program design to discuss the instruction set of the 6502 processor. The programs in this chapter are short and easy to read. You may find yourself reading and agreeing that you understand them, but this is not sufficient. Be sure to execute each of the sample programs. They are written to show you what the processor does when the program is executed. The examples are geared toward this end; they are not necessarily of practical value. In later chapters, examples that may have practical value demand that you have an understanding of the instruction set and of the processor architecture.

The purpose of this chapter is to briefly describe the 6502 architecture and some of the fifty-six operations the microprocessor performs. The busiest piece of hardware in the 6502 is the Arithmetic–Logic Unit, or ALU. This unit is the collection of circuits that performs the arithmetic operations of addition and subtraction, as the A in ALU implies. In the most general sense the function of the ALU is to receive a pair of operands, to combine them according to a well defined set of rules, and then to deliver the result to a memory location.

There are three multipurpose registers available on the 6502. These are the X-register, the Y-register, and the A-register. The A-register is called the accumulator. These registers are eight bits wide. The A-register functions most closely with the ALU. One of the input operands to the ALU is found in A. The other operand is found using one of the thirteen addressing modes available on the 6502. (There is much more to be said about addressing and the 6502 in Chapter 4.) The ALU accepts the operands, performs the requested operation, and places the result in the A-register.

Another register that must be discussed before giving a short example using the ALU and the three multipurpose registers is the P-register. This is the Processor status register. It too is an eight-bit register, but each of the P-register's bits is used to report the status of the 6502. Imagine that the eight bits of the P-register are arranged and named like this:

Bit number →	7	6	5	4	3	2	1	0
Bit name →	N	V	–	B	D	I	Z	C

If you are wondering why they are numbered from right to left, it is because that is the way they are displayed on the screen, as you will see in the first example. Each of these bits can either be on (1) or off (0). Bit number 0 is the Carry flag. The C-flag is set to 1 whenever the sum of two eight-bit numbers cannot be represented in eight bits (and on certain other occasions). Bit number 1 is the Zero flag. The Z-flag is set to 1 whenever the result is 0. Bit number 2 is the Interrupt flag. The I-flag will be pointed out in the first example. Bit number 3 is the Decimal mode flag. Whenever this bit is set to 1 the ALU performs base-ten additions and subtractions. Whenever it is set to 0 the ALU performs hexadecimal arithmetic. Bit number 4 is the Break flag. It will be pointed out in the first example. Bit number 5 is not used, but is always set to 1. Bit number 6 is the oVerflow flag. The status of this bit, the V-flag, is important when signed arithmetic is performed in the 2's-complement notation. For a quick review of 2's-complement notation see Appendix B. Bit number 7 is the Negative flag. The N-flag is a copy of bit 7 of the A-register. The interpretation of this bit very closely depends on the intent of the programmer. Use of the N-flag will be pointed out as the need arises.

USE OF THE PROCESSOR STATUS FLAGS

Decimal Addition

Consider the following sequence:

1. Place a base ten number into the A-register.
2. Add the contents of the A-register to another base ten number.
3. Place the result in the A-register.
4. Display the result and await further instruction.

Addition is accomplished through the use of the ADC (ADd with Carry) instruction. To obtain accurate additions, we must first CLear the Carry. This insures that the contents of the C-flag will not be left to chance from the result of a previous operation. You must CLear the Carry before doing addition because the ADC instruction includes the contents of the C-flag in the calculation. Symbolically we write this as:

$$(A) \leftarrow (A) + (M) + (C)$$

The notation ( ) means "the contents of".

The addition is to be decimal arithmetic so SEt the Decimal status flag to 1. LoaD the Accumulator with a decimal number; ADd with Carry from memory, and place the result in the accumulator. Here is the assembly language program to accomplish the task:

```
1000          * PROGRAM 3.1 ADD
1005          .OR $800
1010 SUM      CLC
1020          SED
1030          LDA #$86
1040          ADC #$13
1050          BRK
```

When the program is assembled the listing is:

PROGRAM 3.1

```
                   1000 * PROGRAM 3.1 ADD
                   1005          .OR $800
0800- 18           1010 SUM      CLC
```

```
0801- F8          1020          SED
0802- A9 86       1030          LDA #$86
0804- 69 13       1040          ADC #$13
0806- 00          1050          BRK


SYMBOL TABLE

0800- SUM
```

Note: If your assembler does not permit convenient access to the Monitor, you may wish to forego use of your assembler altogether, and simply enter the op codes directly from the Monitor.

When the program is executed you will see:

```
0808-    A=99  X=00  Y=00  P=BC  S=F9
```

When the processor executes the BRK instruction at memory location $0806, this causes the contents of the registers to be displayed. Ordinarily we would not want this to be done, but right now the register contents are our primary concern. Therefore, ending this program with a BRK is convenient. A=99 means the contents of the accumulator are $99; the appropriate result. X=00 means the contents of the X-register are $00. P=BC means the contents of the P-register are, in hexadecimal, $BC (remember, $ denotes a hex number). We can determine the contents of the status flags by converting $BC to its binary form. (If you do not recall how to do this, see the discussion in Appendix B.) Figure 3.2 shows the association between the hexadecimal number $BC, its binary representation 1011 1100, and the status flags.

HEX →	B	C
BINARY →	1011	1100
FLAGS →	NV-B	DIZC

For this example, note that we are in the decimal mode, D=1; there was no carry, C=1; and the result is not zero, Z=0. Also the B-flag and the I-flag were set to 1 by the BRK instruction.

One of the skills an assembly language programmer must develop is that of reading the assembled listing. To begin, look at the assembled listing above. Focus your attention on the three left-hand columns. The leftmost column,

$0800, $0801, $0802, $0804, $0806, is the list of the address locations where the program is stored in memory. The second column is the list of the operation codes, op codes for short, $18, $F8, $A9, $69, $00, of each of the instructions in the program. The third column is a list of the operands, $86, $13, for the corresponding op codes, $A9 and $69. In the other columns to the right is a copy of the program.

Note that line 1000 of the program was not assembled. It is merely a comment. The next line, 1010 SUM CLC, was assembled into address location $0800. It contains $18, which is the op code for the CLC instruction. Note that the name of the program, SUM, does not appear in the assembled listing, columns 1, 2, and 3 however it does appear in the symbol table listing provided by most assemblers. The function of a symbol table is to identify the name, SUM, with memory location $0800, whose contents are $18.

The next line shows that memory location $0801 contains F8, the op code for the SED instruction. The next line shows that memory location $0802 contains $A9 (the op code for the LDA instruction) and that memory location $0803 contains $86 (the assembled operand for the LDA instruction).

Note: The $86 is assembled into the location immediately following the op code. This is the meaning of the # symbol in the listing. This "immediate mode-#" of addressing is only one of the thirteen modes available and is explained more fully in the next chapter.

The next line indicates that memory location $0804 contains $69 (the op code for the ADC instruction) and memory location $0805 contains $13. Once again the # has the same effect as noted above. The last line shows that memory location $0806 contains $00, the op code for the BRK instruction.

The next program is a slight modification of the last one. Change the operand of the ADC to #$14, so that you now have:

```
1040          ADC #$14
```

Assemble that program and execute it. Note the changes that occur in the listing. Memory location $0803 now contains $14, the new immediate operand of the ADC instruction. Other changes that occur upon execution of the program are in the registers; namely, A = 00 and P = BD. A = 00 because a three-digit number (in this case 100) will not fit into a two-digit register. The 1 is now in the Carry bit of the P-register, as indicated by P = BD. Convert the contents of the P-register to its binary form and fill in the blanks in the table below.

HEX →	B	D
BINARY →	----	----
FLAGS →	NV-B	DIZC

The C=1 indicates that the Carry bit is on. In summary, 86 + 14 = 100. That is true, but the 1 is in the C-flag and the $00 is in the accumulator. As you can see, the Carry flag is important both before and after an addition. We clear the Carry before addition to be sure that it does not contribute to the sum. After the addition is performed, we can check the contents of the carry to determine the result of the addition.

For the next example, return to the 86 + 13 example, and modify the SED instruction to the CLD instruction. CLD is the mnemonic for CLear Decimal. Assemble the program and execute it. Note the changes that occur. Memory location $0801 now contains $D8, the op code for the CLD instruction. The change that occurs after execution is in the contents of the P-register, which is P=B4. Convert the contents of the P-register to binary and fill in the blanks in Figure 3.4.

HEX →	B	4
BINARY →	----	----
FLAGS →	NV-B	DIZC

The D=0 indicated that the decimal mode was off, therefore the ALU did hexadecimal arithmetic.

Subtraction (Positive Result)

The ALU also does subtraction. The instruction for subtraction is SBC, SuBtract with Carry from the accumulator. The SBC instruction works like this:

```
(A) ← (A) - (M) - 1 + (C)
```

Notice that for subtractions to be done with the expected result the C-flag must be set. The instruction for this is SEC, SEt the Carry. In the notation above, which symbolically shows how the Carry flag affects subtraction, the 1 is often grouped with the Carry flag like this:

```
(A) ← (A) - (1-C)
```

When the grouping is done in this fashion, the (1-C) is referred to as the complement of the Carry. Notation aside, the point is that the C-flag must be set before subtraction.

The following program illustrates the SBC and the SEC instructions in the decimal mode.

PROGRAM 3.2

```
                  1000 * PROGRAM 3.2 SUB
                  1005          .OR $800
0800- 38          1010 SUB      SEC
0801- F8          1020          SED
0802- A9 86       1030          LDA #$86
0804- E9 13       1040          SBC #$13
0806- 00          1050          BRK


SYMBOL TABLE

0800- SUB
```

When the program is executed you will see:

```
0808-   A=73 X=00 Y=00 P=7D S=F9
```

The results are as expected. The accumulator contains \$73 (\$86 − \$13 = \$73). Construct a diagram similar to Figures 3.3 and 3.4 and see that C = 1, the C-flag is set; N = 0, the result is positive.

Program 3.3 performs a subtraction with the Carry flag turned off (CLC). This simulates doing a subtraction without first setting the C-flag and having a spurious zero in the C-flag from a previous operation.

PROGRAM 3.3

```
                  1000 * PROGRAM 3.3 SUB
                  1005          .OR $800
0800- 18          1010 SUB      CLC
0801- F8          1020          SED
0802- A9 86       1030          LDA #$86
0804- E9 13       1040          SBC #$13
0806- 00          1050          BRK

SYMBOL TABLE

0800- SUB
```

When the program is executed you should see:

```
0808-    A=72 X=00 Y=00 P=7D S=F9
```

The contents of the registers show that the accumulator now contains A=72; not the expected result for 86 − 13 = 73. Remember that the arithmetic done by the ALU was:

```
(A)  −  (M)  −1  +  (M)
86   −  13   −1  +   0  = 72
```

The point of these two examples is: Never forget to set the C-flag before subtraction! Also note that as a result of the execution of Program 3.3, the C-flag is now set C=1.

Subtraction (Negative Result)

Program 3.4 attempts to subtract 87 from 86. Note that we have put the SEC instruction back in place, and the decimal mode is set (SED).

PROGRAM 3.4

```
                 1000 * PROGRAM 3.4 SUB
                 1005          .OR $800
0800- 38         1010 SUB      SEC
0801- F8         1020          SED
0802- A9 86      1030          LDA #$86
0804- E9 87      1040          SBC #$87
0806- 00         1050          BRK

SYMBOL TABLE

0800- SUB
```

When the program is executed you should see:

```
0808-    A=99 X=00 Y=00 S=F9
```

Assemble and execute the program. Checking the result in the accumulator, we see A = 99. A surprising (puzzling) result. Note that the N-flag is set N = 1, indicating a negative result. This is consistent with the intent of the subtraction 86 − 87. Also note that the C-flag is now off, C = 0. The explanation for the result requires an understanding of the representation of signed decimal numbers. A full explanation concerning this is in Appendix B.

Change the SED instruction to CLD to set the ALU to do hexadecimal arithmetic. Also change the operand of the SBC instruction to $0A.

PROGRAM 3.5

```
                1000 * PROGRAM 3.5 SUB
                1005          .OR $800
0800- 38        1010 SUB      SEC
0801- D8        1020          CLD
0802- A9 86     1030          LDA #$86
0804- E9 0A     1040          SBC #$0A
0806- 00        1050          BRK
```

```
SYMBOL TABLE

0800- SUB
```

When the program is executed you will see:

```
0808-    A=7C X=00 Y=00 P=75 S=F9
```

The accumulator contains the expected result for hexadecimal subtraction \$86 − \$A = \$7C. (If you are uneasy with this result see Appendix B.) The status register also reflects the appropriate results.

As a last example of subtraction, Program 3.6 changes the operand of the SBC instruction to $87.

PROGRAM 3.6

```
                1000 * PROGRAM 3.6 SUB
                1005          .OR $800
0800- 38        1010 SUB      SEC
0801- D8        1020          CLD
```

```
0802- A9 86     1030          LDA #$86
0804- E9 87     1040          SBC #$87
0806- 00        1050          BRK


SYMBOL TABLE

0800- SUB
```

When the program is executed the results are:

```
0808-    A=FF X=00 Y=00 P=B4 S=F9
```

The result in the A-register is appropriate, since $86 – $87 = –1 in 2's-complement notation. The P-register contains a $B4. Since the binary form of $B is 1011, we know that the N-flag is on. Similarly, since $4 is even, the C-flag is off.

The examples thus far in this chapter have focused on the A-register, the multipurpose register most closely associated with the functioning of the ALU, and the P-register, the processor status register. Undoubtedly you have noticed that there are displayed on the screen three other registers. Two of these, the X-register and the Y-register, are the multipurpose registers whose function is most closely associated with addressing. Specifically, they are most often used as index registers in address calculations. Our purpose in this part of the chapter is to describe their relationship to the architecture of the 6502 and to introduce, in an elementary way, some of the instructions that bear on their use.

The instructions considered here are:

1. a. LDX, LoaD X-register
   b. LDY, LoaD Y-register

2. a. TAX, Transfer from A-register to X-register
   b. TAY, Transfer from A-register to Y-register
   c. TXA, Transfer from X-register to A-register
   d. TYA, Transfer from Y-register to A-register

3. a. INX, INcrement X-register by 1
   b. INY, INcrement Y-register by 1

4. a. DEX, DEcrement X-register by 1
   b. DEY, DEcrement Y-register by 1

A quick scan of the above instructions falsely creates the impression that the X and Y registers are completely interchangeable. X and Y are NOT interchangeable when used for stack manipulation, as we shall see below, nor are they interchangeable when used for addressing, as we shall see in Chapter 4. The purpose of the short example shown below is to demonstrate each of the four kinds of instructions: load, transfer, increment, and decrement.

PROGRAM 3.7

```
                  1000 * PROGRAM 3.7 DEMO
                  1005           .OR $800
0800- 18          1010 X         CLC
0801- A2 05       1020 Y         LDX #$05
0803- A0 15       1030           LDY #$15
0805- A9 00       1040           LDA #$00
0807- 8A          1050           TXA
0808- E8          1060           INX
0809- 88          1070           DEY
080A- 00          1080           BRK


SYMBOL TABLE

0800- X
0801- Y
```

Key-in the example, assemble, and execute it starting at label X. From the assembled listing you can see that $05 was loaded into X, $15 was loaded into Y, and that the accumulator was initialized to $00. The contents of the registers after execution are:

```
080C-   A=05 X=06 Y=14 P=34 S=F9
```

The accumulator contains $05, which was transferred in from X. X contains $06, the result of incrementing X. Y contains $14, the results of decrementing Y. These are the expected results. Analysis of the contents of the P-register show that B = 1, I = 1. C = 0 because of the execution of the CLC instruction.

Now execute the program starting at label Y. The registers are:

```
080C-   A=05 X=06 Y=14 P=35 S=F9
```

Note that the contents of the A, X, and Y registers are the same as before. Analysis of the P-register shows that C = 1. The Carry flag was set by some operation of the 6502, and NOT by the program. The program was executed from line 1020, the line after the CLC instruction. The point is, this second execution of the program from label Y demonstrates that the programmer does not know the status of the C-flag unless it is explicitly set or cleared by the program.

POINTERS

A register that contains an address is called a "pointer register." Such a register is said to "point to" the memory location whose address it contains. The fourth register you have seen displayed on the screen in the examples thus far in this chapter is the S-register, or Stack pointer register. The S-register contains the address of the next available stack location. The idea of a stack has been designed into the architecture of the 6502. Without going too deeply into addressing and memory organization, the stack is a reserved block of memory (256 bytes) that functions as a quick storage and recall area with special rules regarding its use. There are only 256 memory locations available for use with addresses numbered consecutively from 256 to 511. These memory locations are pointed to by the S-register from high (location 511) to low (location 256) consecutively. The S-register serves as a pointer to a location in the stack. The location "pointed to" will vary as a program is executed.

Note: The Stack works opposite the direction most people expect.

The operation of the stack has another, somewhat peculiar, rule to remember. This is the wraparound rule. The S-register counts down from 255 to 0 as memory locations 511 to 256 are pointed to by the S-register. When the stack is used again the S-register contents are decremented from 0 to 255 and once again the S-register points to memory location 511. That is to say the S-register wraps around. The S-register decrements 255, 254, ... 2, 1, 0, 255, 254, ... etc. The wraparound from 0 to 255 occurs without warning; no flags are set. This may seem like a strange way to run a pointer register, but most do operate this way. In fact, the stack is rarely ever half-full in the busiest of programs. People have been known to use the lower half of the stack, $100 up to, say, $180. This is potentially dangerous and you should never be that pressed for space!

Generally the programmer does not need to be concerned with the details of the way the stack (and the stack pointer) handle the bookkeeping. This is done automatically. However, there are ways in which we can affect the stack pointer and stack contents.

STACK

Putting information into a memory location in the stack is referred to as a push. Conversely, retrieving information from a memory location in the stack is referred to as a pull (often called a pop, as in "popping" the stack). Because of the way in which the S-register counts (down after a push and up before a pull) the operation of the stack is said to be Last In First Out, or LIFO. The instructions that bear on the use of the stack are:

1. a. PHA, PusH contents of Accumulator onto the stack
   b. PHP, PusH contents of P-register onto the stack

2. a. PLA, PulL contents of Accumulator from the stack
   b. PLP, PulL contents of P-register from the stack

3. a. TSX, Transfer contents of S-register to X-register
   b. TXS, Transfer contents of X-register to S-register

Note that information can only be transferred in a single instruction between the S and X registers. This is the first case in which the X and Y registers are not interchangeable; there is no TSY nor a TYS instruction. For an illustration of the flow of information through the stack and the registers, consider the following elementary examples.

PROGRAM 3.8

```
                1000 * PROGRAM 3.8 STACK
                1005          .OR $800
0800- 18        1010 STACK    CLC
0801- BA        1020          TSX
0802- 8A        1030          TXA
0803- A8        1040          TAY
0804- A9 86     1050          LDA #$86
0806- 48        1060          PHA
0807- 08        1070          PHP
0808- 38        1080          SEC
0809- A9 87     1090          LDA #$87
080B- 48        1100          PHA
080C- 08        1110          PHP
080D- A9 88     1120          LDA #$88
080F- 48        1130          PHA
```

```
0810- 08        1140        PHP
0811- BA        1150        TSX
0812- 00        1160        BRK


SYMBOL TABLE

0800- STACK
```

Before keying-in this program, the purpose of lines 1020, 1030, 1040 must be explained. Their purpose is to capture the first stack location available to the program and transfer it to the Y-register. Note that to do this the contents of S are first transferred to X, line 1020, then to A, line 1030, and finally they are transferred to Y. Why not do this directly? Because there is no TSY instruction, nor is there a TXY instruction. So the S to X to A to Y transfer is the obvious way to get the first available stack address saved in Y. Saving it will make the search of the stack contents below easier.

Now key-in, assemble, and execute the program. The contents of the registers after execution of the program are shown below.

```
0814-     A=88 X=F7 Y=FD P=B5 S=F3
```

Note: You may observe some differences in the contents of the registers or memory locations NOT discussed in the example. These locations are noncritical, and to some extent depend on what you have been doing with your Apple before executing the examples that discuss the stack. However, if you have any doubt about the contents of any of the noncritical registers or memory locations, cycle your Apple on/off before doing these examples and you should not have any trouble getting the results shown. We have run these examples through many different Apples after having done many different programming tasks, many times without cycling them on/off. We have had no lack of agreement with what is printed in the book and the contents of the noncritical registers and memory locations. Needless to say, the contents of the critical registers and memory locations are assured regardless of what prior task your Apple has been performing!

From the contents of Y we know that stack location $FD contains $86. The PHA instruction in line 1060 pushed the contents of A, $86, into the next available stack location, $FD. Line 1070 pushed the contents of the P-register into the next stack location, $FC. The purpose of lines 1080 and 1090 is to change the contents of A and P, which are then pushed onto the stack, lines

1100 and 1110. Finally, the contents of A are changed again and then the contents of both A and P are pushed onto the stack.

Now let us examine the contents of the stack. Do this by returning to the Monitor. Presumably your assembler allows shifts between it and the Monitor quickly and without disturbing the stack locations filled by the program. We wish to display the contents of stack locations $F8 through $FF.

Note: Remember that stack addresses must be prefixed with a $01 to convert them to memory addresses.

Use the Monitor to display the contents of these memory (stack) locations. The line below shows the contents of the locations.

```
        Monitor command →  *1F8.1FF

    Contents of location →  01F8- B5 88 B5 87 B4 86 67 10
         Stack locations →        F8 F9 FA FB FC FD FE FF
```

From the contents of Y shown above we see that the first available stack location for the program was $FD. Checking the contents of stack location $FD (memory location $01FD) we see the $86 that was loaded into the accumulator (line 1050) and pushed onto the stack (line 1060). Stack location $FC (memory location $01FC) contains $B4, the contents of the P-register at the time line 1070 was executed. Note that the Carry flag is zero. The contents of stack locations $FB and $FA (memory locations $01FB and $01FA) are $87 and $B5 respectively; note that the Carry flag is now set as a result of line 1080. The last stack locations, $F9 and $F8, (memory locations $01F9 and $01F8) contain $88, from lines 1120 and 1130, and the contents of the P-register, $B5, at the time line 1040 was executed. Finally, check the contents of the X-register to see that the next available location in the stack is $F7, as expected at line 1050.

To illustrate the PLA instruction modify Program 3.8 so that it becomes the following example.

PROGRAM 3.9

```
             1000 * PROGRAM 3.9 STACK
             1005          .OR $800
0800- 18     1010 PULL     CLC
0801- BA     1020          TSX
```

```
0802- 8A        1030        TXA
0803- A9 86     1040        LDA #$86
0805- 48        1050        PHA
0806- 08        1060        PHP
0807- 68        1070        PLA
0808- 00        2000        BRK

SYMBOL TABLE

0800- PULL
```

Line 1070 is the PLA instruction, which pulls the contents of the last push instruction executed (line 1060) into the accumulator. Assemble and execute the program. The contents of the registers are shown below.

```
080B-     A=B4 X=FD Y=00 P=B4 S=F8
```

Note that the contents of stack location $FC, which were $B4 after the execution of program 3.8, have been pulled into the accumulator. Use the Monitor to display memory locations $01F8 through $01FF (stack locations $F8 through $FF).

```
01F8-     FD F8 FE 84 FF 86 67 10
```

Notice that after execution of program 3.9 memory location $FC no longer contains $B4. The BRK instruction pushed new information onto the stack and the next available stack location was $FC. More will be said about the BRK instruction in the next part of the chapter.

Add these lines to program 3.9.

```
1080        TAY
1090        PLA
```

Line 1090 transfers the contents of the accumulator (which after execution of the modification of Program 3.9 can be seen to be $B4) into the Y-register, and line 1090 pulls the contents of the next location into the accumulator. Assemble and execute the modified program. The register contents are:

```
080D-     A=86 X=FD Y=B4 P=B4 S=F9
```

Note that the $B4 is now in Y and that the $86 is now in A. Use the Monitor to display memory locations $01F8 through $01FF again.

```
01F8-     BA FD F8 FE 84 FF 67 10
```

Now you see that the contents from the original example have been moved up one memory location, because this time line 2000 is executed the next available stack location is $FD.

THE PROGRAM COUNTER

There is one other register to discuss under the topic of architecture and the instruction set. It is called the Program Counter register, or PC-register. You rarely, if ever, need to think about the PC-register. The most important fact to remember about it is that it always contains the address of the next instruction to be executed. It is very different from the other registers discussed so far. First, you have not seen its contents displayed on the screen. Second, it is a sixteen-bit (two-byte) register. Bits 0 through 7 are referred to as PC Low (PCL); bits 8 through 15 are referred to as PC High (PCH). The purpose of this register is to keep track of the sequence of executable instructions in a program. The sequence only requires your personal management when branches, jumps, returns, or breaks are used in some unusual fashion. Otherwise its operation is automatic.

You have noticed that your programs, when assembled, have been placed sequentially (contiguously) in memory locations from some starting location. The starting location for all programs in this chapter is memory location $0800. When you instruct the 6502 to execute your assembled program, the PC-register is loaded with $0800, and the contents of $0800 are fetched and executed. Then the PC-register is incremented by an amount that depends on the length of the instruction. The contents of this address are then fetched and executed, and the process continues over and over until a break or a branch is executed. It is imperative that when a branch or a jump is executed the contents of the PC-register be properly saved and then restored for a return or a break. The stack is used for saving and retrieving the contents of the PC-register.

Perhaps the easiest way to display the contents of the PC-register is to write a program that uses the JSR instruction, because this instruction pushes the contents of the PC-register onto the stack. Once this is done we can display the stack contents to see what the PC-register contained at the time of the jump. The JSR, Jump to SubRoutine, instruction is three bytes long. Therefore when it is executed the contents of the PC-register are the address of the JSR instruction itself. To get the proper return address stored on the stack, the PC-register must be incremented by two and then pushed onto the stack. Why only two for a three-byte instruction? Remember, it contains the address of the next executable instruction, therefore it already has had one byte added to it and only needs to be incremented by two more. Since the PC-register is two bytes long, two stack locations are required for its storage. The contents of PCH are pushed onto the stack first, the stack pointer register is decremented, and then the contents of PCL are pushed onto the stack. Once the return address is stored in the stack, the second and third bytes of the JSR instruction are loaded into the PC-register and the jump is made.

Shown below is a program using the JSR instruction to display the contents of the PC-register via the stack.

PROGRAM 3.10

```
                    1000 * PROGRAM 3.10 PCR
                    1005          .OR $800
0800- BA            1010 PCR      TSX
0801- 8A            1020          TXA
0802- A8            1030          TAY
0803- 20 09 08      1040          JSR STK
0806- A9 AA         1050          LDA #$AA
0808- 00            1060          BRK
0809- A9 BB         1070 STK      LDA #$BB
080B- A9 CC         1080          LDA #$CC
080D- 00            1090          BRK

SYMBOL TABLE

0800- PCR
0809- STK
```

Lines 1010 through 1030 are the familiar technique for catching the first available stack location in the Y-register. Notice how the JSR instruction is assembled. Memory location $0803 contains the op code for the JSR instruction, $20. Locations $0804 and $0805 contain the address of the label STK. Note that the low-order byte of the address, $09, is stored in location $0804, and the high-order byte of the address, $08, is stored in location $0805. So the jump address is $0809. Checking the address of STK we see that it is in fact $0809 (line 1070 of the program), and the op code of the LDA instruction, $A9, is stored here. To summarize: The JSR instruction is three bytes long. The first byte contains the op code, $20. The second byte contains the low-order byte of the jump address, $09. The third byte contains the high-order byte of the jump address, $08.

```
080F-   A=CC X=FD Y=FD P=B5 S=F7

01F8-   F8 FE 84 FF 05 08 67 10
```

When Program 3.10 is executed analysis of the registers pictured above shows that the Y-register contains $FD, the first available stack location at the time of execution of the JSR instruction. Analysis of stack locations $F8 through $FF also given above shows that stack location $FD (memory location $01FD) contains $08, which is the high-order byte of the PC-register (PCH) pushed onto the stack by the JSR instruction when it was executed. Stack location $FC contains $05, which is the low-order byte of the PC-register, PCL, that was pushed onto the stack by the JSR instruction immediately after PCH. Together they form the return address, $0805, which will be loaded into the PC-register when the example is modified below. A bird's-eye view of this example catches (in the stack) the operation of the JSR instruction midflight (on its way to the "subroutine" STK). Before the jump to STK (memory location $0809) occurred, the next available stack location, $FD, was captured first in the X, then transferrred through the A to the Y-register.

Now modify the program to capture the return address in registers X and Y, and to do a proper return from "subroutine" STK. The modified program is shown below.

PROGRAM 3.1M1

```
                 1000 * PROGRAM 3.10M1 PCR
                 1005           .OR $800
0800- BA         1010 PCR       TSX
0801- 8A         1020           TXA
0802- A8         1030           TAY
0803- 20 07 08   1040           JSR STK
0806- 00         1050           BRK
0807- 68         1060 STK       PLA
0808- A8         1070           TAY
0809- 68         1080           PLA
080A- AA         1090           TAX
080B- 48         1100           PHA
080C- 98         1110           TYA
080D- 48         1120           PHA
080E- 60         1130           RTS


SYMBOL TABLE

0800- PCR
0807- STK
```

Lines 1060 and 1070 capture PCL in the Y-register; lines 1080 and 1090 capture PCH in the X-register. Line 1100 pushes PCH back onto the stack; lines 1110 and 1120 push PCL back onto the stack. Note that if PCH and PCL were not returned to the stack the RTS would not find the proper return address available on the stack. Line 1130 is the RTS instruction, ReTurn from Subroutine. This instruction pulls PCL and PCH from the stack, $0805; increments it by 1, $0806; loads this address into the PC-register. Then the next instruction is fetched (the contents of memory location $0806, $00) and executed (the BRK instruction). Thus the return from "subroutine" STK is accomplished. When Program 3.10M1 is executed, the register contents and the stack contents at the time of the break at line 1050 are:

```
0808-     A=05 X=08 Y=05 P=35 S=F9

01F8-     BA FD F8 FE 84 FF 62 10
```

Note that at the time of the jump to STK, the X-register contains the high-order byte of the return address, $08, and the Y-register contains the low-order byte of the return address, $05. Stack locations $F8 through $FF now contain information different from that in Program 3.10. This is to be expected, because JSR pushed two bytes onto the stack, but RTS pulled them back to accomplish the return, thus the stack is in the same condition as it was before the JSR instruction was executed. Save Program 3.10M1 on disk. You will use it again in Chapter 4.

A more detailed discussion of the BRK instruction, BReaK, can now be given. When the break instruction is executed the following sequence of events occurs:

1. The current contents of the PC-register (the address of the BRK) are incremented by two.
2. The Break flag is set to 1.
3. The contents of the PC-register are pushed onto the stack; PCH first, then PCL.
4. The current contents of the P-register are pushed onto the stack.
5. The Interrupt flag is set to 1.
6. The contents of memory location $FFFF are loaded into PCH and the contents of memory location $FFFE are loaded into PCL. The contents of these two locations make up the interrupt pointer.
7. Execution continues from this address.

You have seen the BRK instruction used many times in the examples in this chapter. The effect of all these steps is to save for future reference the contents of the registers (at the location consistent with number one above) at the time of the break, and and then to display them. This action makes the BRK instruction a convenient debugging aid.

The JMP instruction, JuMP, is similar to the JSR instruction, but JMP is even simpler. The JMP instruction is a three-byte instruction. The first byte contains the op code, $4C. The second and third bytes make up the jump address. This address is loaded into the PC-register, just as it is in the JSR instruction, and off you jump! No saving of return information on the stack. That is to say, there can be no companion return instruction. You must keep track of your journey yourself. (JSR is like GOSUB; JMP is like GOTO.)

The last instructions to be discussed in this chapter are the various branch instructions.

1. a. BCC, Branch if Carry Clear
   If C = 0, the branch is taken.
   b. BCS, Branch if Carry Set
   If C = 1, the branch is taken.

2. a. BNE, Branch if Not Equal to zero
   If Z = 0, the branch is taken.
   b. BEQ, Branch if EQual to zero
   If Z = 1, the branch is taken.

3. a. BPL, Branch if PLus
   If N = 0, the branch is taken.
   b. BMI, Branch if MInus
   If N = 1, the branch is taken.

4. a. BVC, Branch if oVerflow Clear
   If V = 0, the branch is taken.
   b. BVS, Branch if oVerflow Set
   If V = 1, the branch is taken.

Notice that there are four kinds of branch instructions, and each tests a different flag, either C, Z, N, or V. If the value of the flag, a 0 or a 1, matches the condition of the instruction, the branch is taken. Branches are conditional jumps, but the branch address is specified differently. The branch address, which is the address of the next executable instruction, is calculated from a displacement. Branches are two-byte instructions. The first byte contains the op code of the instruction; the second byte contains the displacement of the branch. The displacement is the "distance," the number of bytes, from the end of the branch instruction to the branch address. More will be said about displacement when the relative mode of addressing is explained in Chapter 4. When the flag matches the condition in the branch, the branch is taken. Then the contents of the PC-register are incremented by two (the length of the branch instruction) and by the displacement. A few examples will help make the branch instructions clear. Consider the example shown below.

PROGRAM 3.11

```
                 1000 * PROGRAM 3.11 BRCH
                 1005           .OR $800
0800- 18         1010 BRCH      CLC
0801- 90 07      1020           BCC HERE
0803- A9 11      1030           LDA #$11
0805- A2 22      1040           LDX #$22
0807- A0 33      1050           LDY #$33
0809- 00         1060           BRK
080A- 38         1070 HERE      SEC
080B- A9 AA      1080           LDA #$AA
080D- A2 BB      1090           LDX #$BB
080F- A0 CC      1100           LDY #$CC
0811- 00         1110           BRK

SYMBOL TABLE

0800- BRCH
080A- HERE
```

The branch instruction illustrated here is the BCC instruction. When the example is assembled you can see that the op code for the BCC instruction is stored in location $0801, and it is $90. Location $0802 contains the displacement and it is $07. The branch address then is $0801 + $2 + $07 = $080A, which is the address labeled HERE, and whose contents are $A9 (the op code for the LDA instruction).

When the program is executed, the results are as below.

```
0813-     A=AA X=BB Y=CC P=B5 S=F9
```

First the C-flag is cleared, so the condition of the branch is satisfied and the branch to HERE is taken. You can see that the branch was taken because of the contents of the A, X, and Y registers. Use the editor to set the carry; that is, change line 1010 to

```
1010 SEC
```

When the modified program is assembled and executed the results are:

```
080B-     A=11 X=22 Y=33 P=35 S=F9
```

Note that since the C-flag is set, condition of the branch is not satisfied, so the branch is not taken. The contents of the A, X, and Y registers show that the branch was not taken. Save Program 3.11 on disk. You will use it again in Chapter 4.

SUMMARY

The instructions presented in this chapter were chosen because they illustrate the major architectural features of the 6502 and the operation of the ALU. The instructions not presented in this chapter are illustrated in the other chapters, and a concise summary of all the instructions can be found in Appendix E.

In summary, there are three multipurpose registers: A, X, and Y. There are two special-purpose registers: P and S. P is the program status register: its contents are the status of the seven flags N, V, B, D, I, Z, and C. The S-register contains the address of the next available location in the stack. The stack is the locations in memory from $01FF to $0100. The S-register starts at $FF and decrements; it wraps around. This means that $00 − $01 = $FF in the stack register. The ALU performs only the arithmetic operations addition and subtraction, in two modes, hexadecimal and decimal. The ALU performs more than the simple true/false (branch/no branch) tests illustrated in this chapter by the branch instructions. These other logical operations will be illustrated further in Chapter 6.

Several times in this chapter reference was made to address locations in memory and two modes of addressing were used, but a systematic description of memory and a detailed study of the addressing modes available was purposefully avoided. These are the topics of the next chapter.

CHAPTER 4

ADDRESSING: LEARNING YOUR WAY AROUND MEMORY

The purpose of this chapter is to discuss the various addressing modes available on the 6502 microprocessor. When the 6502 is chosen as the microprocessor many memory organizations are possible. The memory organization we discuss, and the one our examples are drawn from, is that of the Apple II/IIe. Undoubtedly you know that your Apple II/IIe is able to ***address*** 64K of **memory** (using the sixteen bits of the PC-register) and NO more. Let us begin this chapter by seeing why this is a direct result of the eight-bit architecture of the A, X, and Y registers of the 6502. But first you must be able to visualize how any eight-bit memory is organized.

You know that computers are binary machines. This means that the SMALLEST piece of information is stored (is contained in memory) in an electrical circuit that, like the common light switch, is either ***on*** or ***off.*** On is represented as a one (1) and off is represented as a zero (0). This smallest piece of information (a 0 or a 1) is called a bit. When eight bits are grouped together they are called a byte. The byte is the SMALLEST **ADDRESSABLE** piece of information. That is to say, the smallest unit of information that has a number (its address) associated with it is called a byte. You can visualize a byte like this:

A byte →	1	1	0	0	1	1	0	1
Bit number →	7	6	5	4	3	2	1	0
Value of the bit →	2^7	2^6	2^5	2^4	2^3	2^2	2^1	2^0

Remember the powers of 2!

$2^0 = 1$, $2^1 = 2$, $2^2 = 4$, $2^3 = 8$, $2^4 = 16$, $2^5 = 32$, $2^6 = 64$, $2^7 = 128$

Each of the underscores (–) represents the electrical circuits that can be on (1) or off (0). Information in this byte is represented by placing a 1 or a 0 on each of the blanks. In this example the pattern 11001101 is only one of the possible bit patterns in an eight-bit byte. This pattern means that bit 0 is on, bit 1 is off, bit 2 is on, etc. The total number of possible bit patterns is

$$(2^0 + 2^1 + 2^2 + 2^3 + 2^4 + 2^5 + 2^6 + 2^7) + 1 = 2^8 = 256$$

Now if addresses in the Apple II/IIe were only one byte in length we could address only 256 memory locations, because there are only 256 possible combinations of ones and zeros in an eight-bit byte. The Apple II/IIe uses two bytes (the PC-register) to assign addresses to (to keep track of) memory locations. Visualize a two-byte address like this:

An Address

	Location on page Byte # one								Page Byte # zero							
Contents →	0	0	0	1	1	0	0	0	1	1	0	0	1	1	0	1
Bit # →	7	6	5	4	3	2	1	0	7	6	5	4	3	2	1	0

In the Apple II/IIe, byte number 0 is referred to as the page number, and byte number 1 is the memory location on that page. That is, there are 256 addressable pages, and each page contains 256 addressable memory locations. So that in all there are 256 * 256 = 65,536 addressable memory locations. You can address fewer. Now you can see that because the 6502 is designed with only two address bytes (PCH, PCL) only 64K of memory is addressable.

All of the 64K of memory of the Apple II/IIe is addressable, and you can examine (display, read) the contents of all memory locations, but you cannot change the contents of all 64K memory locations. The memory locations whose contents you cannot change are contained in ROM (Read-Only Memory). The contents of ROM locations do NOT change, even when the power is turned off. That is to say, their contents are NOT volatile. This is often convenient. Consider the Monitor program. It begins on page $F8 and location $00 (address $F800) and extends through page $FF and location $FF (address $FFFF). A listing of this program can be found in the *Apple IIe Reference Manual Addendum: Monitor ROM Listing* ***for IIe only.*** If you are using an Apple II this listing is in the *Reference Manual,* Appendix C.

Our main concern in this chapter is addressing memory locations whose content can be changed. These memory locations are contained in RAM (Random-Access Memory). The contents of RAM can be changed; the contents DO vanish when the power is turned off. That is to say, RAM contents are volatile.

ADDRESSING MODES

One powerful advantage of the 6502 over other microprocessors is the large number of addressing modes available. There are thirteen forms (modes) available for specifying the address that instructions use as their operands. All thirteen modes are not available to all fifty-six instructions, but many modes may be available for an instruction. Here is a list of the thirteen available addressing modes:

1. Accumulator
2. Implied
3. (Indirect)
4. Relative
5. Immediate
6. Zero-Page
7. Absolute
8. Zero-Page, X
9. Zero-Page, Y
10. Absolute, X
11. Absolute, Y

12. (Zero-Page), Y

13. (Zero-Page, X)

A compilation of which modes are available to which instructions is given in Appendix E, or in the *Reference Manual for the IIe* Appendix A, or in the *Apple II Reference Manual,* Appendix A.

Accumulator Mode

Perhaps the easiest addressing modes to understand are the ones for which NO address operand is required. The first mode in the list, accumulator, is such a mode. The instructions that use this mode form a unique set (ASL, LSR, ROL, ROR), and they are discussed in Chapter 6. Their primary uses are for bit manipulations and logical operations. They operate only on the contents of the accumulator.

Implied Mode

Implied addressing, the second mode in the list, is another mode for which NO address operand is required. The operand location is implied in the instruction itself. There are eighteen instructions that do not access memory and operate only on the contents of the registers. These instructions are CLC, CLD, CLI, CLV, DEX, DEY, INX, INY, NOP, SED, SED, SEI, TAX, TAY, TSX, TXA, TXS, TYA. There are seven instructions that do access memory but no address operand can be specified. These instructions are BRK, PHA, PHP, PLA, RTI, RTS. Many examples of the use of these instructions have been given in Chapter 3.

(Indirect) Mode

The only instruction that uses the indirect mode of addressing (the third mode in the list) without designating a companion index register is the JMP instruction. There are many instructions that use indirect addressing, but the JMP instruction is the only one that uses indirect addressing without indexing. Indirect addressing is denoted by parentheses. The address in parentheses is the address whose contents are the JMP address. In other words, the address in parentheses is NOT the JMP address; it is only the address from which the JMP address is taken. The following will illustrate the meaning of this.

To save on typing, load Program 3.10M1 from disk. We shall modify it (even though the transfer, pull, and push instructions are not needed here) to illustrate the indirect mode of addressing. The idea in this example is to illustrate the indirect mode of addressing with the JMP instruction. The purpose of this example is not to display the contents of the PC-register (which was the purpose of the transfer, pull, and push instructions in Program 3.10M1). Edit it to look like the program shown below.

PROGRAM 4.1

```
                  1000 * PROGRAM 4.1 JUMPS
                  1005          .OR $800
0800- A9 08       1010 JMPS     LDA #$08
0802- 8D FF 3F    1020          STA $3FFF
0805- A9 11       1030          LDA #$11
0807- 8D FE 3F    1040          STA $3FFE
080A- BA          1050          TSX
080B- 8A          1060          TXA
080C- A8          1070          TAY
080D- 6C FE 3F    1080          JMP ($3FFE)
0810- 00          1090          BRK
0811- 68          1100 STK      PLA
0812- A8          1110          TAY
0813- 68          1120          PLA
0814- AA          1130          TAX
0815- 48          1140          PHA
0816- 98          1150          TYA
0817- 48          1160          PHA
0818- A9 00       1170          LDA #$00
081A- 00          1180          BRK

SYMBOL TABLE

0800- JMPS
0811- STK
```

When the changes are made, assemble the program, but do not execute it yet. Notice that the op code of the JMP in the indirect addressing mode is $6C. Also see how the operand, ($3FFE), was assembled into addresses $080E and $080F. Remember, $3FFE is not the address of the next executable instruction. When lines 1010 through 1040 are executed, location $3FFE contains $11, and location $3FFF contains $08. The next executable instruction after the JMP is the PLA at line 1100 (address $0811). That is to say, the action taken at line 1080 is: the

6502 recognizes an indirect JMP, the contents of $3FFE and $3FFF are loaded into the PC-register, the jump to $0811 is taken, and execution continues from there. Now execute this example. The results are shown below.

```
081C-    A=00 X=10 Y=67 P=37 S=F9
```

The notable result is the contents of the accumulator, 00, which were placed there by the execution of line 1170.

Do not let any indirect jump operands end in FF!

Caution: The indirect address cannot lie across a page boundary. In the above example in line 1080, ($3FFF) could not have been chosen as the address. Had it been chosen, the $11 would be located at $3FFF and the $08 would be located at $4000. The $11 would be on page $3F and the $08 would be on page $40. If the indirect address does lie across a page boundary the JMP will not jump properly. This situation is easy to control: Obey the instruction in the note above!

If an indirect jump does lie across a page boundary, a jump is performed and the results are predictable. See if you can figure it out. This is rumored to be a "technique" used by "master" game programmers to "disguise" their code.

Relative Mode

Only the branch instructions use relative addressing, the fourth mode in the list. Relative addressing means the current contents of the PC-register are added to the operand of a branch instruction only when the condition of the branch is met. The operand of a branch instruction is only one byte long. This is an advantage because a branch instruction can be assembled into two bytes: one byte for the op code, and one byte for the displacement. The disadvantage is that the displacement can only be 127 locations forward, or 127 locations backward. Only seven bits are used to encode the value of the displacement. The eighth bit is used to signify a forward, 0, or a backward, 1, displacement. More information about the representation of negative numbers can be found in Appendix B. A branch that branches backward is the essential structure of a loop. Using branches to construct loops is the topic of Chapter 5. The 127 displacement range may seem very limited, but loops usually do not need to be any longer.

The next example illustrates relative addressing. The idea is to use Program 3.11 to demonstrate forward and backward branching with labels and without labels. Load Program 3.11 and modify it to look like the example shown below. This modification of Program 3.11 demonstrates relative addressing with labels.

PROGRAM 4.2

```
                1000 * PROGRAM 4.2 REL ADR
                1005          .OR $800
0800- A9 DD     1010 TOP      LDA #$DD
0802- 00        1020          BRK
0803- 18        1030 BRCH     CLC
0804- 90 07     1040          BCC HERE
0806- A9 11     1050          LDA #$11
0808- A2 22     1060          LDX #$22
080A- A0 33     1070          LDY #$33
080C- 00        1080          BRK
080D- 38        1090 HERE     SEC
080E- A9 AA     1100          LDA #$AA
0810- A2 BB     1110          LDX #$BB
0812- A0 CC     1120          LDY #$CC
0814- B0 EA     1130          BCS TOP

SYMBOL TABLE

0803- BRCH
080D- HERE
0800- TOP
```

Assemble the program and notice the insertion of line 1130. This is a backward branch to line 1010 labeled TOP. Execute this program from the label BRCH, not from the label TOP. The results are shown below.

```
0804-    A=DD X=BB Y=CC P=B5 S=F9
```

Let us trace the execution of this program. Execution begins at line 1030 which is labeled BRCH. Since the C-flag is cleared at this statement, the branch to HERE is taken and the C-flag is now set; the A, X, and Y registers are loaded with $AA, $BB, and $CC, respectively. The branch to TOP is taken where the A-register is now loaded with $DD. Execution of the program is halted by the BRK at line 1020.

Note how the two branch instructions are assembled. The BCC instruction at line 1040 is assembled with the op code, $90, in location $0804, and the displacement, $07, in location $0805. Since the condition of the branch is met, the address of the next executable instruction is $0804 + $02 + $07 = $080D. (The $02 is added in because the BCC is a two-byte instruction.) The BCS instruction at line 1130 is assembled with the op code, $B0, in location $0814, and the displacement, $EA, in location $0815. To understand why the contents of location $0815 are $EA, you must have a working knowledge of hexadecimal arithmetic. (If you do not, see Appendix B.) Note that $0814 + $02 = $0816, and $0800 − $0816 = $−16. In 2's-complement notation, $−16 is $EA. (This notation is discussed in Appendix B.)

The only assembler known to the authors that does not use labels is the Apple II Miniassembler on the Integer BASIC ROM. For example, the Miniassembler requires that the branch address be specified as the operand of the branch. A popular notation for indicating the current contents of the PC-register is the asterisk, *. So a statement like

```
BCS *+$15
```

means take the current contents of the PC-register, *, and add $15. If your assembler does not use this convention, read its instructions and find out how it does do unlabeled relative addressing. We shall assume that your assembler uses the popular * convention.

Modify Program 4.2 so that it looks like the one shown below.

PROGRAM 4.2M1

```
                 1000 * PROGRAM 4.2M1  REL ADR
                 1005          .OR $800
0800- A9 DD      1010          LDA #$DD
0802- 00         1020          BRK
0803- 18         1030 BRCH     CLC
0804- 90 07      1040          BCC *+$9
0806- A9 11      1050          LDA #$11
0808- A2 22      1060          LDX #$22
080A- A0 33      1070          LDY #$33
080C- 00         1080          BRK
080D- 38         1090          SEC
080E- A9 AA      1100          LDA #$AA
0810- A2 BB      1110          LDX #$BB
```

```
0812- A0 CC     1120          LDY #$CC
0814- B0 EA     1130          BCS *-$14

SYMBOL TABLE

0803- BRCH
```

The branch labels have been stripped off and the operands have been altered to reflect the lack of labels. Look at the assembled code and see that it is exactly the same as the assembled code in Program 4.2. The explanation of the contents of the second byte of each of the branch instructions is the same as in Program 4.2. And the results are the same. (Of course! The machine code is the same, regardless of what the assembler listing is!)

```
0804-    A=DD X=BB Y=CC P=B5 S=F9
```

The assembler used to assemble Program 4.2M1 does decimal to hexadecimal conversions. Hence, all you need to do is count—in decimal—the distance in bytes from where you are to where you wish to branch and use that as the displacement for the branch instruction. Execute this program from the label BRCH. The results are exactly the same as they are for Program 4.2. Some assemblers may not do the decimal to hexadecimal conversion for you, then you must use hexadecimal representations for the displacement. Check the instructions for your assembler or simply try modifying the branch instructions to read

```
1040          BCC *+$9

1130          BCS *-$14
```

Try assembling the program, then check the assembled displacements to see if they were assembled as $07 and $EA. If not, check the instructions and experiment!

Immediate Mode

Next on the list is the immediate mode of addressing. Immediate addressing is indicated by prefixing the operand with a # sign. The # sign indicates that the operand itself is to be used in the execution of the instruction. An operand preceded by a # sign is NOT an address whose contents are to be used in the execution of the instruction. This mode of addressing was used in many examples in Chapters 1, 2, and 3 with the LDA instruction. There are eleven instructions that use the immediate mode of addressing: ADC, AND, CMP, CPX, CPY, EOR, LDA, LDX, LDY, ORA, SBC.

Most of the examples in the first three chapters have used this mode of addressing, so no further examples of its use will appear here. However, if you would like to see an example, review Figure 1.2 in Chapter 1. It contains examples of LDA and LDY in the immediate mode. Program 3.1 in Chapter 3 has ADC in the immediate mode, and Program 3.2 has SBC in the immediate mode. The instructions CMP, CPX, and CPY will be used in this mode in Chapter 5; AND, EOR, and ORA will be used in the immediate mode in Chapter 6.

Zero-Page

Zero-page addressing is a short mode of addressing that can be used only when the first byte of an address is $00, i.e., page zero. The page part of the address, $00, is NOT written in the instruction. It is a short mode because only two bytes are now required for storing the complete instruction in memory. The first byte is the op code, and the second is the zero-page address.

The advantages of this mode are its compactness and, especially, its speed. Zero-page addressing is faster than any other mode. It should be used by the segments of your program that are executed most often. For example, segments contained in long or often-used loops (subroutines) might have their variables in page-zero. The key word is "often." If you can arrange that often-used segments execute faster, your program will be more efficient.

As an example let's rework Program 3.1 to use the ADC instruction in the zero-page addressing mode. The plan is to store the $13 at location $ _ _ on page zero, then, using ADC in the zero-page mode, to do the addition and store the result at location $ _ _ on page zero.

The reason for the underscores, _ _ , in the plan is that you must be careful about using page zero, especially when you wish to interface, "hook," or shake hands with other programs. To point this out more clearly, look on pages 66 and 67 of the *Apple IIe Reference Manual*, or on pages 74 and 75 of the *Apple II Reference Manual*. Here you will see which page-zero locations are used by the Monitor, Applesoft BASIC, DOS, and Integer BASIC. A black dot means this memory location is used by this program. If you wish to run your program, or any of these programs, you must NOT use these locations.

If you are linking your program to other software, check its documentation; we can always hope that the authors have provided a zero-page memory map for their program. Suppose you cannot find any documentation on zero-page memory usage (which is the usual situation), what can you do? One method that is quick, but NOT foolproof, is to run the program in some typical fashion.

In doing this "typical" run, hope that it has used all of the memory locations needed. Now use the Monitor to examine page zero. An indication of an unused memory location is to see a 00 or an FF displayed. You may "reasonably" assume that these locations are unused. No guarantees, just a quick best guess. You could also check in *What's Where in the APPLE?*, by William F. Luebbert, MICRO INK, Inc.

CAUTION: When using page-zero, be sure the locations you intend to use are free.

An efficiently written program makes maximum use of page zero. When you are planning a program we advise you to build a zero-page memory map for your program. This effort will pay off handsomely when you modify the program or link it to another program.

Following the above advice for locating unused memory locations, use the Monitor to display locations $0000 through $0007.

```
0000-    4C 3C D4 4C 3A DB FF FF
```

Locations $0006 and $0007 both contain $FF, so we guess that they are free for our use. Location $0006 will be used to store the $13 and location $0007 will be used to store the result. The modification of Program 3.1 is shown below.

PROGRAM 4.3

```
                    1000 * PROGRAM 4.3 ADD (ZERO-PAGE)
                    1005            .OR $800
0800- 18            1010 SUM        CLC
0801- F8            1020            SED
0802- A9 13         1030            LDA #$13
0804- 85 06         1040            STA $06
0806- A9 86         1050            LDA #$86
0808- 65 06         1060            ADC $06
080A- 85 07         1070            STA $07
080C- 00            1080            BRK

SYMBOL TABLE

0800- SUM
```

Assemble and execute this example. The register contents are the same as those shown in Chapter 3.

```
080E-    A=99 X=00 Y=00 P=BC S=F9
```

Use the Monitor to display the locations $0000 through $0007 again.

```
0000-    4C 3C D4 4C 3A DB 13 99
```

Notice that location $0006 contains the $13, and that $0007 contains $99, the result.

Absolute Mode

Absolute addressing is a longer mode of addressing than is zero-page addressing because it requires three bytes of memory to store an instruction in this mode. The op code requires one byte and the address now requires two bytes; a byte to specify the page and another to specify the location on the page.

Program 4.3 will be reworked to use the ADC instruction in the absolute addressing mode. The caution mentioned above for using page zero locations applies in general to all memory locations. The procedure for finding available memory locations is the same. Scanning for blocks of 00s or FFs, we find that locations $4000 through $400F are usually available unless you are using graphics.

```
4000- 00 00 FF FF 00 00 FF FF
```

Editing Program 4.3 to use the the first two locations we have:

PROGRAM 4.4

```
                1000 * PROGRAM 4.4 ADD  ABSOLUTE
1005            .OR $800
0800- 18        1010 SUM     CLC
0801- F8        1020         SED
0802- A9 13     1030         LDA #$13
0804- 8D 00 40  1040         STA $4000
0807- A9 86     1050         LDA #$86
0809- 6D 00 40  1060         ADC $4000
```

```
080C- 8D 01 40 1070          STA $4001
080F- 00       1080          BRK

SYMBOL TABLE

0800- SUM
```

Assemble and execute Program 4.4. The register contents are the same as before

```
0811-    A=99 X=00 Y=00 P=BC S=F9
```

Using the Monitor, again display the locations $4000 through $400F.

```
4000-    13 99 FF FF 00 00 FF FF
4008-    00 00 FF FF 00 00 FF FF
```

You can see that location $4000 contains the $13, and that $4001 contains $99, the result.

Indexed Modes

The six remaining modes are indexed modes of addressing. An indexed mode of addressing is one that requires two operands to determine the address used in the execution of the instruction. The address used in the execution of the instruction is called the target address; it is also called the effective address. The method of calculating the target address differs from one index mode to another.

There are two indexed addressing modes available for page zero. They are (Zero Page,X) and (Zero Page,Y). (Zero Page,X) is the primary indexed mode because it is used by sixteen of the fifty-six instructions. (Zero Page, Y) is used only by LDX and STX. To understand how a target address is calculated for (Zero Page, X) addressing, consider the ADC instruction used in this mode.

```
ADC operand1,X
```

The target address, TA, is the sum of operand1, a zero page address, plus the contents of the X-register.

TA = operand1 + (X)

(Remember: the parentheses around the X mean "the contents of X.")

To illustrate this indexed addressing mode, let's again rework Program 4.4 using the ADC in this mode. We have determined that the page zero location

$6F is a safe location to use in this example for the storage of the $13. (If you try this example and something "strange" happens, it means that $6F was not "safe" for the assembler that you are using. Find a "safe" location on page zero and use it instead of $6F.) Edit Program 4.4, or enter the op codes via the Monitor.

PROGRAM 4.5

```
                     1000 * PROGRAM 4.5 ADD  ZERO-PAGE,X
1005                 .OR $800
0800- 18             1010 SUM     CLC
0801- F8             1020         SED
0802- A9 13          1030         LDA #$13
0804- 85 6F          1040         STA $6F
0806- A9 86          1050         LDA #$86
0808- A2 5A          1060         LDX #$5A
080A- 75 15          1070         ADC $15,X
080C- 85 06          1080         STA $06
080E- 00             1090         BRK

SYMBOL TABLE

0800- SUM
```

Assemble and execute Program 4.5. The register contents are shown below.

```
0810-    A=99 X=5A Y=00 P=BC S=F9
```

Note that the contents of the X-register are now $5A. The target address of the ADC instruction was calculated by the 6502 in the following manner.

TA = operand1 + (X)
TA = $15 + $5A = $6F

When the ADC instruction is executed, the contents of $006F, $13, are fetched and added to the contents of the accumulator, $86; then the result, $99, is stored in location $0006. Use the Monitor to display the contents of these locations.

```
0000-    4C 3C D4 4C 3A DB 99 01
```

You can see that ($006F) = $13, and ($0006) = $99.

Since only two instructions use (Zero Page,Y) and since it is very similar to (Zero Page,X) no examples will be given for it. However, if you wish to work through one, just change all the Xs to Ys and execute the program again.

The most often used modes of indexed addressing are the next two in the list, 10 and 11. The Absolute,X mode is used by fifteen instructions, and the Absolute,Y mode is used by nine instructions. The absolute indexed mode is similar to the zero-page indexed mode in that operand1 is added to the contents of the index register to calculate the target address. But the difference is that operand1 is now any non-zero-page address. To understand how the target address is calculated for Absolute,X addressing, consider the ADC instruction in this mode.

```
ADC operand1, X
```

The target address is a non-zero-page address plus the contents of the X-register. Modifying Program 4.4 to illustrate Absolute,X we have:

PROGRAM 4.6

```
                1000 * PROGRAM 4.6 ADD  ABSOLUTE,X
1005            .OR $800
0800- 18        1010 SUM     CLC
0801- F8        1020         SED
0802- A9 13     1030         LDA #$13
0804- 8D 00 40  1040         STA $4000
0807- A9 86     1050         LDA #$86
0809- A2 20     1060         LDX #$20
080B- 7D E0 3F  1070         ADC $3FE0,X
080E- 8D 01 40  1080         STA $4001
0811- 00        1090         BRK

SYMBOL TABLE

0800- SUM
```

Assemble and execute Program 4.6. The register contents are shown below.

```
0813-    A=99 X=20 Y=00 P=BC S=F9
```

Note that the contents of the X-register are now $20. The target address of the ADC instruction is

```
TA = operand1 + (X)
TA =  $3FE0   + $20 = $4000
```

When this ADC instruction is executed, the contents of $4000, $13, are fetched and added to the contents of the accumulator, $86, and the result, $99, is stored in location $4001.

The Absolute,Y works in the same way, but the Y-register is used as the index register. Since this mode is so similar to the one just illustrated no example will be given. If you wish to do one, change all the Xs to Ys and execute the program again.

The next addressing mode to be discussed is (Zero Page,Y). This indexed addressing mode is very different from the four indexed modes discussed thus far. There are three differences to be remembered. First, the zero-page address in parentheses is *ONLY* the first part of an adjacent *PAIR* of addresses. Second, it is the *CONTENTS* of this pair that are used to calculate the target address. Third, the *LEAST* significant Byte (LB) of the address that is used to calculate the target address is stored in the part SHOWN in the instruction and the *MOST* significant byte (or High Byte, HB) of the address that is used to calculate the target address is stored in the part *NOT SHOWN* in the instruction. To restate this third difference again: The PAGE part of this address is stored in the part of the pair *NOT SHOWN* in the instruction, and the *LOCATION ON THIS PAGE* is stored in the part of the pair *SHOWN* in the instruction. Once this *INDIRECT* part of the target address is formed it must be added to the contents of the Y-register.

Note: This process of putting the low byte first, high byte second is standard procedure used on the 6502. This addressing practice is referred to as Low Byte–High Byte (LBHB).

The ADC instruction will be used again to show how the target address is calculated for this indirect indexed addressing mode. This example will use the memory locations we know are safe because they were used in the examples above. It will use zero-page locations $06 and $07 as the zero-page pair to store the indirect part of the target address, $3FE0, and the Y-register will contain $20. To properly arrange the page part of the target address, $3F must be stored in $07, and the location on page $3F, $E0, must be stored in $06. The remainder of the target address, $20, must be put in the Y-register. The target address calculation looks like this:

		Seen in inst.		Not seen in inst.				
TA	=	(06)	+	(07)	+	(Y)		
		Location on page		Page part				
TA	=	$E0	+	$3F00	+	$20	=	$4000
TA	=	$4000						

Editing Program 4.6 to accomplish this produces Program 4.7 shown below.

PROGRAM 4.7

```
                1000 * PROGRAM 4.7 ADD  (ZERO PAGE),Y
                1005          .OR $800
0800- 18        1010 SUM      CLC
0802- A9 3F     1030          LDA #$3F
0804- 85 07     1040          STA $07
0806- A9 E0     1050          LDA #$E0
0808- 85 06     1060          STA $06
080A- A9 13     1070          LDA #$13
080C- 8D 00 40  1080          STA $4000
080F- A9 86     1090          LDA #$86
0811- A0 20     1100          LDY #$20
0813- 71 06     1110          ADC ($06),Y
0815- 8D 01 40  1120          STA $4001
0818- 00        1130          BRK

SYMBOL TABLE

0800- SUM
```

Assemble and execute Program 4.7. The register contents are shown below.

```
081A-    A=99 X=00 Y=20 P=BC S=F9
```

The registers contain the same information as they did in Program 4.6. Use the Monitor to display the contents of the locations shown below.

```
4000-    13 99 4B 20 0A 52 53 20
```

Use the information to see how the target address was calculated.

The last addressing mode to be discussed is (Zero Page,X). This is another indirect mode of addressing. The ADC instruction will be used again to show how the target address is calculated. This indirect mode also uses a zero-page pair of locations. They contain the target address of the instruction, with the page and the location on the page stored in the pair in reverse order. The ADC instruction found in Program 4.8 is

```
ADC ($C8,X)
```

The target address for this instruction is calculated as follows:

TA = (C8 + (X))
TA = (C8 + 20)
TA = (E8)

	Location on page		Page part		
TA =	(E8)	+	(E9)		
	Contents of $E8		Contents of $E9		
TA =	$07	+	$4000	=	$4007

TA = $4007

Editing Program 4.7 to illustrate the ADC instruction in this indexed indirect mode produces Program 4.8 shown below:

PROGRAM 4.8

```
                 1000 * PROGRAM 4.8 ADD  (ZERO PAGE,X)
                 1005           .OR $800
0800- 18         1010 SUM       CLC
0801- F8         1020           SED
0802- A9 40      1030           LDA #$40
```

```
0804- 85 E9      1040          STA $E9
0806- A9 07      1050          LDA #$07
0808- 85 E8      1060          STA $E8
080A- A9 13      1070          LDA #$13
080C- 8D 07 40 1080          STA $4007
080F- A9 86      1090          LDA #$86
0811- A2 20      1100          LDX #$20
0813- 61 C8      1110          ADC ($C8,X)
0815- 8D 01 40 1120          STA $4001
0818- 00         1130          BRK

SYMBOL TABLE

0800- SUM
```

Assemble and execute Program 4.8. The register contents are shown below.

```
081A-    A=99 X=20 Y=00 P=BC S=F9
```

Use the Monitor to display the contents of the locations shown below, then use this information to see how the target address was calculated.

```
4000-    13 99 4B 20 0A 52 53 13
```

In summary, there are thirteen addressing modes available on the 6502. Even though all modes are not available for all instructions, this is (most often) not a handicap. A compilation of the modes available to each instruction is given in Appendix E. The examples given in this chapter were chosen to illustrate the structure of each addressing mode, not necessarily the most powerful use nor the most typical. Many of the examples in the following chapters use the indexed modes and the indexed indirect modes in typical settings.

CHAPTER 5

BRANCHES, LOOPS, AND NESTING

The purpose of this chapter is to illustrate the construction of loops and the use of branches to control loops. These are fundamental constructs because they provide for different pathways through a program and for repetitive use of program segments.

A loop is a program segment that contains a backward branch to an earlier statement in the program. An example of a backward branch was given in Program 4.2. The BCS TOP at statement 1130 is a backward branch to the label TOP in statement 1010. Because of the BRK at statement 1020 no loop was formed.

A LOOP

To properly illustrate a backward branch used to construct a loop, consider this problem. Often the contents of memory need to be cleared, or initialized, to some specific value. We wish to write a program to initialize 256 consecutive memory locations to a value. If the starting address of the 256 locations has the form $XY00, then page XY will be initialized to the chosen value.

It is convenient to divide the construction of loops into four stages: (1) Initialization is done before entry into the loop. Most often this is the few lines of coding just above the top of the loop. (2) The body of the loop is the part of the coding that is executed over and over as the loop grinds onward. (3) Loop control is usually done by incrementing or decrementing a counter, which sets a flag in the P-register. The control part of the loop is also executed over and over as the loop grinds onward. (4) Testing for an exit from the the loop is usually done at the bottom of the loop. Testing the appropriate flag that was set in the loop control step is done by a branch instruction at the bottom of the loop that branches to the top of the loop. When the test FAILS, the loop is exited. That is to say, when the branch condition is TRUE the next executable statement is the one at the top of the loop. When the branch condition is FALSE the next executable is the one below the branch.

Consider the program shown below, which copies the number $11 into memory locations $4000 through $40FF.

PROGRAM 5.1

```
                  1000 * PROGRAM 5.1 MEM FILL
                  1005          .OR $0800      SET ORIGIN AT $0800
0800- A9 11       1010 BEGIN    LDA #$11       LOAD FILL VALUE
0802- A0 00       1020          LDY #$00       INIT Y
0804- 99 00 40    1030 TOP      STA $4000,Y    STORE VALUE AT $4000+(Y)
0807- C8          1040          INY            SET Z-FLAG
0808- D0 FA       1050          BNE TOP        TEST Z BRANCH IF PG NOT FILLED
080A- 00          1060 DONE     BRK            STOP CALL MONITOR

SYMBOL TABLE

0800- BEGIN
080A- DONE
0804- TOP
```

The initialization stage consists of the statements 1010 and 1020. Statement 1010 loads the fill value, $11, into the accumulator. Line 1020 initializes the index register, Y, to $00. Statement 1030 is the top of the loop and it stores the contents of the accumulator at location \$4000 + (Y). On entry into the loop the target address is calculated like this:

TA = \$4000 + (Y)

TA = \$4000 + \$00 = \$4000

Statement 1040 is the only statement in the body of the loop. It increments the Y register by one, \$01, and sets the Z-flag each time 1040 is executed. This is the characteristic of the INY instruction that is used to control the loop. The loop control statement is line 1050. The Y-register is incremented each time the loop is executed. Testing for an exit from the loop is done each time the loop executes statement 1050. The Z-flag is tested, and if the contents of Y are not equal to zero, that is if Z=0, the branch to TOP is taken. If you are wondering how the contents of the Y-register ever return to zero, remember wrap-around. That is to say, the contents of the Y-register go \$00, \$01, \$03, . . . , \$FE, \$FF, \$00. On the 256th iteration of the loop, the address calculation for the target address of the STA is

TA = \$4000 + (Y)

TA = \$4000 + \$FF = \$40FF

THEN (Y), \$FF, incremented by \$01, \$FF + \$01 = \$00, and the test fails. The branch "falls through." The next instruction executed is the BRK instruction.

Key-in, assemble, and execute the program. When you get Program 5.1 working save it. You will use it again in Program 5.2. The contents of the registers at the end of execution of the program are shown below.

```
080C-    A=11 X=00 Y=00 P=37 S=F9
```

Note that A contains the fill pattern "11," Y is zeroed, and that the Z-flag is set to 1.

(P) =	3	7
	0011	0111
	NV-B	DIZC

Use the Monitor to see that memory alocations \$4000 through \$40FF have been filled with the "11" pattern. A few lines of the results are shown below.

```
4000-    11 11 11 11 11 11 11 11
```

Same pattern through

```
40F8-    11 11 11 11 11 11 11 11
4100-    FF FF 00 00 FF FF 00 00
```

Now modify line 1030 so that the starting location on the page is not $00. For example, choose $4064 and change the fill value to "22." Assemble and execute the program again. The contents of the registers are shown below.

```
080C-    A=22 X=00 Y=00 P=37 S=F9
```

Only the contents of the A-register change. The new fill pattern is "22." If you have not turned off your Apple since you executed Program 5.1, and you examine memory locations $4000 through $4067, you will see the "11" pattern from $4000 through $4063, and the "22" pattern from $4064 through $4163. A few lines with these results are shown below.

```
4000-    11 11 11 11 11 11 11 11
```

Same pattern through

```
4060-    11 11 11 11 22 22 22 22
4068-    22 22 22 22 22 22 22 22
```

Same pattern through

```
4160-    22 22 22 22 FF FF 00 00
```

However, if you restart your Apple and execute only the modification to Program 5.1 you will see the start up pattern for your RAM from $4000 through $4063, and the "22" pattern takes over through $4164.

We shall make one further modification to the program. Now suppose you do not wish to pattern 256 locations at a time, but only wish to pattern part of them. We wish to pattern only the memory locations from $4000 to some stopping address that is less than $40FF. The method of stopping the loop will be to load Y with the number of locations to be filled and then decrement Y in the loop.

PROGRAM 5.1M2

```
1000 * PROGRAM 5.1M2 MEM FILL
1005          .OR $0800      SET ORIGIN AT $0800
```

```
0800- A9 33     1010 BEGIN  LDA #$33      LOAD FILL VALUE
0802- A0 10     1020        LDY #$10      LOAD STOPPING VALUE
0804- 99 6F 40  1030 TOP    STA $406F,Y   STORE VALUE AT $406F+(Y)
0807- 88        1040        DEY           SET N & Z
0808- D0 FA     1050        BNE TOP       TEST Z BRANCH IF NOT DONE
080A- 00        1060 DONE   BRK           STOP CALL MONITOR

SYMBOL TABLE

0800- BEGIN
080A- DONE
0804- TOP
```

Note that when Program 5.1M2 is executing, memory location $407F is filled first (TA = $406F + $10 = $407F). Then Y is decremented ($10 - $01 = $0F). The second time the loop is performed location $407E is filled (TA = $406F + $0F = $406E). That is to say the pattern "33" is filled from the high address, $407F, down to the low address, $4070. In other words the filling process is done "backwards."

Modify Program 5.1 to reflect these changes. Assemble and execute the program. The contents of the registers are shown below.

```
080C-    A=33 X=00 Y=00 P=37 S=F9
```

Use the Monitor to display memory locations $4000 through $4167. If you have not turned off your Apple after executing Program 5.1 and its first modification you will see

```
4000-    11 11 11 11 11 11 11 11
```

Same pattern through

```
405F-    11 11 11 11 11 11 11 11
4060-    11 11 11 11 22 22 22 22
4068-    22 22 22 22 22 22 22 22
4070-    33 33 33 33 33 33 33 33
4078-    33 33 33 33 33 33 33 33
4080-    22 22 22 22 22 22 22 22
```

Same pattern through

```
4160-    22 22 22 22 FF FF 00 00
```

Next we wish to present an example that will fill more than 256 memory locations at a time. To do this we must change the method of addressing. Indexed addressing was used in Programs 5.1 and 5.1M2 (see line 1030). The method used in the next example is post-indexed addressing (see line 1170 of Program 5.2).

NESTED LOOPS AND THE COMPARE INSTRUCTIONS

Nested loops will be used to accomplish the filling of more than one page of memory. Loops are said to be nested if one loop is contained inside another loop. That is to say, the body of one loop, the outer loop, contains another loop, the inner loop. Program 5.2 loops over not only the locations on a page, but also several pages of memory. The program shown below contains an outside loop (TOPOUT) that loops over the pages. The inside loop (TOPIN) loops the locations on the page, and actually stores the value in each location on the page. The outside loop merely keeps track of the page on which the inside loop is working. The program permits starting at any location (LSTART) on an initial page. It then fills the remainder of the initial page and every location on the remaining pages.

```
PROGRAM 5.2               1000 * PROGRAM 5.2 FILL PAGES
                   1005          .OR $0800      SET ORIGIN AT $0800
                   1010 * INITIALIZATION
3FF8-              1020 PSTART .EQ $3FF8     STARTING PAGE
3FF9-              1030 PSTOP  .EQ $3FF9     STOPPING PAGE
0008-              1040 PAGE   .EQ $08       CURRENT PAGE
3FFB-              1050 LSTART .EQ $3FFB     STARTING LOC. ON 1ST PG.
0800- A9 40        1060 BEGIN  LDA #$40      STARTING PAGE
0802- 85 09        1070        STA PAGE+1    STORE IT
0804- 8D F8 3F     1080        STA PSTART    AGAIN FOR SAFE KEEPING
0807- A9 24        1090        LDA #$24      INIT. START PAGE LOC.
0809- 85 08        1100        STA PAGE      STORE IT
080B- A9 70        1110        LDA #$70      STOPPING PAGE
080D- 8D F9 3F     1120        STA PSTOP     STORE IT
0810- A0 00        1130        LDY #$00      STARTING LOC. ON 1ST PG.
                   1140 * TOP OF OUTER LOOP
0812- A9 52        1150 TOPOUT LDA #$52      RELOAD FILL VALUE
                   1160 * TOP OF INNER LOOP
0814- 91 08        1170 TOPIN  STA (PAGE),Y STORE VALUE AT PAGE+Y
                   1180 * INNER LOOP CONTROL
```

```
0816- C8        1190          INY           AND SET N & Z
                1200 * TEST INSIDE LOOP
0817- D0 FB     1210          BNE TOPIN     FINISHED WITH THIS PAGE?
0819- 84 08     1220          STY PAGE      STORE IT
                1230 * OUTER LOOP CONTROL
081B- E6 09     1240          INC PAGE+1    INC TO NEXT PAGE
081D- AD F9 3F  1250          LDA PSTOP     LOAD STOPPING PAGE
0820- C5 09     1260          CMP PAGE+1    SET N, Z & C
                1270 * TEST OUTSIDE LOOP
0822- D0 EE     1280          BNE TOPOUT    FINISHED ALL PAGES?
0824- 00        1290 DONE     BRK           STOP AND CALL MONITOR

SYMBOL TABLE

0800- BEGIN
0824- DONE
3FFB- LSTART
0008- PAGE
3FF8- PSTART
3FF9- PSTOP
0814- TOPIN
0812- TOPOUT
```

The purpose of line 1220 is to store the $00 in the Y-register in location PAGE. This stops the filling on a page boundary.

Outer loop control is done in this example using the CMP instruction, which compares memory and accumulator. The CMP instruction SUBTRACTS the contents of the memory location specified by the operand (PAGE + 1) FROM the contents of the accumulator (PSTOP). The N, Z, and C flags are set according to the result of the subtraction. Neither the contents of the memory location nor the contents of the accumulator are changed, nor is the result of the subtraction kept. The CMP instruction has the largest number of addressing modes available of the three compare instructions.

The other compare instructions are CPX and CPY. The action taken by these instructions is similar to the CMP instruction. Each instruction SUBTRACTS the contents of the specified memory location FROM the indicated register (the X-register for CPX, and the Y-register for CPY).

In the outer loop control section of the example, PAGE + 1 is incremented by 1 (line 1240); PSTOP is loaded into the accumulator (line 1250); the subtraction is performed and the flags are set (line 1260). Line 1280 tests the Z-flag; if it is not zero the branch to TOPOUT is taken.

Key-in the program, assemble, and execute it. The register contents are shown below.

```
0826-    A=70 X=00 Y=00 P=37 S=F9
```

If you have not turned off your Apple, then the results are:

```
3FF8-    40 70 FF FF FF FF FF FF
4000-    11 11 11 11 11 11 11 11
4008-    11 11 11 11 11 11 11 11
4010-    11 11 11 11 11 11 11 11
4018-    11 11 11 11 11 11 11 11
4020-    11 11 11 11 52 52 52 52
4028-    52 52 52 52 52 52 52 52
```

Same pattern through

```
6FF8-    52 52 52 52 52 52 52 52
7000-    7F 7F 00 00 7F 7F 00 00
```

The pattern "52" begins at location $4020 and ends at location $6FFF. Location $3FF8 contains $40, the starting page; location $3FF9 contains the stopping page. Save this program; you will need it again in Chapter 10.

To see an interesting effect, do not reload the fill value into the accumulator at the top of the outer loop, line 1150. Instead, load the accumulator with the current page number, and reset line 1090 to 00. This modification is shown below. Assemble and execute the program. Can you predict what will be in memory after the execution of this program?

PROGRAM 5.2M1

```
                  1000 * PROGRAM 5.2M1        FILL PAGES MOD1
                  1005          .OR $0800     SET ORIGIN AT $0800
                  1010 * INITIALIZATION
3FF8-             1020 PSTART .EQ $3FF8       STARTING PAGE
3FF9-             1030 PSTOP  .EQ $3FF9       STOPPING PAGE
0008-             1040 PAGE   .EQ $08         CURRENT PAGE
3FFB-             1050 LSTART .EQ $3FFB       STARTING LOC. ON 1ST PG.
0800- A9 40       1060 BEGIN  LDA #$40        STARTING PAGE
0802- 85 09       1070        STA PAGE+1      STORE IT
0804- 8D F8 3F    1080        STA PSTART      AGAIN FOR SAFE KEEPING
```

```
0807- A9 00          LDA #$00     INIT. START PAGE LOC.
0809- 85 08          STA PAGE     STORE IT
080B- A9 70          LDA #$70     STOPPING PAGE
080D- 8D F9 3F       STA PSTOP    STORE IT
0810- A0 00          LDY #$00     STARTING LOC. ON 1ST PG.
           * TOP OF OUTER LOOP
0812- A5 09    TOPOUT LDA PAGE+1  RESET THE FILL VALUE
           * TOP OF INNER LOOP
0814- 91 08    TOPIN  STA (PAGE),Y STORE VALUE AT PAGE+Y
           * INNER LOOP CONTROL
0816- C8             INY          AND SET N & Z
           * TEST INSIDE LOOP
0817- D0 FB          BNE TOPIN    FINISHED WITH THIS PAGE?
0819- 84 08          STY PAGE     RESET LOC ON PG TO $00
           * OUTER LOOP CONTROL
081B- E6 09          INC PAGE+1   INC TO NEXT PAGE
081D- AD F9 3F       LDA PSTOP    LOAD STOPPING PAGE
0820- C5 09          CMP PAGE+1   SET N, Z & C
           * TEST OUTSIDE LOOP
0822- D0 EE          BNE TOPOUT   FINISHED ALL PAGES?
0824- 00       DONE  BRK          STOP AND CALL MONITOR
```

```
SYMBOL TABLE

0800- BEGIN
0824- DONE
3FFB- LSTART
0008- PAGE
3FF8- PSTART
3FF9- PSTOP
0814- TOPIN
0812- TOPOUT
```

The contents of the registers are shown below.

```
0826-    A=70 X=00 Y=00 P=37 S=F9
```

Here is a list of a few of the memory locations filled by this program.

```
3FF8-    40 70 FF FF FF FF FF FF
4000-    40 40 40 40 40 40 40 40
4008-    40 40 40 40 40 40 40 40
```

Same pattern through

```
40F8-    40 40 40 40 40 40 40 40
4100-    41 41 41 41 41 41 41 41
```

Same pattern through

```
41F8-    41 41 41 41 41 41 41 41
4200-    42 42 42 42 42 42 42 42
```

Same pattern through

```
42F8-    42 42 42 42 42 42 42 42
4300-    43 43 43 43 43 43 43 43
```

See how the patterns progress;
they keep going up to

```
6EF8-    6E 6E 6E 6E 6E 6E 6E 6E
6F00-    6F 6F 6F 6F 6F 6F 6F 6F
```

Same 6F pattern through

```
6FF8-    6F 6F 6F 6F 6F 6F 6F 6F
7000-    7F 7F 00 00 7F 7F 00 00
```

In this example, the fill value is the page number. In the next example, we will use the idea of incrementing the accumulator and storing its contents at a location to fill a table.

TABLE BUILDING

To further illustrate the use of nested loop, we wish to construct an 8 by 8 table. That is, the table will have eight columns and eight rows. The table is to look like this:

```
11 12 13 14 15 16 17 18
21 22 23 24 25 26 27 28
31 32 33 34 35 36 37 38
41 42 43 44 45 46 47 48
51 52 53 54 55 56 57 58
61 62 63 64 65 66 67 68
71 72 73 74 75 76 77 78
81 82 83 84 85 86 87 88
```

An 8 by 8 table was chosen because memory is displayed in eight columns by the Apple Monitor. Therefore it will be easy for you to see the table on the screen.

To build this table an outside loop is required to count off the row locations, and an inside loop is required to count off the column locations. As in the first two examples in this chapter the Y-register will be used as the index register.

The program shown below will build an 8 by 8 table starting at location $4000.

PROGRAM 5.3

```
                1000 * PROGRAM 5.3 BUILD TABLE
                1005        .OR $0800     SET ORIGIN AT $0800
                1010 * INITIALIZATIONS
0008-           1020 TABLE  .EQ $08       STARTING ADDRESS OF TABLE
3FF8-           1030 LR     .EQ $3FF8     LENGTH OF A ROW
3FF9-           1040 LC     .EQ $3FF9     LENGTH OF A COLUMN
3FFA-           1050 LRS    .EQ $3FFA     KEEP LR SAFE
3FFB-           1060 LCS    .EQ $3FFB     KEEP LC SAFE
0800- A9 40     1070 BEGIN  LDA #$40      PAGE OF TABLE
0802- 85 09     1080        STA TABLE+1   STORE IT
0804- A9 00     1090        LDA #$00      LOC ON PAGE FOR TABLE
0806- 85 08     1100        STA TABLE     STORE IT
0808- A9 08     1110        LDA #$08      NUMBER OF ROWS
080A- 8D F8 3F  1120        STA LR        STORE IT
080D- 8D FA 3F  1130        STA LRS       AGAIN TO KEEP IT SAFE
0810- A9 08     1140        LDA #$08      NUMBER OF COLUMNS
0812- 8D F9 3F  1150        STA LC        STORE IT
0815- 8D FB 3F  1160        STA LCS       AGAIN TO KEEP IT SAFE
0818- A0 00     1170        LDY #$00      INIT LOC COUNTER
081A- A9 11     1180        LDA #$11      INIT FILL VALUE
081C- AE FB 3F  1190 TOPOUT LDX LCS       RELOAD NO. OF COLUMNS
081F- 8E F9 3F  1200        STX LC        RESET NO. OF COLUMNS
0822- 91 08     1210 TOPIN  STA (TABLE),Y STORE VALUE AT TABLE+Y
0824- 18        1220        CLC           CLEAR CARRY FOR ADDITION
0825- 69 01     1230        ADC #$01      INC ACCUM TO NEXT COL VALUE
0827- C8        1240        INY           INC Y TO NEXT LOC
0828- CE F9 3F  1250        DEC LC        COUNT COLUMNS SET N, Z & C
082B- D0 F5     1260        BNE TOPIN     FINISHED THIS ROW?
```

```
082D- 18        1270        CLC           CLEAR CARRY FOR ADDITION
082E- 69 08     1280        ADC #$08      INC ACCUM TO NEXT COL VALUE
0830- CE F8 3F  1290        DEC LR        COUNT ROWS SET N, Z &C
0833- D0 E7     1300        BNE TOPOUT    FINISHED TABLE?
0835- 00        1310 DONE   BRK           STOP AND CALL MONITOR

SYMBOL TABLE

0800- BEGIN
0835- DONE
3FF9- LC
3FFB- LCS
3FF8- LR
3FFA- LRS
0008- TABLE
0822- TOPIN
081C- TOPOUT
```

When you key-in, assemble, and execute the program these will be the results:

```
Register contents:
082D-    A=91 X=08 Y=40 P=36 S=F9

Memory contents:
3FF8-    00 00 08 08 FF FF FF FF
4000-    11 12 13 14 15 16 17 18
4008-    21 22 23 24 25 26 27 28
4010-    31 32 33 34 35 36 37 38
4018-    41 42 43 44 45 46 47 48
4020-    51 52 53 54 55 56 57 58
4028-    61 62 63 64 65 66 67 68
4030-    71 72 73 74 75 76 77 78
4038-    81 82 83 84 85 86 78 88
```

Let us take a closer look at some aspects of this program. LR and LC have been saved a second time in LRS and LCS (lines 1130 and 1169) as a reminder. They serve no logical purpose in this example and these two lines may be eliminated, if you wish. When the last element in any row is filled, the accumulator will have the value R9, where R is the number of the row in the accumulator when the inside loop finishes. To get the first value in the next row, R+1, we need to add $08 to the current contents of the accumulator, that is:

(A) at the end of the inside loop →	R9
Add 08 →	+ 08
(A) at the top of the inside loop on reentry →	/R+1/1

Specifically at the end of the first row:

(A) →	19
Add 08 →	+ 08
(A) upon first entry of inside loop →	21

At the end of the second row:

(A) →	29
Add 08 →	+ 08
(A) upon 2nd entry of inside loop →	31

and so on for all eight iterations of the outside loop.

The addition of $08 advances the value in the accumulator to the value at the beginning of the next row. This addition is done at statement 1210. Save Program 5.3 to disk before proceeding.

Before going on to modifications to Program 5.3 we shall modify Program 5.1 so that it can be used to clear page $40 to zeros. To do this, load Program 5.1 as the working file for your assembler. Add the ORigin directive (.OR) for your assembler. For this example, CLEAR will be assembled into locations starting at $6000. Change the fill value to $00, and change the BRK instruction in line 1150 to the RTS instruction. Now execution of the program will fill page $40 with zeros and return to your assembler instead of calling the Monitor when it executes. Test your modification for proper execution and save it to disk with the file name CLEAR. You will need to CLEAR page $40 between execution of the modifications to Program 5.3. The CLEAR program is shown below.

```
                1000 * PROGRAM CLEAR
                1010            .OR $6000
6000- A9 00     1020 BEGIN  LDA #$00     LOAD FILL VALUE
6002- A0 00     1030        LDY #$00     INIT Y
6004- 99 00 40  1040 TOP    STA $4000,Y  STORE VALUE AT $4000+Y
6007- C8        1050        INY          SET N & Z
6008- D0 FA     1060        BNE TOP      TEST Z BRANCH IF PG NOT FILLED
600A- 60        1070 DONE   RTS          RETURN

SYMBOL TABLE

6000- BEGIN
600A- DONE
6004- TOP
```

Alternatively, you could use HGR2, which begins at $F3D8, to clear the screen to black. HGR2 also toggles the soft switch at $C052, which sets the full screen display. (If you are working with a split screen display this characteristic of HGR2 would be annoying.)

Program 5.3 has no flexibility. This program can construct only an 8 by 8 table. We wish to modify this program so that it will build any table up to eight columns and as many rows as we wish. The modified program is shown below.

PROGRAM 5.3M1

```
                  1000 * PROGRAM 5.3M1 BUILD TABLE MOD1
                  1005         .OR $0800      SET ORIGIN AT $0800
                  1010 * INITIALIZATIONS
3FF8-             1020 LR      .EQ $3FF8     LENGTH OF A ROW
3FF9-             1030 LC      .EQ $3FF9     LENGTH OF A COLUMN
3FFA-             1040 LCS     .EQ $3FFA     KEEP LC SAFE
3FFB-             1050 CNTR    .EQ $3FFB     POSITION COUNTER
3FFC-             1060 KEEP    .EQ $3FFC     KEEP ACCUMULATOR HERE
0800- A9 04       1070 BEGIN   LDA #$04      NUMBER OF ROWS
0802- 8D F8 3F    1080         STA LR        STORE IT
0805- A9 04       1090         LDA #$04      NUMBER OF COLUMNS
0807- 8D F9 3F    1100         STA LC        STORE IT
080A- 8D FA 3F    1110         STA LCS       AGAIN TO KEEP IT SAFE
080D- A0 00       1120         LDY #$00      INIT LOC COUNTER
080F- A9 11       1130         LDA #$11      INIT FILL VALUE
0811- A2 08       1140 TOPOUT  LDX #$08      RESET COUNTER
0813- 8E FB 3F    1150         STX CNTR      STORE IT
0816- AE FA 3F    1160         LDX LCS       RELOAD NO. OF COLUMNS
0819- 8E F9 3F    1170         STX LC        RESET NO. OF COLUMNS
081C- 99 00 40    1180 TOPIN   STA $4000,Y   STORE VALUE AT TABLE+(Y)
081F- 18          1190         CLC           CLEAR CARRY FOR ADDITION
0820- 69 01       1200         ADC #$01      INC ACCUM TO NEXT COL VALUE
0822- C8          1210         INY           INC Y TO NEXT LOC
0823- CE FB 3F    1220         DEC CNTR      COUNT POSITIONS
0826- CE F9 3F    1230         DEC LC        COUNT COLUMNS SET N, Z & C
0829- D0 F1       1240         BNE TOPIN     FINISHED THIS ROW?
082B- 8D FC 3F    1250         STA KEEP      KEEP ACCUM FOR LATTER
082E- 18          1260         CLC           CLEAR CARRY FOR ADDITION
082F- 98          1270         TYA           PUT CURRENT ADDRESS INTO A
0830- 6D FB 3F    1280         ADC CNTR      ADD ON LEFT OVER ADDRESSES
```

```
0833- A8       1290        TAY          PUT UPDATED ADDRESS BACK INTO Y
0834- AD FC 3F 1300        LDA KEEP     RESTORE ACCUMULATOR
0837- 18       1310        CLC          CLEAR CARRY FOR ADDITION
0838- 6D FB 3F 1320        ADC CNTR     ADD ON LEFT OVER POSITIONS
083B- 69 08    1330        ADC #$08     INC ACCUM TO NEXT COL VALUE
083D- CE F8 3F 1340        DEC LR       COUNT ROWS SET N, Z & C
0840- D0 CF    1350        BNE TOPOUT   FINISHED TABLE?
0842- 00       1360 DONE   BRK          STOP AND CALL MONITOR

SYMBOL TABLE

0800- BEGIN
3FFB- CNTR
0842- DONE
3FFC- KEEP
3FF9- LC
3FFA- LCS
3FF8- LR
081C- TOPIN
0811- TOPOUT
```

Locations LR and LC are used to store the length of a row and and the length of a column, respectively. These locations are used to count off the rows and columns as they are filled. The example is set up to build a 4 by 4 table; lines 1070 through 1110 put the 4s into these locations.

The accumulator must now be used to do, not only the addition for the fill value, but also some of the addition for the addressing. CNTR is used to do the address updating when a row is only partially filled, line 1280, and to update the fill value when a row is only partially filled, line 1370. The purpose of line 1250 is to KEEP the current contents of the accumulator, the last fill value plus one, safe while the address updating is done, lines 1270 through 1290, and then to restore this value, line 1300, and update it, lines 1320 and 1330.

If you have not turned off your Apple since you ran Program 5.3, you need to run—load, assemble and execute—CLEAR before running Program 5.3M1. And if you have not turned off your Apple since you last ran CLEAR (it still exists starting at location $6000), then you can execute CLEAR from the Monitor by keying-in 6000G. If you do not run CLEAR before running Program 5.3M1 you will not "see" anything happen, because 5.3 put an 11 in the first row, first column, and a 12 in the first row, second column, etc. Program 5.3M1 does the same thing, but only in the 4 by 4 block in the table. Therefore nothing changes in this table. Save Program 5.3M1 to disk, run CLEAR, then run Program 5.3M1. The results are shown below.

Register contents:

```
084E-    A=51 X=04 Y=20 P=36 S=F9
```

Memory contents:

```
3FF8-    00 00 04 04 04 45 FF FF
4000-    11 12 13 14 00 00 00 00
4008-    21 22 23 24 00 00 00 00
4010-    31 32 33 34 00 00 00 00
4018-    41 42 43 44 00 00 00 00
4020-    00 00 00 00 00 00 00 00
```

This example will also fill tables that are not square. Change the number of rows to $0B and the number of columns to $07. Run the program again; these results are shown below.

Register contents:

```
A=C1 X=07 Y=58 P=36 S=F9
```

Memory contents:

```
3FF8-    00 00 0B 07 00 00 00 00
4000-    11 12 13 14 15 16 17 00
4008-    21 22 23 24 25 26 27 00
4010-    31 32 33 34 35 36 37 00
4018-    41 42 43 44 45 46 47 00
4020-    51 52 53 54 55 56 57 00
4028-    61 62 63 64 65 66 67 00
4030-    71 72 73 74 75 76 77 00
4038-    81 82 83 84 85 86 87 00
4040-    91 92 93 94 95 96 97 00
4048-    A1 A2 A3 A4 A5 A6 A7 00
4050-    B1 B2 B3 B4 B5 B6 B7 00
4058-    00 00 00 00 00 00 00 00
```

This chapter gave you some experience with branches used to construct and control simple loops. It also showed you how to nest loops and how to manipulate elements in a table. In the next chapter some of the examples will use the elements in a table as input to examples on arithmetic.

CHAPTER 6

LOGICAL OPERATIONS AND BIT MANIPULATIONS

The purpose of this chapter is to illustrate two classes of instructions that are used primarily to change or to test a single bit. Remember that a bit is the smallest piece of information processed by a digital computer. Its value is either a 1 or a 0. A byte is eight bits grouped together and is the smallest addressable unit of information processed by a digital computer. Since only bytes (eight bits) can be moved, stored, fetched, or processed by the 6502 ALU, there must be instructions that easily allow for the processing, changing, and testing of single bits in a byte. There are two classes of instructions that do this: (1) logical operations and (2) bit shifts and rotations.

The instructions that perform logical operations are AND, EOR, and ORA. There is one instruction that performs a logical test; it is the BIT instruction. There are four instructions that move all the bits in a byte; they are ASL, LSR, ROL, and ROR.

AND

Before going too deeply into use of these instructions, let's look at the meaning of the logical operation AND. This operation is performed at the bit level and requires two bits. The table below shows all possible combinations of the required bits in the guide row and column and the result is in the body of the table.

	AND	Mem bit 0	Mem bit 1
Acc bit	0	0	0
	1	0	1

Acc Bit	AND	Mem Bit	=	Result in table
0	AND	0	=	0
0	AND	1	=	0
1	AND	0	=	0
1	AND	1	=	1

That is all there is to the AND instruction at the bit level. This is the way the AND instruction works in the 6502:

(A) ← (A) AND (Memory)

That is, the contents of the accumulator are ANDed bit by bit with the contents of a memory location, then the result is stored in the accumulator. Consider this short program.

```
LDA #$33
AND #$BB
BRK
```

Here is what happens.

(A) in hex	→	3	3
(A) in binary	→	0011	0011
(M) in binary	→	1011	1011
(A) AND (M)	→	0011	0011
(A) after AND	→	3	3

Key-in and run this example; the results of its execution are shown below.

PROGRAM 6.1

```
                1000 * PROGRAM 6.1 LOGICAL AND
                1005          .OR $800     SET ORIGIN AT $800
0800- A9 33     1010 AND      LDA #$33
0802- 29 BB     1020          AND #$BB
0804- 00        1030          BRK

SYMBOL TABLE

0800- AND
```

Register contents:

0806- A=33 X=00 Y=00 P=35 S=F9

Note that AND sets the N and the Z flags.

```
(P) in hex    →       3         5
(P) in binary → 0 0 1 1   0 1 0 1
The flags     → N V - B   D I Z C
```

Z=0 indicating a nonzero result; N=0 indicating that bit 7 of the accumulator is off.

EOR

This operation is also performed bit by bit on a byte in the accumulator and a byte in memory. This is called the Exclusive OR, EOR. The table below shows all possible combinations of the bits.

EOR		Mem bit 0	Mem bit 1
Acc bit	0	0	1
	1	1	0

Acc Bit	AND	Mem Bit	=	Result in table
0	AND	0	=	0
0	AND	1	=	1
1	AND	0	=	1
1	AND	1	=	0

The EOR instruction is sometimes remembered as "one OR the other, but not both."

Edit Program 6.1 to do EOR in line 1020. Key-in and run Program 6.2; the program and the results of its execution are shown below.

PROGRAM 6.2

```
                1000 * PROGRAM 6.2 LOGICAL EOR
                1005          .OR $800      SET ORIGIN AT $800
0800- A9 33     1010 EOR      LDA #$33
0802- 49 BB     1020          EOR #$BB
0804- 00        1030          BRK

SYMBOL TABLE

0800- EOR
```

Register contents:

```
0806-   A=88 X=00 Y=00 P=B5 S=F9
```

Here is what happened.

```
(A) in binary → 0011  0011
(M) in binary → 1011  1011
(A) EOR (M)   → 1000  1000
(A) after EOR →    8     8
```

Note that EOR sets the N and the Z flags.

```
(P) in hex    →       B        5
(P) in binary → 1 0 1 1  0 1 0 1
The flags     → N V - B  D I Z C
```

ORA

There are two slightly different OR instructions. The other OR instruction is called the Inclusive OR, ORA. This operation is also performed bit by bit on a byte in memory and a byte in the accumulator. The table below shows all possible combinations of the bits.

ORA		Mem bit 0	Mem bit 1
Acc bit	0	0	1
	1	1	1

Acc Bit	AND	Mem Bit	=	Result in table
0	AND	0	=	0
0	AND	1	=	1
1	AND	0	=	1
1	AND	1	=	1

The ORA instruction is sometimes remembered as "one OR the other, OR both."

Edit Program 6.2 to do ORA in line 1020. Key-in the changes and run Program 6.3; the program and the results of its execution are shown below.

PROGRAM 6.3

```
                1000 * PROGRAM 6.3 LOGICAL ORA
                1005          .OR $800      SET ORIGIN AT $800
0800- A9 33     1010 ORA      LDA #$33
0802- 09 BB     1020          ORA #$BB
0804- 00        1030          BRK

SYMBOL TABLE
0800- ORA
```

Register contents:

```
0806-   A=BB X=00 Y=00 P=B5 S=F9
```

Here is what happened.

(A) in binary → 0011 0011
(M) in binary → 1011 1011
(A) ORA (M) → 1011 1011
(A) after ORA → B B

Note that ORA sets the N and the Z flags.

```
(P) in hex    →        B         5
(P) in binary →  1 0 1 1   0 1 0 1
The flags     →  N V - B   D I Z C
```

Z=0 indicating a nonzero result; N=1 indicating that bit 7 of the accumulator is on.

BIT

The fourth logical instruction, BIT, only tests the contents of the accumulator with the contents of a memory location. Neither the contents of the accumulator nor the contents of memory are changed. Only the flags are changed, and the manner in which they are set is unusual. The BIT instruction ANDs (A) with (M). The Z-flag is set according to the result of the operation; Z=1 if (A) AND (M) is zero (0000), and Z=0 if (A) AND (M) is not zero (a 1 appears anywhere in the byte). N and V are set according to bits 7 and 6 of (M). N=bit 7 of (M); V=bit 6 of (M). Another peculiarity of the BIT instruction is that it has only two addressing modes: (1) zero page, (2) absolute. Edit Program 6.3 to do the BIT instruction in line 1020; also change the contents of the accumulator to $77. Key-in the changes and run Program 6.4; the program and the results of its execution are shown below.

PROGRAM 6.4

```
                1000 * PROGRAM 6.4 LOGICAL BIT
                1005         .OR $800      SET ORIGIN AT $800
0800- A9 BB     1010 BIT     LDA #$BB
0802- 85 07     1020         STA $07
0804- A9 77     1030         LDA #$77
0806- 24 07     1040         BIT $07
0808- 00        1050         BRK

SYMBOL TABLE

0800- BIT
```

Register contents:

```
080A-    A=77 X=00 Y=00 P=B5 S=F9
```

Memory contents:

```
0000- 4C 3C D4 4C 3A DB 00 BB
```

```
(A) in binary  →  0111  0111
(M) in binary  →  1011  1011
(A) AND (M)    →  0011  0011(result is 'lost')
(A) after BIT  →  0111  0111(same as before)
```

Note that BIT sets the N, V and Z flags.

```
(P) in hex     →     B      5
(P) in binary  →   1011   0101
The flags      →   NV-B   DIZC
```

Z=0 indicating the result is not zero; N=1 indicating bit 7 of (M) is 1, and V=0 indicating bit 6 of (M) is 0.

The four instructions that move all the bits within a byte will be illustrated next. When no operand is written for these instructions the contents of the accumulator are shifted or rotated. When an operand is written the contents of the specified memory location are shifted or rotated. First let's look at the shift instructions.

ASL

The instruction that shifts bits to the left is the ASL (Arithmetic Shift Left) instruction. This instruction sets the N, Z, and C flags. The carry bit is most easily visualized as being situated to the left of the accumulator. The zero creator is most easily visualized as being situated to the right of the accumulator. It has an endless pile of zeros to place into bit 0 of the accumulator when the ASL instruction is executed. Here is the picture, and an example that shows the result of an ASL.

	Carry bit	Accumulator (Memory loc)		Pile of zeros
(A) in hex →		4	3	
(A) in binary →	_	0100	0011	0
Bit number →		7654	3210	

Perform an ASL on (A)—first shift.

(A) in binary →	0	1000	0110	0
(A) in hex →		8	6	

Perform another ASL on (A)—second shift.

(A) in binary →	1	0000	1100	0
(A) in hex →		0	C	

Perform another ASL on (A)—third shift.

(A) in binary →	0	0001	1000	0
(A) in hex →		1	8	

Perform another ASL on (A)—fourth shift.

(A) in binary →	0	0011	0000	0
(A) in hex →		3	0	

The four examples shown below do 1, 2, 3, and 4 ASLs. In these examples no operand for the ASL instruction is specified, therefore the contents of the accumulator, $43, are shifted. The results of the executions are also shown.

PROGRAM 6.5

```
                1000 * PROGRAM 6.5   MOVE BITS IN BYTE
                1005          .OR $800      SET ORIGIN AT $800
0800- A9 43     1010 ASL      LDA #$43
0802- 0A        1020          ASL
0803- 00        1030          BRK

SYMBOL TABLE
0800- ASL
```

Register contents:

```
0805-   A=86 X=00 Y=00 P=B4 S=F9
```

```
(P) in hex    →       B        4
(P) in binary → 1 0 1 1  0 1 0 0
The flags     → N V - B  D I Z C
```

PROGRAM 6.5M1

```
                1000 * PROGRAM 6.5M1 MOVE BITS IN BYTE
                1005          .OR $800      SET ORIGIN AT $800
0800- A9 43     1010 ASL      LDA #$43
0802- 0A        1020          ASL
0803- 0A        1021          ASL
0804- 00        1030          BRK

SYMBOL TABLE

0800- ASL
```

Register contents:

```
0806-   A=0C X=00 Y=00 P=35 S=F9
```

```
   (P) in hex →       3        4
(P) in binary → 0 0 1 1  0 1 0 0
    The flags → N V - B  D I Z C
```

PROGRAM 6.5M2

```
                1000 * PROGRAM 6.5M2 MOVE BITS IN BYTE
                1005          .OR $800      SET ORIGIN AT $800
0800- A9 03     1010 ASL      LDA #$03
0802- 0A        1020          ASL
0803- 0A        1021          ASL
0804- 0A        1022          ASL
0805- 00        1030          BRK

SYMBOL TABLE

0800- ASL
```

Register contents:

```
0807-   A=18 X=00 Y=00 P=34 S=F9
```

```
   (P) in hex →       3         4
(P) in binary →  0 0 1 1   0 1 0 0
    The flags →  N V - B   D I Z C
```

PROGRAM 6.5M3

```
                1000 * PROGRAM 6.5M3 MOVE BITS IN BYTE
                1005          .OR $800      SET ORIGIN AT $800
0800- A9 43     1010 ASL      LDA #$43
0802- 0A        1020          ASL
0803- 0A        1021          ASL
0804- 0A        1022          ASL
0805- 0A        1023          ASL
0806- 00        1030          BRK

SYMBOL TABLE

0800- ASL
```

Register contents:

```
0808-  A=30 X=00 Y=00 P=34 S=F9
```

The P-flags for this program are the same as in Program 6.5M2.

Note that a single ASL is multiplication by 2 in hex. However you must be cautious about a 1 showing up in the Carry flag. When a 1 does show up in the Carry flag, the result of the multiplication is no longer represented in the accumulator (memory location) alone. This is the meaning of overflow, but ASL does not set the V-flag; only ADC and SBC do that.

Here is a summary of the ASL operations, viewed as multiplications by two.

First ASL	\$43 × \$02 \$86	
Second ASL	\$86 × \$02 10\$C	(This is eight-bit overflow because the 1 is in the carry flag.)
Third ASL	\$10C × \$002 \$218	(But the Carry flag cannot hold a 2. In fact, the Carry flag had a 0 shifted into it.)
Fourth ASL	\$18 × \$02 \$30	

LSR

The instruction that shifts bits to the right is the LSR (Logical Shift Right) instruction. For this instruction, visualize the carry bit as being situated to the right of the accumulator (memory location), and the endless pile of zeros on the left of the accumulator (memory location). These zeros are placed into bit 7 of the accumulator (memory location) when an LSR is executed. Execution of LSR sets the N, Z, and C flags. Since zeros are always shifted into bit 7, N is always set to zero. Here is the picture.

	Pile of zeros	Accumulator (Memory loc)		Carry bit
(M) in hex →		5	1	
(M) in binary →	0	0101	0001	
	_	----	----	_
Bit number →		7654	3210	

First shift.
Perform an LSR on (M).

(M) in binary →	0	0010	1000	1
	_	----	----	_
(M) in hex →		2	8	

Second shift.
Perform another LSR on (M).

(M) in binary →	1	0001	0100	0
	_	----	----	_
(M) in hex →		1	4	

Note that a single LSR is equivalent to division by two with the result truncated to an integer. That is:

$51/$2 → (5*16 + 1)/2 = 81/2 = 40.5 → 40 → 2*16 + 8 → $28

The two examples shown do 1 and 2 LSRs. In these examples the operand is the memory location $3FF8. The contents of this memory location ($51) are shifted. The results of the executions are shown.

PROGRAM 6.6

```
                1000 * PROGRAM 6.6   MOVE BITS IN BYTE
                1005        .OR $800      SET ORIGIN AT $800
0800- A9 51     1010 LSR    LDA #$51
0802- 8D F8 3F  1020        STA $3FF8
0805- 4E F8 3F  1030        LSR $3FF8
0808- 00        1040        BRK

SYMBOL TABLE

0800- LSR
```

Register contents:

```
080A-    A=51 X=00 Y=00 P=35 S=F9
```

Memory contents:

```
3FF8- 28
```

(P) in hex	→	3	5
(P) in binary	→	0 0 1 1	0 1 0 1
The flags	→	N V - B	D I Z C

PROGRAM 6.6M1

```
                1000 * PROGRAM 6.6M1 MOVE BITS IN BYTE
                1005          .OR $800      SET ORIGIN AT $800
0800- A9 51     1010 LSR      LDA #$51
0802- 8D F8 3F  1020          STA $3FF8
0805- 4E F8 3F  1030          LSR $3FF8
0808- 4E F8 3F  1040          LSR $3FF8
080B- 00        1050          BRK
```

SYMBOL TABLE

```
0800- LSR
```

Register contents:

```
080D-    A=51 X=00 Y=00 P=34 S=F9
```

Memory contents:

```
3FF8- 14
```

(P) in hex	→	3	4
(P) in binary	→	0 0 1 1	0 1 0 0
The flags	→	N V - B	D I Z C

ROL

There are two rotate instructions: ROL and ROR. The instruction that rotates bits to the left is the ROL, Rotate One bit Left. This instruction sets the N, Z, and C flags. This instruction is a rotate because bits are never lost, as they are in a shift. The bits are circulated through the accumulator (memory location) and the Carry bit clockwise one bit for each ROL. Visualize the Carry bit centered above the accumulator (memory location). Here is the picture.

```
                (Carry) →      _
 Contents of Acc or Mem →  ---- ----
             Bit number →  7654 3218
```

Here is an example of how this works.

```
          (C) →      1
                     -

(A) in binary →  0101 0110
                 ---- ----
   Bit number →  7654 3210
   (A) in Hex →     5    6
```

First Rotation.
Perform an ROL on (A).

```
          (C) →      0
                     -

(A) in binary →  1010 1101
                 ---- ----
   Bit number →  7654 3210
   (A) in Hex →     A    D
```

Second rotation.
Perform another ROL on (A).

```
          (C) →      1
                     -

(A) in binary →  0101 1010
                 ---- ----
   Bit number →  7654 3210
   (A) in Hex →     5    A
```

The two examples shown below do 1 and 2 ROLs. In these examples no operand is specified for the ROL, therefore the contents on the accumulator ($56) are rotated left. Initially the Carry bit is set.

PROGRAM 6.7

```
                  1000 * PROGRAM 6.7   MOVE BITS IN BYTE
                  1005          .OR $800     SET ORIGIN AT $800
0800- 38          1010 ROL      SEC
0801- A9 56       1020          LDA #$56
0803- 2A          1030          ROL
0804- 00          1040          BRK

SYMBOL TABLE

0800- ROL
```

Register contents:

```
0806-    A=AD X=00 Y=0 P=B4 S=F9
```

(P) in hex	→	B	4
(P) in binary	→	1 0 1 1	0 1 0 0
The flags	→	N V - B	D I Z C

PROGRAM 6.7M1

```
                  1000 * PROGRAM 6.7M1 MOVE BITS IN BYTE
                  1005          .OR $800     SET ORIGIN AT $800
0800- 38          1010 ROL      SEC
0801- A9 56       1020          LDA #$56
0803- 2A          1030          ROL
0804- 2A          1035          ROL
0805- 00          1040          BRK
```

```
SYMBOL TABLE
0800- ROL
```

Register contents:

```
0807-    A=5A X=00 Y=00 P=35 S=F9
```

(P) in hex	→	3	5
(P) in binary	→	0 0 1 1	0 1 0 1
The flags	→	N V - B	D I Z C

ROR

The last instruction to be illustrated in this chapter is the ROR, Rotate One bit Right. This instruction sets the N, Z, and C flags. No bits are lost because they are circulated through the accumulator (memory location) and the Carry bit counterclockwise one bit for each ROR. As in the ROL case, visualize the Carry bit centered above the accumulator (memory location).

(C) → 1

(M) in binary →	0101	0110
Bit number →	7654	3210
(M) in hex →	5	6

Perform an ROR on (M)—first rotation.

(C) → 0

(M) in binary →	1010	1011
Bit number →	7654	3210
(M) in hex →	A	B

Perform another ROR on (M)—second rotation.

```
                (C) →         1
                              -

(M) in binary → 0101  0101
                ----  ----
  Bit number →  7654  3210
  (M) in hex →     5     5
```

The two examples shown below do 1 and 2 RORs. In these examples the operand is the memory location $3FF8. The contents of this memory location, $56, are rotated. Initially the Carry bit is set.

PROGRAM 6.8

```
                 1000 * PROGRAM 6.8   MOVE BITS IN BYTE
                 1005          .OR $800     SET ORIGIN AT $800
0800- 38         1010 ROR      SEC
0801- A9 56      1020          LDA #$56
0803- 8D F8 3F   1030          STA $3FF8
0806- 6E F8 3F   1040          ROR $3FF8
0809- 00         1050          BRK

SYMBOL TABLE

0800- ROR
```

Register contents:

```
080B-   A=56 X=00 Y=00 P=B4 S=F9
```

Memory contents:

```
3FF8- AB
```

```
(P) in hex    →        B        4
(P) in binary →  1 0 1 1  0 1 0 0
The flags     →  N V - B  D I Z C
```

PROGRAM 6.8M1

```
                1000 * PROGRAM 6.8M1 MOVE BITS IN BYTE
                1005          .OR $800      SET ORIGIN AT $800
0800- 38        1010 ROR      SEC
0801- A9 56     1020          LDA #$56
0803- 8D F8 3F  1030          STA $3FF8
0806- 6E F8 3F  1040          ROR $3FF8
0809- 6E F8 3F  1050          ROR $3FF8
080C- 00        1060          BRK

SYMBOL TABLE

0800- ROR
```

Register contents:

```
080E-   A=56 X=00 Y=00 P=35 S=F9
```

(P) in hex	→	3	5
(P) in binary	→	0 0 1 1	0 1 0 1
The flags	→	N V - B	D I Z C

SUMMARY

Bit operations are important because they allow you to determine the contents of any bit of a memory location. For example, BIT (along with branch instructions) allows for program control based on the contents of a single bit. As an alternative, an appropriate number of shift and rotate instructions can bring any bit into the Carry. Then the BCS, BCC instructions can be used to control the program.

SECTION

III

LINKAGE

CHAPTER 7

SUBROUTINE LINKAGE

Assembly language programming presents challenges (and opportunities) that the Applesoft programmer does not have. Among other things, you must decide where the program will be located in memory, and where each of the variables will be stored. As a result, you must know a little more about memory organization and usage than was necessary for writing Applesoft programs. Table 7.1 provides an outline of the Apple memory, and the pages ahead give a brief description of the more significant parts.

TABLE 7.1 Apple Memory

Address	*Usage*
$0000–$00FF	*Page 0*
$0100–$01FF	*Page 1; System stack*
$0200–$02FF	*Page 2; Input buffer*
$0300–$03FF	*Page 3; $300–$3CF: Free space $3D0–$3FF: System usage*
$0400–$07FF	*Text and Low-Resolution Graphics page 1*
$0800–$1FFF	*Typically used for Applesoft program and variable storage*
$0800–$0BFF	*Text and Low-Resolution Graphics page 2*
$2000–$3FFF	*High-Resolution Graphics page 1*
$4000–$5FFF	*High-Resolution Graphics page 2*
$6000–$95FF	*Program and variable storage*
$9600–$FFFF	*System usage*

HOW MEMORY LOCATIONS ARE USED

Page Zero

Page zero consists of the first 256 bytes of Apple memory, with addresses $00–$FF. These memory locations are especially useful because the 6502 architecture allows them to be accessed more rapidly than other memory locations. For example, the page zero reference LDA $06 requires three machine cycles, but the reference LDA $306 requires four cycles. Further, certain addressing modes are available only through page zero.

Because speed of execution is usually important to assembly language programmers, they like to use page zero as much as possible. When you are designing a program, you will probably want to place many of your variables there. Do so with caution. The programmers who wrote Applesoft, DOS, and the Monitor have used many of these memory locations. Since your machine language programs will usually use subroutines in one of these programs, or will be called as subroutines by an Applesoft program, you must be careful that your use of page zero does not interfere with its use by DOS or ProDOS, Applesoft, or the Monitor.

Very few page zero locations are left untouched by all three of DOS, Applesoft, and the Monitor. While we make no guarantees, we believe the following are safe: $6–$9, $19, $1E, $1F, $CE, $CF, $D7, $E3, $EB–$EF, $F9–$FF.

Tables in the Apple reference manuals indicate usage of page zero memory. Be careful; the tables are incomplete. For example, in the Apple II reference manual memory locations $1A–$1D are not shown to be used by Applesoft. In fact, they are used by the high-resolution plotting routines. All manuals show location $D6 to be unused by Applesoft, but it is the "mystery location." (If the high bit of $D6 is a 1, then all immediate-execution Applesoft commands have the effect of-RUN.)

Your assembler probably also uses some page zero locations. This is a temporary problem if you test program segments as they are assembled. The usage of page zero by your program and by your assembler may be in conflict, causing some strange behavior. If this occurs, you will have to exit the assembler, test the assembled code, then reenter the assembler.

Clearly, we cannot use page zero indiscriminately. On the other hand, it is inconvenient to be restricted to only the few "safe" locations listed above. If we exercise some care, we can expand the list of memory locations available to us. For example, if graphics commands will not be used by a machine language program or by the Applesoft program that calls it, the machine language program can use page zero locations $1A–$1C, $26, $27, $30, and others. We recommend that you seek a source of information on zero-page usage. Several articles on the subject have been published in computer magazines, and the book *What's Where in the Apple,* by W. F. Luebbert, is an excellent reference.

Page 1

Page 1 is a term used to refer to the 256 bytes of memory addressed as $100–$1FF. It has no speed advantages like those of page zero, and has no merit over any other section of memory. It is used as the Apple system stack (see Chapter 3) and, as a result, should be considered to be off-limits for program or variable storage.

Page 2

Page 2 ($200–$2FF) is used as the Apple's input buffer. As a program line, or input requested by a program, is typed from the keyboard, it is stored in page 2. Then, when the RETURN key is pressed the input is taken from page 2, subjected to some processing (determined by the type of input), and stored elsewhere in memory. Then page 2 is unused, as it awaits further input.

If you are in need of an area of memory for temporary data storage, you may use page 2. Be careful, since any data stored there is subject to destruction the next time you touch the keyboard.

Actually, since page 2 has no real advantages over other areas of memory, there is no reason to use it unless you are extremely pressed for memory.

Page 3

Page 3 ($300–$3FF) is a more satisfactory area for storage of variables and short machine language programs. While it does not have the speed advantage associated with page zero, page 3 is still a desirable area of memory, since part of it ($300–$3CF) is usually unused. DOS, ProDOS, and the Monitor use locations $3D0–$3FF, so it is best to avoid their use.

Page 4 and Beyond

Page 1 of text (and page 1 of low-resolution graphics) occupies $400–$7FF (except for a few bytes which are reserved for use by peripherals). If you want to write a program that will write directly to the screen, you will do so by storing data in this range of memory. The addressing of the text page is discussed in Chapter 10.

Applesoft programs usually reside in memory beginning at $801, with their variables and arrays usually following the program. The amount of memory required is obviously dependent on the length of the program and on the number of variables and arrays. Page two of text, and page two of low-resolution graphics, is drawn from $800–$BFF.

High-resolution graphics page one draws its display from the memory range $2000–$3FFF; high-resolution graphics page 2 occupies $4000–$5FFF.

Memory from $6000 to the beginning of DOS ($9600 on a 48K system) often goes unused. Applesoft programs that are long, relocated, or have many variables or arrays may overwrite this area of memory. Otherwise it is a prime area for use by machine language programs.

ACCESSING MACHINE LANGUAGE PROGRAMS

BLOAD

The most direct way to access a machine language program is to BLOAD it from disk, then CALL it. This was done in Program 2.7, repeated below as Program 7.1. The machine language program TONE ROUTINE is the product of the source file which was given as Program 2.6. Notice that the program has no internal references except for branches. As a result the program is relocatable (location independent). That is, it can be loaded to any free memory locations. Line 10 of Program 7.1 could be changed to read

```
10 PRINT CHR$(4); "BLOAD TONE ROUTINE, A$6000"
```

as long as line 60 is changed to reference the routine at this new address:

```
60 CALL 24576
```

PROGRAM 7.1

```
1  REM PROGRAM 7.1
2  REM MELODY
10  PRINT  CHR$ (4);"BLOAD TONE ROUTINE,A$300"
20  PRINT  CHR$ (4);"BLOAD TONE ROUTINE,A$300"
30  FOR I = 1 TO 6
40  READ DUR: POKE 6,DUR: REM DURATION OF NOTE
50  READ PITCH: POKE 7,PITCH
60  CALL 768
70  NEXT I
80  DATA  64,203,64,171,64,128,128,102,64,128,255,102
```

The part of memory just below DOS (or ProDOS) is a good location for storing a machine language program. When this is done, the program can be protected from being overwritten by Applesoft variables and strings by setting HIMEM to a value just below the start of the program. For example, Program 7.2 loads the TONE ROUTINE at $9500 (decimal 38144), and sets HIMEM so that the routine is protected.

PROGRAM 7.2

```
1  REM PROGRAM 7.2
2  REM MELODY
10  PRINT  CHR$ (4);"BLOAD TONE ROUTINE,A$300"
20  HIMEM: 38144
30  FOR I = 1 TO 6
40  READ DUR: POKE 6,DUR: REM  DURATION OF NOTE
50  READ PITCH: POKE 7,PITCH
60  CALL 38144
70  NEXT I
80  DATA 64,203,64,171,64,128,128,102,64,128,255,102E
```

There are occasions when it is convenient to use BRUN to BLOAD a machine language and begin execution of the program. This allows the machine language program to do some initial bookkeeping as it is loaded. Programs 7.5 and 7.6 will illustrate the technique.

POKE

As an alternate, we can arrange for an Applesoft program to load a machine language program through the use of the POKE command. The binary file which is the TONE ROUTINE is given in Table 7.2.

TABLE 7.2 Tone Routine in Hex and in Decimal

The File in Hex	*The File in Decimal*
AD 30 C0 A6 07 88 D0 04	173, 48 192, 166, 7, 136, 208, 4
C6 06 F0 05 CA D0 F6 F0	198, 6, 240, 5, 202, 208, 246, 240
EF 60	239, 96

Program 7.3 reads the code for the subroutine from a DATA statement, then POKEs it into memory. Note that while the approach is suitable for this example, it would not be appropriate for a longer file.

PROGRAM 7.3

```
1  REM PROGRAM 7.3
2  REM MELODY
3  REM ENTERS MACHINE LANGUAGE SUBROUTINE
10  FOR I = 0 TO 17
20  READ X: POKE 768 + I,X
30  NEXT I
40  FOR I = 1 TO 6
50  READ DUR: POKE 6,DUR: REM DURATION OF NOTE
60  READ PITCH: POKE 7,PITCH
70  CALL 768
80  NEXT I
90  REM DATA FOR MACHINE LANGUAGE SUBROUTINE
100  DATA 173,48,192,166,7,136,208,4
110  DATA 198,6,240,5,202,208,246,240
120  DATA 239,96
130  REM DATA FOR TUNE
140  DATA 64,203,64,171,64,128,128,102,64,128,255,102
```

Even for short subroutines, the POKE approach is inconvenient. In this case we first obtained a hexadecimal dump of the binary file, then converted the numbers into decimal form. (Yes, you could use PEEK to obtain the decimal form directly.) Then the decimal numbers must be typed into a DATA statement. Each of these steps is cumbersome and provides opportunity for error.

Hiding a Machine Language Subroutine

It is possible to have a machine language program loaded (and saved) along with the Applesoft program that calls it. Again, this approach is not without its disadvantages. We will illustrate with Program 7.4. The listing shows (in line 40) that the program calls a machine language program at location 2225 ($8C3). How did it get there? When the Applesoft program is first typed in, it will be found that the end of the program is at 2220. The end of the program is given by PEEK(175) + 256*PEEK(176).

With the Applesoft program in memory, we next BLOAD TONE ROUTINE, A2225. Next, we change the pointer that identifies the end of the Applesoft program: POKE 175,195: POKE 176, 8 (2243 = 195 + 256*8). Now the pointer identifies the end of the Applesoft program as being beyond the end of the machine language routine. Finally, SAVE PROGRAM 7.4. DOS will save the TONE ROUTINE along with the Applesoft program. The commands RUN PRO-

GRAM 7.4 or LOAD PROGRAM 7.4 will bring both the Applesoft and the machine language routines into memory.

WARNING: Any editing of the Applesoft program (adding, deleting, or changing program lines) will subject the machine language program to dislocation, or destruction. This approach should be used only with well developed Applesoft programs, which are not likely to be edited.

PROGRAM 7.4

```
1  REM PROGRAM 7.4
2  REM HIDDEN PROGRAM
10  FOR I = 1 TO 6
20  READ DUR: POKE 6,DUR: REM  DURATION OF NOTE
30  READ PITCH: POKE 7,PITCH
40  CALL 2225
50  NEXT I
60  DATA 64,203,64,171,64,128,128,102,64,128,255,102
```

& (Ampersand)

The most common way of accessing a machine language program is to use the CALL command. The CALL must specify the location (in decimal) at which execution of a machine language program is to begin. Thus CALL 768 causes execution to begin at location 768 ($300) and CALL −151 causes execution to begin at location 65185 (65336 − 151). The earlier examples in this book have used CALL to access machine language programs from Applesoft.

The ampersand (&) symbol provides another means to transfer control to a machine language program. & is a reserved word in Applesoft, and is a valid Applesoft command. When the command is executed, control is transferred to whatever machine language program is resident at $3F5. When DOS 3.3 is in control, that program is just

```
JMP $FF58
```

and the program at $FF58 is

```
RTS
```

As a result, an & is nonproductive, unless provision has been made for some worthwhile activity at $3F5

Note: ProDOS does not automatically store a JMP at $3F5.

Memory locations $3F0–$3FF have been reserved for various jump instructions. The addresses of power-up, interrupt, and similar routines are stored here. Space is available at $3F5–$3F7 for a jump instruction that will be called through the & instruction. For example, if you provide the command

```
3F5- 4C 6E A5    JMP $A56E
```

then the & instruction (either in an Applesoft program or as an immediate-execution command) will result in a CATALOG, since the DOS CATALOG instruction lives at address $A56E. (This can be a good use of & if you have many disks to catalog.)

Remember that the & command is intended as a means of extending the Applesoft language. Many utility programs that use & have been published in computer magazines. Our purpose here is primarily to show how to effectively use it. Providing a valuable utility program is a secondary concern. The program we present is brief, but illustrates &, along with the display screen soft switches, indirect and indexed addressing, loops, and TXTPTR.

Soft Switches

Program 7.5 will allow & to access the display screen soft switches. The soft switches are eight memory locations that control the source and type of screen display. The switches and their effects are shown in Table 7.3 and in Appendix F.

The program segment below illustrates the use of the soft switches. The effect of the commands will be to display page one of high-resolution graphics, in full screen mode. Other display modes can be displayed through similar means.

```
BIT $C050
BIT $C052
BIT $C054
BIT $C055
```

TABLE 7.3 Effects of Soft Switches

Location	*Effect*
$C050	Display graphics
$C051	Display text
$C052	Full screen
$C053	Mixed screen
$C054	Page 1
$C055	Page 2
$C056	Lo-res graphics
$C057	Hi-res graphics

Note that here we are displaying the graphics page, in contrast to the commands HGR or HGR2, which display and clear the graphics pages.

While the program segment above uses BIT to set the soft switches, other commands (e.g., LDA $C050, STA $C055) would be just as effective.

Further use of soft switches is shown in Chapters 10 and 11.

TXTPTR

CHARGET is an Applesoft subroutine that begins at $B1. Its purpose is to read the contents of memory locations pointed to by the contents of TXTPTR ($B8, $B9). Usually TXTPTR is pointing at the input buffer ($200 - $2FF) or at an Applesoft program. When an Applesoft program transfers control to a machine language program, TXTPTR provides a way for the machine language program to read information from the Applesoft program. Programs 7.5 and 7.6 illustrate this technique.

PROGRAM 7.5

```
0001 * PROGRAM 7.5
1000          .OR $300
1010 * SET UP & VECTOR ON BRUN
```

```
0300- A9 4C    1020          LDA #$4C
0302- 8D F5 03 1030          STA $3F5
0305- 18       1040          CLC
0306- AD 72 AA 1050          LDA $AA72
0309- 69 17    1060          ADC #$17     * $17 PLUS
030B- 8D F6 03 1070          STA $3F6     * DESTINATION OF
030E- AD 73 AA 1080          LDA $AA73    * OF FILE MOST
0311- 69 00    1090          ADC #$00     * RECENTLY BLOADED
0313- 8D F7 03 1100          STA $3F7
0316- 60       1110          RTS          RETURN TO BASIC
               1120 *--------------------------------
               1130 * INTERPRET & COMMAND STRING
0317- A0 00    1140          LDY #$00
0319- B1 B8    1150 A        LDA ($B8),Y  READ CHARACTER
031B- A2 08    1160          LDX #$08     TEST AGAINST 8 COMMANDS
031D- CA       1170 B        DEX
031E- 30 10    1180          BMI RET      NO MATCH, QUIT
0320- DD 31 03 1190          CMP DATA,X
0323- D0 F8    1200          BNE B        NOT A MATCH
0325- 9D 50 C0 1210          STA $C050,X  TOGGLE SOFT SWITCH
0328- E6 B8    1220          INC $B8      *
032A- D0 02    1230          BNE C        * INCREMENT TXTPTR
032C- E6 B9    1240          INC $B9      *
032E- D0 E9    1250 C        BNE A        ALWAYS
0330- 60       1260 RET      RTS
0331- 47 54 46
0334- 4D 31 32
0337- 4C 48    1270 DATA     .AS /GTFM12LH/


SYMBOL TABLE

0319- A
031D- B
032E- C
0331- DATA
0330- RET
```

NOTE: The .AS in the above program is the S-C Assembler's directive that stores the character string GTFM12LH in sequential location starting at the current location ($0331). The slashes are the delimiters that denote the beginning and the end of the character string. The equivalent directive for the Big Mac or DOS Tool Kit assemblers is ASC.

PROGRAM 7.6

```
1  REM PROGRAM 7.6
2  REM DEMONSTRATES &
10  PRINT  CHR$ (4);"BRUN AMPERSOFT,A$300"
20  & H1FG
30  INPUT A$
40  & T
50  INPUT A$
60  & 2LG
70  INPUT A$
80  & T1
```

Program 7.6 illustrates the use of & to call a machine language program, AMPERSOFT, which results from Program 7.5. Since the two programs are linked, we will discuss them together.

Line 10 of Program 7.6 will BRUN AMPERSOFT. As a result, AMPERSOFT is loaded and the program is executed, beginning at the specified address ($300 in this case). AMPERSOFT is relocatable, so it could be loaded elsewhere if you wish.

AMPERSOFT has two parts: a bookkeeping phase and a soft switching phase. BRUN actually executes only the first (bookkeeping) part of AMPERSOFT. The RTS at line 1120 will return control to the Applesoft program. The initial part of AMPERSOFT (lines 1030–1120) sets the JMP address that is required by &. The destination address of the most recently BLOADed file is read from $AA72–$AA73 (in this case that would be $300), and an offset is added to account for the length of the bookkeeping phase of AMPERSOFT. When control is returned to Applesoft, the contents of $3F5–$3F7 will be 4C 17 03, or

```
$3F5- 4C 17 03  JMP $317
```

Whenever Applesoft encounters an &, it will transfer control to the machine language program that is located at $317. That program is the soft-switch phase of AMPERSOFT.

Lines 20, 40, 60, 80 of Program 7.6 illustrate the Applesoft side of the & command. The characters G, T, F, M, 1, 2, L, H are used to identify the soft switches to be toggled, as shown in Table 7.3.

The order in which the switches are accessed is not important, and the number of switches accessed with a single & is arbitrary. The INPUT A$ in lines 30, 50, 70 provides a request for input, to postpone further access to the soft switches. The input is ignored.

The machine language side of the & is more complex. The program must (1) read each of the characters which follow the &, (2) decide which soft switch should be toggled, and (3) toggle the switch. Further, we don't want the program to bomb if an extraneous character should appear; it would be better either to print "SYNTAX ERROR," or to take no visible action.

When Applesoft reads the &, it advances TXTPTR ($B8, $B9) so that it is pointing at the byte that follows the keycode for &. It is at this point that the machine language program takes over.

After setting the Y-register to zero (line 1140), we use TXTPTR to load the accumulator with the contents of the byte that immediately follows the & (line 1150). Lines 1160 through 1200 then try to match the contents of the accumulator with the code for one of the characters G, T, F, M, 1, 2, L, H. The X-register is used to identify the character being tested. (X will contain 0, 1, 2, 3, 4, 5, 6, 7 as we are testing G, T, F, M, 1, 2, L, H, respectively.)

If a match is obtained, the contents of X provide an index to the proper soft switch for line 1210:

```
1210 STA $C050,X
```

Then TXTPTR is incremented (lines 1220–1240) and a forced branch (line 1250) directs control to line 1150, where the next byte is read.

If no match is found, we can assume that either an extraneous character has been read, or that we have reached the end of the & string of command characters. In either case, when the X-register is decremented past zero (line 1170), the N-flag will be set. Then line 1180 (BMI RET) will return control to the Applesoft program without incrementing TXTPTR. Applesoft will immediately read the byte pointed to by TXTPTR. If that byte is at the end of the command string, its contents will be either $3A (:) or $00 (end-of-Applesoft-line code). In this case Applesoft will continue execution of the remainder of the program.

If the unmatched character is not the expected $3A or $00, then Applesoft will print "SYNTAX ERROR," and exit the program.

Modify Program 7.5 to require a specific syntax from the & command string. For example, you could require that consecutive characters be separated by commas. The modified program would then confirm that the commas were present before proceeding.

CTRL-Y and USR

& permits the extension of the Applesoft language to include a user defined command. CTRL-Y and USR also provide extensions. We will devote less discussion to these two, since they behave in a manner that is similar to &, but are generally less valuable.

CTRL-Y permits extension of the Monitor. If you type CTRL-Y (press CTRL and Y, then RETURN) while in the Monitor, you will initiate a JMP to memory location $3F8. At that location you should have a JMP to a machine language subroutine. For example, if you have

```
$3F8-   4C 6E A5    JMP $A56E
```

then CTRL-Y is the CATALOG command. If you are testing a machine language program that turns on the graphics screen and displays some graphics images, then you might want to have CTRL-Y access a machine language program that sets the display screen to TEXT, page 1. That way you can easily return to the text screen each time you test the graphics program.

USR provides another means of extending Applesoft. The syntax for use is USR(aexpr), where aexpr is an arithmetic expression. Forms such as USR(5) or USR(2*X) are acceptable. When Applesoft encounters USR(aexpr), it transfers control to the machine language program that resides at $000A, after evaluating aexpr and storing the result as a floating-point number in the Main Floating-Point accumulator (MFP). (More on floating point numbers in Chapter 8.) It is incumbent on you to see that an appropriate machine language program is at $000A. Since page zero locations are in heavy demand, USR is best utilized by having location $000A provide a jump to a machine language program. For example,

```
000A-   4C 00 03    JMP $300
```

USR is not a frequently used means of passing control to machine language programs. It can be very useful in cases that require floating-point numbers to be passed from an Applesoft program to a machine language program.

Programs 7.7 and 7.8 illustrate the use of USR. Program 7.7 makes use of floating-point subroutines, which are discussed in Chapter 8, so this example may not be entirely clear as you read it. If that is the case, return to it after reading Chapter 8.

Program 7.7 is a subroutine that multiplies a given number by ***. The number is found in the Main Floating-Point Accumulator (put there by USR), then multiplied by 2*** and by .5, and the result left in the Main Floating-Point Accumulator. On return from the subroutine, the answer is found as the value of USR. Program 7.8 illustrates the way in which USR can be used within an Applesoft program.

PROGRAM 7.7

```
                1000 * PROGRAM 7.7  USR
                1010        .OR $300
0300- A9 64     1020        LDA #$64      .5 STORED
0302- A0 EE     1030        LDY #$EE        AT $EE64
0304- 20 7F E9  1040        JSR $E97F     MULT BY .5
0307- A9 6B     1050        LDA #$6B      2*PI STORED
0309- A0 F0     1060        LDY #$F0        AT $F068
030B- 20 7F E9  1070        JSR $E97F     MULT BY 2*PI
030E- 60        1080        RTS
```

PROGRAM 7.8

```
1  REM PROGRAM 7.8  USR
10  POKE 10,76: POKE 11,0: POKE 12,3
20  FOR I = 768 TO 782
30  READ X: POKE I,X
40  NEXT I
50  INPUT "ENTER A NUMBER X ";X
60  PRINT "X TIMES PI = "; USR (X)
70  PRINT : PRINT "PI = "; USR (1)
80  PRINT : INPUT "RADIUS OF CIRCLE ";RAD
90  PRINT "CIRCUMFERENCE = ";RAD *  USR (2)
100  DATA  169,100,160,238
110  DATA  32,127,233,169,107
120  DATA  160,240,32,127,233,96
```

The linkage of machine language programs to Applesoft programs is an important part of assembly language. It is not always necessary to pass variables to the machine language program. In those cases CALLs are as effective as any process.

The most common way to pass variables to a machine language program seems to be the POKE and CALL approach. In many cases & might be a better choice. Experiment with its use in some of the examples given earlier in this book. Following the discussion of floating-point subroutines in Chapter 8, you may find further uses for USR.

CHAPTER 8

USING APPLESOFT FLOATING-POINT SUBROUTINES

All of the discussion so far has been directed toward working with numbers that are integers. A lot of programming requires nothing more, but there are many other occasions when it is necessary to perform calculations with numbers that have fractional parts. Of course, the processor can deal only with 0s and 1s. If it is necessary to perform calculations with numbers that are not integers, we first must establish a way of representing those numbers as strings of 0s and 1s. We will use the standard Applesoft floating-point form to represent such numbers. We also need algorithms and subroutines that will perform the desired calculations. Fortunately, most of this work has been done, and the results are available in the Applesoft floating-point ROM subroutines. If you are not familiar with Applesoft packed and unpacked excess $80 floating-point notation, read Appendix C before going any further.

If we wish to have a floating-point calculation performed by an assembly language program, we will make the appropriate numbers available in floating-point form, and then call the Applesoft subroutine that performs the arithmetic.

THE FLOATING-POINT ACCUMULATORS

Before accessing these Applesoft routines you most know how two areas of page zero are organized for their use. The locations $9D, $9E, $9F, $A0, $A1, $A2 together are called the Main Floating-point ACcumulator, or MFAC. Locations $A5, $A6, $A7, $A8, $A9, $AA together are called the Secondary Floating-point ACcumulator, or SFAC. These are new uses of the word accumulator. MFAC and SFAC are zero page locations used to communicate with the Applesoft floating-point subroutines that are on pages $D0 through $F7 of ROM. These locations, MFAC and SFAC, are not the same as the 6502's accumulator. To avoid confusion, throughout the rest of this chapter, we will refer to the 6502's accumulator simply as A.

Imagine that MFAC and SFAC are laid out like this:

```
   MFAC →  __  __  __  __  __  __
Address →  $9D $9E $9F $A0 $A1 $A2
Purpose →  EXP <-  Mantissa -> SGN
   SFAC →  __  __  __  __  __  __
Address →  $A5 $A6 $A7 $A8 $A9 $AA
Purpose →  EXP  <- Mantissa -> SGN
```

Location $9D ($A5) of MFAC (SFAC) holds the power of two with $80 added to it; this is the "excess" of excess $80 notation. This location is the EXPonent, or EXP, of the floating-point number. Locations $9E through $A1 ($A6 through $A9) make up the mantissa, which is the fractional part of MFAC (SFAC). Location $A2 ($AA) is used to denote the SiGN, or SGN, of the number. Only the high bit (leftmost bit) of $A2 ($AA) is used. The rest of the bits in this byte do not have any meaning. If the high bit of $A2 ($AA) is off (is equal to zero), the number in MFAC (SFAC) is positive. If the high bit is set (is equal to one), the number in MFAC (SFAC) is negative. Each hex digit of the mantissa indicates the reciprocal power of sixteen (the place value) it is to be multiplied by in the conversion to base ten.

Here is an example of what this means. Suppose that either MFAC or SFAC contains 84 AD 00 00 00; then the conversion to base ten goes like this:

```
MFAC address -->   9    D     9    E    9    F    A    0    A    1
SFAC address -->   A    5     A    6    A    7    A    8    A    9
    Contents -->   8    4     A    D    0    0    0    0    0    0
                   -    -     -    -    -    -    -    -    -    -
                      EXP    <---      M a n t i s s a        --->
 Place Value -->     84-80     -1    -2   -3    -4    -5    -6    -7    -8
                   2         16    16    16    16    16    16    16    16
                        4
Conversion            2    *(10/16 + 13/256 + 0/4096 + 0/65536 + ...)
             to         16 *(10/16 + 13/256 + 0 + 0 + 0 + 0 + 0 + 0)
                 base       (10 + 13/16)
                     ten    (10 + 0.8125)
                             10.8125
```

Note that the EXP is multiplied by the sum of all the reciprocal powers of sixteen.

A word about zero is required: The Applesoft floating-point routines consider a representation to be zero if EXP is zero, regardless of the value of the mantissa.

NORMALIZATION

There is one other peculiar, but easy to understand, aspect of MFAC (SFAC) that must be understood before these locations can be used to communicate with the Applesoft floating-point subroutines: normalization. This means that the floating point representation of the number must have the high bit (leftmost bit) of the mantissa set. If you have an excess $80 notation of a number that is not normalized, for example 5 —> 84 50 00 00 00, it must be normalized before it is used in any calculation. Shift left the bits in the mantissa; for each shift left, decrease the EXP byte by one. Keep shifting and decreasing until a 1 appears in the high bit of $9E ($A6). In the representation of 5 shown above only one shift/decrease is required to normalize the representation of 5 —> 83 A0 00 00 00.

Normalization is not something that must be done by hand. In Program 8.1, lines 1020 through 1130 initialize MFAC and SFAC with the unnormalized representation of +5 given in the paragraph above.

PROGRAM 8.1

```
                    1000 * PROGRAM 8.1 NORMALIZATION
                    1005            .OR $800       SET ORIGIN AT $800
E82E-               1010 NORM       .EQ $E82E
0800- A9 84         1020 BEGIN      LDA #$84       EXP
0802- 85 9D         1030            STA $9D
0804- 85 A5         1040            STA $A5
0806- A9 50         1050            LDA #$50       MANTISSA, HI
0808- 85 9E         1060            STA $9E
080A- 85 A6         1070            STA $A6
080C- A9 00         1080            LDA #$00       MANTISSA, SIGN
080E- A2 03         1090            LDX #$03
0810- 95 9F         1100 LOOP       STA $9F,X
0812- 95 A7         1110            STA $A7,X
0814- CA            1120            DEX
0815- 10 F9         1130            BPL LOOP
0817- 20 2E E8      1140            JSR NORM
081A- 00            1150            BRK

SYMBOL TABLE

0800- BEGIN
0810- LOOP
E82E- NORM
```

Note that the SGN bytes are clear, indicating that the number is positive. The JSR (line 1140) is to the normalization routine, NORM, which begins at $E82E. This routine normalizes MFAC, but not SFAC. The BRK leaves us in the Monitor and the contents of the registers, MFAC ($9D through $A2) and SFAC ($A5 through $AA), can be displayed.

Registers:

```
081C-    A=83 X=50 Y=00 P=B0 S=DC
```

Memory:

```
009D- 83 A0 00 00 00 00
00A5- 84 50 00 00 00 00
```

Note that MFAC is now normalized, 83 A0 00 00 00 00; but SFAC, 84 50 00 00 00 00, is not.

CALCULATING; MULT

Program 8.2 loads MFAC and SFAC with +8 −> 84 80 00 00 00 00. Lines 1020 through 1130 initialize MFAC and SFAC. Note that the SGN bytes are set to 00, indicating the number is positive. Lines 1160 through 1180 need further explanation.

PROGRAM 8.2

```
                    1000 * PROGRAM 8.2 MFAC & SFAC
                    1005          .OR $800      SET ORIGIN AT $800
E982-               1010 MULT     .EQ $E982
0800- A9 84         1020 BEGIN    LDA #$84      EXP
0802- 85 9D         1030          STA $9D
0804- 85 A5         1040          STA $A5
0806- A9 80         1050          LDA #$80      MANTISSA, HI
0808- 85 9E         1060          STA $9E
080A- 85 A6         107           STA $A6
080C- A9 00         1080          LDA #$00      MANTISSA, SIGN
080E- A2 03         1090          LDX #$03
0810- 95 9F         1100 LOOP     STA $9F,X     FILL MANTISSA
0812- 95 A7         1110          STA $A7,X
0814- CA            1120          DEX
0815- 10 F9         1130          BPL LOOP
0817- 85 AB         1140          STA $AB       SET $AB AND
0819- 85 AC         1150          STA $AC         $AC TO 0
081B- A5 9D         1160          LDA $9D       ALSO SETS Z
081D- 20 82 E9      1170          JSR MULT      (MFAC)*(SFAC) -> (MFAC)
0820- 00            1180          BRK


SYMBOL TABLE

0800- BEGIN
0810- LOOP
E982- MULT
```

Registers:

```
0822-    A=87 X=40 Y=00 P=0 S=D8
```

Memory:

```
009D- 87 80 00 00 00 00
00A5- 84 80 00 00 00 00
```

This example uses the Applesoft MULTiplication subroutine that starts at $E982. Using this as an entry point requires that:

1. Byte $AB has been properly initialized. It should receive

   [SGN(MFAC)]   EOR   [SGN(SFAC)]

   We will shortly describe a subroutine which loads SFAC. As it does so, it also sets the value of $AB for us.
2. Byte $AC is an extra (extension, guard) byte that provides greater accuracy to the result of the multiplication. In general, it provides this extended accuracy for any floating-point operation. Its place value is sixteen to the minus nine power, 1/68,719,476,736. Since such accuracy is not required for this example, we load $AC with 0.
3. The EXP of MFAC must be loaded in the 6502's accumulator just before the MULT subroutine is called; line 1180 satisfies this requirement.

   The multiplication is performed and the result is placed in MFAC.

   $8*8 = 64 -> 87\ 80\ 00\ 00\ 00 -> 2^7 * (8/16) = 64$

Usually you will not load MFAC and SFAC by hand as was done in this example. There are Applesoft subroutines that perform these tasks. The true purpose of the example was to familiarize you with MFAC, SFAC, and excess $80 notation. We will not be loading MFAC and SFAC by hand in any of the later examples.

UNPACKING AND PACKING

Several floating-point numbers are already stored in the computer (see Table 8.7 for a partial list). Use the Monitor to examine the contents of locations $EE64 through $EE68. You should see

```
EE64- 80 00 00 00 00
```

displayed on your screen. These five numbers define the number +1/2 in PACKED excess $80 notation. A packed number is one whose sign is stored in the high bit of the second byte (the first byte of the mantissa). In this example this byte has hex 00 –> binary 0000 0000. Note that the high bit is clear. This means the number is positive. Packed format is the way the Applesoft interpreter stores numbers in its variable storage area. You can quickly convert (UNPACK) to the MFAC (SFAC) format by (1) storing the first byte of the mantissa in the sign byte (of course, only the high bit is important), and (2) ORAing the first byte of the mantissa with $80. For example,

```
First byte of mantissa in binary → 0000 0000
       ORA       $80 in binary → 1000 0000
       ----------------------------------
               Result in binary → 1000 0000
                  Result in hex →    8    0
```

The unpacked format of +1/2 as it would appear in MFAC or SFAC is:

```
MFAC (SFAC) format → 80 80 00 00 00 00
 (Unpacked format)   EXP <Mantissa> SGN
```

Note that the leftmost bit of SGN is clear; this means the number is positive.

Locations $E937 through $E93B contain the packed representation of −1/2.

```
$E937- 80 80 00 00 00
```

The high bit of the second byte is set, indicating that the number is negative. To unpack it, store the first byte of the mantissa in the sign byte and ORA the first byte of the mantissa with $80:

```
First byte of mantissa in binary → 1000 0000
       ORA       $80 in binary → 1000 0000
       ----------------------------------
               Result in binary → 1000 0000
                  Result in hex →    8    0
```

```
MFAC (SFAC) format → 80 80 00 00 00 00
 (Unpacked)          EXP <Mantissa> SGN
```

Note that the leftmost bit of SGN is set, so this number is negative.

There is an Applesoft subroutine that will unpack a floating-point number and MOVe the unpacked result into MFAC. This subroutine also initializes location $AB and loads the MFAC EXP into the 6502's accumulator. The subroutine, MOVMI (MOVe MFAC In), is located at $EAF9. (Remember that we are now referring to the 6502's accumulator simply as A.) To use MOVMI, A must be loaded with the low byte of the address of the beginning of the number, and Y must be loaded with the high byte of the address of the beginning of the number.

When MOVMI returns, the number has been unpacked and placed into MFAC, location $AB has been initialized, and EXP has been loaded into A. In Program 8.3, lines 1030 and 1040 establish the beginning address of 1/2 in Y and A, $EE64. Statement 1050 calls MOVMI. The next two statements, 1060 and 1070, load Y and A with the beginning address of −1/2. The Applesoft entry point named LMULT unpacks the number −1/2 into SFAC, resets $AB, and then yields control to the MULTiplication subroutine used in Program 8.2.

PROGRAM 8.3

```
                  1000 * PROGRAM 8.3 UNPK & MULT
EAF9-             1010 MOVMI   .EQ $EAF9
E97F-             1020 LMULT   .EQ $E97F
0800- A0 EE       1030 BEGIN   LDY #$EE
0802- A9 64       1040         LDA #$64
0804- 20 F9 EA    1050         JSR MOVMI
0807- A0 E9       1060         LDY #$E9
0809- A9 37       1070         LDA #$37
080B- 20 7F E9    1080         JSR LMULT
080E- 00          1090         BRK

SYMBOL TABLE

0800- BEGIN
E97F- LMULT
EAF9- MOVMI
```

The results of running Program 8.3 are shown below.

Registers:

```
0810-    A=7F X=40 Y=00 P=34 S=F9
```

Memory:

```
009D- 7F 80 00 00 00 80
00A5- 80 80 00 00 00 80
```

Note the result of the multiplication in MFAC:

$$(1/2)*(-1/2) = (-1/4) \rightarrow \text{7F 80 00 00 00 80} \rightarrow (-2^{-1})*(8/16)$$
$$= (-1/4)$$

Notice that Program 8.3 used MOVMI to unpack a floating-point number and store it in MFAC. The LMULT subroutine unpacked a second number, stored it in SFAC, then transferred control to a MULTiplication routine that returned the product of MFAC and SFAC.

There are other subroutines that pack and unpack floating-point numbers, and copy floating-point numbers from one location to another. These are summarized in Table 8.5.

WHAT IS IN A NAME?

Throughout this chapter we are describing ways to access Applesoft floating-point subroutines. It is easier to describe the subroutines if they are given names, and we have done so. So for as we know, neither Apple Computer nor Microsoft (which wrote the Applesoft floating point package) has published an "official" set of names for the subroutines.

As you read other references, you may encounter different labels. For example, the main floating-point accumulator (MFAC) is sometimes called FAC or MFP. The secondary floating-point accumulator is sometimes called ARG or SFP. The MULT routine has been called FMULTT, and the EXP routine has been called FPWRT.

We do not like to see a proliferation of labels. However, the labels we have seen elsewhere generally did not fit our desire to have short, consistent, descriptive labels. As a result, we have introduced our own.

THE FLOATING-POINT REPRESENTATION OF A NUMBER

The last two programs used the multiplication subroutine of Applesoft to illustrate the format of floating-point numbers in memory (five bytes, packed excess $80). In the Program 8.2, the conversion from base-ten to packed notation was done by hand and the result was loaded directly into MFAC and SFAC. In Program 8.3, floating-point numbers that already exist in Applesoft were used to load MFAC and SFAC.

If we are to perform meaningful calculations, we must have a way to provide the floating point form of any arbitrary number. The easiest way to place floating-point numbers into memory in packed notation is to use an Applesoft program to do the conversion.

Applesoft recognizes three types of variables: 1) Real, 2) Integer—%, 3) String—$. We shall focus our attention on real type variables. The last part of this chapter describes integer storage and representation. If you understand the format of real variables the others are a snap!

Example 8.4 identifies several variable names and the values to be converted.

```
10  REM EXAMPLE 8.4
20  REM SIMPLE VARIABLES
100 A = 12:B = 12.73:C = -0.00321:
    D = -2.9388E - 7
```

Type NEW, or FP, then key-in the program and RUN it. When it is run the variables are packed into memory. To locate their address, enter the Monitor (CALL −151) and examine the contents of locations $69 through $6C. These four bytes point to the beginning address ($69–low byte, $6A–high byte) and the ending address plus one ($6B–low byte, $6C–high byte) of the simple variable table. In this example we find the following:

```
0069 - 54 08 70 08
```

This tells us that the simple variables have been packed into memory starting at $853 and ending at $86E. The contents of these locations are:

```
0854- 41 00 84 40 00 00 00
085b- 42 00 84 4B AE 14 7B
0862- 43 00 78 D2 5E DD 03
0869- 44 00 6B 9D C6 8F 46
```

The information in these bytes is organized like this:

A = 12 →	41	00	84	40	00	00	00
Address →	$854	$855	$856	$857	$858	$859	$85A
	char1 of name1 "A"	char2 of name1 " "	EXP 2^4	←	Mantissa		→
				*(12/16 + 0 + ...) 12			

Each simple variable in Applesoft requires seven bytes of memory for storage. The first two bytes contain the name of the variable, and the next five bytes contain its value in packed format, ready for use by MOVMI. (If you would like to see how to convert a number to packed excess $80 notation by hand, see Appendix C.) The rest of the values of the variables defined in statement 120 are:

B = 12.73 →	42	00	84	4B	AE	14	7B
Address →	$85B	$85C	$86D	$85E	$85F	$860	$861
C = −0.00321 →	43	00	78	D2	5E	DD	03
Address →	$862	$863	$864	$865	$866	$867	$868
D = −2.9388E-7 →	44	00	6B	9D	C6	8F	46
Address →	$869	$86A	$86B	$86C	$86D	$86E	$86F

You can recover the memory area occupied by the program by keying-in only the variable names and their values. When you press RETURN at the end of the line, Applesoft begins packing the variables, starting at location $803. Here is an example of this technique.

PROGRAM 8.4M1

```
]FP
]A=12:B=12.73:C=-0.00321:D=-2.9388E-7

]CALL -151

*69.6C

0069- 03 08 1F 08
*803.81E

0803- 41 00 84 40 00
0808- 00 00 42 00 84 4B AE 14
0810- 7B 43 00 78 D2 5E DD 03
0818- 44 00 6B 9D C6 8F 46
*
```

APPLESOFT ARRAY STORAGE

If there are more than a few variables to pack into memory, there is a more convenient method for using Applesoft to pack the variables. Program 8.5 uses an array designated A to organize the packing. Array storage is organized differently because the values all have the same name, A, and differ only in their position in memory. Key-in and RUN the Applesoft program shown in the example. You can use this program to have Applesoft pack any number of variables.

PROGRAM 8.5

```
10  REM EXAMPLE 8.5 1-D ARRAYS
100  INPUT "N: NUMBER OF VARIABLES
     TO BE CONVERTED.    ";N%
110 N% = N% - 1
120  DIM A(N%)
130  FOR I = 0 TO N%
140  PRINT "I = ";I: INPUT A(I)
150  PRINT
160  NEXT I

]RUN
N: NUMBER OF VARIABLES TO BE CONVERTED.  4
I = 0
?12

I = 1
?12.73

I = 2
?-0.00321

I = 3
?-2.9388E-7

]CALL-151

*6B.6E
06B- A4 08 BF 08

*8A4.8BE
08A4- 41 00 1B 00
08A8- 01 00 04 84 40 00 00 00
08B0- 84 4B AE 14 7B 78 D2 5E
08B8- DD 03 6B 9D C6 8F 46
```

Call the Monitor and display the contents of locations $6B and $6C. These locations contain the starting address of the array information, $8A4 (your address may be different). Locations $6D and $6E contain the ending location plus one, $8BF. A listing of the contents pointed to by these locations is shown above. The first several bytes of the array block (the header) describe how the entire block is organized. For this example the header is seven bytes long. The information in the header is organized like this:

Header →	41	00	1B	00	01	00	04
Address →	$8A4	$8A5	$8A6	$8A7	$8A8	$8A9	$8AA
	char1 of name "A".	char2 of name " "	LENGTH of this block		# of DIMs	Range of right most index	

If the array has more than one dimension, each index requires two bytes for its range. Since our array has only one DIMension, only two bytes are required. If an array has three DIMensions then the header is 5 + 3*2 = 11 bytes long. The length of an array block is contained in the third and fourth bytes of the heading and is easily calculated. For this example: (1 DIMension) * (4, its range) = (4 variables), (4 variables) * (5 bytes per variable) = (20 bytes for variables), (20 bytes for variables) + (7 bytes for header) = ($1B the length of this block).

The remainder of the block is organized like this:

I	Starting address	Contents packed	Base ten value
0	$8A4+$7=$8AB	84 40 00 00 00	12
1	$8AB+$5=$8B0	84 4B AE14 7B	12.73
2	$8B0+$5=$8B5	78 D2 5E DD03	−0.00321
3	$8B5+$5=$8BA	6B 9D C6 8F 46	−2.9388E−7

FLOATING-POINT CALCULATIONS

Now that you have seen an easy way of obtaining the packed form of numbers, and have copied routines to load and store the contents of MFAC and SFAC, we will show how to use the floating-point calculating subroutines. Each of the following examples illustrates a floating-point calculation. The examples also illustrate various ways of providing floating-point numbers for use by the subroutines; and show how the results of the subroutines can be read, or made available to other subroutines, or passed to an Applesoft BASIC program.

Program 8.3 used MULT after MFAC and SFAC had been loaded. The other floating-point operations (addition, subtraction, division, exponentiation) have a similar organization to MULTiplication. For all the operations except exponentiation there are two entry points. One entry point is provided for the case when MFAC and SFAC are already loaded and only the operation needs to be performed. (This is the only way exponentiation is organized.) A second entry point is usually provided for the case in which MFAC is already loaded by MOVMI, but SFAC needs to be loaded and then the operation performed. (Each of these begin with a JSR MOVSI—see Table 8.5.) The result of the operation is always placed in MFAC. Table 8.1 shows the entry points for these operations.

TABLE 8.1 Two Operand Subroutines

Name	*Entry Point*	*Action Taken*
1. ADD	$E7C1	(MFAC) ← (SFAC) + (MFAC)
MFAC and SFAC already loaded; do the ADDition.		
2. LADD	$E7BE	(MFAC) ← [Y,A] + (MFAC)
MFAC is already loaded; (Y,A) points to the memory location of the packed number to be ADDed to (MFAC).		
3. SUB	$E7AA	(MFAC) ← (SFAC) − (MFAC)
MFAC and SFAC already loaded; (SFAC will have (MFAC) SUBtracted from it.		
4. LSUB	$E7A7	(MFAC) ← [Y,A] − (MFAC)
MFAC is already loaded; (Y,A) points to the memory location of the packed number that will have (MFAC) SUBtracted from it.		
5. MULT	$E982	(MFAC) ← (SFAC) * (MFAC)
MFAC and SFAC already loaded; do the MULTiplication.		
6. LMULT	$E97F	(MFAC) ← [Y,A] * (MFAC)
MFAC is already loaded; (Y,A) points to the memory location of the packed number to be MULTiplied by (MFAC).		
7. DIV	$EA69	(MFAC) ← (SFAC) / (MFAC)
MFAC and SFAC already loaded; DIVide (SFAC) by (MFAC)		
8. LDIV	$EA66	(MFAC) ← [Y,A] / (MFAC)
MFAC is already loaded; (Y,A) points to the memory location of the packed number that will be DIVided by (MFAC).		
9. POWER	$EE97	(MFAC) ← (SFAC)
MFAC and SFAC already loaded; (SFAC) is raised to the (MFAC) power.		

Note: In this table, and in the other tables in this chapter, the notation [Y,A] is used to indicate that Y must contain the high byte of the address (the page part), and A must contain the low byte of the address (the location on the page) of the first byte of the floating-point number. In short, Y and A point to the floating-point number.

Program 8.6 demonstrates the Applesoft subroutine LSUB (subroutine 4 in Table 8.1).

PROGRAM 8.6

```
                1000 * PROGRAM 8.6  LSUB & MOVE
                1010           .OR $300
E7A7-           1020 LSUB      .EQ $E7A7
EAF9-           1030 MOVMI     .EQ $EAF9
0300- A0 03     1040 BEGIN  LDY /DATAX    VAR ADDR, HI
0302- A9 0F     1050        LDA #DATAX    VAR ADDR, LO
0304- 20 F9 EA  1060        JSR MOVMI     COPY TO MFAC
0307- A0 03     1070        LDY /DATAY    VAR ADDR, HI
0309- A9 14     1080        LDA #DATAY    VAR ADDR, LO
030B- 20 A7 E7  1090        JSR LSUB      (Y,A) -> MFAC,
                1091 *                    SFAC - MFAC ->MFAC
030E- 00        1100        BRK
030F- 84 40 00
0312- 00 00     1110 DATAX  .HS 8440000000
0314- 78 D2 5E
0317- DD 03     1120 DATAY  .HS 78D25EDD03

SYMBOL TABLE

0300- BEGIN
030F- DATAX
0314- DATAY
E7A7- LSUB
EAF9- MOVMI
```

Note that the .HS in the above program is the S-C assembler directive that stores a hex string of digits (8440000000) starting at the current location ($030F). The equivalent directive for the Big Mac assembler is HEX. The DOS Tool Kit does not have an identical directive, but its DFB directive can be use to perform this task.

In Program 8.6, the two operands are stored as part of the program (lines 1110, 1120). We obtained the floating-point form of the numbers from the Applesoft BASIC program given as Program 8.4. Note that the labels DATAX and DATAY identify the start of each of the floating-point numbers. In lines 1040 and 1050 the high and low bytes of the address are loaded into the Y and A registers. The "/" in LDY /DATAX designates the high-order byte of the address identified by DATAX. Similarly, the "#" in LDA #DATAX designates the low-order byte of the address. This use of "/" and "#" is common is 6502 assemblers.

Lines 1040 through 1060 load the MFAC with 12 → 84 40 00 00 00. Lines 1070 and 1080 change the contents of Y and A so that they point to −0.00321 → 78 D2 5E DD 03. The subroutine LSUB (line 1090) loads SFAC with the number pointed to by (Y,A), then performs the subtraction SFAC − MFAC: −0.00321 − 12 = −12.00321 → 84 C0 0D 25 ED BF, and the result is placed in MFAC. The BRK leaves us in the Monitor, where we can examine the contents of MFAC:

```
9D- 84 C0 0D 25 ED BF
```

A word about the .OR statement in line 1030 in Program 8.6: Applesoft stores BASIC programs starting at $0801. The Applesoft variables are loaded at the next available location. (In Program 8.5 this is location $08A4.) The assembler we are using begins loading the machine language (assembled) program at $0800, but the destination address can be changed by the .OR (ORigin) statement. Your assembler should have a similar directive; use it in place of .OR. We have moved the origin of Program 8.6 because we will soon be linking assembly language programs to Applesoft BASIC programs. We want to avoid a collision between the Applesoft program and our assembled program, so the beginning of the assembled program has been moved to $300.

Printing the Results of a Calculation

Program 8.7 demonstrates the Applesoft subroutine LDIV which starts at $EA66. It is subroutine 8 in Table 8.1.

PROGRAM 8.7

```
                1000 * PROGRAM 8.7  LDIV & PRNTFAC
                1010          .OR $300
EA66-           1020 LDIV    .EQ $EA66
EAF9-           1030 MOVMI   .EQ $EAF9
ED2E-           1040 PRNTFAC .EQ $ED2E
```

```
0300- A0 03    1050 BEGIN  LDY /DATAX    VAR ADDR, HI
0302- A9 12    1060        LDA #DATAX    VAR ADDR, LO
0304- 20 F9 EA 1070        JSR MOVMI     (Y,A) -> MFAC
0307- A0 03    1080        LDY /DATAY    VAR ADDR, HI
0309- A9 17    1090        LDA #DATAY    VAR ADDR, LO
030B- 20 66 EA 1100        JSR LDIV      (Y,A) -> SFAC
               1101 *                    SFAC/MFAC -> MFAC
030E- 20 2E ED 1110        JSR PRNTFAC   PRINT MFAC
0311- 60       1120        RTS
0312- 78 D2 5E
0315- DD 03    1130 DATAX  .HS 78D25EDD03
0317- 6B 9D C6
031A- 8F 46    1140 DATAY  .HS 6B9DC68F46

SYMBOL TABLE

0300- BEGIN
0312- DATAX
0317- DATAY
EA66- LDIV
EAF9- MOVMI
ED2E- PRNTFAC
```

This example is organized very much like Program 8.6 MFAC is loaded using MOVMI with −0.00321, then Y and A are set to point to −2.9388E-7. The division is performed

```
(-2.9388E-7)/(-0.00321) = 9.1551402E-05 -> 73 BF FF 48 DF 4F
```

and the result is placed in MFAC. The jump to PRNTFAC causes the contents of MFAC to be printed on the screen. Note that as PRNTFAC is printing the contents of MFAC, it changes these contents. If PRNTFAC is used to display a result that is needed for later calculations, a copy of that result should be made (in SFAC, for example) before calling PRNTFAC. (See Table 8.5 for a listing of copy routines.)

Storage of Calculated Results

It would be unusual to have a machine language program that performed a single floating-point calculation. Typically, the results of calculations are stored for later use by the program.

Program 8.8 demonstrates the Applesoft subroutine POWER, starting at $EE97 (subroutine 9 in Table 8.1). It also shows how the results of a calculation can be copied from MFAC to another memory location (for later access).

PROGRAM 8.8

```
                   1000 * PROGRAM 8.8 POWER & MOVES
                   1010           .OR $300
E9E3-              1011 MOVSI     .EQ $E9E3
EAF9-              1020 MOVMI     .EQ $EAF9
EB2B-              1040 MOVMO     .EQ $EB2B
EE97-              1060 POWER     .EQ $EE97
0300- A0 03        1070 BEGIN     LDY /DATAX      VAR ADDR, HI
0302- A9 19        1080           LDA #DATAX      VAR ADDR, LO
0304- 20 F9 EA     1090           JSR MOVMI       (Y,A) -> MFAC
0307- A0 03        1100           LDY /DATAY      VAR ADDR, HI
0309- A9 1E        1110           LDA #DATAY      VAR ADDR, LO
030B- 20 E3 E9     1120           JSR MOVSI       (Y,A) -> SFAC
030E- 20 97 EE     1130           JSR POWER       (SFAC) (MFAC) -> MFAC
0311- A0 03        1140           LDY /DATAZ      VAR ADDR, HI
0313- A2 23        1150           LDX #DATAZ      VAR ADDR, LO
0315- 20 2B EB     1160           JSR MOVMO       MFAC -> (Y,X)
0318- 00           1170           BRK
0319- 84 4B AE
031C- 14 7B        1180 DATAX     .HS 844BAE147B
031E- 84 40 00
0321- 00 00        1190 DATAY     .HS 8440000000
0323- 00 00 00
0326- 00 00        1200 DATAZ     .HS 0000000000

SYMBOL TABLE

0300- BEGIN
0319- DATAX
031E- DATAY
0323- DATAZ
EAF9- MOVMI
EB2B- MOVMO
E9E3- MOVSI
EE97- POWER
```

To use POWER, both MFAC and SFAC must be loaded before it is called. The subroutine that MOVes SFAC In is located at $E9E3. It works like MOVMI, except that SFAC is loaded instead of MFAC. (It also sets $AB properly.) The operation performed is (SFAC) to the (MFAC) power. In this example we calculate 12 to the 12.73, which is 5.469873E13 → AE C6 FE 2A 1D 00. Then the example packs the result and moves it to storage designated by DATAZ.

When the example is executed, the BRK will leave the Monitor in control. Examine the contents of locations $323 through $327 to confirm that the calculation is correct.

Suggestions

1. Modify Program 8.8 so that −0.00321 is loaded into MFAC and 12 is loaded into SFAC. Call POWER to perform 12 to the

−0.00321 = 0.9920551 → 80 FD F7 54 02 00.

As an alternative, have the result printed (use PRNTFAC) and use a more familiar calculation, say 2 to the third power, so that you can easily confirm the calculation.

2. The examples given here perform only one calculation (multiplication or division, etc.). The subroutines need not be used in isolation, but can be used sequentially to perform more complex calculations. Write a subroutine to do a calculation like 24.7* `(215.4^12 - 73).`

SINGLE-OPERAND SUBROUTINES

Many Applesoft subroutines require only one operand; these subroutines are listed in Table 8.2.

Most of the one-operand subroutines use only MFAC. MFAC is loaded, a subroutine is called, and the result is placed into MFAC. The exceptions are the subroutines SGNA and RND. SGNA sets (A) = $01 if (MFAC) > 0; sets (A) = $00 if (MFAC) = $00, and sets (A) = $FF if (MFAC) < 0. RND generates a "random number" in locations $C9 through $CD. RND is the topic of Program 8.14.

LINKAGE TO APPLESOFT PROGRAMS

One of the purposes of this chapter is to demonstrate means of linking an Applesoft BASIC program to a machine language program. Such linkage usually requires

TABLE 8.2 One-Operand Subroutines

	Name	*Entry Point*	*Action Taken*
1.	LOG	$E941	(MFAC) <– LOG(MFAC)
2.	SGNA	$EB82	(A) <– SGN(MFAC)
3.	SGN	$EB90	(MFAC) <– SGN(MFAC)
4.	ABS	$EBAF	(MFAC) <– ABS(MFAC)
5.	INT	$EC23	(MFAC) <– INT(MFAC)
6.	SQR	$EE8D	(MFAC) <– SQR(MFAC)
7.	MMFAC	$EED0	(MFAC) <– –(MFAC)
8.	EXP	$EF09	(MFAC) <– EXP(MFAC)
9.	RND	$EFAE	($C9 – $CD) <– a random number
10.	COS	$EFEA	(MFAC) <– COS(MFAC)
11.	SIN	$EFF1	(MFAC) <– SIN(MFAC)
12.	TAN	$F03A	(MFAC) <– TAN(MFAC)
13.	ATN	$F09E	(MFAC) <– ATN(MFAC)

a means of passing variables between the two programs. The next programs show several ways this can be done.

If an Applesoft BASIC program stores a variable in an easily identified location, then that variable can be read by a machine language program. The BASIC command LOMEM: permits the specification of the location of the beginning of the simple variable table. As a result, the locations at which simple variables are stored can be known when the floating-point subroutine is written.

Programs 8.9A and 8.9 illustrate this process, and also illustrate the use of the Applesoft floating-point subroutine SQR. The BASIC program (Example 8.9A) defines values for variables X and Z1, and calls a machine language subroutine that will calculate Z1 = SQR(X). When control is returned to the BASIC program, the value of Z1 is printed.

```
10  REM PROGRAM 8.9A
100  LOMEM: 8192
110 X = 12: Z1 = 0
120  CALL 768
130  PRINT Z1
```

PROGRAM 8.9

```
                 1000 * PROGRAM 8.9 SQR; USES LOMEM
                 1010 * LINK WITH EXAMPLE 8.9A
                 1020            .OR $300
EAF9-            1030 MOVMI      .EQ $EAF9
EB2B-            1040 MOVMO      .EQ $EB2B
EE8D-            1050 SQR        .EQ $EE8D
0300- A0 20      1060 BEGIN      LDY #$20      ADDR OF
0302- A9 02      1070            LDA #$02        VAR #1
0304- 20 F9 EA   1080            JSR MOVMI     (Y,A) -> MFAC
0307- 20 8D EE   1090            JSR SQR       SQR(MFAC) -> MFAC
030A- A0 20      1100            LDY #$20      ADDR OF
030C- A2 09      1110            LDX #$09        VAR #2
030E- 20 2B EB   1120            JSR MOVMO     MFAC -> (Y,X)
0311- 60         1130            RTS

SYMBOL TABLE

0300- BEGIN
EAF9- MOVMI
EB2B- MOVMO
EE8D- SQR
```

When one 110 of the BASIC program is executed, space is allocated for variables X and Z1, and the numbers 12 and 0 are stored there in packed form. So that the machine language program will be able to find X and know where to store the value calculated for Z1, line 100 of the BASIC program sets LOMEM at 8192. By doing so, LOMEM establishes the beginning of the simple variable table at 8192 ($2000). The first seven bytes of the table will be used for the first variable defined (X) and the next seven bytes will be used for the second variable defined (Z1). When lines 100 and 110 have been executed, locations $2000–$200D will contain

```
2000- 58 00 84 40 00 00 00
2007- 5A 31 00 00 00 00 00
```

Note that two bytes are used for the first two characters of the name of the variable, and the packed floating-point form of its value occupies the next five bytes.

When line 120 (of Program 8.9A) transfers control to the machine language subroutine (Program 8.9), the value of X is available, starting at $2002. In Program 8.9, lines 1060–1080 unpack the number and store it in MFAC. Line 1090 calculates the square root of the number and stores the result in MFAC. Lines 1100–1130 copy the contents of MFAC to the bytes reserved for the value of Z1. When control is returned to the BASIC program, the value of Z1 can be printed.

Note: This method of providing floating-point numbers to a machine language subroutine provides an opportunity to pass variables between machine language programs and BASIC programs, but it does require knowledge of exactly where the value of a variable is to be found and stored.

Locating a Variable in the Variable Table

Program 8.10 passes one variable from a BASIC program to a machine language program, and passes another variable back to the BASIC program (8.10A). Further, the passing of variables is done without knowing exactly where the variables are stored. The program calls VARFND, a subroutine that locates a simple variable. On entry to the subroutine, locations \$81 and \$82 must contain the first two characters of the name of the simple variable. If the variable name does not appear in the variable table, the subroutine creates the variable. The subroutine will exit with the address of the first byte of the value of the variable in (Y,A).

```
10  REM PROGRAM 8.10A
100 X = 12
110  CALL 768
120  PRINT Z1
```

PROGRAM 8.10

```
                1000 *PROGRAM 8.10 LOG AND VARFND
                1010 *LINK WITH EXAMPLE 8.10A
                1020        .OR $300
E053-           1030 VARFND .EQ $E053
E941-           1040 LOG    .EQ $E941
EAF9-           1050 MOVMI  .EQ $EAF9
EB2B-           1060 MOVMO  .EQ $EB2B
0300- A9 58     1070 BEGIN  LDA #$58      ASCII CODE FOR X
```

```
0302- 85 81     1080        STA $81      1ST CHAR OF VAR NAME
0304- A9 00     1090        LDA #$00     NULL CHARACTER
0306- 85 82     1100        STA $82      2ND CHAR OF VAR NAME
0308- 20 53 E0  1110        JSR VARFND   LOCATE THE VARIABLE
                1111 *                   ADDR IN (Y,A)
030B- 20 F9 EA  1120        JSR MOVMI    (Y,A) -> MFAC
030E- 20 41 E9  1130        JSR LOG      LOG(MFAC) -> MFAC
0311- A9 5A     1140        LDA #$5A     ASCII CODE FOR "Z"
0313- 85 81     1150        STA $81      1ST CHAR OF VAR NAME

0315- A9 31     1160        LDA #$31     ASCII CODE FOR "1"
0317- 85 82     1170        STA $82      2ND CHAR OF VAR NAME
0319- 20 53 E0  1180        JSR VARFND   CREATE THE VARIABLE
                1181 *                   ADDR IN (Y,A)
031C- AA        1190        TAX          MOVMO REQUIRES (Y,X)
031D- 20 2B EB  1200        JSR MOVMO    MFAC -> (Y,X)
0320- 60        1210        RTS

SYMBOL TABLE

0300- BEGIN
E941- LOG
EAF9- MOVMI
EB2B- MOVMO
E053- VARFND
```

Lines 1070–1100 identify the variable name as "X." Note that the variable name must be identified with two characters. If only one is needed, the second is set to the null character, with ASCII code 0. Line 1110 calls VARFND, which returns with the address of the value of X in (Y,A).

After the value of LOG(X) has been calculated (lines 1120, 1130), lines 1140–1170 identify the variable name Z1. Line 1180 creates the variable, since it was not previously defined, and returns with the address of its value in (Y,A). Line 1190 arranges to have this address in (Y,X), so that line 1200 can store the contents of MFAC as the value of Z1.

On return to the BASIC program, the value of Z1 (2.48490665) can be printed.

Note on VARFND: VARFND can be used to locate simple integer variables also. It is again necessary that $81, $82 contain the name of the variable, but the high-order bits of $81 and $82 must be set to 1. For example, to identify the simple integer variable INT%,

```
LDA #$C9      ASCII "I"  (HIGH BIT SET)
STA $81
LDA #$CE      ASCII "N"  (HIGH BIT SET)
STA $82
```

Note that only the first two characters are used.

One Subroutine, Many Variables; Use of &

There are times when a machine language program might be called to perform a calculation several times, and be expected to use different variables as operands on each occasion. Program 8.11 shows one way to permit this. The program includes a BASIC program that uses the format & var1, var2 to identify the variables to be used by the machine language program. In this example, the machine language subroutine performs the calculation var2 = EXP(var1).

```
10  REM PROGRAM 8.11A
100  POKE 1013,76
110  POKE 1014,0
120  POKE 1015,3
130 X = 1.23
140  & X,Y
150  PRINT Y
160  & X ^ 2 + 2 * Y,Z
170  PRINT Z
```

PROGRAM 8.11

```
              1000 * PROGRAM 8.11 EXP, FRMEVL, PTRGET
              1010 * LINK WITH EXAMPLE 8.11A
              1020         .OR $300
DD7B-         1030 FRMEVL .EQ $DD7B
DEBE-         1040 CHKCOM .EQ $DEBE
DFE3-         1050 PTRGET .EQ $DFE3
EB2B-         1060 MOVMO  .EQ $EB2B
EF09-         1070 EXP    .EQ $EF09
0300- 20 7B DD 1080 BEGIN  JSR FRMEVL    EXPR AT TXTPTR
              1081 *                     IS PUT IN MFAC
0303- 20 09 EF 1090        JSR EXP       EXP(MFAC) -> MFAC
```

```
0306-  20 BE DE 1100        JSR CHKCOM     CONFIRM COMMA
0309-  20 E3 DF 1110        JSR PTRGET     ADDR OF VAR AT TXTPTR
                1111 *                      IS PUT IN (Y,A)
030C-  AA       1120        TAX            MOVMO REQUIRES (Y,X)
030D-  20 2B EB 1130        JSR MOVMO      MFAC -> (Y,X)
0310-  60       1140        RTS

SYMBOL TABLE

0300- BEGIN
DEBE- CHKCOM
EF09- EXP
DD7B- FRMEVL
EB2B- MOVMO
DFE3- PTRGET
```

Note that the BASIC program (8.11A) calls the machine language program twice. The first time, Y is defined as EXP(X), or EXP(1.23). The second time, Z is defined as EXP(X^2+2*Y). In preparation for the use of &, lines 100–120 of the BASIC program store the code JMP $300 at addresses $3F5–$3F7 (1013–1015).

When the machine language program is called, it must determine which variable is to be used for calculation, and arrange to move the value of that variable into MFAC. This is done by FRMEVL. This subroutine reads the expression that immediately follows &, evaluates it, and stores the result in MFAC.

After line 1090 performs the calculation EXP(var1), line 1100 checks to see that a comma is present. (FRMEVL interpreted the comma as the end of var1.) If no comma is found, the program will terminate with the message "SYNTAX ERROR."

Each of FRMEVL and PTRGET uses the contents of $B8, $B9 as a pointer into the BASIC program. This pointer, called TXTPTR, identifies the location of the next character to be read. TXTPTR is constantly being incremented as characters are read.

After the calculation of EXP(var1) is completed, the machine language program must store the contents of MFAC as var2. First PTRGET is called (line 1110). This subroutine increments TXTPTR so that it is pointing at var2. The name of the variable is read, and the location of the variable is determined. If the variable name has not yet been used, the variable is created and assigned a value of 0.

Next, the contents of MFAC are copied into the memory locations that are reserved for the value of var2. When the machine language program returns control to the BASIC program, the calculated value of var2 can be printed.

If the machine language program defined by Program 8.11 is assembled at $300, running Program 8.11A results in the following:

```
]RUN
3.42122954
4252.91145
```

INTEGER TO FLOATING-POINT CONVERSIONS

On many occasions we must work with both real (floating-point) and integer values. In these cases it is convenient to have subroutines that convert one of these types of numbers to the other. Table 8.3 contains the Applesoft subroutines that do conversions between excess $80 and 2's-complement hexadecimal integer notation. The only exception is CIYM.

Program 8.12 shows how to use CIAYM to convert a 2-byte hex integer in A and Y, −5 −> FF FB, to excess $80 notation (−5 −> 83 A0 00 00 00 FF) in MFAC.

PROGRAM 8.12

```
                  1000 * PROGRAM 8.12 CIAYM
                  1005          .OR $800      SET ORIGIN
E2F2-             1010 CIAYM    .EQ $E2F2
0800- A9 FF       1020 BEGIN    LDA #$FF  HEX REP.
0802- A0 FB       1030          LDY #$FB  OF -5
0804- 20 F2 E2    1040          JSR CIAYM
0807- 00          1050          BRK

SYMBOL TABLE

0800- BEGIN
E2F2- CIAYM
```

Registers:

```
0809-   A=83 X=05 Y=00 P=B4 S=F9
```

Memory:

```
009D- 83 A0 00 00 00 FF
```

Modify Program 8.12 to convert +5 –> 00 05 to excess $80 notation, +5 –> 83 A0 00 00 00 00, in MFAC. Here are the results when the program is run with this modification.

Registers:

```
0809–     A=83 X=05 Y–00 P=B4 S=F9
```

Memory:

```
009D- 83 A0 00 00 00 00
```

TABLE 8.3 Conversion Subroutines

Name	*Entry Point*	*Action Taken*
1. CPMIL	$EBF2	(Ext–>MFAC) –> ($85,$86)
The extension byte is rounded into MFAC and then MFAC is converted to a 2-byte integer in $85,$86. See Table 8.4 for rounding only.		
2. CLIM	$DEE9	[$A0,$A1] –> MFAC
$A0,$A1 contain the starting address of a two-byte integer that is converted to excess $80 notation in MFAC.		
3. CPMI	$E108	(MFAC) –> ($A0,$A1)
MFAC must be positive and less than 32,768; the two-byte integer is formed in $A0,$A1.		
4. CMI	$E10C	(MFAC) –> ($A0,$A1)
MFAC must be between –32,768 and 32,768; the two-byte integer is formed in (A0,A1). If integer is negative, it is in 2's-complement notation.		
5. CIAYM	$E2F2	(A,Y) –> (MFAC)
The integer in A and Y is converted to excess $80 notation in MFAC.		
6. CIYM	$E301	(Y) –> (MFAC)
The integer in Y, not in 2's-complement notation, is converted to excess $80 notation in MFAC.		
7. CMIX	$E6FB	(MFAC) –> (X)
MFAC is converted to a one-byte integer in X.		
8. CMIL	$E752	(MFAC) –> ($50,$51)
MFAC is converted to a two-byte integer in locations $50,$51.		
9. CIAM	$EB93	(A) –> (MFAC)
The integer in A is converted to excess $80 notation in MFAC.		
10. CMIE	$EBF2	(MFAC) –> ($9E,$9F,$A0,$A1)
MFAC is converted to a four-byte integer in locations $9E through $A1.		

The subroutine CMI, starting at $E10C, converts MFAC into a two-byte integer in $A0,$A1. Program 8.13 loads 2*PI = 6.283185308 −> 83 49 0F DA A2 into MFAC and converts it to 00 06 in $A0,$A1.

PROGRAM 8.13

```
                  1000 * PROGRAM 8.13 CONVERSION CMI
                  1005            .OR $800      SET ORIGIN
E10C-             1010 CMI        .EQ $E10C
EAF9-             1020 MOVMI      .EQ $EAF9
0800- A0 F0       1030 BEGIN      LDY #$F0   PAGE PART OF 2*PI
0802- A9 6B       1040            LDA #$6B   LOC ON PAGE OF 2*PI
0804- 20 F9 EA    1050            JSR MOVMI  MOVE IT TO MFAC
0807- 20 0C E1    1060            JSR CMI    DO THE CONV INTO A0,A1
080A- 00          1070            BRK        CALL MONITOR

SYMBOL TABLE

0800- BEGIN
E10C- CMI
EAF9- MOVMI
```

Registers:

```
080C-   A=48 X=9D Y=00 P=36 S=F9
```

Memory:

```
009D- 83 00 00 00 06 49
00A5- 8C FF A0 00 00 00
```

The subroutine CMIE, starting at $EBF2, converts MFAC into a four-byte integer in $E9 through $A1. The largest integer we could find in ROM is 1,000,000,000 −> 9E 6E 6B 28 00, which begins at $ED14. Program 8.14 moves this value into MFAC and converts it to 3B 9A CA 00 in $9E through $A1.

PROGRAM 8.14

```
                  1000 * PROGRAM 8.14 CONVERSION CMIE
                  1005            .OR $800      SET ORIGIN
EAF9-             1010 MOVMI      .EQ $EAF9
EBF2-             1020 CMIE       .EQ $EBF2
```

```
0800- A0 ED     1030 BEGIN  LDY #$ED    PAGE PART OF 1 BILLION
0802- A9 14     1040        LDA #$14    LOC ON PAGE OF 1 BILLION
0804- 20 F9 EA  1050        JSR MOVMI   MOVE IT TO MFAC
0807- 20 F2 EB  1060        JSR CMIE    DO THE CONV INTO 9E-A1
080A- 00        1070        BRK         CALL MONITOR

SYMBOL TABLE

0800- BEGIN
EBF2- CMIE
EAF9- MOVMI
```

Registers:

```
080C-   A=1D X=9D Y=00 P=76 S=F9
```

Memory:

```
009D- 9E 3B 9A CA 00 6E
00A5- 8C FF A0 00 00 00
```

The subroutine CLIM, starting at $DEE9, uses $A0,$A1 to point to the memory location of a two-byte integer to be converted to excess $80 notation in MFAC. Program 8.15 puts a +5 -> 00 05 in locations $4000 and $4001, then loads $A0,$A1 with the address ($4000) and does the conversion.

PROGRAM 8.15

```
                1000 * EXAMPLE 8.15 CONVERSION CLIM
                1005        .OR $800      SET ORIGIN
DEE9-           1010 CLIM   .EQ $DEE9
0800- A9 00     1020 BEGIN  LDA #$00    INITIALIZE
0802- 8D 00 40  1030        STA $4000   LOC WITH THE
0805- A9 05     1040        LDA #$05    INTEGER TO BE
0807- 8D 01 40  1050        STA $4001   CONVERTED
080A- A9 40     1060        LDA #$40    ESTABLISH ITS
080C- 85 A1     1070        STA $A1     ADDRESS FOR
080E- A9 00     1080        LDA #$00    USE WITH THE
0810- 85 A0     1090        STA $A0     SUBROUTINE CLIM
0812- 20 E9 DE  1100        JSR CLIM    DO CONV INTO MFAC
0815- 00        1110        BRK         CALL MONITOR

SYMBOL TABLE
```

```
0800- BEGIN
DEE9- CLIM
```

Registers:

```
0817-    A=83 X=05 Y=00 P=B4 S=F9
```

Memory:

```
009D- 83 A0 00 00 00 00
00A5- 8C FF A0 00 00 00
```

Modify Program 8.15 to convert −31,482 −> 85 06 to excess $80 notation in MFAC, 8F F5 F4 00 00 FF. The results are:

Registers:

```
0817-    A=8F X=7A Y=00 P=B4 S=F9
```

Memory:

```
009D- 8F F5 F4 00 00 FF
00A5- 8C FF A0 00 00 00
```

MISCELLANEOUS SUBROUTINES

Table 8.4 contains subroutines that, by their nature, did not seem to belong in any of the previous tables. Only the normalization subroutine, entry 7 in this table, has been used in an example. Because their use is similar in many ways to subroutines already illustrated, no further examples from this table are given.

MEMORY MOVE SUBROUTINES

Most examples in this chapter used subroutines that moved data from one memory location to another. Table 8.5 contains a summary of the subroutines that can be used to copy floating-point numbers from one memory location to another.

The pair of subroutines in Table 8.6 uses the stack for storage. Their use is somewhat tricky, so they will be illustrated.

To illustrate saving (MFAC) on the stack, we shall move SQR(2) = 1.414213562 −> 81 35 04 F3 34 into MFAC, then call MSTAK, located at $DE10, to pack the extension byte into MFAC and push it onto the stack.

TABLE 8.4 Odds and Ends

	Name	*Entry Point*	*Action Taken*
1.	NOT	$DE98	(MFAC) <− NOT(MFAC)
2.	OR	$DF4F	(MFAC) <− (SFAC) OR (MFAC)
3.	AND	$DF55	(MFAC) <− (SFAC) AND (MFAC)
4.	COMP	$DF6A	(SFAC) is compared to (MFAC)

MFAC is set to 1 if the result of the comparison is true. MFAC is set to 0 if the comparison is false. The contents of location $16 determines the type of comparison to be done according to:

Contents of $16	Comparison to be done	Shorthand Reminder
1	(SFAC) > (MFAC)	< = >
2	(SFAC) = (MFAC)	4 2 1
3	(SFAC) > or = (MFAC)	
4	(SFAC) < (MFAC)	
5	(SFAC) < > (MFAC)	
6	(SFAC) < or = (MFAC)	

5.	MULTI	$E2B6	(Y,X) <− ($AE,$AD) * (accum,$64)

The hex integer in $AE,$AD is multiplied by the hex integer in A and $64.

6.	ADDH	$E7A0	(MFAC) <− (MFAC) + 1/2
7.	NORM	$E82E	(MFAC) <− normalized(MFAC)
8.	MULTT	$EA39	(MFAC) <− (MFAC) * 10
9.	DIVT	$EA55	(MFAC) <− (MFAC)/10
10.	ROUND	$EB72	(MFAC) <− (ext)

The extension byte, $AC, is rounded into MFAC.

11.	COMPA	$EBB2	[Y,A] − (MFAC)

(A) = $01 if the subtraction is negative; (A) = $00 if the subtraction is zero; (A) = $FF if the subtraction is positive.

The program first moves SQR(2) to MFAC (lines 1040–1060). Next the stack pointer is saved in location $06 (so that we will be able to confirm the operation of MSTAK. Following the jump to MSTAK, the BRK instruction (line 1100) leaves us in the Monitor.

TABLE 8.5 Moves

	Name	*Entry Point*	*Action Taken*
1.	MOVSI	$E9E3	[Y,A] -> (SFAC)
2.	MOV5S	$E9E7	[$5F,$5E] -> (SFAC)
3.	MOVMI	$EAF9	[Y,A] -> (MFAC)
4.	MOV5M	$EAFD	[$5F,$5E] -> (MFAC)
5.	MOVM98	$EB1E	(MFAC) -> ($98,$99,$9A,$9B,$9C)
6.	MOVM93	$EB21	(MFAC) -> ($93,$94,$95,$96,$97)
7.	MOVMZ Move (MFAC) to the zero-page location pointed to by X.	$EB23	(MFAC) -> [X]
8.	MOVM8	$EB27	(MFAC) -> [$86,$85]
9.	MOVMO	$EB2B	(MFAC) -> [Y,X]
10.	MOVSM	$EB53	(SFAC) -> (MFAC)
11.	MOVMS	$EB63	(MFAC) -> (SFAC)

TABLE 8.6 Stack Moves

	Names	*Entry Point*	*Action Taken*
1.	MSTAK	$DE10	(ext->MFAC) then PUSH (MFAC) onto the stack. This takes six bytes.
	This subroutine ends with a JMP instead of an RTS. The JMP address is stored in ($5E,$5F) by the subroutine itself. When you use it with STAKS, put the return address on the stack, page part first, before calling MSTAK.		
2.	STAKS	$DE47	PULL stack, six bytes, into SFAC.
	This subroutine must be called with a JMP and not with a JSR. (You do see why don't you? The stack is used to store the return address for a JSR.) It concludes with an RTS, so there must be a proper return address on the stack before STAKS is called.		

PROGRAM 8.16

```
                1000 * EXAMPLE 8.16 STACK SAVES
                1005         .OR $800     SET ORIGIN
DE10-           1010 MSTAK   .EQ $DE10
EAF9-           1020 MOVMI   .EQ $EAF9
0006-           1030 SAVE    .EQ $06
0800- A0 E9     1040 BEGIN   LDY #$E9    PAGE PART OF SQR(2)
0802- A9 32     1050         LDA #$32    LOC ON PG OF SQR(2)
0804- 20 F9 EA  1060         JSR MOVMI   MOVE IT TO MFAC
0807- BA        1070         TSX         PUT NEXT STACK ADDRESS IN X
0808- 8E 00 40  1080         STX SAVE    SAVE IT
080B- 20 10 DE  1090         JSR MSTAK   PUSH MFAC ONTO THE STACK
080E- 00        1100         BRK         CALL THE MONITOR

SYMBOL TABLE

0006- SAVE
0800- BEGIN
EAF9- MOVMI
DE10- MSTAK
```

When we executed this example, we found location $06 contained $FD. To see that MSTAK had the desired effect, we examine the six bytes of MFAC and the six stack locations $F9–$FD. (Remember, the stack pointer $FD is really pointing at $1FD.) MSTAK also put the address of the next executable instruction in locations $5E, $5F. In Program 8.16, this is the address of the BRK instruction (line 1100).

When the example is assembled and executed the results are:

Registers:

```
0810-   A=81 X=79 Y=35 P=B4 S=F3
```

Memory:

```
009D- 81 B5 04 F3 34 35

01F0- B5 9F BA FD F8 FE 84 FF
01F8- 81 B5 04 F3 34 35 62 10

005E- 0E 08
```

Program 8.17 shows how to use STAKS. The program will load SQR(2) into MFAC, then transfer it to the stack by using MSTAK. Then STAKS recovers the number, putting it in SFAC.

Before MSTAK is used, a return address is pushed onto the stack. This address is used to direct program flow upon return from STAKS.

PROGRAM 8.17

```
                 1000 * PROGRAM 8.17  MSTAK AND STAKS
                 1005          .OR $800      SET ORIGIN
DE10-            1010 MSTAK   .EQ $DE10
DE47-            1020 STAKS   .EQ $DE47
EAF9-            1030 MOVMI   .EQ $EAF9
0800- A0 E9      1040 BEGIN   LDY #$E9      LOCATION OF
0802- A9 32      1050         LDA #$32        SQR(2)
0804- 20 F9 EA   1060         JSR MOVMI
0807- A9 08      1070         LDA /END      SET UP
0809- 48         1080         PHA             THE RETURN
080A- A9 14      1090         LDA #END        FROM
080C- 48         1100         PHA             STAKS
080D- 20 10 DE   1110         JSR MSTAK     MFAC -> STACK
0810- 4C 47 DE   1120         JMP STAKS     NOTE JMP NOT JSR
0813- 60         1130         RTS           THIS IS NOT USED
0814- 00         1140 END     BRK

SYMBOL TABLE

0800- BEGIN
0814- END
EAF9- MOVMI
DE10- MSTAK
DE47- STAKS
```

Note that when this program is executed, the RTS in line 1130 will never be encountered. The address of END is on the stack and provides the destination when STAKS returns. Check MFAC and SFAC to confirm that they each contain the same thing (81 B5 04 F3 34 35, or SQR(2)).

FLOATING-POINT NUMBERS

Several times in the examples in this chapter we have used the packed excess $80 representation of floating-point numbers that are contained in the Applesoft ROMs. Table 8.7 contains these and a few more. Some of these are useful for application and some are good only for testing purposes.

TABLE 8.7 Floating-Point Numbers in ROM

	Base Ten Value	*Starting Address*	*Contents*
1.	1/4	$F070	7F 00 00 00 00
2.	1/2	$EE64	81 00 00 00 00
3.	−1/2	$E937	80 80 00 00 00
4.	SQR(1/2)	$E920	80 35 04 F3 34
5.	SQR(2)	$E932	81 35 04 F3 34
6.	1	$E913	81 00 00 00 00
7.	10	$EA50	84 20 00 00 00
8.	2*PI	$F06B	83 49 0F DA A2
9.	PI/2	$F066	81 49 0F DA A2
10.	NAT. LOG(2)	$E93C	80 31 72 17 F8
11.	1 BILLION	$ED14	9E 6E 6B 28 00
12.	−32,768	$E0FE	90 80 00 00 20
13.	0.434255942	$E919	7F 5E 56 CB 79
14.	0.576584541	$E91E	80 13 9B 0B 64
15.	0.961800759	$E923	80 76 38 93 16
16.	1.442695041	$EEDB	81 38 AA 3B 29
17.	2.885390074	$E928	82 38 AA 3B 20
18.	−42.78203928	$EA46	86 AB 20 CE E7
19.	2.980232E-8	$EE84	9C 00 00 00 0A
20.	1.014753E-37	$EE69	FA 0A 1F 00 00

INTEGER STORAGE BY APPLESOFT

The integer variable type is recognized in Applesoft by the % at the end of a name. Integer values are stored in memory in 2's-complement notation. Here is a program that shows how dimensioned integer variables are stored.

```
100  REM PROGRAM 8.18
110  REM INTEGER STORAGE
```

```
120  INPUT "N: NUMBER OF VARIABLES
     TO BE CONVERTED.   ";N%
130 N% = N% - 1
140  DIM AI%(N%)
150  FOR I = 0 TO N%
160  PRINT "I = ";I: INPUT AI%(I)
170  PRINT
180  NEXT I

]RUN
N: NUMBER OF VARIABLES TO BE CONVERTED.   4
I = 0
?123

I = 1
?-123

I = 2
?32767

I = 3
?-32767

]CALL-151

*6B.6E
006B- B2 08 C1 08

*8B2.8C0
08B2- C1 C9 0F 00 01 00
08B8- 04 00 7B FF 85 7F FF 80
08C0- 01
```

Initialize the Applesoft pointers with the FP command, then enter the values. Call the Monitor and find the beginning address, $865, and the ending address, $873, of the integer storage block. The information in the header, the first seven bytes for this example, is organized just like it is for floating-point variables:

Header →	C1	C9	0F	00	01	00	04
Address →	$865	$866	$867	$868	$869	$86A	$86B
	CHAR1 name "A"	CHAR2 name "I"	LENGTH of this block		# of DIMs	RANGE of right most index	

The remainder of the block is organized differently than it is for floating-point storage—only two bytes are used for each integer. The remainder of the block is organized like this:

I	Starting Address	Contents 2's complement	Base ten value
0	\$865+\$7=\$86C	00 7B	123
1	\$86C+\$2=\$86E	FF 85	−123
2	\$86E+\$2=\$870	7F FF	32767
3	\$860+\$2=\$872	80 01	−32767

ADDITIONAL EXAMPLES

Each of the examples given earlier in this chapter focused on the use of a single floating-point subroutine. Each of the next two examples combines several of the types of subroutines presented so far.

SIN (at \$EFF1) is a one-operand subroutine listed in Table 8.2. It calculates the trigonometric sine of the number found in the MFAC, and stores the result in MFAC. SIN assumes that the number found in MFAC is specified in radians. Programs 8.19 and 8.19A illustrate a way of specifying an angular measurement in degrees rather than radians, and having the sine of the angle calculated.

Remember how to convert degrees to radians?

Radians = (PI/2)∗(Degrees/90)

PI is not stored in Applesoft ROM, but PI/2 and 2∗PI are. PI/2 begins at \$F066, and 2∗PI begins at \$F06B. In Program 8.19 the conversion from degrees to radians is done using PI/2. The arithmetic is:

R = D∗(PI/2)/(180/2), or
R = (D/90)∗(PI/2)

Since PI/2 is provided in ROM, we need provide only the values of D and 90. The BASIC program (Program 8.19A) will pass the value of D via the USR function. The integer 90 will be provided as a divisor by loading that number in the Y register and using CYIM to convert it to a floating-point number in MFAC.

```
10  REM PROGRAM 8.19A
100  POKE 10,76
```

```
110  POKE 11,0
120  POKE 12,3
130  PRINT USR(40)
```

PROGRAM 8.19

```
                1000 * PROGRAM 8.19 SIN(DEGREES)
                1010 * LINK WITH EXAMPLE 8.19A
E301-           1020 CIYM    .EQ $E301
E97F-           1030 LMULT   .EQ $E97F
EA69-           1040 DIV     .EQ $EA69
EB63-           1050 MOVMS   .EQ $EB63
EFF1-           1060 SIN     .EQ $EFF1
                1070         .OR $300
0300- 20 63 EB  1080         JSR MOVMS     MFAC -> SFAC
0303- A0 5A     1090         LDY #$5A      DECIMAL 90
0305- 20 01 E3  1100         JSR CIYM      90 -> MFAC
0308- A5 A2     1110         LDA $A2       SET $AB TO
030A- 45 AA     1120         EOR $AA        EOR OF SIGN OF
030C- 85 AB     1130         STA $AB        MFAC AND SFAC
030E- A5 9D     1140         LDA $9D       ALSO SETS Z
0310- 20 69 EA  1150         JSR DIV       D/90 -> MFAC
0313- A0 F0     1160         LDY #$F0      ADDR OF
0315- A9 66     1170         LDA #$66        PI/2
0317- 20 7F E9  1180         JSR LMULT     RADIAN MEASURE
031A- 20 F1 EF  1190         JSR SIN       SIN(MFAC) -> MFAC
031D- 60        1200         RTS

SYMBOL TABLE

E301- CIYM
EA69- DIV
E97F- LMULT
EB63- MOVMS
EFF1- SIN
```

A TABLE OF RANDOM NUMBERS

The last program in this chapter develops a table of numbers. This can be a useful device. Once a table is available, values can usually be read from it much more rapidly than they could be recalculated.

The table that is developed here consists of random numbers and makes use of the RND subroutine. Before considering Program 8.20, first note the behavior of RND. If X is negative, RND(X) uses the value of X to calculate a "random" number. (Since it is calculated, the result is predictable, and hence is not really random.) If X is zero, RND(X) returns the most recently calculated random number. If X is positive, RND(X) ignores X, but uses the value of the most recently calculated random number as it calculates the next one. The number used to start the calculation is sometimes called the "seed."

If RND (at $EFAE) is called from a machine language program, the number in MFAC is used in the way RND(X) uses X. When RND has completed its calculations, the result is stored in MFAC, with a copy placed in locations $C9 through $CD. If MFAC contains zero when RND is called, the number in $C9 through $CD is moved to MFAC, and RND branches to an RTS. If MFAC contains a negative number, RND uses that number to start the calculation of a random number. If MFAC contains a positive number, the contents of $C9 through $CD are copied to MFAC, then used to calculate a random number.

Program 8.20 generates a table of random numbers that is stored beginning at $4000 (page 2 of high-resolution graphics). The random number seed and the number of entries for the table are passed from an Applesoft program (Program 8.20A).

```
10  REM EXAMPLE 8.20A RANDOM
100 POKE 1013,76: POKE 1014,0: POKE 1015,3: REM SET UP & JUMP
100 A = 3
110 & - 2,A ^ 2 + 4
120  REM -2 PROVIDES THE SEED
130  REM A^2+4 IS THE LENGTH OF THE TABLE
```

PROGRAM 8.20

```
                1000 * PROGRAM 8.20
                1010 * LINK WITH PROGRAM 8.20A
0006-           1020 LEN     .EQ $06
0007-           1030 LOC     .EQ $07
0008-           1040 PAGE    .EQ $08
DD7B-           1050 FRMEVL  .EQ $DD7B
DEBE-           1060 CHKCOM  .EQ $DEBE
E6FB-           1070 CMIX    .EQ $E6FB
EB2B-           1080 MOVMO   .EQ $EB2B
EFAE-           1090 RND     .EQ $EFAE
                1100         .OR $300
```

```
0300- A9 40              LDA #$40      ADDRESS
0302- 85 08              STA PAGE        OF
0304- A9 00              LDA #$00        TABLE
0306- 85 07              STA LOC         STORAGE
0308- 20 7B DD           JSR FRMEVL    EVALUATE FORMULA
               *                         AT TXTPTR
030B- 20 FB E6           JSR CMIX      INT(MFAC) -> X
030E- 86 06              STX LEN       LENGTH OF TABLE
0310- 20 BE DE           JSR CHKCOM    CONFIRM COMMA
0313- 20 7B DD           JSR FRMEVL    READ NEXT FORMULA
0316- 20 AE EF      LOOP JSR RND       GENERATE A RANDOM NUMBER
0319- A4 08              LDY PAGE      DESTINATION
031B- A6 07              LDX LOC        ADDRESS
031D- 20 2B EB           JSR MOVMO     MFAC -> (Y,X)
0320- 18                 CLC           READY TO
0321- A5 07              LDA LOC       INC DESTINATION
0323- 69 05              ADC #$05      FOR NEXT RANDOM
0325- 85 07              STA LOC          NUMBER
0327- C6 06              DEC LEN       COUNT DOWN
0329- D0 EB              BNE LOOP        TO 0
032B- 60                 RTS           TABLE COMPLETE

SYMBOL TABLE

DEBE- CHKCOM
E6FB- CMIX
DD7B- FRMEVL
0006- LEN
0007- LOC
0316- LOOP
EB2B- MOVMO
0008- PAGE
EFAE- RND
```

CHAPTER 9

PROGRAM INTERACTION: AN EXTENDED EXAMPLE

Assembly language programs are useful for a variety of reasons. Some of the more valuable applications are those performing duties similar to those provided by Applesoft BASIC commands. When such programs are linked to BASIC, they give the opportunity to extend it.

In this chapter we will develop an assembly language subroutine that provides such an extension to BASIC. The example was chosen because it illustrates the process of developing such routines; because it is an example of a very close, interactive linkage between BASIC and assembly language; and because it provides a useful extension of BASIC. We will begin with a fundamental statement of the problem and the goals, then develop the routine through to its implementation in an application program.

THE PROBLEM

Applesoft provides the capability of accepting user-defined variables in a program. By using INPUT, GET, or PEEK(−16384), the computer can accept keyboard input and interpret it as a numeric or string variable. However, there is no provision for the input of a function that can be used for calculation later in the program. This capability would be useful in educational or scientific software.

We will develop a procedure that will permit user input of functions. We will provide for linkage of the subroutine to BASIC. The subroutine will be relocatable, and will permit the identification (and re-identification) of one or several functions.

There are several things that must be done. The program must accept the keyboard input, put it in a form that Applesoft can use, store it somewhere in memory, and tell the Applesoft interpreter where it can be found.

Background

As a step in developing our assembly language program, let's see how Applesoft handles functions. First, consider an example.

```
10 DEF FN F(X) = COS(X)
```

Enter this one-line program, RUN it, then enter the Apple Monitor (CALL −151) and look at the hexadecimal form of the program and variables. Type 800.821 to see the display shown below.

```
800- 00 11 08 0A 00 B8 C2 46
808- 28 58 29 D0 DE 28 58 29
810- 00 00 00 0A C6 00 0C 08
818- 1D 08 DE 58 00 00 00 00
820- 00 00
```

Table 9.1 interprets the contents of this area of memory. The contents of memory locations $800–$813 were established by typing in the one line of the program. Notice that COS(X) does not appear in the same form as we typed, but is coded, or tokenized. Instead of storing the characters C, O, S, Applesoft uses the token $DE (decimal 222) to represent the cosine function. (See the *Applesoft Reference Manual* for a complete list of BASIC tokens.)

The contents of $814–$822 were established when the program was run. When Applesoft encountered the DEF FN F(X) = COS(X) statement, it set up

TABLE 9.1

800- 00	Beginning-of-program code
801- 11	Pointer to next
802- 08	program line (at $811)
803- 0A	Line number $000A
804- 00	(decimal 10)
805- B8	Token for DEF
806- C2	" " FN
807- 46	Code for F
808- 28	" " (
809- 58	" " X
80A- 29	" ")
80B- D0	Token for =
80C- DE	" " COS
80D- 28	Code for (
80E- 58	" " X
80F- 29	" ")
810- 00	
811- 00	End-of-program code
812- 00	
813- 0A	
814- C6	Code for F (high bit set)
815- 00	Second letter of function name
816- 0C	Address of function ($80C)
817- 08	
818- 1D	Address of argument
819- 08	variable X ($81D)
81A- DE	First byte of function
81B- 58	Code for X
81C- 00	Second letter of variable name
81D- 00	Exponent of variable
81E- 00	
81F- 00	Mantissa of variable
820- 00	
821- 00	

the function pointer ($814–$81A). This pointer has a structure that is similar to that of string pointers. Table 9.2 shows how the pointers to string variables and functions are organized.

When the variable X was encountered, space was allocated and X was given the initial value of 0.

TABLE 9.2

String Pointers			*Function Pointers*		
NAME	(pos)	1st byte	NAME	(neg)	1st byte
	(neg)	2nd byte		(pos)	2nd byte
Length one byte			Function address	high byte	
Address high byte				low byte	
low byte			Variable address	high byte	
0				low byte	
0			First byte of function		

If we wish to make a function available for use by Applesoft we must (1) input the function, (2) tokenize the function, and (3) set up the function pointer. Fortunately we can arrange for most of the work to be done by the BASIC program that calls our subroutine. If a program line is encountered that contains

```
20 DEF FN F(X) = X
```

then a function pointer is established that points to the memory location at which the tokenized function begins. Since the inclusion of such a line requires little effort, yet handles a major part of our task, we will have such a line in the BASIC program. Note, however, that the pointer identifies (in this case) a very short function (one byte). In order to reserve space for the storage of a longer function we will use the program line

```
20 DEF FN F(X) = X :::::::::::::::::::::
```

When the function is received and tokenized, it will be stored in this reserved area.

The input of the function is most easily handled by use of a string input so that a variable length sequence of characters can be received. Again, this is easily done by a BASIC program line:

```
30 INPUT "ENTER F(X) = "; F$
```

With the function received as a string F$, it is time for the assembly language program to take over. It must tokenize the string just received and store the tokenized function starting at the memory location identified by the function pointer.

If the machine language subroutine is called immediately after the function string is entered, the string (which has been stored in the string storage area of memory) will still be available in the keyboard input buffer (page 2 of memory: \$200–\$2FF). This is fortunate, because the Applesoft tokenize routine (TKNZ, which begins at \$D559) expects to find keyboard input there. We will use TKNZ to put the input string in a form that Applesoft can use for calculation.

Our subroutine will use several Applesoft and Monitor subroutines, which we will review before considering the program itself. As Applesoft steps through a program, TXTPTR (\$B8, \$B9) points at the character or token that is to be read. The subroutine CHARGET (\$B1) will first increment TXTPTR by one, then load the accumulator with the contents of the memory location pointed at by TXTPTR. CHARGOT (\$B7) loads the accumulator with the contents of the memory location pointed at by TXTPTR, but does not increment TXTPTR. The two routines (CHARGET, CHARGOT) also set the Carry and Zero flags to classify the contents of the accumulator, but that is not of direct consequence to us now.

We will also use the Applesoft routine FNFIND. PTRGET (\$DFE3) locates the memory location of the variable (real, integer, or string pointer) whose name is pointed at by TXTPTR. On return from PTRGET, memory locations \$9B and \$9C will contain the address of the variable's name. FNFIND (\$DFEA), which is a part of PTRGET, performs the same type of duty for functions. When we call FNFIND, we must be sure that TXTPTR is pointing to the first byte of the name of the function, and that the accumulator and memory location \$14 contain the first byte (negative) of the name of the function. On return from FNFIND, locations \$9B, \$9C will contain the address of the function pointer.

The last Applesoft subroutine we will use is TOKEN (\$D559). This routine tokenizes the input string that is pointed to by TXTPTR, and stores the result in the keyboard buffer.

THE SUBROUTINE

We can now turn to the outline of the machine language program. This routine must accomplish several things for us. It must (1) find the function pointer (we will use FNFIND to handle this task); (2) tokenize the string (use TOKEN) and store it in a suitable location; and (3) store the first byte of the tokenized function as the last byte of the function pointer.

The subroutine is intended to be called from Applesoft immediately after a string has been received. Applesoft will store the string and set up the string pointer. Although the string will be put in regular string storage, just below HIMEM, it will also remain in the input buffer (page 2) beginning at \$200, until it is overwritten by later input. Our tokenizing routine will expect to find the string here (at \$200).

One question must yet be resolved: How is the subroutine to be accessed from BASIC? Several methods are available. We will use the & vector method, since this makes it easy to pass the name of the function to the subroutine. We will thus be able to use the subroutine repeatedly to identify several different functions.

Two temporary pointers are defined for use by the routine. FNPTR ($FD, $FE) will contain the address of the function pointer. FNADR ($FB, $FC) will contain the address of the tokenized function.

Lines 1080–1110 locate the function pointer. JSR CHARGOT, in line 1080, reads the first byte of the function name. The first byte of the function name must be negative (high bit set to 1); this is arranged by the ORA #$80 in line 1090. With this byte in the accumulator and in memory location $14, we can jump to the subroutine FNFIND. This Applesoft subroutine will locate the function pointer (or create one if no function by this name has previously been defined). On return from FNFIND, locations $9B, $9C will contain the address of the function pointer. Lines 1140–1170 save this address in FNPTR, FNPTR+1 for later use. Then lines 1200–1250 read the address of the function from the function pointer (established by the BASIC program) and store the address in FNADR, FNADR+1.

We can now turn to the task of tokenizing the function. Since this process will modify TXTPTR, its contents are first saved on the stack (lines 1280–1310). Location $B8 is then set to 0 (lines 340–1350) in preparation for the call to Applesoft subroutine TKNZ (line 1370). TKNZ will read the input line at $200 (the string is still there), tokenize it, and store the result, again at $200. On return from TKNZ, the Y-register will contain a number that is 5 larger than the length of the tokenized function.

We subtract 3, that leaves a result which is 2 larger than the length of the tokenized function (lines 1410–1440). This allows us to store the function and two extra bytes in the position previously occupied by the dummy function (lines 1460–1590). The two extra bytes are the codes for ":" and "REM". We then store the first byte of the function as the last byte of the function pointer (lines 1630–1650), and restore TXTPTR to its earlier value (lines 1680–1710). The task is complete, and function is ready for later use.

```
00B7-          1000 CHARGOT .EQ $B7
00FB-          1010 FNADR   .EQ $FB
00FD-          1020 FNPTR   .EQ $FD
D559-          1030 TKNZ    .EQ $D559
DFEA-          1040 FNFIND  .EQ $DFEA
               1050         .OR $300
               1060 *--------------------------------
               1070 * LOCATE  FUNCTION POINTER
```

```
0300- 20 B7 00 1080        JSR CHARGOT  READ 1ST BYTE OF FN LABEL
0303- 09 80    1090        ORA #$80     SET HIGH BIT
0305- 85 14    1100        STA $14      STORE FOR ACCESS BY FNFIND
0307- 20 EA DF 1110        JSR FNFIND   LOCATE OR CREATE FN POINTER
               1120 *-------------------------------
               1130 * FNPTR, FNPTR+1 GET ADDRESS OF FUNCTION POINTER
030A- A5 9B    1140        LDA $9B
030C- 85 FD    1150        STA FNPTR
030E- A5 9C    1160        LDA $9C
0310- 85 FE    1170        STA FNPTR+1
               1180 *-------------------------------
               1190 * FNADR, FNADR+1 GET ADDRESS OF FUNCTION
0312- A0 02    1200        LDY #$02
0314- B1 FD    1210        LDA (FNPTR),Y
0316- 85 FB    1220        STA FNADR
0318- C8       1230        INY
0319- B1 FD    1240        LDA (FNPTR),Y
031B- 85 FC    1250        STA FNADR+1
               1260 *-------------------------------
               1270 * SAVE TXTPTR WHEN CALLING TKNZ
031D- A5 B8    1280        LDA $B8
031F- 48       1290        PHA
0320- A5 B9    1300        LDA $B9
0322- 48       1310        PHA
               1320 *-------------------------------
               1330 * TOKENIZE THE STRING
0323- A9 00    1340        LDA #$00
0325- 85 B8    1350        STA $B8      NEEDED FOR TKNZ SUBROUTINE
               1360 *-------------------------------
0327- 20 59 D5 1370        JSR TKNZ     TOKENIZE THE STRING
               1380 *-------------------------------
               1390 * SUBTRACT 5 FROM Y TO GET THE
               1400 * LENGTH OF THE TOKENIZED STRING
032A- 98       1410        TYA
032B- 18       1420        CLC
032C- E9 03    1430        SBC #$03     LENGTH+2
032E- A8       1440        TAY
               1450 *-------------------------------
               1460 * STORE A "REM"
032F- A9 B2    1470        LDA #$B2     TOKEN FOR "REM"
0331- 91 FB    1480        STA (FNADR),Y
0333- 88       1490        DEY
```

```
                  * STORE A ":"
0334- A9 3A                LDA #$3A      CODE FOR ":"
0336- 91 FB                STA (FNADR),Y
0338- 88                   DEY
                  *-------------------------------
                  * STORE TOKENIZED FUNCTION
0339- B9 00 02    A        LDA $200,Y
033C- 91 FB                STA (FNADR),Y
033E- 88                   DEY
033F- 10 F8                BPL A
                  *-------------------------------
                  * SET LAST BYTE OF FUNCTION POINTER
                  * TO THE FIRST BYTE OF THE FUNCTION
0341- AD 00 02             LDA $200
0344- A0 06                LDY #$06
0346- 91 FD                STA (FNPTR),Y
                  *-------------------------------
                  * RESTORE TXTPTR
0348- 68                   PLA
0349- 85 B9                STA $B9
034B- 68                   PLA
034C- 85 B8                STA $B8
                  *-------------------------------
034E- 60                   RTS

SYMBOL TABLE

0339- A
00B7- CHARGOT
00FB- FNADR
DFEA- FNFIND
00FD- FNPTR
D559- TKNZ
```

Access from Applesoft

The following BASIC program segment illustrates the use of this subroutine.

```
10 PRINT CHR$(4); "BRUN FNINPT"
20 DEF FN F(X) = x : : : : : : : :
30 INPUT "ENTER F(X) = ";F$ : &F
```

As the subroutine is loaded in line 10, it makes the & connection. Line 20 causes the function pointer to be established. The function in line 20 is a dummy, used to allow Applesoft to complete the function pointer. Line 20 also provides a location where a variable length function can later be stored. (If you anticipate long functions, then provide more colons; excess colons will be interpreted as multiple-statement indicators.) Line 30 receives the function and calls the subroutine via &F. The name of the input string and the name of the function need not agree, but it is important that the function name given with the & be the same as that which appears in an earlier DEF FN statement.

After entering the program, run it and enter a function, say COS(X∧2 − 4). Then list the program. You will find line 20 is modified to define the new function. The function definition is immediately followed by ": REM", as provided by lines 1470–1520 of the assembly language program. This has been provided so that the function can be redefined, using functions of different length. To see this in action, type RUN 20, and enter a short function, say X∧3. Then list the program again.

It is possible to use the subroutine repeatedly, to define different functions. To the BASIC program above, add the following.

```
25 DEF FN Y(X) = X : : : : : : : : :
40 INPUT "ENTER Y(X) = Y: &Y
```

The program will now accept two user-defined functions.

Notes

There are several resources you can turn to for additional information about CHARGET, TXTPTR, and other Applesoft and Monitor internal locations. *CALL A.P.P.L.E* has published several articles in their monthly magazine, and also some compilations of articles: *All About Applesoft, More About Applesoft*. S-C Software offers a complete disassembly of Applesoft, with comments (you must have the S-C Macro Assembler to access this). Articles on Applesoft appear with some regularity in several magazines: *CALL A.P.P.L.E, MICRO, Softalk*, etc.

SECTION

IV

GRAPHICS

CHAPTER 10

INTRODUCTION TO THE SCREEN: ORGANIZATION AND ADDRESSING

The purpose of this chapter is to introduce you to the organization of the screen and its relationship to the memory locations whose contents are displayed on the screen. We will first consider the TEXT screen, then the low-resolution graphics screen, and finally the high-resolution graphics screen.

TEXT DISPLAY

There are two areas of memory that may be used to display text on the screen. Memory locations $0400 through $07FF are called the primary text page, or page 1 of text. (Note that the use of the word page here is different from its use in earlier chapters, where it meant the 256 locations that make up a page of memory.) The primary text page is made up of the four pages of memory $04, $05, $06, and $07. The next four pages of memory, consisting of memory locations $0800 through $0BFF, are used as the secondary text page (also called page 2 of text).

Although it is possible to display text on either of the two text pages, only page 1 is supported by Applesoft BASIC or the Monitor. We will begin by using this text page, but will later explain how page 2 of text may be used.

Note: In our discussions we are assuming a forty-column display. Things change somewhat when the eighty-column mode is used (see the reference manual supplied with your eighty-column card for further information.)

If we want to display messages on the text screen, we might begin by using the character output subroutine that is provided in the Apple Monitor. COUT begins at $FDED, and will output the character whose ASCII code is in the accumulator. In order to print a message, we could load the accumulator with the ASCII code for each character of the message, then jump to COUT. For example:

Assembler code	ASCII code →	What appears on the screen
LDA #$C8	$C8 →	H
JSR COUT		
LDA #$C5	$C5 →	E
JSR COUT		
LDA #$CC	$CC →	L
JSR COUT		
LDA #$CC	$CC →	L
JSR COUT		
LDA #$CF	$CF →	0
JSR COUT		

(A list of ASCII codes is given in the reference manual.)

Although this process is effective, it is a cumbersome way to print messages. For greater efficiency we might use a loop such as the following:

```
        LDY #$00
LOOP    LDA MESG,Y
```

HALF PRICE BOOKS®

Half Price Books
1835 Forms Drive
Carrollton, TX 75006
OFS OrderID 39643187

Thank you for your order, Main Address!

Thank you for shopping with Half Price Books! Please contact Support@hpb.com. if you have any questions, comments or concerns about your order (113-8586307-3169009)

Visit our stores to sell your books, music, movies games for cash.

SKU	ISBN/UPC	Title & Author/Artist	Shelf ID	Qty	OrderSKU
S479416354	9780201052091	Assembly Language for the Applesoft Progra... Myers, Roy E.,Finley, Clarence W.	DB 25.15.6	1	

SHIPPED STANDARD TO:
Main Address
800 Avondale Ave
1033872-1-0010
Grandview Heights OH 43212
j1gg094j97htty5@marketplace.amazon.com

ORDER# **113-8586307-3169009**
AmazonMarketplaceUS

```
        BEQ END
        JSR COUT
        INY
        BNE LOOP
END     RTS
MESG    .DA #$C8,#$C5,#$CC,#$CC,#$CF,#$00
```

Note that the .DA is the S-C Assembler directive that creates the constants $C8, $C5, $CC, $CF, $00 in memory, starting at the current location. The label (MESG) is associated with the address of the first constant in the string ($C8). The directive to accomplish this task using Big Mac is DA. The DOS Tool Kit does not have an identical directive, but its DFB directive can be used to perform this task.

The loop will consecutively load the accumulator with the ASCII codes of each of the characters in the message, then jump to COUT. A null character (with ASCII code 0) is used to signal the end of the message. Note that, at most, 256 characters can be printed in a message. After the 256th character, the Y-register will have been incremented to 0 and the BNE LOOP test will fail.

Program 10.1 shows how the above loop can be used to print a message. The program accesses several Monitor subroutines in addition to COUT. HOME is the Monitor routine that clears page 1 of text and moves the cursor to the top of the screen. VTAB reads the contents of memory location $25 (which we label CV) to identify the vertical position on the screen at which printing should take place. (CV should contain a number from $0 through $17.) COUT uses this value and reads the contents of memory location $24 (labeled as CH) to identify the horizontal screen position.

Lines 1080 through 1120 identify CH and CV, and JSR to (call) VTAB. The remainder of the program consists of the loop described above. Note that it is necessary to set CH and CV only once. As COUT prints each character of the message, it also increments CH (and CV if necessary).

PROGRAM 10.1

```
              1000 * PROGRAM 10.1
              1010 * PRINTING ON TEXT PAGE 1
0024-         1020 CH      .EQ $24
0025-         1030 CV      .EQ $25
FDED-         1040 COUT    .EQ $FDED
FC22-         1050 VTAB    .EQ $FC22
FC58-         1060 HOME    .EQ $FC58
              1070         .OR $300
              1080 *------------------------------
```

```
0300- 20 58 FC 1090         JSR HOME      CLEAR SCREEN
0303- A9 0E    1100         LDA #$0E      SET
0305- 85 24    1110         STA CH         HORIZONTAL POSITION
0307- A9 05    1120         LDA #$05      SET
0309- 85 25    1130         STA CV         VERTICAL POSITION
030B- 20 22 FC 1140         JSR VTAB
030E- A2 00    1150         LDX #$00
0310- BD 1C 03 1160 LOOP    LDA MESG,X    READ A CHARACTER
0313- F0 06    1170         BEQ END       IF END OF MESSAGE
0315- 20 ED FD 1180         JSR COUT      PRINT IT
0318- E8       1190         INX           INC INDEX
0319- D0 F5    1200         BNE LOOP      GET NEXT CHARACTER
031B- 60       1210 END     RTS
031C- C5 D8 C1
031F- CD D0 CC
0322- C5 A0 B1
0325- B0 AE B1 1220 MESG    .AS -/EXAMPLE 10.1/
0328- 00       1230         .DA 0

SYMBOL TABLE

0024- CH
FDED- COUT
0025- CV
031B- END
FC58- HOME
0310- LOOP
031C- MESG
FC22- VTAB
```

Note that the .AS directive used above stores the hex form of the ASCII string of characters (Program 10.1) in sequence starting at the current location. The slashes are delimiters that mark the beginning and end of the string. The dash (minus sign) preceding the string indicates that the high bit of each byte (character) is set (1). The directive to accomplish this task, using either Big Mac or DOS Tool Kit, is ASC. In Program 10.1 the .DA directive is used to create the null character that signals the end of the message.

The message printing routine in Program 10.1 can be used in a variety of settings. If several messages are to be printed, it would be best to replace line 1140 with

```
1140 LOOP LDA (ADDR),Y
```

Then when a message is to be printed, its address can be stored in ADDR and ADDR+1 (any two consecutive, unused page-zero locations could be used). A jump to the subroutine will print the designated message.

TEXT Screen Addressing

After executing Program 10.1, enter the Monitor and list the contents of memory locations $68E through $699. You should find the following.

```
068E- C5 D8 C1 CD D0 CC C5 A0 B1 B0 AE B1
```

Note that the memory contents correspond exactly to the ASCII codes of the message that was printed. Memory locations $68E through $699 are a part of text page 1. Their contents determine exactly what is displayed on the 15th through the 26th positions of the 5th line of the text display. (If any screen scrolling has taken place, the memory contents will have changed.)

Figure 10.1 shows the addressing structure of TEXT page 1. Note that the addresses listed for the leftmost byte of each screen line are not consecutive (or logical?). However, once the address of the leftmost position in a screen line is known, the other positions in that line are numbered consecutively.

With Figure 10.1 available for reference, we could display messages on the text screen by storing the ASCII character codes in appropriate screen memory locations (that is what COUT does). Program 10.2 does this. Compare it with Program 10.1.

PROGRAM 10.2

```
                1000 * PROGRAM 10.2
                1010 * PRINTS BY STORING ASCII CODES
0026-           1020 BASL    .EQ $26
0027-           1030 BASH    .EQ $27
FC58-           1040 HOME    .EQ $FC58
                1050         .OR $300
                1060 *--------------------------------
0300- 20 58 FC  1070         JSR HOME      CLEAR SCREEN
0303- A9 80     1080         LDA #$80      SET BASE
0305- 85 26     1090         STA BASL       ADDRESS TO
0307- A9 06     1100         LDA #$06       $0680
0309- 85 27     1110         STA BASH        (VTAB 6)
030B- A0 0E     1120         LDY #$0E      HTAB
```

L#	Pag1 Hex	Pag1 Dec	Pag2 Hex	Pag2 Dec
0	$400	1204	$800	2048
1	$480	1152	$880	2176
2	$500	1280	$900	2304
3	$580	1408	$980	2432
4	$600	1536	$A00	2560
5	$680	1664	$A80	2688
6	$700	1792	$B00	2816
7	$780	1920	$B80	2944
8	$428	1064	$828	2088
9	$4A8	1192	$8A8	2216
10	$528	1320	$928	2344
11	$5A8	1448	$9A8	2472
12	$628	1576	$A28	2600
13	$6A8	1704	$AA8	2728
14	$728	1832	$B28	2856
15	$7A8	1960	$BA8	2984
16	$450	1104	$850	2128
17	$4D0	1232	$850	2256
18	$550	1360	$950	2384
19	$5D0	1488	$9D0	2512
20	$650	1616	$A50	2640
21	$6D0	1744	$AD0	2768
22	$750	1872	$B50	2896
23	$7D0	2000	$BD0	3024

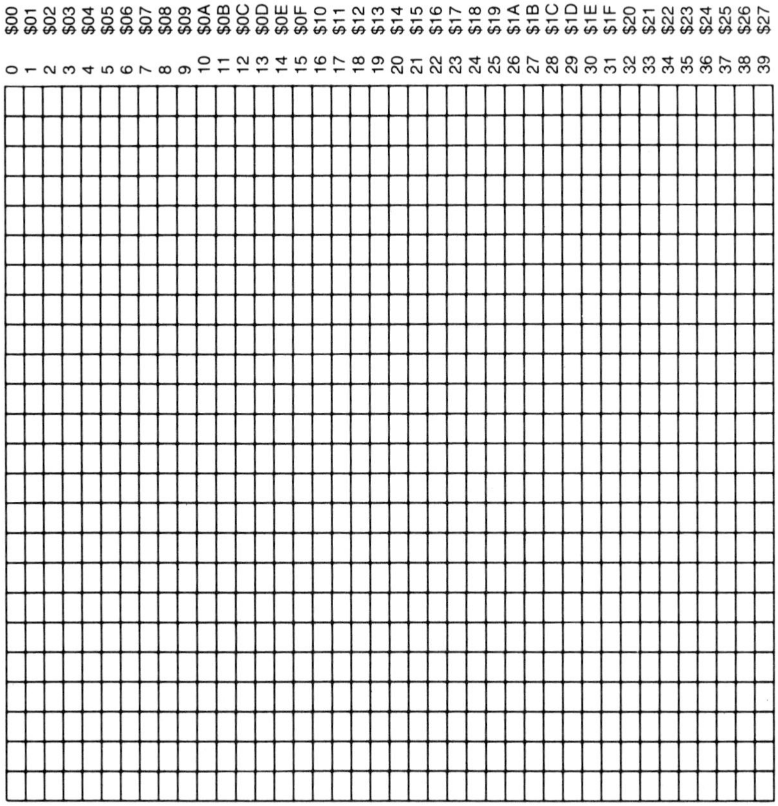

FIGURE 10.1 Text page/Lo-res page addresses

```
030D- A2 00     1130          LDX #$00
030F- BD 1B 03  1140 LOOP     LDA MESG,X     READ A CHARACTER
0312- F0 06     1150          BEQ END        IF END OF MESSAGE
0314- 91 26     1160          STA (BASL),Y   PRINT CHARACTER
0316- C8        1170          INY            INC HTAB
0317- E8        1180          INX            INC INDEX
0318- D0 F5     1190          BNE LOOP       GET NEXT CHARACTER
031A- 60        1200 END      RTS
031B- C5 D8 C1
031E- CD D0 CC
0321- C5 A0 B1
```

```
0324- B0 AE B2 1210 MESG   .AS -/EXAMPLE 10.2/
0327- 00 00    1220        .DA 00

SYMBOL TABLE

0027- BASH
0026- BASL
031A- END
FC58- HOME
030F- LOOP
031B- MESG
```

Extended Example: Printing on Page 2 of Text

As noted above, the secondary text page consists of memory locations $0800–$0BFF. This text page is not directly supported by Applesoft or the Monitor. It is not frequently needed. We are considering it here as we illustrate screen addressing techniques.

Program 10.3 displays several messages on page 2 of text. In order to do this, the program must do several things:

1. Set the display switches to show this text screen.
2. Clear this section of memory ($800–$BFF) so that the display is black.
3. Print the messages by storing the appropriate ASCII codes in the proper memory locations.

We will consider these tasks separately, developing routines which are combined as Program 10.3.

Page two of text can be displayed by toggling the appropriate soft switches. In this case, we must toggle the switches for TEXT ($C051) and the switch for PAGE 2 ($C055). This can be done by

```
BIT $C051
BIT $C055
```

Toggling these soft switches will cause page 2 of text to be displayed, but the screen contents will be unpredictable. The display screen will interpret the contents of memory locations $800–$BFF as text. This section of memory may contain an Applesoft program, a machine language program, data, or garbage. In order to have page 2 of text displayed as a blank (black) screen, it is necessary to clear the screen. HOME ($FC58) performs this task for page 1 of text, but is not effective for page 2.

Clearing the screen really means displaying a screen full of blank spaces (ASCII code $A0). We could imitate the behavior of HOME, but that would not be efficient. Rather, we will simply store the code $A0 in each memory location from $800 through $BFF.

```
CLEAR LDA #$04       4 PAGES OF MEMORY
      STA NPGS
      LDA #$08       STARTING WITH PAGE 8
      STA PAGE+1
      LDY #$00       INITIALIZE Y AND
      STY PAGE         COMPLETE PAGE ADDRESS
      LDA #$A0       FILL VALUE (SPACE)
LOOP  STA (PAGE),Y STORE IT AT (PAGE)+Y
      INY            NEXT BYTE
      BNE LOOP       IF NOT END OF PAGE
      INC PAGE+1     NEXT PAGE
      DEC NPGS       COUNTER
      BNE LOOP       IF NOT DONE
      RTS
```

We use NPGS to identify the number of pages yet to be cleared, and decrement NPGS from 4 to 0. PAGE and PAGE + 1 identify the page currently being cleared.

There is a significant difference between the above subroutine and the method by which HOME clears text page 1. We have stored $A0 in each of the 1024 memory locations from $800 to $BFF. HOME stores $A0 in in each of 960 memory locations (forty characters in each of twenty-four lines), not in all of the 1024 memory locations from $400 through $7FF. DOS uses the memory locations that are not cleared (and not displayed).

With page 2 of text displayed and cleared, we can turn to the printing of specific messages. We will use a modification of the printing method of Program 10.2 (lines 1140–1200 of that program).

```
       STY INDX
PLOOP  LDY INDX
       LDA (MESG),Y READ A CHARACTER
       BEQ END        IF END OF STRING
       LDY CH         GET HTAB
       STA (BASL),Y STORE CHARACTER
       INC CH         FOR NEXT HTAB
       INC INDX       FOR NEXT CHARACTER
```

```
        BNE PLOOP     IF NOT NOT DONE
END     RTS           MESSAGE PRINTED
```

INDX is a zero-page location that is an index into the message. It identifies the character to be printed next. CH identifies the horizontal screen location at which the next character is to be printed. MESG and MESG+1 are zero-page locations that are used to identify the address of the message that is to be printed.

Before calling this routine, it is necessary to identify the address of the message (MESG, MESG+1), identify the horizontal print location (CH), and identify the vertical print position (specify BASL, BASH).

As in Program 10.2, BASL and BASH identify the base address (address of the memory location that controls the leftmost position) of the print line. Figure 10.1 gives the base addresses of the screen lines of text page 1. The corresponding base addresses for text page 2 are each exactly $400 higher (as indicated in Table 10.1 later in this chapter).

For a given vertical print position (VTAB) there are two ways of obtaining the base address (BASL, BASH): calculate the value of BASL and BASH; or find the values of BASL and BASH in an address table. The Apple Monitor obtains BASL and BASH (for text page 1) by calculation, performed by the subroutine BASCALC, at location $FBC1 through $FBD8. (See the Monitor disassembly in the *Apple Reference Manual*.) A similar routine can (easily?) be written for page two of text. (Study the disassembly of BASCALC, then try it.)

In Program 10.3 we illustrate the use of a look-up table for obtaining BASL and BASH. The base addresses of each screen line (twenty-four addresses, or forty-eight bytes) are given in the table ADDR. In order to obtain the base address of a specific screen line, we load the X-register with 2*VTAB, then

```
LDA ADDR,X
STA BASH
INX
LDA ADDR,X
STA BASL
```

Note: VTAB can have values of 0 through 23, so the X-register should be loaded with an even integer between 0 and 46.

PROGRAM 10.3

```
                  1000 * EXAMPLE 10.3
                  1010 * PRINTING ON TEXT PAGE 2
0007-             1020 INDX   .EQ $07
```

```
0008-          1030 NPGS   .EQ $08
0008-          1040 MESG   .EQ $08
0024-          1050 CH     .EQ $24
0026-          1060 PAGE   .EQ $26
0026-          1070 BASL   .EQ $26
0027-          1080 BASH   .EQ $27
C000-          1090 KBD    .EQ $C000
C010-          1100 STROBE .EQ $C010
C051-          1110 TEXT   .EQ $C051
C054-          1120 PAG1   .EQ $C054
C055-          1130 PAG2   .EQ $C055
               1140        .OR $6000
               1150 *--------------------------------
6000- 2C 51 C0 1160 BEGIN BIT TEXT     DISPLAY TEXT
6003- 2C 55 C0 1170        BIT PAG2       PAGE2
6006- 20 60 60 1180        JSR CLEAR    CLEAR SCREEN
               1190 *PRINT FIRST MESSAGE
6009- A9 08    1200        LDA #$08     HTAB
600B- 85 24    1210        STA CH
600D- A9 60    1220        LDA /M1      HI BYTE OF ADDRESS
600F- A0 7A    1230        LDY #M1      LO BYTE OF ADDRESS

6011- A2 02    1240        LDX #$02     VTAB*2
6013- 20 3C 60 1250        JSR PRINT
               1260 *PRINT SECOND MESSAGE
6016- A9 0B    1270        LDA #$0B     HTAB
6018- 85 24    1280        STA CH
601A- A9 60    1290        LDA /M2      HI BYTE OF ADDRESS
601C- A0 87    1300        LDY #M2      LO BYTE OF ADDRESS

601E- A2 08    1310        LDX #$08     VTAB*2
6020- 20 3C 60 1320        JSR PRINT
               1330 *PRINT THIRD MESSAGE
6023- A9 0E    1340        LDA #$0E     HTAB
6025- 85 24    1350        STA CH
6027- A9 60    1360        LDA /M3      HI BYTE OF ADDRESS
6029- A0 99    1370        LDY #M3      LO BYTE OF ADDRESS
602B- A2 0E    1380        LDX #$0E     VTAB*2
602D- 20 3C 60 1390        JSR PRINT
               1400 *--------------------------------
6030- AD 00 C0 1410 .1     LDA KBD      READ KEYBOARD
6033- 10 FB    1420        BPL .1       IF NO KEYPRESS
```

```
6035- 2C 10 C0 1430        BIT STROBE   CLEAR STROBE
6038- 2C 54 C0 1440        BIT PAG1     DISPLAY PAGE 1
603B- 60       1450        RTS          DONE
               1460 *------------------------------
603C- 84 08    1470 PRINT STY MESG
603E- 85 09    1480        STA MESG+1
6040- BD A8 60 1490        LDA ADDR,X
6043- 85 27    1500        STA BASH
6045- E8       1510        INX
6046- BD A8 60 1520        LDA ADDR,X
6049- 85 26    1530        STA BASL
604B- A0 00    1540        LDY #$00
604D- 84 07    1550        STY INDX
604F- A4 07    1560 PLOOP LDY INDX
6051- B1 08    1570        LDA (MESG),Y READ A CHARACTER
6053- F0 0A    1580        BEQ END      IF END OF STRING
6055- A4 24    1590        LDY CH       GET HTAB
6057- 91 26    1600        STA (BASL),Y STORE CHARACTER
6059- E6 24    1610        INC CH       FOR NEXT HTAB
605B- E6 07    1620        INC INDX     FOR NEXT CHARACTER
605D- D0 F0    1630        BNE PLOOP    IF NOT NOT DONE
605F- 60       1640 END    RTS          MESSAGE PRINTED
               1650 *------------------------------
6060- A9 04    1660 CLEAR  LDA #$04     4 PAGES OF MEMORY
6062- 85 08    1670        STA NPGS
6064- A9 08    1680        LDA #$08     STARTING WITH PAGE 8
6066- 85 27    1690        STA PAGE+1
6068- A0 00    1700        LDY #$00     INITIALIZE Y AND
606A- 84 26    1710        STY PAGE       COMPLETE PAGE ADDRESS
606C- A9 A0    1720        LDA #$A0     FILL VALUE (SPACE)
606E- 91 26    1730 LOOP   STA (PAGE),Y STORE IT AT (PAGE)+Y
6070- C8       1740        INY          NEXT BYTE
6071- D0 FB    1750        BNE LOOP     IF NOT END OF PAGE
6073- E6 27    1760        INC PAGE+1   NEXT PAGE
6075- C6 08    1770        DEC NPGS     COUNTER
6077- D0 F5    1780        BNE LOOP     IF NOT DONE
6079- 60       1790        RTS
               1800 *------------------------------
607A- C5 D8 C1
607D- CD D0 CC
6080- C5 A0 B1
6083- B0 AE B3 1810 M1     .AS -/EXAMPLE 10.3/
```

```
6086- 00        1820        .HS 00
6087- D0 D2 C9
608A- CE D4 C9
608D- CE C7 A0
6090- CD C5 D3
6093- D3 C1 C7
6096- C5 D3     1830 M2     .AS -/PRINTING MESSAGES/
6098- 00        1840        .HS 00
6099- CF CE A0
609C- D4 C5 D8
609F- D4 A0 D0
60A2- C1 C7 C5
60A5- A0 B2     1850 M3     .AS -/ON TEXT PAGE 2/
60A7- 00        1860        .HS 00
                1870 *BASE ADDRESS TABLE FOR TEXT PAGE 2
60A8- 08 00 08
60AB- 80 09 00
60AE- 09 80 0A
60B1- 00 0A 80
60B4- 0B 00 0B
60B7- 80        1880 ADDR   .HS 08000880090009800A000A800B000B80
60B8- 08 28 08
60BB- A8 09 28
60BE- 09 A8 0A
60C1- 28 0A A8
60C4- 0B 28 0B
60C7- A8        1890        .HS 082808A8092809A80A280AA80B280BA8
60C8- 08 50 08
60CB- D0 09 50
60CE- 09 D0 0A
60D1- 50 0A D0
60D4- 0B 50 0B
60D7- D0        1900        .HS 085008D0095009D00A500AD00B500BD0

SYMBOL TABLE

60A8- ADDR
0027- BASH
0026- BASL
6000- BEGIN
0024- CH
6060- CLEAR
```

```
605F- END
0007- INDX
C000- KBD
606E- LOOP
607A- M1
6087- M2
6099- M3
0008- MESG
0008- NPGS
C054- PAG1
C055- PAG2
0026- PAGE
604F- PLOOP
603C- PRINT
C010- STROBE
C051- TEXT
```

Notes on Program 10.3

1. Note the exit routine (lines 1410–1450). Since this program is for illustrative purposes only, it seemed desirable to return the display screen to text page 1 on exit. Lines 1410 and 1420 cause a wait until a key is pressed. Then the keyboard strobe is cleared (line 1430), so that later keypresses can be properly read, and the display screen is set to page 1 (line 1440).
2. Most applications do not require the use of text page 2. However, if page 2 of high-resolution graphics is to be displayed in mixed mode, the four lines of text displayed at the bottom of the screen are taken from text page 2.
3. The use of page 2 of text is in conflict with any Applesoft program that is currently in memory, since program storage usually begins at memory location $0801. If you wish to use page 2 of text and have an Applesoft program in memory, it is necessary to relocate the Applesoft program.

   Say you have an Applesoft program PROG stored on disk. If you LOAD PROG or RUN PROG, the program is loaded into memory and stored at the destination specified by the contents of locations 103 and 104 ($67, $68). Typically location 103 contains a 1 and location 104 contains an 8, and the program is stored beginning at location $801 (decimal 2049).

   By changing the contents of locations 103 and 104, you can control the destination of PROG. For example, if you store a 1 ($01) in location 103 and a 64 ($40) in location 104, then LOAD PROG will cause the program to be located at 16385 ($4001). An Applesoft program can be made to relocate itself if a line like the following is used at the beginning of the program.

```
1  IF  PEEK(103) < > 1 OR PEEK(104) < > 64 OR PEEK(16384)
< > 0 THEN POKE 103,1: POKE 104,64: POKE 16384,0: PRINT
CHR$(4); "RUN PROG"
```

This line will cause PROG to be loaded at 16385 ($4001). Since the byte that immediately precedes the start of the program must contain the start of program code (0), it was necessary to confirm that location 16384 ($4000) does contain a 0.

Other destinations for Applesoft programs are clearly available, simply by modifying the above program line.

4. Note that Program 10.3 makes no provision for moving to a lower screen line if a message is too long to fit on a designated line. Further, no provision is made for scrolling the screen. Provision of these features is not a trivial task, but would be an interesting challenge.

5. As an alternate to obtaining BASL and BASH from an address table, we could load the accumulator with VTAB (between $0 and $17), then call BASCALC (at $FBC1). On return from this subroutine, BASL and BASH will be set to the proper base address for printing on text page 1. The corresponding page 2 address can then be obtained by adding $04 to BASH.

LOW-RESOLUTION GRAPHICS

Very few commercially available programs use Lo-res graphics, and you probably will not have much interest in it. But if you want a display that shows colored rectangles, Lo-res is THE way to go. Lo-res graphics occupies the same area of memory as TEXT. There are two Lo-res graphics pages: The PRIMARY Lo-res graphics page starts at $0400 and runs through $07FF. The SECONDARY Lo-res graphics page starts at $0800 and runs through $0BFF. Each block of Table 10.1 is vertically divided in half and you can choose the color of the top half separate from the bottom half according to the table shown at the top of page 199.

Each byte in memory holds two hex digits. A single hex digit in a byte is called a nibble. The left nibble sets the bottom color of a block and the right nibble sets the top color of a block. The example shown below uses the Monitor subroutine KEYIN located at $FD1B. KEYIN waits for a keypress. When it finds

TABLE 10.1 Lo-Res Colors

Hex	*Dec*	*Color*	*Hex*	*Dec*	*Color*
$0	0	Black	$8	8	Brown
$1	1	Magenta	$9	9	Orange
$2	2	Dark blue	$A	10	Gray 2
$3	3	Purple	$B	11	Pink
$4	4	Dark green	$C	12	Light green
$5	5	Gray 1	$D	13	Yellow
$6	6	Medium blue	$E	14	Aquamarine
$7	7	Light blue	$F	15	White

one, it places the keycode into the accumulator. (You can find the keycodes in Appendix B.)

PROGRAM 10.4

```
                 1000 *PROGRAM 10.4 LO-RES COLORS
C050-            1010 GR      .EQ $C050
C054-            1020 PAG1    .EQ $C054
C056-            1030 LORES   .EQ $C056
F836-            1040 CLRTOP  .EQ $F836
FD1B-            1050 KEYIN   .EQ $FD1B
                 1060         .OR $300
0300- 2C 50 C0   1070 BEGIN   BIT GR        TOGGLE GRAPHICS
0303- 2C 54 C0   1080         BIT PAG1      TOGGLE PAGE 1
0306- 2C 56 C0   1090         BIT LORES     TOGGLE LO-RES
0309- 20 36 F8   1100         JSR CLRTOP    CLEAR SCREEN TO BLACK
030C- A2 00      1110         LDX #$00      SET X
030E- 20 1B FD   1120 LOOP    JSR KEYIN     GET A COLOR
0311- 9D 00 04   1130         STA $0400,X   STORE IT AT $400+X
0314- E8         1140         INX           INC X TO NEXT BLOCK
0315- E0 28      1150         CPX #$28      END OF ROW?
0317- D0 F5      1160         BNE LOOP      NO? KEEP GOING
0319- 60         1170         RTS
```

```
SYMBOL TABLE

0300- BEGIN
F836- CLRTOP
C050- GR
FD1B- KEYIN
030E- LOOP
C056- LORES
C054- PAG1
```

Line 1130 stores the keycode at location $0400 plus the contents of X, so that it is displayed on the screen.

When you run Program 10.4 the screen stays black until you press a key, then the key's color is displayed in the top row of the screen. If the first key pressed is the E-key, its keycode, $C5, is displayed in the upper lefthand corner block as the colors gray 1 over light green. That is, left nibble is C -> light green appears on the bottom; the right nibble is 5 -> gray 1 appears on the top. If you press the RETURN key in the next block you will see yellow over brown, $8D.

The example will end after forty keypresses; if you would like to "see" more keys, run the program again, or modify the program to fill the next row on the screen.

The next "row" (of two-high blocks) starts with memory location $0480 and extends to $04A7. Note that these are the same memory locations that are used for the second line of the TEXT screen. The addressing of the low-resolution graphics screen (page 1 or 2) is the same as the addressing structure of the TEXT screen (page 1 or 2).

Notes

1. The subroutines that Applesoft uses to draw images on the low-resolution graphics screen are actually part of the Monitor. If it is useful to draw low-resolution images from a machine language program, these subroutines can be accessed, as indicated in Table 10.2.

2. The subroutines listed above are effective only for low-resolution graphics page 1. The use of low-resolution graphics page 2 requires that you develop images by storing color codes in appropriate memory locations (as in Program 10.4). If you wish to do this, note that the addressing structure of page 2 of low-resolution graphics parallels that of low-resolution graphics page 1, with the address of each memory location being higher by $0400.

TABLE 10.2 Lo-Res subroutines

	Name	*Entry Point*	*Action Taken*
1.	CLRSCR	$F832	Clears the entire (full screen) low-res screen.
2.	CLRTOP	$F836	Clears the top (mixed screen) low-res screen.
3.	SETCOL	$F864	Set color to use for plotting. Color number ($0–$F) is found in X.
4.	PLOT	$F800	Plots a block whose vertical position is found in A and whose horizontal position is found in Y.
5.	HLINE	$F819	Draws a horizontal line of blocks at vertical position given in A, from horizontal position given in Y rightward to horizontal position given in $2C.
6.	VLINE	$F828	Draws a vertical line of blocks at horizontal position given in Y, from vertical position given in A downward to vertical position given in $2C.
7.	SCRN	$F871	Reads the color of the block whose vertical position is given in A and whose horizontal position is given in Y. The color is returned in A.

HIGH-RESOLUTION GRAPHICS

The high-resolution graphics pages are located in a different area of memory from the TEXT/Lo-res graphics areas. The PRIMARY Hi-res graphics page runs from $2000 through $3FFF. The SECONDARY Hi-res page runs from $4000 through $5FFF. So there are two 8K blocks of memory for use in Hi-res graphics applications.

Before reading the next paragraph look at Figure 10.1 and remember how the blocks on the right side of the figure are organized. Look at Figure 10.6 (given later in this chapter) and note its similarity to Figure 10.1 (both are arranged as 40 by 24 blocks). Also note their differences: (1) The line numbers increase by one in Figure 10.1, whereas the line numbers increase by eight in Figure 10.6; and (2) the address of each block is different. Now look at Figure 10.6 and visualize each block as being divided into eight horizontal slices (see Figure 10.4) to accommodate the "missing" addresses.

Focus your attention on the upper lefthand block of Figure 10.1 (TEXT/Lo-res screen) and use the addresses for page 2. This is what you should see:

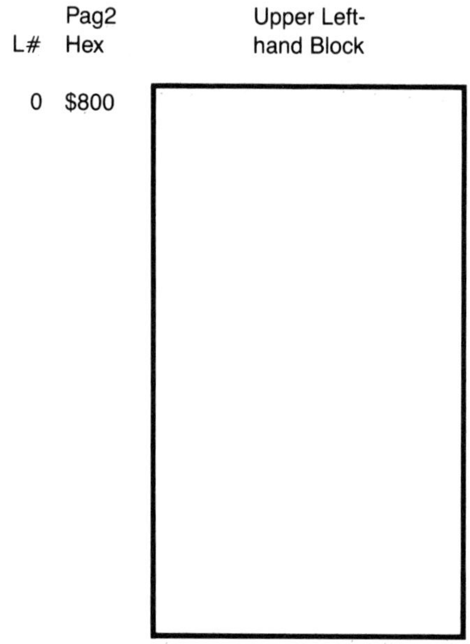

FIGURE 10.2 The upper lefthand corner block of the TEXT/Lo-res screen

Figure 10.2 will be used to develop the upper lefthand corner block of the Hi-res screen (see Figure 10.6). The Hi-res screen can be visualized as 40 by 24 blocks, but each block must first be divided horizontally into eight slices.

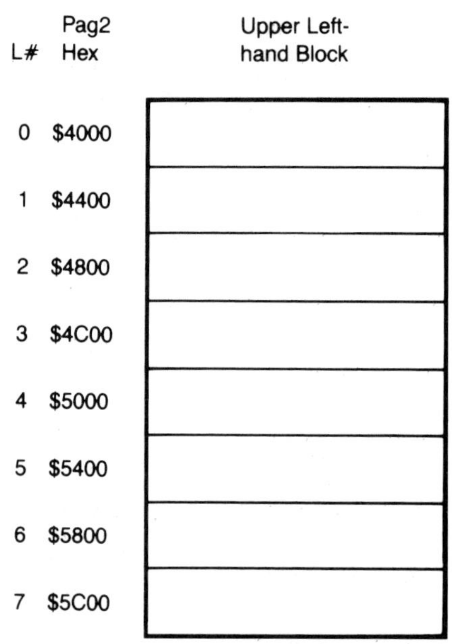

FIGURE 10.3 Divide Figure 10.2 into eight horizontal slices

Now vertically divided into seven segments.

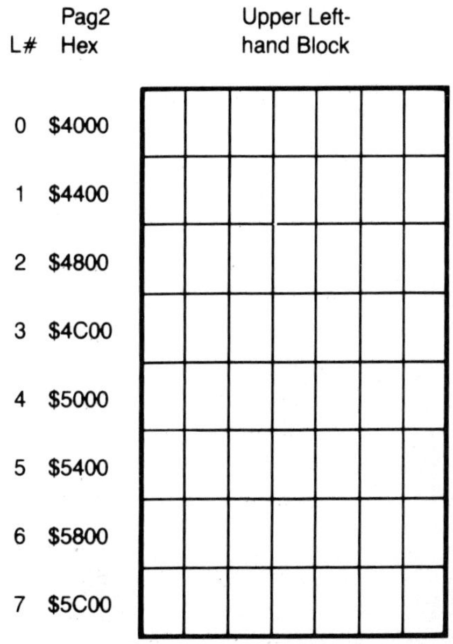

FIGURE 10.4 The upper lefthand corner block of the Hi-res screen

Each of the smaller blocks in the larger block in Figure 10.2 represents a single dot of light on the Hi-res screen. Each of these dots of light is called a "pixel," which is the acronym for "picture element." Whether or not a pixel is lighted (on) depends on wheter the contents of the corresponding bit in the byte ($4000, for example) are on (1).

Complication Number 1: The high bit (number 7) is NOT displayed on the Hi-res screen. It is used to select the color (color bit) of the pixels in the byte. (Remember, eight bits to a byte, but seven vertical segments on the screen.)

Imagine that location $4000 contains $D5.

```
Contents
of $4000        In binary
   $D5       →  1101 0101
Bit number → 7654 3210
```

Complication number 2: The bit numbers and their contents must be reversed from the way we imagined them in the earlier chapters.

Contents of $4000	Reversed in binary
$D5	⟶ 1010 1011
Bit number	⟶ 0123 4567

Now clip off the high bit.

Contents of $4000	Reversed in binary
$D5	⟶ 1010 101
Bit number	⟶ 0123 456

When $D5 is stored in location $4000 and page 2 of the hi-res screen is displayed, this is what you will see:

Address	Line #								
		0	1	2	3	4	5	6	← Column number
		0	1	2	3	4	5	6	← Bit number (See note below)
		V	G	V	G	V	G	V	← Color bit off (0)
		B	O	B	O	B	O	B	← Color bit on (1)
$4000	0	1	0	1	0	1	0	1	← $D5 with hi-bit clipped off
$4400	1								
$4800	2								
$4C00	3								
$5000	4								
$5400	5								
$5800	6								
$5C00	7								

FIGURE 10.5 Upper lefthand corner block on the Hi-res screen

Program 10.5 is a reworking of Program 10.4 to make it illustrate the structure of the Hi-res graphics pages. It uses page 2 of Hi-res graphics, but page 1 works exactly the same way, except that the addresses are different. Assemble and execute Program 10.5 so that you can see what is happening as you read.

PROGRAM 10.5

```
                  1000 * PROGRAM 10.5 HI-RES COLORS
F3D8-             1010 HGR2    .EQ $F3D8
FD1B-             1020 KEYIN   .EQ $FD1B
                  1030         .OR $300
0300- 20 D8 F3    1040 BEGIN   JSR HGR2      DISPLAY HI-RES PAGE 2
0303- A2 00       1050         LDX #$00      INIT X
0305- 20 1B FD    1060 LOOP    JSR KEYIN     GET A KEYCODE
0308- 9D 00 40    1070         STA $4000,X   STORE IT
030B- E8          1080         INX           INC TO NEXT VALUE
030C- E0 27       1090         CPX #$27      END OF ROW?
030E- D0 F5       1100         BNE LOOP      NO, KEEP GOING
0310- 60          1110         RTS           STOP

SYMBOL TABLE

0300- BEGIN
F3D8- HGR2
FD1B- KEYIN
0305- LOOP
```

As your first keypress, choose the U-key and repeat it across the top of the screen. The keycode for U is $D5, so memory locations $4000 through $4027 all contain $D5. (You can check this by calling the Monitor and listing these locations.) What you should see on the screen is a continuous line made up of a short blue bar followed by a white dot, followed by an orange bar, white dot, blue bar, etc. This pattern repeats across the top line of the screen.

If you have a monochrome screen, you see a broken line that looks like this: white dot, black dot, white dot, black dot, white dot, black dot, white dot, white dot (these two white dots smear together to give a short white bar that probably appears brighter than the white dots) black dot, etc. This pattern repeats across the top line of the screen.

To understand what is going on you must look at each bit in the bytes. Each picture element, a dot or pixel, is on if the corresponding bit in memory is on (1). If a bit is on you see a white (or colored) pixel. However, only seven bits of a byte are displayed on the screen. The high bit, bit number seven, is used to control the color of the dot. Each bit can display one of two colors (see Figure 10.5). The colors are violet or blue if the COLUMN number is even, and green or orange if the COLUMN number is odd. The colors violet and green occur when the high bit contains a 0; blue and orange occur when the high bit contains 1. To see this arrangement, let's imagine a few more screen locations adjacent to the upper left corner.

```
                       11111111112222222222333333
     Column number → 01234567890123456789012345678901234
  Color if hi-bit=0 → VGVGVGVGVGVGVGVGVGVGVGVGVGVGVGVGVGV
  Color if hi-bit=1 → BOBOBOBOBOBOBOBOBOBOBOBOBOBOBOBOBOB
          Contents → 10101011010101101010110101011010101
      What you see → <blue>ww<orn>ww<blu>ww<orn>ww<blu>w
        Bit number → 01234560123456012345601234560123456
      Byte address → <$4000><$4001><$4002><$4003><$4004>
```

Now you can see what happened when you entered the string of U's:

```
                     h
                     i
                     b
                     i
                     t
   U → $D5 → 1010101 1
Bit number → 0123456 7
```

Note that the bit numbers are reversed from the way we have been looking at them in earlier chapters!

The high bit is on, so the blue-orange color line is chosen. The blue-on/orange-off/blue-on pattern smears together to produce the blue bar seen on the screen. At the byte borders, the blue and the orange bits are both on, side by side. This produces the white dot you see on the screen.

If you have a monochrome screen, the odd and even pixels do not smear together and you can see the black dot where the bit is off.

How would you produce a solid blue line across the top of the screen? The high bit must be set in each byte, and the bit pattern must look like this:

```
BOBOBOBOBOBOBOBOBOBOBOBOBOBOBO
1010101010101010101010101010
<$4000><$4001><$4003><$4004>
```

```
($4000) = 1 1010101 → $D5 → key U
($4001) = 1 0101010 → $AA → key *
```

If you run Program 10.5 again and enter U*U*U*U*U*U*U*U* . . . as the keystrokes, you will see a solid blue line across the top of the screen. In monochrome you see white dot, black dot repeated across the top of the screen. How would you produce an orange line? Try *U*U*U*U*U*U*U*U. . . .

Addressing the High-Resolution Graphics Screen

Figure 10.6 shows the addressing pattern of the high-resolution graphics pages.

The addresses of all eight lines of the upper left block of the Hi-res screen page 2 are given in Figure 10.5.

The next example displays everything that can happen on the screen as the contents of a byte are changed from $00 to $FF, which is everything that can be stored in the byte. Let's move down to line 96 on Hi-res page 2 (the byte in column 0 is $4228) and out to byte column $14. The address of this byte is $4228 + $14 = $423C.

Program 10.6 uses the KEYIN subroutine to wait until you are ready to increment the contents of $423C. Each keypress increments the contents of $423C by one.

PROGRAM 10.6

```
                  1000 * PROGRAM 10.6 SEE THE DOTS
F3D8-             1010 HGR2    .EQ $F3D8
FD1B-             1020 KEYIN   .EQ $FD1B
                  1030         .OR $7000
7000- 20 D8 F3 1040 BEGIN   JSR HGR2     CLEAR SCREEN TO BLACK
7003- A2 00       1050         LDX #$00     STARTING VALUE
7008- 8E 3C 42 1070 LOOP    STX $423C    PUT IT IN THE BYTE
700B- 20 1B FD 1080         JSR KEYIN    WAIT FOR A KEYPRESS
700E- 20 D8 F3 1090         JSR HGR2     CLEAR SCREEN EACH TIME
7014- E8          1110         INX          INC TO NEXT VALUE
7018- D0 EE       1130         BNE LOOP     DO ALL VALUES!
701A- 60          1140         RTS
```

```
SYMBOL TABLE

7000- BEGIN
F3D8- HGR2
FD1B- KEYIN
7008- LOOP
```

The Applesoft subroutine HGR2 begins at $F3D8; it is used to set up and clear page 2 to black. Key-in, assemble, and execute Program 10.6. Table 10.3 summarizes what you see on a color screen after each key press.

If you have trouble seeing the dots in Program 10.6, Program 10.6M1 should alleviate the problem. In this modification the contents of $423C are repeated in the seven bytes below it. This should make it easier to see what is going on.

L#	Pag1 Hex	Pag1 Dec	Pag2 Hex	Pag2 Dec
0	$2000	8192	$4000	16384
8	$2080	8320	$4080	16512
16	$2100	8448	$4100	16640
24	$2180	8576	$4180	16767
32	$2200	8704	$4200	16896
40	$2280	8832	$4280	17024
48	$2300	8960	$4300	17152
56	$2380	9088	$4380	17280
64	$2028	8232	$4028	16424
72	$20A8	8360	$40A8	16552
80	$2128	8488	$4128	16680
88	$21A8	8616	$41A8	16808
96	$2228	8744	$4228	16936
104	$22A8	8872	$42A8	17064
112	$2328	9000	$4328	17192
120	$23A8	9128	$43A8	17320
128	$2050	8272	$4050	16464
136	$20D0	8400	$40D0	16592
144	$2150	8528	$4150	16720
152	$21D0	8656	$41D0	16848
160	$2250	8784	$4250	16976
168	$22D0	8912	$42D0	17104
176	$2350	9040	$4350	17232
184	$23D0	9168	$43D0	17360

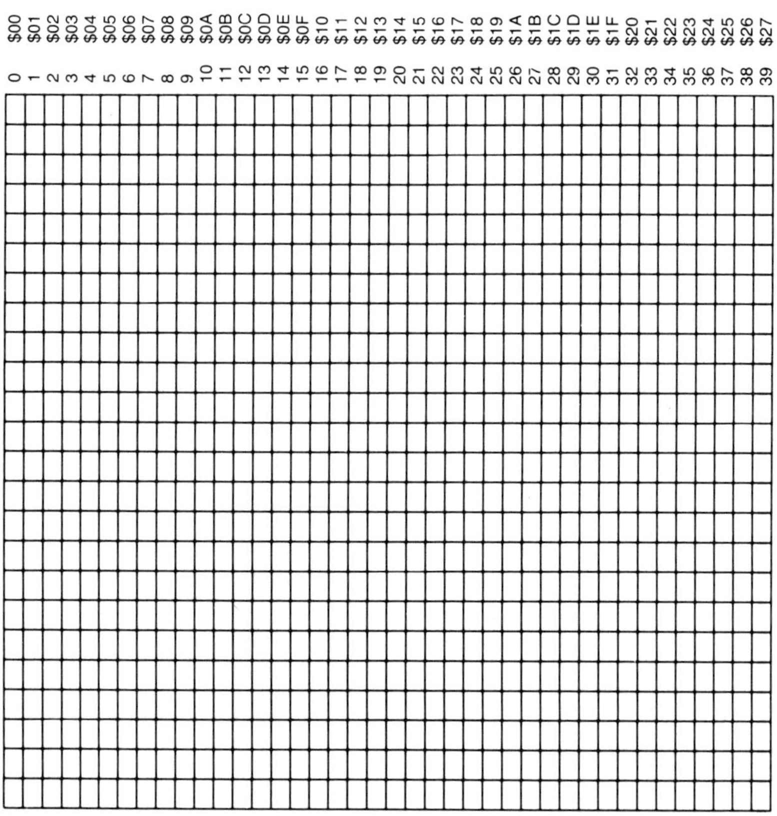

FIGURE 10.6 Hi-res page addresses

TABLE 10.3 Seeing the pixels

Byte address	→	< $ 4 2 3 C >	h			
Bit number	→	0 1 2 3 4 5 6	i			
Place value	→	1 2 4 8 1 2 4	b			
Color hi-bit = 0	→	V G V G V G V	i			
Color hi-bit = 1	→	B O B O B O B	t			What you see
Keypress		Contents			Hex	in color
1		1 0 0 0 0 0 0	0	→	01	Violet dot
2		0 1 0 0 0 0 0	0	→	02	Green dot
3		1 1 0 0 0 0 0	0	→	03	White fat dot
4		0 0 1 0 0 0 0	0	→	04	Violet dot
5		1 0 1 0 0 0 0	0	→	05	Violet bar
6		0 1 1 0 0 0 0	0	→	06	White fat dot
7		1 1 1 0 0 0 0	0	→	07	VWG smear
8		0 0 0 1 0 0 0	0	→	08	Green dot
9		1 0 0 1 0 0 0	0	→	09	V G dots
10		0 1 0 1 0 0 0	0	→	0A	Green bar
11		1 1 0 1 0 0 0	0	→	0B	WG bar
12		0 0 1 1 0 0 0	0	→	0C	White fat dot
13		1 0 1 1 0 0 0	0	→	0D	VW smear
14		0 1 1 1 0 0 0	0	→	0E	White bar
15		1 1 1 1 0 0 0	0	→	0F	White bar
16		0 0 0 0 1 0 0	0	→	10	Violet dot
17		1 0 0 0 1 0 0	0	→	11	V dot blk bar V dot
.					.	
.		You can see the			.	
.		pattern now.			.	
.		The next			.	
.		interesting			.	
.		patterns occur			.	
.		when the hi-bit			.	
.		comes on and			.	
.		the colors			.	
.		change.			.	
.					.	
127		1 1 1 1 1 1 1	0	→	7F	V dot blk bar V dot
128		0 0 0 0 0 0 0	1	→	80	All black!
129		1 0 0 0 0 0 0	1	→	81	Blue dot
130		0 1 0 0 0 0 0	1	→	82	Orange dot
131		1 1 0 0 0 0 0	1	→	83	White fat dot
.					.	
.		Got the			.	
.		picture?			.	
.					.	

If you have trouble seeing the dots in Program 10.6, Program 10.6M1 should alleviate the problem. In this modification the contents of $423C are repeated in the seven bytes below it. This should make it easier to see what is going on.

PROGRAM

```
                 1000 * PROGRAM 10.6M1 SEE THE BARS
F3D8-            1010 HGR2    .EQ $F3D8
FD1B-            1020 KEYIN   .EQ $FD1B
                 1040         .OR $7000
7000- 20 D8 F3   1050 BEGIN   JSR HGR2      CLEAR SCREEN TO BLACK
7003- A2 00      1060         LDX #$00      STARTING VALUE
7008- 8E 3C 42   1080 LOOP    STX $423C     PUT IT IN THE BYTE
700B- 8E 3C 46   1090         STX $463C     AND ALL THE BYTES IN THE BLOCK
700E- 8E 3C 4A   1100         STX $4A3C                 "
7011- 8E 3C 4E   1110         STX $4E3C                 "
7014- 8E 3C 52   1120         STX $523C                 "
7017- 8E 3C 56   1130         STX $563C                 "
701D- 8E 3C 5E   1150         STX $5E3C                 "
7020- 20 1B FD   1160         JSR KEYIN     WAIT FOR KEYPRESS
7023- 20 D8 F3   1170         JSR HGR2      CLEAR SCREEN EACH TIME
702C- D0 DA      1200         BNE LOOP      DO ALL VALUES!
702E- 00         1210         RTS
SYMBOL TABLE

7000- BEGIN
F3D8- HGR2
7FFF- KEEP
FD1B- KEYIN
7008- LOOP
```

Run Program 10.6M1. Table 10.3 explains what you see in the eight slices.

What should be clear, to those of you with color screens, is that no pixel on the screen is white! In fact there are only red, green, and blue pixels. To get a white dot to appear on a color screen you must turn two colored pixels side by side. They add up to a fat white dot. But even then the left and the right ends of the white dot will show some color. You may need a magnifying glass to see the colored fringes. Alternatively, you can view the screen from across the room with a pair of binoculars!

If you have a monochrome screen, you see each pixel that is on in Table 10.3 as a white dot. Two white dots on together appear as a slightly brighter white bar.

Bit Pattern Images: A Letter

Enough of this dot business, let's build something. We suggest an A in the middle of the screen. The layout for our A is shown below.

```
                                                         h
                                                         i
                          Place value -> 12481241248124 b
 Left Right    Contents    Color -> BOBOBOBOBOBOBO i if hi bit=1
 byte  byte       L  R      Color -> VGVGVGVGVGVGVG t if hi bit=0
$55BB $55BC -->  00 01 ----------> 00000001000000 0
$59BB $59BC -->  00 02 ----------> 00000010100000 0
$5DBB $5DBC -->  20 04 ----------> 00000100010000 0
$423B $423C -->  20 04 ----------> 00000100010000 0
$463B $463C -->  60 07 ----------> 00000111110000 0
$4A3B $4A3C -->  20 04 ----------> 00000100010000 0
$4E3B $4E3C -->  20 04 ----------> 00000100010000 0
```

For a review of binary-to-hex conversion, see Appendix B.

Note that defining the "middle" of the screen presents us with some decisions. There is an even number of byte columns, 40, across the screen. We have decided to put the left "half" (three of the seven bit columns of the A) in byte column $13; and the other "half" (four of the seven bit columns) in byte column $14. There is an even number of rows down the screen, 192. We have decided to use rows 93 through 99.

Refer to Figure 10.7. It gives the line numbers and the corresponding addresses of the left edge of the screen for high-resolution graphics pages one and two. The byte at the left edge of the screen on line 93 is $55A8; move over to column $13. The address of this byte is $55A8 + $13 = $55BB. Program 10.7 stores the appropriate values in the fourteen bytes needed to build an A. To see how the contents are determined, let's look at the crossbar in the A.

	Top Third				Middle Third				Bottom Third		
L#	Hex	Pag1	Pag2	L#	Hex	Pag1	Pag2	L#	Hex	Pag1	Pag2
0	$00	$2000	$4000	64	$40	$2028	$4028	128	$80	$2050	$4050
1	$01	$2400	$4400	65	$41	$2428	$4428	129	$81	$2450	$4450
2	$02	$2800	$4800	66	$42	$2828	$4828	130	$82	$2850	$4850
3	$03	$2C00	$4C00	67	$43	$2C28	$4C28	131	$83	$2C50	$4C50
4	$04	$3000	$5000	68	$44	$3028	$5028	132	$84	$3050	$5050
5	$05	$3400	$5400	69	$45	$3428	$5428	133	$85	$3450	$5450
6	$06	$3800	$5800	70	$46	$3828	$5828	134	$86	$3850	$5850
7	$07	$3C00	$5C00	71	$47	$3C28	$5C28	135	$87	$3C50	$5C50
8	$08	$2080	$4080	72	$48	$20A8	$40A8	136	$88	$20D0	$40D0
9	$09	$2480	$4480	73	$49	$24A8	$44A8	137	$89	$24D0	$44D0
10	$0A	$2880	$4880	74	$4A	$28A8	$48A8	138	$8A	$28D0	$48D0
11	$0B	$2C80	$4C80	75	$4B	$2CA8	$4CA8	139	$8B	$2CD0	$4CD0
12	$0C	$3080	$5080	76	$4C	$30A8	$50A8	140	$8C	$30D0	$50D0
13	$0D	$3480	$5480	77	$4D	$34A8	$54A8	141	$8D	$34D0	$54D0
14	$0E	$3880	$5800	78	$4E	$38A8	$58A8	142	$8E	$38D0	$58D0
15	$0F	$3C80	$5C80	79	$4F	$3CA8	$5CA8	143	$8F	$3CD0	$5CD0
16	$10	$2100	$4100	80	$50	$2128	$4128	144	$90	$2150	$4150
17	$11	$2500	$4500	81	$51	$2528	$4528	145	$91	$2550	$4550
18	$12	$2900	$4900	82	$52	$2928	$4928	146	$92	$2950	$4950
19	$13	$2D00	$4D00	83	$53	$2D28	$4D28	147	$93	$2D50	$4D50
20	$14	$3100	$5100	84	$54	$3128	$5128	148	$94	$3150	$5150
21	$15	$3500	$5500	85	$55	$3528	$5528	149	$95	$3550	$5550
22	$16	$3900	$5900	86	$56	$3928	$5928	150	$96	$3950	$5950
23	$17	$3D00	$5D00	87	$57	$3D28	$5D28	151	$97	$3D50	$5D50
24	$18	$2180	$4180	88	$58	$21A8	$41A8	152	$98	$21D0	$41D0
25	$19	$2580	$4580	89	$59	$25A8	$45A8	153	$99	$25D0	$45D0
26	$1A	$2980	$4980	90	$5A	$29A8	$49A8	154	$9A	$29D0	$49D0
27	$1B	$2D80	$4D80	91	$5B	$2DA8	$4DA8	155	$9B	$2DD0	$4DD0
28	$1C	$3180	$5180	92	$5C	$31A8	$51A8	156	$9C	$31D0	$51D0
29	$1D	$3580	$5580	93	$5D	$35A8	$55A8	157	$9D	$35D0	$55D0
30	$1E	$3980	$5980	94	$5E	$39A8	$59A8	158	$9E	$39D0	$59D0
31	$1F	$3D80	$5D80	95	$5F	$3DA8	$5DA8	159	$9F	$3DD0	$5DD0
32	$20	$2200	$4200	96	$60	$2228	$4228	160	$A0	$2250	$4250
33	$21	$2600	$4600	97	$61	$2628	$4628	161	$A1	$2650	$4650
34	$22	$2A00	$4A00	98	$62	$2A28	$4A28	162	$A2	$2A50	$4A50
35	$23	$2E00	$4E00	99	$63	$2E28	$4E28	163	$A3	$2E50	$4E50
26	$24	$3200	$5200	100	$64	$3228	$5228	164	$A4	$3250	$5250
37	$25	$3600	$5600	101	$65	$3628	$5628	165	$A5	$3650	$5650
38	$26	$3A00	$5A00	102	$66	$3A28	$5A28	166	$A6	$3A50	$5A50
39	$27	$3E00	$5E00	103	$67	$3E28	$5E28	167	$A7	$3E50	$5E50
40	$28	$2280	$4280	104	$68	$22A8	$42A8	168	$A8	$22D0	$42D0
41	$29	$2680	$4680	105	$69	$26A8	$46A8	169	$A9	$26D0	$46D0
42	$2A	$2A80	$4A80	106	$6A	$2AA8	$4AA8	170	$AA	$2AD0	$4AD0
43	$2B	$2E80	$4E80	107	$6B	$2EA8	$4EA8	171	$AB	$2ED0	$4ED0
44	$2C	$3280	$5280	108	$6C	$32A8	$52A8	172	$AC	$32D0	$52D0
45	$2D	$3680	$5680	109	$6D	$36A8	$56A8	173	$AD	$36D0	$56D0
46	$2E	$3A80	$5A80	110	$6E	$3AA8	$5AA8	174	$AE	$3AD0	$5AD0
47	$2F	$3E80	$5E80	111	$6F	$3EA8	$5EA8	175	$AF	$3ED0	$5ED0
48	$30	$2300	$4300	112	$70	$2328	$4328	176	$B0	$2350	$4350
49	$31	$2700	$4700	113	$71	$2728	$4728	177	$B1	$2750	$4750
50	$32	$2B00	$4B00	114	$72	$2B28	$4B28	178	$B2	$2B50	$4B50
51	$33	$2F00	$4F00	115	$73	$2F28	$4F28	179	$B3	$2F50	$4F50
52	$34	$3300	$5300	116	$74	$3328	$5328	180	$B4	$3350	$5350
53	$35	$3700	$5700	117	$75	$3728	$5728	181	$B5	$3750	$5750
54	$36	$3B00	$5B00	118	$76	$3B28	$5B28	182	$B6	$3B50	$5B50
55	$37	$3F00	$5F00	119	$77	$3F28	$5F28	183	$B7	$3F50	$5F50
56	$38	$2380	$4380	120	$78	$23A8	$43A8	184	$B8	$23D0	$43D0
57	$39	$2780	$4780	121	$79	$27A8	$47A8	185	$B9	$27D0	$47D0
58	$3A	$2B80	$4B80	122	$7A	$2BA8	$4BA8	186	$BA	$2BD0	$4BD0
59	$3B	$2F80	$4F80	123	$7B	$2FA8	$4FA8	187	$BB	$2FD0	$4FD0
60	$3C	$3300	$5300	124	$7C	$33A8	$53A8	188	$BC	$33D0	$53D0
61	$3D	$3780	$5780	125	$7D	$37A8	$57A8	189	$BD	$37D0	$57D0
62	$3E	$3B80	$5B80	126	$7E	$3BA8	$5BA8	190	$BE	$3BD0	$5BD0
63	$3F	$3F80	$5F80	127	$7F	$3FA8	$5FA8	191	$BF	$3FD0	$5FD0

FIGURE 10.7 Hi-res screen line numbers and the addresses of the left edge of the screen

```
                                    h       h
                                    i       i
                                    b       b
                                    i       i
           Place value --> 1248124 t 1248124 t
     Contents in binary --> 0000011 0 1110000 0
        Contents in hex -->    0  6      7  0
      Swap the nibbles -->    6  0      0  7
               Address -->   $463B    $463C
```

Since we have free choice over the high bit, we have set it to 0.

PROGRAM 10.7

```
                  1000 * PROGRAM 10.7 BUILD AN A WITH HI-BIT OFF
F3D8-             1010 HGR2    .EQ $F3D8
FD1B-             1020 KEYIN   .EQ $FD1B
                  1025         .OR $800
0800- 20 D8 F3 1030 BEGIN   JSR HGR2     CLEAR PAGE 2 TO BLACK
0803- A9 01    1040         LDA #$01     TOP OF THE A
0805- 8D BC 55 1050         STA $55BC    ITS BYTE
0808- A9 40    1060         LDA #$40     NEXT LINE OF A
080A- 8D BB 59 1070         STA $59BB    ITS BYTE
080D- A9 02    1080         LDA #$02     NEXT LINE OF A
080F- 8D BC 59 1090         STA $59BC    ITS BYTE
0812- A9 20    1100         LDA #$20     DO ALL THESE AT ONCE
0814- 8D BB 5D 1110         STA $5DBB    TOP LEFT LEG
0817- 8D 3B 42 1120         STA $423B    NEXT DOT DOWN LEFT LEG
081A- 8D 3B 4A 1130         STA $4A3B    BOTTOM LEFT LEG
081D- 8D 3B 4E 1140         STA $4E3B    BOTTOM DOT ON LEFT LEG
0820- A9 04    1150         LDA #$04     DO ALL THESE AT ONCE
0822- 8D BC 5D 1160         STA $5DBC    TOP RIGHT LEG
0825- 8D 3C 42 1170         STA $423C    NEXT DOT DOWN LEFT LEG
0828- 8D 3C 4A 1180         STA $4A3C    BOTTOM RIGHT LEG
082B- 8D 3C 4E 1190         STA $4E3C    BOTTOM DOT ON RIGHT LEG
082E- A9 60    1200         LDA #$60     LEFT CROSS BAR
0830- 8D 3B 46 1210         STA $463B    ITS BYTE
0833- A9 07    1220         LDA #$07     RIGHT CROSS BAR
0835- 8D 3C 46 1230         STA $463C    ITS BYTE
0838- 20 1B FD 1240         JSR KEYIN    WAIT FOR KEY PRESS TO RETURN
083B- 60       1250         RTS
```

```
SYMBOL TABLE

0800- BEGIN
F3D8- HGR2
FD1B- KEYIN
```

Clearly, this is not an efficient way to generate images on the high-resolution graphics screen. That is not the intent of the example. Rather, it is intended to show how the graphics screen addressing is organized, and how the contents of specific memory locations are related to the image that is displayed.

In Chapter 11 we shall use this bit pattern to illustrate an animation technique.

Bit Pattern Images: A Gremlin

In Chapter 12 we discuss the development of a classic "shoot-em-up" game. The target is a "gremlin." The data that make up the gremlin cannot be stored

```
                Address -->   $4**0  $4??1
                                  136    136
Base-ten place values --> 12386241248624
     Hex place values --> 12481241248124
               Base                           Base
L#   **         10  Hex                    Hex   10       ??
32  $4200 -->   48  30        11   11     0C   12 <-- $4201
33  $4600 -->  124  7C      11111111111   3F   63 <-- $4601
34  $4A00 -->   68  44      1   111   1   23   35 <-- $4A01
35  $4E00 -->   70  46     11   111   11  63   99 <-- $4E01
36  $5200 -->   70  46     11   111   11  63   99 <-- $5201
37  $5600 -->  126  7E     1111111111111  7F  127 <-- $5601
38  $5A00 -->  120  78       111111111    1F   31 <-- $5A01
39  $5E00 -->   72  48       1  111  1    13   19 <-- $5E01
40  $4280 -->   78  4E     111  111  111  73  115 <-- $4281
41  $4680 -->   14   E     111       111  70  112 <-- $4681
42  $4A80 -->  126  7E     1111111111111  7F  127 <-- $4A81
43  $4E80 -->    4   4      1         1   20   32 <-- $4E81
44  $5280 -->    4   4      1         1   20   32 <-- $5281
45  $5680 -->    4   4      1         1   20   32 <-- $5681
46  $5A80 -->    4   4      1         1   20   32 <-- $5A81
47  $5E80 -->   14   E     111       111  70  112 <-- $5E81
```

on the Hi-res screen directly, as was done for the A in Program 10.7, because we plan later to make the gremlin move across the screen. The gremlin will be stored "out of sight" in the program area and then moved to the Hi-res screen for display. The facing display shows the layout of the gremlin as it will appear on the Hi-res screen.

Most assemblers provide directives that allow for the storage of data. Some assemblers permit base ten values in their data directives, and some allow only hex values. Both place value systems are shown in the gremlin layout. If base ten place values are used it is not necessary to swap the nibbles to get the contents of a byte. The only price to pay for this convenience is larger numbers in the addition.

The program that contains the gremlin data is shown below.

PROGRAM 10.8

```
                 1000 * PROGRAM 10.8 SCREEN ADDRESSING
                 1010 * AND THE GREMLIN
7FFE-            1020 WIDTH  .EQ $7FFE
7FFF-            1030 HEIGHT .EQ $7FFF
0006-            1040 BASET  .EQ $06
000A-            1050 BASEB  .EQ $0A
FD1B-            1060 KEYIN  .EQ $FD1B
F3D8-            1070 HGR2   .EQ $F3D8
                 1080        .OR $7000
7000- A9 42      1090 GREM   LDA #$42       PAGE PART
7002- 85 07      1100        STA BASET+1    OF TOP
7004- 85 0B      1110        STA BASEB+1    AND BOTTOM
7006- A9 00      1120        LDA #$00       LOC ON PAGE
7008- 85 06      1130        STA BASET      OF TOP
700A- A9 80      1140        LDA #$80       LOC ON PAGE
700C- 85 0A      1150        STA BASEB      OF BOTTOM
700E- A9 08      1160        LDA #$08       GREMLIN IS EIGHT
7010- 8D FF 7F   1170        STA HEIGHT     BYTES HIGH
7013- 20 D8 F3   1180        JSR HGR2       CLEAR SCREEN TO BLACK
7016- A2 00      1190        LDX #$00       INIT X, GET GREMLIN INDEX
7018- A9 02      1200 LOOPO  LDA #$02       THE WIDTH OF GREMLIN
701A- 8D FE 7F   1210        STA WIDTH      STORE IT
701D- A0 00      1220        LDY #$00       INIT Y, SEND GREMLIN INDEX
701F- 20 1B FD   1230 LOOPI  JSR KEYIN      WAIT FOR KEYPRESS
```

```
7022- BD 49 70 1240          LDA DATGT,X    GET TOP OF GREMLIN
7025- 91 06    1250          STA (BASET),Y  SEND TOP TO SCREEN
7027- BD 59 70 1260          LDA DATGB,X    GET BOTTOM OF GREMLIN
702A- 91 0A    1270          STA (BASEB),Y  SEND BOTTOM TO SCREEN
702C- E8       1280          INX            INC TO NEXT GET BYTE
702D- C8       1290          INY            INC TO NEXT SEND BYTE
702E- CE FE 7F 1300          DEC WIDTH      KEEP TRACK OF WHICH PART
7031- D0 EC    1310          BNE LOOPI      MOVED BOTH SIDES OF GREMLIN?
7033- 18       1320          CLC            CLEAR CARRY FOR ADD
7034- A5 07    1330          LDA BASET+1    NEED TO ADD
7036- 69 04    1340          ADC #$04       $04 TO TOP TO STEP DOWN TO
7038- 85 07    1350          STA BASET+1    NEXT SCREEN LINE
703A- A5 0B    1360          LDA BASEB+1    DO SAME THING
703C- 69 04    1370          ADC #$04       TO BOTTOM OF
703E- 85 0B    1380          STA BASEB+1    GREMLIN
7040- CE FF 7F 1390          DEC HEIGHT     KEEP TRACK OF WHICH LINE
7043- D0 D3    1400          BNE LOOPO      MOVED 8 SLICES OF GREMLIN?
7045- 20 1B FD 1410          JSR KEYIN      WAIT FOR KEYPRESS TO RTN
7048- 60       1420          RTS
               1430 * DATA STORAGE OF THE GREMLIN. DATA IS

               1440 * STORED IN PAIRS BY LINE. LEFT BYTE, RIGHT BYTE.

               1450 * NEXT PAIR IS NEXT LINE, ETC.
7049- 30 0C 7C
704C- 3F 44 23
704F- 46 63    1460 DATGT   .DA #48,#12,#124,#63,#68,#35,#70,#99
7051- 46 63 7E
7054- 7F 78 1F
7057- 48 13    1470         .DA #70,#99,#126,#127,#120,#31,#72,#19
7059- 4E 73 0E
705C- 70 7E 7F
705F- 04 20    1480 DATGB   .DA #78,#115,#14,#112,#126,#127,#4,#32
7061- 04 20 04
7064- 20 04 20
7067- 0E 70    1490         .DA #4,#32,#4,#32,#4,#32,#14,#112

SYMBOL TABLE

000A- BASEB
0006- BASET
7059- DATGB
```

```
7049- DATGT
7000- GREM
7FFF- HEIGHT
F3D8- HGR2
FD1B- KEYIN
701F- LOOPI
7018- LOOPO
7FFE- WIDTH
```

The data directive for the assembler used in Program 10.8 is .DA; the # in front of each number means that it is a base ten number. (A prefix of #$ would signify a number given in hexadecimal form.) The hex equivalent is assembled into memory. Note how lines 1460 through 1490 are assembled into locations $7049 through $7068. The DATa for the Top of the Gremlin is in lines 1460 and 1470. It is organized in pairs by line. The first pair (#48, #12) is the top line of the gremlin; the next pair (#124, #63) is the second line, etc. The same organization is followed for the DATa for the Bottom of the Gremlin in lines 1480 and 1490.

The program copies a byte for the top left and a byte for the bottom left of the gremlin from the data area to the screen; then bytes for the top right and the bottom right are moved from the data area to the screen. Lines 1090, 1100, and 1120 establish the page part of the top left and the bottom left of the gremlin. Lines 1120 through 1160 establish the location on the page of these parts. The height of the top and of the bottom is eight bytes. The outer loop (lines 1200 through 1400) steps down through the eight slices (X=0, 1, 2, 3, 4, 5, 6, 7) in the top and the bottom of the gremlin. The inside loop (lines 1230 through 1310) steps left to right (Y = 0, 1) across the gremlin. The bottom of the outer loop (lines 1320 through 1400) increments the base address of the gremlin on the screen.

The purpose of the instruction, JSR KEYIN, at the top of the inner loop is to cause the program to wait for a keypress, so that you can see each part of the gremlin as it is moved to the screen. If you remove the JSR KEYIN, the gremlin appears instantly on the screen.

You should design some other bit pattern images, and write programs to position the images at various locations on the high-resolution graphics screen. Consider ways to animate such images. (Draw the image—erase it—draw again in a nearby position—erase—etc.) You will find that the screen addressing pattern is a hurdle to reasonable animation. In the next two chapters we will demonstrate several animation techniques.

CHAPTER 11

HIGH-RESOLUTION GRAPHICS

In this chapter we will give examples of assembly language programs that generate graphic displays. The intention is to demonstrate the use of the assembly language instructions that were presented in earlier chapters, and to illustrate graphics techniques. The first examples use Applesoft subroutines to draw lines and plot points. Later examples discard the Applesoft subroutines in favor of techniques that provide increased speed, and plot points in a manner that is more useful in our specific application.

HI-RES SUBROUTINES

Recall from Chapter 10 how Apple II Hi-res graphics are organized: the display screen consists of 192 rows of individual dots (pixels). Each row has 280 pixels in it. The ability to generate a graphic image rests on the ability to turn pixels on or off.

A portion of the Apple memory is set aside to support the graphics display. Memory with addresses in the range $2000–$3FFF is used for high-resolution graphics page 1, and the range $4000–$5FFF is used for high-resolution graphics page 2. Each pixel on the graphics screen corresponds to a bit in the graphics memory. A pixel is turned on if the corresponding bit is on. The ability to turn pixels on or off thus rests on the ability to identify the corresponding bit and turn it on or off.

Undoubtedly Chapter 10 convinced you that the addressing of individual pixels is not a simple matter. Rather than tackle the problem directly, we will first access the Applesoft subroutines that perform the task. Later in this chapter the addressing of individual pixels will be considered.

If we are writing an Applesoft program to turn on the dot at screen location (135,76), we

1. Identify the graphics screen to be used (HGR or HGR2).
2. Identify the HCOLOR to be used (HCOLOR = 0,1,2,3,4,5,6,7).
3. Plot the dot (HPLOT 135,76).

If we are writing an assembly language program to turn on the dot at screen location (135,76), we must accomplish the same tasks. In the next several pages we will detail each of these steps.

HGR and HGR2

The Applesoft commands HGR and HGR2 perform several tasks. Each displays a graphics screen, identifies that screen as the one to be used for plotting, and clears the screen to black. If we are content with the functioning of these commands we can use them as subroutines (JSR $F3E2 for HGR; JSR $F3D8 for HGR2). On the other hand, if we wish to control the graphics activity more directly, we can do so.

Displaying a graphics screen is a matter of toggling the appropriate soft switches. Table 11.1 shows the memory locations of the soft switches and the function of each.

To display high-resolution graphics page, 1 we could use the following commands:

```
BIT HIRES
BIT MIXEDSCR
BIT PAG1
BIT GR
```

TABLE 11.1 Soft Switches

Variable Name	*Function*	*Memory Location*
GR	Display graphics	$C050
TEXT	Display text	$C051
FULLSCR	Display all text or graphics	$C052
MIXEDSCR	Display mixed graphics/text	$C053
PAG1	Display page 1 of text or graphics	$C054
PAG2	Display page 2 of text or graphics	$C055
LORES	Display lores mode	$C056
HIRES	Display hires mode	$C057

In each of the above commands the result of the logical operation BIT is ignored. It is the mere accessing of the memory location that toggles the soft switch. Other commands such as LDA or STA would have the same effect as BIT.

To identify the graphics screen to be used for plotting we must store a $20 (for high-resolution graphics page 1) or a $40 (for high-resolution graphics page 2) in memory location $E6. This location will be referenced by the Applesoft plotting routines.

Clearing the screen to black is most easily done by calling the Applesoft subroutine HCLR at $F3F2. Clearing the screen to other colors is possible. The examples given in Chapter 1 showed how to do this.

HCOLOR

The Applesoft subroutine SETHCOL at location $F6EC will set the color to be used for plotting. To use the subroutine, load the X-register with the number of the HCOLOR you wish to use for plotting (HCOLOR = 0,1,2,3,4,5,6,7) and jump to the subroutine. For example, to set the plotting color to violet (HCOLOR= 2),

```
LDX #$02
JSR SETHCOL
```

Any future calls to HPLOT subroutines (described below) will use HCOLOR = 2.

Actually, the setting of plotting color can easily be done directly. The HCOLOR number (0,1,2,3,4,5,6,7) is really an index into a table of color codes, as indicated in Table 11.2.

TABLE 11.2 HCOLOR Index

HCOLOR	*Color Code*	*Color*
0	$00	Black1
1	$2A	Violet
2	$55	Blue
3	$7F	White1
4	$80	Black2
5	$AA	Orange
6	$D5	Blue
7	$FF	White2

It is necessary that the proper color code be stored in location $E4. If we wish to specify HCOLOR= 2, we may do so by

```
LDA #$55
STA $E4
```

HPLOT

We will consider the Applesoft HPLOT command as two Applesoft subroutines: HPLOT (at $F457) and HLIN (at $F53A). The HPLOT subroutine can be used to plot individual points; HLIN is a subroutine used to plot lines.

Before calling the HPLOT subroutine it is necessary to load the A-, X-, and Y-registers as follows:

A: vertical coordinate
X: low byte of horizontal coordinate
Y: high byte of horizontal coordinate

For example, to plot a dot at screen location (135,76), which has hex coordinates ($87,$4C), we could use the following (assuming that the color code and plotting screen have been specified):

```
LDA #$4C   VERTICAL COORD (DECIMAL 76)
LDY #$00   HORIZ COORD HIGH
JSR HPLOT
```

While HPLOT will plot a dot at the location specified by the contents of the A-, X-, and Y-registers, HLIN will draw a line from the dot most recently plotted to a newly specified screen location. Before calling the HLIN subroutine it is necessary to load the A-, X-, and Y-registers as follows:

A: low byte of horizontal coordinate
X: high byte of horizontal coordinate
Y: vertical coordinate

Note that the registers are not used as they are for HPLOT.

To plot a line from screen location 135,76 to 275,145, we could first plot a dot at location 135,76, as described above, then reload the A-, X-, and Y-registers to identify screen location 275,145 and jump to the HLIN subroutine. Program 11.1 demonstrates the procedure.

PROGRAM 11.1

```
                  1000 * PROGRAM 11.1
                  1010 * DRAW A RECTANGLE
00E4-             1020 COLOR  .EQ $E4
F3D8-             1030 HGR2   .EQ $F3D8
F457-             1040 HPLOT  .EQ $F457
F53A-             1050 HLIN   .EQ $F53A
                  1055        .OR $800
0800- A9 7F       1060        LDA #$7F
0802- 85 E4       1070        STA COLOR    WHITE
0804- 20 D8 F3    1080        JSR HGR2     PAGE 2
0807- A9 46       1090        LDA #$46     VERTICAL
0809- A2 64       1100        LDX #$64     HORIZ LOW
080B- A0 00       1110        LDY #$00       "   HIGH
080D- 20 57 F4    1120        JSR HPLOT    POINT AT 100,70
0810- A9 0E       1130        LDA #$0E     HORIZ LOW
0812- A2 01       1140        LDX #$01       "   HIGH
0814- A0 46       1150        LDY #$46     VERTICAL
0816- 20 3A F5    1160        JSR HLIN     LINE TO 270,70
0819- A9 0E       1170        LDA #$0E     HORIZ LOW
081B- A2 01       1180        LDX #$01       "   HIGH
081D- A0 7D       1190        LDY #$7D     VERTICAL
081F- 20 3A F5    1200        JSR HLIN     LINE TO 270,125
0822- A9 64       1210        LDA #$64     HORIZ LOW
0824- A2 00       1220        LDX #$00       "   HIGH
```

```
0826- A0 7D     1230        LDY #$7D      VERTICAL
0828- 20 3A F5  1240        JSR HLIN      LINE TO 100,125
082B- A9 64     1250        LDA #$64      HORIZ LOW
082D- A2 00     1260        LDX #$00        "   HIGH
082F- A0 46     1270        LDY #$46      VERTICAL
0831- 20 3A F5  1280        JSR HLIN      LINE TO 100,70
0834- 60        1290        RTS


SYMBOL TABLE
00E4- COLOR
F3D8- HGR2
F53A- HLIN
F457- HPLOT
```

There are a number of Applesoft subroutines that are of value when writing programs that produce graphic images. Table 11.3 lists the more useful ones.

BIT PATTERN ANIMATION

We can display a graphic image in motion if we follow this sequence:

1. Draw the image at a specified location.
2. Calculate the new position for the image.
3. Erase the current image.
4. Go to step 1.

One-Dimensional Animation

If the consecutive locations of the image are close together and if only a short time is required for each of the above steps, then an image can be made to appear to move smoothly. Program 11.2 illustrates the process by having a dot move from the left side to the right side of the graphics screen.

PROGRAM 11.2

```
1000 * PROGRAM 11.2
1010 * MOVE A DOT ACROSS THE SCREEN
```

TABLE 11.3 High Resolution Graphics Subroutines

Name	*Entry Point*
HGR	$F3E2

HGR $F3E2
Sets display screen soft switches to Page 1, Mixed-screen, High-resolution, Graphics mode; stores $20 in location $E6, establishing $2000–$3FFF as the section of memory to be used by plotting subroutines; and clears this section of memory.

HGR2 $F3D8
Sets display screen soft switches to Page 2, Full-screen, High-resolution, Graphics mode; stores $40 in location $E6, establishing $4000–$5FFF as the section of memory to be used by plotting subroutines; and clears this section of memory.

HCLR $F3F2
Clears the graphics screen currently designated by the contents of $E6. To clear page 1 ($2000–$3FFF), store $20 in $E6 and enter the subroutine. To clear page 2 ($4000–$5FFF), store $40 in $E6 before entering the subroutine.

BKGND $F3F6
Colors the graphics screen currently designated by the contents of $E6 (as in HCLR above), using the color code in $1C. Consult the color codes in Table 11.2.

SETHCOL $F6EC
Sets the color to be used by subsequent plotting subroutines. The color number (0–7) in the X-register is used to select the color code (as in Table 11.2). This color code is stored in $E4.

HPOSN $F411
Positions the "high-res cursor." Actually it calculates the values of BASL, BASH, the OFFSET, and the BITMASK in order to identify the byte and bit corresponding to a designated screen location. On entry, the high byte of the horizontal position is in the Y-register, the low byte is in the X-register, and the vertical position is in the A-register. HPOSN also transfers the color code in the reference location $E4 to the location $1C, where it is accessed by plotting subroutines.

HPLOT $F457
First calls HPOSN (above), then reads the color code in $1C and plots a single dot at the designated screen location. On entry, the registers should be as for HPOSN.

HLIN $F53A
Draws a line from the most recently plotted point to the point designated by the contents of the X-, Y-, and A-registers. On entry, the high byte of the horizontal position should be in the X-register, the low byte in the A-register, and the vertical position in the Y-register. HLIN uses the color code that is stored in $1C.

```
0000-        1020 XPOSL  .EQ $00
0001-        1030 XPOSH  .EQ $01
0002-        1040 YPOS   .EQ $02
0005-             1070 ENDFLG .EQ $05
00E4-             1080 COLOR  .EQ $E4
C051-             1090 TEXT   .EQ $C051
C054-             1100 PAGE1  .EQ $C054
F3D8-             1110 HGR2   .EQ $F3D8
F457-             1120 HPLOT  .EQ $F457
FC58-             1130 HOME   .EQ $FC58
FCA8-             1140 WAIT   .EQ $FCA8
                  1145        .OR $800
                  1150 *INITIALIZATION
0800- A9 00       1160        LDA #$00
0802- 85 05       1170        STA ENDFLG
0804- 85 00       1180        STA XPOSL     START AT LEFT
0806- 85 01       1190        STA XPOSH       OF SCREEN
0808- A9 14       1200        LDA #$14      SET VERTICAL
080A- 85 02       1210        STA YPOS      SCREEN POSITION
080C- 20 D8 F3    1220        JSR HGR2      PAGE 2
                  1230 *
                  1240 *MAIN CONTROL LOOP
080F- 20 2E 08    1250 REPT   JSR DRAW
0812- 20 4A 08    1260        JSR INC.POSITION
0815- 20 5C 08    1270        JSR COMPARE
0818- A9 30       1280        LDA #$30      PAUSE TO
081A- 20 A8 FC    1290        JSR WAIT      DECREASE SPEED
081D- 20 3C 08    1300        JSR ERASE
0820- A5 05       1310        LDA ENDFLG
0822- F0 EB       1320        BEQ REPT
                  1330 *END MAIN CONTROL LOOP
                  1340 *EXIT
0824- 20 58 FC    1350        JSR HOME
0827- 2C 54 C0    1360        BIT PAGE1
082A- 2C 51 C0    1370        BIT TEXT
082D- 60          1380        RTS
082E- A9 7F       1390 DRAW   LDA #$7F
0830- 85 E4       1400        STA COLOR     WHITE1
0832- A5 02       1410        LDA YPOS      VERTICAL
0834- A6 00       1420        LDX XPOSL     HORIZ LOW
0836- A4 01       1430        LDY XPOSH       "   HIGH
0838- 20 57 F4    1440        JSR HPLOT     DRAW THE DOT
```

```
083B- 60          1450          RTS
083C- A9 00       1460 ERASE    LDA #$00
083E- 85 E4       1470          STA COLOR     BLACK
0840- A5 02       1480          LDA YPOS      VERTICAL
0842- A6 03       1490          LDX OLDXL     HORIZ LOW
0844- A4 04       1500          LDY OLDXH       "   HIGH
0846- 20 57 F4    1510          JSR HPLOT     DRAW THE DOT
0849- 60          1520          RTS
                  1530 INC.POSITION
084A- A5 00       1540          LDA XPOSL     HORIZ LOW
084C- 85 03       1550          STA OLDXL     SAVE FOR ERASE
084E- 18          1560          CLC
084F- 69 01       1570          ADC #$01      INC HORIZ LOW
0851- 85 00       1580          STA XPOSL     SAVE NEW VALUE
0853- A5 01       1590          LDA XPOSH     HORIZ HIGH
0855- 85 04       1600          STA OLDXH     SAVE FOR ERASE
0857- 69 00       1610          ADC #$00      INC HORIZ HIGH
0859- 85 01       1620          STA XPOSH     IF CARRY IS SET
085B- 60          1630          RTS
                  1640 COMPARE
                  1650 *HAS THE DOT CROSSED THE SCREEN?
085C- A5 01       1660          LDA XPOSH     HORIZ HIGH
085E- F0 08       1670          BEQ RET       IF HORIZ < 256
0860- A5 00       1680          LDA XPOSL     IF HORIZ > 255
0862- C9 18       1690          CMP #$18      IS HORIZ = 280?
0864- D0 02       1700          BNE RET       IF NOT
0866- 85 05       1710          STA ENDFLG    SIGNAL EXIT
0868- 60          1720 RET      RTS


SYMBOL TABLE

00E4- COLOR
085C- COMPARE
082E- DRAW
0005- ENDFLG
083C- ERASE
F3D8- HGR2
FC58- HOME
F457- HPLOT
084A- INC.POSITION
0004- OLDXH
```

```
0003- OLDXL
C054- PAGE1
080F- REPT
0868- RET
C051- TEXT
FCA8- WAIT
0001- XPOSH
0000- XPOSL
0002- YPOS
```

NOTES AND SUGGESTIONS

1. You may notice that Program 11.2 uses page zero memory locations (0–5) that are generally accessed by Applesoft. No harm is done, unless the program is to be called by an Applesoft program. If this use is intended, other locations should be used.
2. The program immediately displays and clears the text page when the animated dot reaches the right screen boundary (lines 350–1380). You might provide a pause, or a "WAIT FOR KEYPRESS" routine before switching from the display of the graphics page.
3. Can you animate the dot from right to left? The process is similar. Try animation in the vertical direction.
4. It was necessary to include a delay loop in this program (lines 1280–1290). Without it the animation is far too fast to be seen. in some of the later examples in this chapter the delay is not needed, because the image being animated is more complex.

Two-Dimensional Animation

Program 11.2 provides animation in one direction only (horizontal). If the INC.POSITION subroutine added an increment to the Y position as well as to the X position, the program would provide animation in two directions. Program 11.3 gives this type of mobility.

PROGRAM 11.3

```
1000 * PROGRAM 11.3
1010 * 2-D ANIMATION
```

```
0001-            1020 DATA   .EQ $01
0001-            1030 XPOS   .EQ $01
0002-            1040 YPOS   .EQ $02
0003-            1050 DLX    .EQ $03
0004-            1060 DLY    .EQ $04
0005-            1070 OLDX   .EQ $05
0006-            1080 OLDY   .EQ $06
00E0-            1090 XHI    .EQ $E0
0020-            1100 XLO    .EQ $20
0090-            1110 YHI    .EQ $90
0020-            1120 YLO    .EQ $20
00E4-            1130 COLOR  .EQ $E4
F3D8-            1140 HGR2   .EQ $F3D8
F457-            1150 HPLOT  .EQ $F457
FCA8-            1160 WAIT   .EQ $FCA8
                 1170        .OR $6000
                 1175 *INITIALIZATION
6000- A9 70      1180 INIT   LDA #$70      INITIAL
6002- 85 01      1190        STA XPOS        HORIZONTAL POSITION
6004- A9 80      1200        LDA #$80      INITIAL
6006- 85 02      1210        STA YPOS        VERTICAL POSITION
6008- A9 01      1220        LDA #$01
600A- 85 03      1230        STA DLX       INITIAL
600C- 85 04      1240        STA DLY         INCREMENTS
600E- 20 D8 F3   1250        JSR HGR2
                 1260 *
                 1270 *MAIN CONTROL LOOP
6011- 20 30 60   1280 REPT   JSR DRAW
6014- A9 30      1290        LDA #$30      PAUSE TO
6016- 20 A8 FC   1300        JSR WAIT      DECREASE SPEED
6019- 20 3E 60   1310        JSR INC.POSITION
601C- 20 22 60   1320        JSR ERASE
601F- 4C 11 60   1330        JMP REPT
                 1335 *END MAIN CONTROL LOOP
                 1336 *
6022- A9 00      1430 ERASE  LDA #$00
6024- 85 E4      1440        STA COLOR     BLACK
6026- A5 06      1450        LDA OLDY      VERTICAL
6028- A6 05      1460        LDX OLDX      HORIZONTAL LOW
602A- A0 00      1470        LDY #$00      HORIZONTAL HIGH
602C- 20 57 F4   1480        JSR HPLOT     DRAW THE DOT
602F- 60         1490        RTS
```

```
6030- A9 7F      1500 DRAW    LDA #$7F
6032- 85 E4      1510         STA COLOR      WHITE1
6034- A5 02      1520         LDA YPOS       VERTICAL
6036- A6 01      1530         LDX XPOS       HORIZONTAL LOW
6038- A0 00      1540         LDY #$00       HORIZONTAL HIGH
603A- 20 57 F4   1550         JSR HPLOT      DRAW THE DOT
603D- 60         1560         RTS
                 1570 INC.POSITION
603E- A5 01      1580         LDA XPOS       HORIZ
6040- 85 05      1590         STA OLDX       SAVE FOR ERASE
6042- 18         1600         CLC
6043- 65 03      1610         ADC DLX        XPOS = XPOS + DLX
6045- 85 01      1620         STA XPOS       NEW HORIZ
6047- C9 E0      1630         CMP #XHI       AT RIGHT BOUNDARY
6049- F0 04      1640         BEQ .1         IF SO BOUNCE
604B- C9 20      1650         CMP #XLO       AT LEFT BOUNDARY
604D- D0 09      1660         BNE .2         IF NOT CHECK VERT
604F- A9 FF      1670 .1      LDA #$FF
6051- 18         1680         CLC
6052- 45 03      1690         EOR DLX        NEGATE
6054- 69 01      1700         ADC #$01        DLX
6056- 85 03      1710         STA DLX
6058- A5 02      1720 .2      LDA YPOS       VERT
605A- 85 06      1730         STA OLDY       SAVE FOR ERASE
605C- 18         1740         CLC
605D- 65 04      1750         ADC DLY        YPOS = YPOS + DLY
605F- 85 02      1760         STA YPOS       NEW VERT
6061- C9 90      1770         CMP #YHI       AT BOTTOM BOUNDARY
6063- F0 04      1780         BEQ .3         IF SO, BOUNCE
6065- C9 20      1790         CMP #YLO       AT TOP BOUNDARY
6067- D0 09      1800         BNE .4
6069- A9 FF      1810 .3      LDA #$FF
606B- 18         1820         CLC
606C- 45 04      1830         EOR DLY        NEGATE
606E- 69 01      1840         ADC #$01        DLY
6070- 85 04      1850         STA DLY
6072- 60         1860 .4      RTS

SYMBOL TABLE

00E4- COLOR
0001- DATA
```

```
0003- DLX
0C04- DLY
6030- DRAW
6022- ERASE
F3D8- HGR2
F457- HPLOT
603E- INC.POSITION
.01=604F, .02=6058, .03=6069, .04=6072
6000- INIT
0005- OLDX
0006- OLDY
6011- REPT
FCA8- WAIT
00E0- XHI
0020- XLO
0001- XPOS
0090- YHI
0020- YLO
0002- YPOS
```

NOTES AND SUGGESTIONS

1. As in Program 11.2 a dot is set in motion. The dot will move only within the rectangle bounded on the left by XMIN, on the right by XMAX, on the top by YMIN, and on the bottom by YMAX. Between successive HPLOTs we add DELX and DELY to XPOS and YPOS respectively. Each of DELX and DELY are given an initial value of 1. When the dot touches the left or right boundaries, DELX is changed in sign. When the dot touches the top or bottom boundaries, DELY is changed in sign. As a result, the dot will appear to bounce off the boundaries.
2. To make the programming a little easier, one-byte values are used for the horizontal limits of the rectangle within which the dot bounces. This means the far right columns (256 through 279) are never used. Can you see how to extend the motion to this part of the graphics screen?
3. Note the process by which DLX and DLY are negated (lines 1610–1710 and 1810–1850). Work out the bit manipulation for several values of DLX and DLY. In this example, DLX and DLY can only attain the values 1 and -1 ($FF).
4. Use the HPLOT and HLIN subroutines (as in Program 11.1) to draw a rectangle around the region within which the dot bounces.

Animated Bit Pattern

We will next arrange to animate a graphic image by moving each of the dots that make up the image. The image we will use is the upper case letter A. As shown in Figure 11.1, the letter consists of sixteen dots. The letter is initially positioned at approximately the screen center. The screen locations of the dots that make up the letter are indicated in Figure 11.1, and are listed in Table 11.4.

Table 11.4 identifies initial values of DELX and DELY for each dot. With sixteen dots and increments of +1, −1 ($01, $FF) and +2, −2 ($02, $FE) we are able to assign a unique velocity to each dot. As a result, the dots in the bit pattern will not move as a unit, but instead will be moving separately. The image will be a recognizable letter A only when the dots return to their original positions.

Note that while there is a clear pattern evident in the assignment of the values $02, $01, $FF, $FE to DELY, it may appear that the assignment of values to DELX was done in a disorganized manner. While the present arrangement is not the only one that would work, there is some reason for it. We will be arranging that the dots bounce off the top, bottom, left, and right boundaries. In doing so, we want each dot to exactly attain each of the extreme positions. That is never a problem when increments of +1, −1 ($01, $FF) are used, since the dots will move through every possible X and Y value until an extreme position is

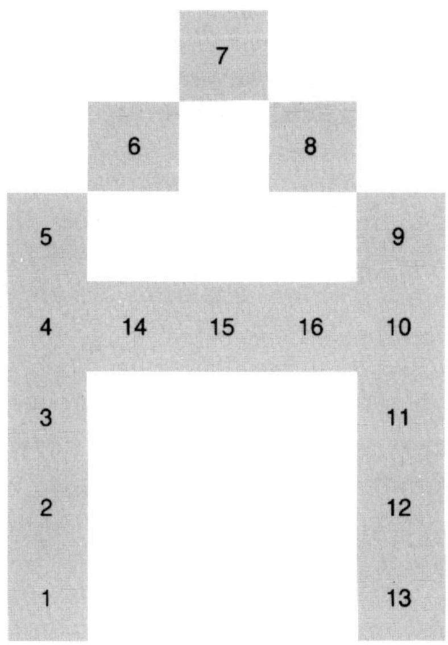

FIGURE 11.1

TABLE 11.4

POINT	*XPOS*	*YPOS*	*DLS*	*DLY*
1	$8A	$63	$02	$02
2	$8A	$62	$01	$01
3	$8A	$61	$02	$02
4	$8A	$60	$01	$01
5	$8A	$5F	$02	$02
6	$8B	$5E	$01	$01
7	$8C	$5D	$02	$02
8	$8D	$5E	$01	$01
9	$8E	$5F	$FE	$FE
10	$8E	$60	$FF	$FF
11	$8E	$61	$FE	$FE
12	$8E	$62	$FF	$FF
13	$8E	$63	$FE	$FE
14	$8B	$61	$FF	$FF
15	$8C	$61	$FE	$FE
16	$8D	$61	$FF	$FF

reached. On the other hand, when increments of +2, −2 ($02, $FE) are used, the dots will skip positions as the X and Y values are incremented. The assignment in Table 11.4 was made to assure that each dot would attain each extreme position.

Program 11.4 animates the dots in the bit pattern. Several components of the program were lifted from Program 11.3, but we will comment only on the new parts. Program 11.4 follows the model of Program 11.3 in animating the dot whose position (XPOS, YPOS, OLDX, OLDY) and velocity (DELX, DELY) are available in memory locations $01–$06. Since sixteen dots will be animated, the data corresponding to each dot will be copied into memory locations $01–$06 when it is needed. Other methods for accessing the data could be used. We are using this method because it will allow us to easily increase the number of dots to be animated without the need for cumbersome addressing techniques.

PROGRAM 11.4

```
                    1000 * PROGRAM 11.4
                    1010 * ANIMATED BIT PATTERN
0001-               1020 DATA    .EQ $01
```

```
0001-              1030 XPOS    .EQ $01
0002-              1040 YPOS    .EQ $02
0003-              1050 DLX     .EQ $03
0004-              1060 DLY     .EQ $04
0005-              1070 OLDX    .EQ $05
0006-              1080 OLDY    .EQ $06
0007-              1090 ENDFLG  .EQ $07
0090-              1100 XHI     .EQ $90
0020-              1110 XLO     .EQ $20
0091-              1120 YHI     .EQ $91
0021-              1130 YLO     .EQ $21
000B-              1140 COUNTR  .EQ $0B
000C-              1150 PNTR    .EQ $0C
000E-              1160 CNTR    .EQ $0E
00E4-              1170 COLOR   .EQ $E4
C051-              1180 TEXT    .EQ $C051
C054-              1190 PAGE1   .EQ $C054
F3D8-              1200 HGR2    .EQ $F3D8
F457-              1210 HPLOT   .EQ $F457
FC58-              1220 HOME    .EQ $FC58
                   1230         .OR $6000
                   1240 *INITIALIZATION
6000- A9 00        1250         LDA #$00
6002- 85 0E        1260         STA CNTR
6004- 85 07        1270         STA ENDFLG
6006- 20 D8 F3     1280         JSR HGR2
6009- 20 2F 60     1290         JSR INIT.PNTR
                   1300 *
                   1310 * MAIN CONTROL LOOP
600C- 20 3C 60     1320 REPT    JSR COPY.DATA.IN
600F- 20 87 60     1330         JSR ERASE
6012- 20 95 60     1340         JSR DRAW
6015- 20 52 60     1350         JSR INC.POSITION
6018- 20 47 60     1360         JSR COPY.DATA.OUT
601B- 20 A3 60     1370         JSR BOOKKEEPING
601E- A5 07        1380         LDA ENDFLG
6020- D0 03        1390         BNE EXIT
6022- 4C 0C 60     1400         JMP REPT
                   1410 * END MAIN CONTROL LOOP
                   1420 *
                   1430 *
                   1440 EXIT
```

```
6025- 20 58 FC 1450        JSR HOME      CLEAR SCREEN
6028- 2C 54 C0 1460        BIT PAGE1     DISPLAY PAGE 1
602B- 2C 51 C0 1470        BIT TEXT      OF TEXT
602E- 60       1480        RTS           END PROGRAM
               1490 INIT.PNTR
602F- A9 D8    1500        LDA #DATA0    LOW BYTE OF DATA
6031- 85 0C    1510        STA PNTR      STORAGE ADDRESS
6033- A9 60    1520        LDA /DATA0    HIGH BYTE OF DATA
6035- 85 0D    1530        STA PNTR+1    STORAGE ADDRESS
6037- A9 00    1540        LDA #$00      START DRAW CYCLE
6039- 85 0B    1550        STA COUNTR    OVER AGAIN
603B- 60       1560        RTS
               1570 COPY.DATA.IN
603C- A0 05    1580        LDY #$05      MOVE 6 NUMBERS
603E- B1 0C    1590 .1     LDA (PNTR),Y FROM STORAGE
6040- 99 01 00 1600        STA DATA,Y    TO WORKSPACE
6043- 88       1610        DEY
6044- 10 F8    1620        BPL .1
6046- 60       1630        RTS
               1640 COPY.DATA.OUT
6047- A0 05    1650        LDY #$05      MOVE 6 NUMBERS
6049- B9 01 00 1660 .1     LDA DATA,Y    FROM WORKSPACE
604C- 91 0C    1670        STA (PNTR),Y TO STORAGE
604E- 88       1680        DEY
604F- 10 F8    1690        BPL .1
6051- 60       1700        RTS
               1710 INC.POSITION
6052- A5 01    1720        LDA XPOS      HORIZ
6054- 85 05    1730        STA OLDX      SAVE FOR ERASE
6056- 18       1740        CLC
6057- 65 03    1750        ADC DLX       XPOS = XPOS + DLX
6059- 85 01    1760        STA XPOS      NEW HORIZ
605B- C9 90    1770        CMP #XHI      AT RIGHT BOUNDARY
605D- F0 04    1780        BEQ .1        IF SO BOUNCE
605F- C9 20    1790        CMP #XLO      AT LEFT BOUNDARY
6061- D0 09    1800        BNE .2        IF NOT CHECK VERT
6063- A9 FF    1810 .1     LDA #$FF
6065- 18       1820        CLC
6066- 45 03    1830        EOR DLX       NEGATE
6068- 69 01    1840        ADC #$01       DLX
606A- 85 03    1850        STA DLX
606C- A5 02    1860 .2     LDA YPOS      VERT
```

```
606E- 85 06    1870        STA OLDY     SAVE FOR ERASE
6070- 18       1880        CLC
6071- 65 04    1890        ADC DLY      YPOS = YPOS + DLY
6073- 85 02    1900        STA YPOS     NEW VERT
6075- C9 91    1910        CMP #YHI     AT BOTTOM BOUNDARY
6077- F0 04    1920        BEQ .3       IF SO, BOUNCE
6079- C9 21    1930        CMP #YLO     AT TOP BOUNDARY
607B- D0 09    1940        BNE .4
607D- A9 FF    1950 .3     LDA #$FF
607F- 18       1960        CLC
6080- 45 04    1970        EOR DLY      NEGATE
6082- 69 01    1980        ADC #$01      DLY
6084- 85 04    1990        STA DLY
6086- 60       2000 .4     RTS
6087- A9 00    2010 ERASE  LDA #$00
6089- 85 E4    2020        STA COLOR    BLACK
608B- A5 06    2030        LDA OLDY
608D- A6 05    2040        LDX OLDX
608F- A0 00    2050        LDY #$00     HORIZ HIGH
6091- 20 57 F4 2060        JSR HPLOT
6094- 60       2070        RTS
6095- A9 7F    2080 DRAW   LDA #$7F
6097- 85 E4    2090        STA COLOR    WHITE1
6099- A5 02    2100        LDA YPOS
609B- A6 01    2110        LDX XPOS
609D- A0 00    2120        LDY #$00     HORIZ HIGH
609F- 20 57 F4 2130        JSR HPLOT
60A2- 60       2140        RTS
               2150 *GET BASH
               2160 BOOKKEEPING
60A3- E6 0B    2170        INC COUNTR   COUNT NUMBER OF
60A5- A5 0B    2180        LDA COUNTR   DOTS DRAWN SO FAR
60A7- C9 10    2190        CMP #$10     ALL DOTS DONE?
60A9- F0 1A    2200        BEQ .1       IF SO, START OVER
60AB- 18       2210        CLC
60AC- A5 0C    2220        LDA PNTR     POINT
60AE- 69 06    2230        ADC #$06     TO
60B0- 85 0C    2240        STA PNTR     DATA
60B2- A5 0D    2250        LDA PNTR+1   FOR
60B4- 69 00    2260        ADC #$00     NEXT
60B6- 85 0D    2270        STA PNTR+1   DOT
60B8- AD 00 C0 2280        LDA $C000    KEYPRESS?
```

```
60BB- 10 1A     2290          BPL .2        IF NOT, RETURN
60BD- AD 10 C0 2300          LDA $C010     CLEAR KEYBOARD STROBE
60C0- A9 01     2310          LDA #$01
60C2- 85 07     2320          STA ENDFLG    SET EXIT FLAG
60C4- 60        2330          RTS
60C5- 20 2F 60 2340 .1       JSR INIT.PNTR
60C8- E6 0E     2350          INC CNTR      NUMBER OF CYCLES
60CA- A5 0E     2360          LDA CNTR
60CC- C9 E1     2370          CMP #$E1      BACK TO ORIGINAL?
60CE- D0 07     2380          BNE .2
60D0- 20 0C FD 2390          JSR $FD0C     WAIT FOR KEYPRESS
60D3- A9 01     2400          LDA #$01
60D5- 85 0E     2410          STA CNTR      RESET
60D7- 60        2420 .2       RTS
60D8- 8A 63 01
60DB- 02 00 00 2430 DATA0    .DA #$8A,#$63,#$01,#$02,#$00,#$00
60DE- 8A 62 FE
60E1- 01 00 00 2440 DATA1    .DA #$8A,#$62,#$FE,#$01,#$00,#$00
60E4- 8A 61 FE
60E7- 02 00 00 2450 DATA2    .DA #$8A,#$61,#$FE,#$02,#$00,#$00
60EA- 8A 60 02
60ED- 01 00 00 2460 DATA3    .DA #$8A,#$60,#$02,#$01,#$00,#$00
60F0- 8A 5F FF
60F3- 02 00 00 2470 DATA4    .DA #$8A,#$5F,#$FF,#$02,#$00,#$00
60F6- 8B 5E FF
60F9- 01 00 00 2480 DATA5    .DA #$8B,#$5E,#$FF,#$01,#$00,#$00
60FC- 8C 5D 02
60FF- 02 00 00 2490 DATA6    .DA #$8C,#$5D,#$02,#$02,#$00,#$00
6102- 8D 5E 01
6105- 01 00 00 2500 DATA7    .DA #$8D,#$5E,#$01,#$01,#$00,#$00
6108- 8E 5F FF
610B- FE 00 00 2510 DATA8    .DA#$8E,#$5F,#$FF,#$FE,#$00,#$00
610E- 8E 60 02
6111- FF 00 00 2520 DATA9    .DA #$8E,#$60,#$02,#$FF,#$00,#$00
6114- 8E 61 FE
6117- FE 00 00 2530 DATA10   .DA #$8E,#$61,#$FE,#$FE,#$00,#$00
611A- 8E 62 FE
611D- FF 00 00 2540 DATA11   .DA #$8E,#$62,#$FE,#$FF,#$00,#$00
6120- 8E 63 01
6123- FE 00 00 2550 DATA12   .DA #$8E,#$63,#$01,#$FE,#$00,#$00
6126- 8B 61 FF
6129- FF 00 00 2560 DATA13   .DA #$8B,#$61,#$FF,#$FF,#$00,#$00
```

```
612C- 8C 61 02
612F- FE 00 00 2570 DATA14 .DA #$8C,#$61,#$02,#$FE,#$00,#$00
6132- 8D 61 01
6135- FF 00 00 2580 DATA15 .DA #$8D,#$61,#$01,#$FF,#$00,#$00


SYMBOL TABLE

60A3- BOOKKEEPING .01=60C5, .02=60D7
000E- CNTR
00E4- COLOR
603C- COPY.DATA.IN .01=603E
6047- COPY.DATA.OUT .01=6049
```

PNTR is a two-byte (PNTR, PNTR+1) variable that points to the byte of memory at which the data for a given dot begin. The subroutine INIT.PNTR sets PNTR so that it identifies the beginning of the data table. Subroutine COPY.DATA.IN copies six consecutive bytes into the DATA workspace ($01–$06). A dot is then ready. After the dot is erased and redrawn, its position can be incremented. This process duplicates the subroutines of Program 11.3. Next COPY.DATA.OUT puts the workspace DATA values back into the data table, ready for future use.

The subroutine BOOKKEEPING serves several functions. First, COUNTR is incremented. This variable keeps track of the number of dots that have been drawn. If COUNTR is less than 16, PNTR is incremented by 6 so that it points to the beginning of the data for the next dot. Then a check is made to see if a key has been pressed (a signal to end the program).

When COUNTR is incremented to 16, all dots have been drawn. A branch to AGAIN arranges to start the entire cycle over again. PNTR is reset. The variable CNTR is checked. If it has reached 225, then all the dots have returned to their original positions. (The key value for CNTR is determined by the positions of the boundaries against which the dots will bounce.) Animation ceases until a keypress gives the signal to resume motion.

There is one visible defect in Program 11.4. When the bit pattern returns to its original position, a couple of dots are not visible. To see the cause, note that each dot is erased from its old position (OLDX,OLDY), then redrawn in its new position (XPOS,YPOS). Assume that dot number 10 is occupying position P and dot number 8 is occupying position Q, but is about to be moved to position P. When it is moved, position Q is erased and position P is drawn (it is drawn again, since dot number 10 is there). When dot number 10 is moved, its old position (P) will be erased. That means dot number 8 will not be visible.

BITMASKING TECHNIQUES

Before developing a method of correcting this problem, we will look at the HPLOT subroutine. It is listed below. You can see it (without labels and variables) at $F457.

```
HPLOT    JSR HPOSN
         LDA COLOR
         EOR (BASL),Y
         AND BITMASK
         EOR (BASL),Y
         STA (BASL),Y
         RTS
```

The first thing HPLOT does is to jump to the HPOSN subroutine. This accomplishes several tasks:

1. HPOSN identifies the address of the leftmost byte of the row in which the HPLOT is to occur. This address is stored in BASL ($26) and BASH ($27).
2. Within the plotting row identified by BASL and BASH, HPOSN identifies the byte that is to be affected. On return from the subroutine, the Y-register is an index to this byte, so that (BASL),Y will identify the address of the byte.
3. HPOSN identifies the bit position to be affected within the plotting byte. The corresponding bit (and bit 7) are turned On in BITMASK ($30). The other bits in BITMASK are Off. (Bit 7 is turned on in order to accommodate colors. See the *Apple II Reference Manual* for some background.)

To illustrate the effect of HPOSN, assume we wish to plot a dot at (94,123) (HPLOT 94,123). We can do this, assuming the color has been specified, with the following:

```
LDA #$7B     * VERTICAL   (DEC 123)
LDX #$5E     * HORIZONTAL LOW   (DEC 94)
LDY #$00     * HORIZONTAL HIGH
JSR HPLOT
RTS
```

As we have seen, the first action taken by HPLOT will be to call HPOSN. The contribution of HPOSN in this case will be to

1. Identify the base address of the plotting row, which is $2F28. BASL will receive $28 and BASH will receive $2F.
2. Identify the byte index, which is $13. (The designated point is in the thirteenth byte from the left of the screen.) On return from HPOSN, the Y-register will contain $13.
3. Identify the bit to be turned on, which is bit number 2. BITMASK will receive the number 132 (binary 10000100). (Note that bit number 2 is the third bit, since the first bit is number 0.)

We will use two examples to illustrate the function served by the remaining parts of HPLOT. In each case we will show the changes that take place in the Accumulator and in the screen display byte (BASL),Y.

Example 1: Plotting (in white; HCOLOR= 3) in a position which is initially black.

	BITMASK	Screen Display Byte (BASL) , Y	Color	Accumulator
JSR HPOSN	10000100	01000000	01111111	XXXXXXXX
LDA COLOR				01111111
EOR (BASL) , Y				00111111
AND BITMASK				00000100
EOR (BASL) , Y				01000100
STA (BASL) , Y		01000100		
RTS				

Note that bit 6 of the display byte was on before the HPLOT occurred. It was not changed when dot 2 was plotted.

Example 2: Plotting (in black; HCOLOR= 0) in a position that is initially white.

	BITMASK	Screen Display Byte (BASL) , Y	Color	Accumulator
JSR HPOSN	10000100	01000100	00000000	XXXXXXXX
LDA COLOR				00000000
EOR (BASL) , Y				01000100
AND BITMASK				00000100
EOR (BASL) , Y				01000000
STA (BASL) , Y		01000000		
RTS				

Try a few examples of your own. We will not be using colors other than white and black, but you might experiment to see how the other colors work. The color codes are given in Table 11.2.

The use of EOR and AND in HPLOT permits a general purpose point-plotting subroutine to handle the plotting of a variety of colors. We can design special purpose plotting subroutines that provide features that HPLOT does not offer. The program segment listed below is an example.

```
JSR HPOSN
LDA BITMASK
EOR (BASL),Y
STA (BASL),Y
RTS
```

We will give two examples to show the effect of this subroutine.

Example 3: Plotting a dot in a position that is initially OFF (black).

	BITMASK	Screen Display Byte (BASL),Y	Accumulator
JSR HPOSN	10000100	01000000	XXXXXXXX
LDA BITMASK			10000100
EOR (BASL),Y			11000100
STA (BASL),Y		11000100	

Note that while no COLOR was specified or accessed, a dot was plotted in the position indicated by the BITMASK. Bit 6 of the screen display byte, that was On before the plotting subroutine, remains On. Note also that while bit 7 gets turned On, it is not displayed. Again, it is strictly for color control.

Example 4: Plotting a dot in a position that is already ON.

	BITMASK	Screen Display Byte (BASL),Y	Accumulator
JSR HPOSN	10000100	01000100	XXXXXXXX
LDA BITMASK			10000100
EOR (BASL),Y			11000000
STA (BASL),Y		11000000	

In this case, while no COLOR was specified or accessed, the dot indicated by the BITMASK was changed from ON to OFF.

The subroutine above has the effect of a complementary plot. As with HPLOT, BITMASK identifies the bit pattern at which plotting occurs. If the indicated bit is ON, the subroutine turns it OFF. If the bit is OFF, it is turned ON. This is a convenient tool, one that will correct the shortcoming encountered in Program 11.4.

COMPLEMENTARY DRAWING

Recall the difficulty with Program 11.4: Some dots did not appear when the bit pattern returned to its original position. The reason for this is that each dot is erased from its old position (OLDX,OLDY), then redrawn in its new position (XPOS,YPOS). Occasionally one dot moves into a position that is about to be vacated by another dot. To illustrate this problem, assume dot number 10 is drawn in position P and dot number 8 is drawn in position Q, but is about to be moved to position P. When it is moved, position Q is erased and position P is drawn (it was already drawn for dot number 10). When dot number 10 is moved, its old position (P) will be erased. As a result, no trace of dot number 8 remains.

If we use the complementary draw subroutine instead of HPLOT, the problem disappears. If dot number 10 occupies P and dot number 8 occupies Q and is about to move to P, then when dot number 8 is moved from Q, the complementary draw will erase Q. When dot number 8 is moved to P, the complementary draw will erase P (which was ON for dot number 10). Then when dot number 10 is moved from P, the complementary draw will turn P ON again. As a result, dot number 8 is visible. And all the other dots will be visible also.

While a listing of the amended program is not given, here are the changes to make to Program 11.4 in order to provide for complementary drawing. We will refer to the amended program as Program 11.5.

1. Replace the identification of HPLOT with

```
HPOSN    .EQ $F411
```

   and define BTMSK as

```
BTMSK    .EQ $30
```

2. Rewrite DRAW as follows:

```
DRAW   LDA YPOS
       LDX XPOS
       LDY #$00        HORIZ HIGH
       JSR HPOSN       GET ADDRESS, BITMASK
       LDA BTMSK
       EOR (BASL),Y    BITMASK EOR SCREEN
       STA (BASL),Y    SAVE TO SCREEN
       RTS
```

3. Rewrite ERASE as follows:

```
ERASE LDA FLAG         DON'T ERASE ON
      BEQ RET          FIRST CYCLE
      LDA OLDY
      LDX OLDX
      LDY #$00         HORIZ HIGH
      JSR HPOSN        GET ADDRESS, BITMASK
      LDA BTMSK
      EOR (BASL),Y     BITMASK EOR SCREEN
      STA (BASL),Y     SAVE TO SCREEN
      RTS
```

4. Insert additional lines into Program 11.4:

```
1015 FLAG  .EQ $00
1255       STA FLAG        INITIALIZE TO ZERO
2365       STA FLAG        SET TO NONZERO
```

FLAG was not needed in Program 11.4 because the ERASE always resulted in drawing in black, which was the background color. Since ERASE now results in a complementary draw, we will skip ERASE the first time through the erase-draw cycle (since there is nothing to erase).

To make this program a little more interesting, you can increase the size of the data set. The result can be a pleasant looking animation, with swirling dots coalescing to form a name or graphics image. The present structure of the program will limit the number of dots to less than 256; but larger numbers are not desirable, since the resulting animation would be extremely slow.

Speeding Up Animation

The animation provided by Program 11.5 is satisfactory. The dots move smoothly, with good speed, and the image is clear. However, if a large number of dots is to be animated the movement of dots could become unreasonably slow. We can achieve a noticeable increase in speed, and thus be able to animate many more dots, by avoiding the use of the HPOSN subroutine and arranging to achieve its results through more efficient methods. In fact, the result we will achieve provides movement that is almost too fast for the 16 dots we have been working with. We have had very satisfactory animation with more than 150 dots. In those cases we were animating a name or object.

Of course, in the process of gaining speed, we must sacrifice something. In this case we are sacrificing compactness. Rather than obtaining byte location and bit location through calculation, as is done in HPOSN, we will look up the values in long reference tables (look-up tables). We will trade a 3-byte call to an Applesoft subroutine (JSR HPOSN) for a 32-byte subroutine and 650 bytes of tables.

Our reference tables will provide the same results as we obtained from HPOSN:

1. We must identify the address of the leftmost byte of the row in which the HPLOT is to occur. We will again store the result in BASL ($26) and BASH ($27).
2. Within the plotting row identified by BASL and BASH, we must identify the byte that is to be affected. We will load the Y-register with an index to this byte so that once more (BASL),Y will identify the address of the byte. We will call this index the Y-offset, and will refer to the corresponding table as the OFFSET table.
3. We must identify the bit position to be affected within the plotting byte. The corresponding bit will be turned ON in BITMASK ($30) (We will not turn on bit 7 as HPOSN does, since color is not important here. If you are using colors, you may need to turn on bit 7 to achieve the desired color—it is easily done.) The other bits in BITMASK are OFF.

We will consider each of these tasks separately.

BASE ADDRESS TABLES

Table 10.5 lists the base addresses of all 192 high-resolution graphics lines. The first column contains the base addresses for the top third of the screen. The second and third columns give base addresses for the middle and bottom thirds of the screen. Look over the lists. You should notice some consistent patterns.

These patterns provide the basis for formulas that can be used to calculate the base address associated with a given horizontal plotting position. Before you start developing such formulas, remember: that is what HPOSN does. Our intention is to use the table of addresses in order to save calculation time. We will store the addresses in two tables, which we will call TBLYL (low part of the addresses) and TBLYH (high part of the addresses).

We will use no calculation to obtain the value of BASH or BASL. TBLYH will have the high byte of each address in it. TBLYL will have all 192 low addresses in it. They can be accessed by the following routine.

```
LDY YPOS
LDA TBLYL, Y
STA BASL
LDA TBLYH, Y
STA BASH
```

OFFSET Table

Next we must identify the byte that is to be affected within the plotting row. There are forty bytes on each plotting line, so it might seem that the offset table would need forty entries. On the other hand, there are 280 positions in each plotting line. Plotting the first 7 positions will result in modifying the first byte only (offset 0). Plotting in the eighth through fourteenth positions will affect the second byte (offset 1). And so on.

If we want to avoid calculation, we will have an offset table that has 280 entries in it. The first 7 entries will be 0s; the next 7 entries will be 1s, and so on. The last 7 entries will have 39s ($27). Then, for a given horizontal position XPOS, we might try the following routine to obtain the offset.

```
LDX XPOS
LDY OFFSET, X
STY OFFSET
```

You will note that the above routine will access only 256 of the numbers in our 280-byte table. That is all right if you are willing to give up the use of the right margin of the screen. (We will do so in the program we are developing.) If you want to use the entire width, it will be necessary to use two tables: TBLXL (for positions 0 through 255) and TBLXH (for positions 256 through 279). Access to the tables can then be controlled by way of a two-byte X position: XPOSL,

XPOSH. If XPOSH is 0, read from TBLXL. If XPOSH is 1, read from TBLXH. Thus:

```
       LDA XPOSH
       BNE HERE
       LDY TBLXL,X
       BPL CONT      ALWAYS
HERE   LDY TBLXH,X
CONT   STY OFFSET
```

BITMASK Table

We must now obtain the bit mask, which identifies the specific bit to be affected within the plotting byte. While this could be accomplished through the use of another table, we will instead do a little arithmetic. Algebraically we can say that

BIT POSITION = XPOS − 7*OFFSET

We can easily multiply by factors of 2, 4, 8, etc. (use ASL), and will take advantage of this by noting that

7*OFFSET = 8*OFFSET − OFFSET

The following subroutine will obtain the BITMASK when provided with the horizontal plotting position XPOS. (Again we assume that XPOS is a one-byte value.)

```
LDA OFFSET
ASL             MULTIPLY
ASL             OFFSET
ASL             BY 8
SEC
SBC OFFSET
STA TEMP        7*OFFSET
LDA XPOS
SEC
SBC TEMP        XPOS - 7*OFFSET
TAX
LDA MASKTBL,X
```

MASKTBL will have seven numbers in it. Each number, in binary form, will have all positions zero except for the bit position that we want to plot. The entries of the table are thus 1, 2, 4, 8, 16, 32, 64.

We can combine the three functions of HPOSN into a single subroutine, HPOSN1. Before entering the subroutine we will load the X- and Y-registers with the horizontal and vertical coordinates of the point that is to be plotted.

```
*GET BASH AND BASL
        LDA TBLYH,Y   READ TABLE
        STA BASH      STORE IT
        LDA TBLYL,Y   READ TABLE
        STA BASL      STORE IT
*GET OFFSET
        LDY OFFSET,X READ TABLE
        STY OFFSET     STORE IT
*GET BITMASK
        TYA
        ASL           MULTIPLY
        ASL           OFFSET
        ASL           BY 8
        SEC
        SBC OFFSET
        STA TEMP      7*OFFSET
        TXA
        SBC TEMP      XPOS - 7*OFFSET
        TAX
        LDA MASKTBL,X
        RTS
```

On return from the subroutine, BASL and BASH will be loaded as they would be by HPOSN. The Y-register will have the OFFSET in it, and the Accumulator will have the BITMASK. Since XPOS and YPOS are not referenced directly by the subroutine HPOSN1, we can use it for ERASE as well as for DRAW.

The task remaining is to update the previous program (Program 11.5) so that these newer features are added. It will be fairly easy to modify the source file to provide for HPOSN1. The onerous task is to type in all of the data for the tables. We can ease that burden too. For the price of a small delay (not noticeable) at the start of the program, before the graphics begins, we can have a subroutine fill the tables for us. This is done in lines 2770–3070 of Program 11.6, which shows the updated form of the earlier programs.

PROGRAM 11.6

```
                1000 * PROGRAM 11.6
                1010 * FASTER ANIMATION
0000-           1020 FLAG    .EQ $00
0001-           1030 DATA    .EQ $01
0001-           1040 XPOS    .EQ $01
0002-           1050 YPOS    .EQ $02
0003-           1060 DLX     .EQ $03
0004-           1070 DLY     .EQ $04
0005-           1080 OLDX    .EQ $05
0006-           1090 OLDY    .EQ $06
0007-           1100 ENDFLG  .EQ $07
0009-           1110 LINNUM  .EQ $09
000A-           1120 INDX    .EQ $0A
000B-           1130 COUNTR  .EQ $0B
000C-           1140 PNTR    .EQ $0C
000E-           1150 CNTR    .EQ $0E
000F-           1160 NDOTS   .EQ $0F
0010-           1170 OFFSET  .EQ $10
0090-           1180 XHI     .EQ $90
0020-           1190 XLO     .EQ $20
0091-           1200 YHI     .EQ $91
0021-           1210 YLO     .EQ $21
0026-           1220 BASL    .EQ $26
0027-           1230 BASH    .EQ $27
0030-           1240 TEMP    .EQ $30
00E6-           1250 HPAGE   .EQ $E6
C051-           1260 TEXT    .EQ $C051
C054-           1270 PAGE1   .EQ $C054
F3D8-           1280 HGR2    .EQ $F3D8
F411-           1290 HPOSN   .EQ $F411
FC58-           1300 HOME    .EQ $FC58
                1310         .OR $6000
                1320 *INITIALIZATION
6000- 20 FF 60  1330         JSR FILL.TABLES
6003- A9 00     1340         LDA #$00
6005- 85 0E     1350         STA CNTR
6007- 85 07     1360         STA ENDFLG
6009- 85 00     1370         STA FLAG
600B- 20 D8 F3  1380         JSR HGR2
```

```
600E- 20 34 60 1390        JSR INIT.PNTR
               1400 *
               1410 * MAIN CONTROL LOOP
6011- 20 41 60 1420 REPT   JSR COPY.DATA.IN
6014- 20 8C 60 1430        JSR ERASE
6017- 20 9C 60 1440        JSR DRAW
601A- 20 57 60 1450        JSR INC.POSITION
601D- 20 4C 60 1460        JSR COPY.DATA.OUT
6020- 20 C8 60 1470        JSR BOOKKEEPING
6023- A5 07    1480        LDA ENDFLG
6025- D0 03    1490        BNE EXIT
6027- 4C 11 60 1500        JMP REPT
               1510 * END MAIN CONTROL LOOP
               1520 *
               1530 *
               1540 EXIT
602A- 20 58 FC 1550        JSR HOME      CLEAR TEXT SCREEN
602D- 2C 54 C0 1560        BIT PAGE1     DISPLAY PAGE 1
6030- 2C 51 C0 1570        BIT TEXT      OF TEXT
6033- 60       1580        RTS           END PROGRAM
               1590 INIT.PNTR
6034- A9 C2    1600        LDA #DATA0    LOW BYTE OF DATA
6036- 85 0C    1610        STA PNTR      STORAGE ADDRESS
6038- A9 63    1620        LDA /DATA0    HIGH BYTE OF DATA
603A- 85 0D    1630        STA PNTR+1    STORAGE ADDRESS
603C- A9 00    1640        LDA #$00      START DRAW CYCLE
603E- 85 0B    1650        STA COUNTR    OVER AGAIN
6040- 60       1660        RTS
               1670 COPY.DATA.IN
6041- A0 05    1680        LDY #$05      MOVE 6 NUMBERS
6043- B1 0C    1690 .1     LDA (PNTR),Y FROM STORAGE
6045- 99 01 00 1700        STA DATA,Y    TO WORKSPACE
6048- 88       1710        DEY
6049- 10 F8    1720        BPL .1        TIL Y IS NEGATIVE
604B- 60       1730        RTS
               1740 COPY.DATA.OUT
604C- A0 05    1750        LDY #$05      MOVE 6 NUMBERS
604E- B9 01 00 1760 .1     LDA DATA,Y    FROM WORKSPACE
6051- 91 0C    1770        STA (PNTR),Y TO STORAGE
6053- 88       1780        DEY
6054- 10 F8    1790        BPL .1
6056- 60       1800        RTS
```

```
                  INC.POSITION
6057- A5 01                LDA XPOS     HORIZ
6059- 85 05                STA OLDX     SAVE FOR ERASE
605B- 18                   CLC
605C- 65 03                ADC DLX      XPOS = XPOS + DLX
605E- 85 01                STA XPOS     NEW HORIZ
6060- C9 90                CMP #XHI     AT RIGHT BOUNDARY?
6062- F0 04                BEQ .1       IF SO BOUNCE
6064- C9 20                CMP #XLO     AT LEFT BOUNDARY?
6066- D0 09                BNE .2       IF NOT CHECK VERT
6068- A9 FF       .1       LDA #$FF
606A- 18                   CLC
606B- 45 03                EOR DLX      NEGATE
606D- 69 01                ADC #$01      DLX
606F- 85 03                STA DLX
6071- A5 02       .2       LDA YPOS     VERT
6073- 85 06                STA OLDY     SAVE FOR ERASE
6075- 18                   CLC
6076- 65 04                ADC DLY      YPOS = YPOS + DLY
6078- 85 02                STA YPOS     NEW VERT
607A- C9 91                CMP #YHI     AT BOTTOM BOUNDARY?
607C- F0 04                BEQ .3       IF SO, BOUNCE
607E- C9 21                CMP #YLO     AT TOP BOUNDARY?
6080- D0 09                BNE .4
6082- A9 FF       .3       LDA #$FF
6084- 18                   CLC
6085- 45 04                EOR DLY      NEGATE
6087- 69 01                ADC #$01      DLY
6089- 85 04                STA DLY
608B- 60          .4       RTS
608C- A5 00       ERASE    LDA FLAG     DON'T ERASE ON
608E- F0 0B                BEQ .1       FIRST CYCLE
6090- A4 06                LDY OLDY
6092- A6 05                LDX OLDX
6094- 20 A8 60             JSR HPOSN1   GET ADDRESS, BITMASK
6097- 51 26                EOR (BASL),Y BITMASK EOR SCREEN
6099- 91 26                STA (BASL),Y SAVE TO SCREEN
609B- 60          .1       RTS
609C- A4 02       DRAW     LDY YPOS
609E- A6 01                LDX XPOS
60A0- 20 A8 60             JSR HPOSN1   GET ADDRESS, BITMASK
60A3- 51 26                EOR (BASL),Y BITMASK EOR SCREEN
```

```
60A5- 91 26    2230        STA (BASL),Y SAVE TO SCREEN
60A7- 60       2240        RTS
               2250 *GET BASH
60A8- B9 42 62 2260 HPOSN1 LDA TBLYH,Y
60AB- 85 27    2270        STA BASH
60AD- B9 02 63 2280        LDA TBLYL,Y
60B0- 85 26    2290        STA BASL
               2300 *GET OFFSET
60B2- BC 42 61 2310        LDY OFFTBL,X
60B5- 84 10    2320        STY OFFSET
               2330 *GET BITMASK
60B7- 98       2340        TYA
60B8- 0A       2350        ASL          MULTIPLY
60B9- 0A       2360        ASL          OFFSET
60BA- 0A       2370        ASL          BY 8
60BB- 38       2380        SEC
60BC- E5 10    2390        SBC OFFSET
60BE- 85 30    2400        STA TEMP     7*OFFSET
60C0- 8A       2410        TXA
60C1- E5 30    2420        SBC TEMP     XPOS - 7*OFFSET
60C3- AA       2430        TAX
60C4- BD 3B 61 2440        LDA MASKTBL,X
60C7- 60       2450        RTS
               2460 BOOKKEEPING
60C8- E6 0B    2470        INC COUNTR   COUNT NUMBER OF
60CA- A5 0B    2480        LDA COUNTR   DOTS DRAWN SO FAR
60CC- C9 0F    2490        CMP #NDOTS   ALL DOTS DONE?
60CE- F0 1A    2500        BEQ .1       IF SO, START OVER
60D0- 18       2510        CLC
60D1- A5 0C    2520        LDA PNTR     POINT
60D3- 69 06    2530        ADC #$06     TO
60D5- 85 0C    2540        STA PNTR     DATA
60D7- A5 0D    2550        LDA PNTR+1   FOR
60D9- 69 00    2560        ADC #$00     NEXT
60DB- 85 0D    2570        STA PNTR+1   DOT
60DD- AD 00 C0 2580        LDA $C000    KEYPRESS?
60E0- 10 1C    2590        BPL .2       IF NOT, RETURN
60E2- AD 10 C0 2600        LDA $C010    CLEAR KEYBOARD STROBE
60E5- A9 01    2610        LDA #$01
60E7- 85 07    2620        STA ENDFLG   SET EXIT FLAG
60E9- 60       2630        RTS
60EA- 20 34 60 2640 .1     JSR INIT.PNTR
```

```
60ED- E6 0E    2650         INC CNTR     NUMBER OF CYCLES
60EF- A5 0E    2660         LDA CNTR
60F1- 85 00    2670         STA FLAG     SET TO NONZERO
60F3- C9 E1    2680         CMP #$E1     BACK TO ORIGINAL POSITION?
60F5- D0 07    2690         BNE .2       IF NOT
60F7- 20 0C FD 2700         JSR $FD0C    WAIT FOR KEYPRESS
60FA- A9 01    2710         LDA #$01
60FC- 85 0E    2720         STA CNTR     RESET
60FE- 60       2730 .2      RTS
               2740 FILL.TABLES
               2750 *LOAD OFFTBL
60FF- 18       2760         CLC
6100- A9 00    2770         LDA #$00     INITIAL VALUE TO TABLE
6102- A0 00    2780         LDY #$00     INDEX TO TABLE
6104- A2 06    2790 .1      LDX #$06
6106- 99 42 61 2800 .2      STA OFFTBL,Y
6109- C8       2810         INY
610A- F0 07    2820         BEQ .3       OFFTBL HOLDS 256 NUMBERS
610C- CA       2830         DEX
610D- 10 F7    2840         BPL .2       UNTIL 7 NUMBERS STORED
610F- 69 01    2850         ADC #$01     INCREASE NO TO BE STORED
6111- D0 F1    2860         BNE .1       ALWAYS
               2870 *LOAD TBLYL AND TBLYH
6113- A9 40    2880 .3      LDA #$40     DESIGNATE HIGH
6115- 85 E6    2890         STA HPAGE     RES PAGE 2
6117- A9 00    2900         LDA #$00     START AT TOP
6119- 85 09    2910         STA LINNUM    OF SCREEN
611B- 85 0A    2920         STA INDX     INDEX TO TABLE STORAGE
611D- A0 00    2930 .4      LDY #$00     HORIZONTAL HIGH BYTE
611F- A2 00    2940         LDX #$00     HORIZONTAL LOW BYTE
6121- 20 11 F4 2950         JSR HPOSN
6124- A4 0A    2960         LDY INDX     TABLE INDEX
6126- A5 26    2970         LDA BASL     BASE ADDRESS LOW BYTE
6128- 99 02 63 2980         STA TBLYL,Y
612B- A5 27    2990         LDA BASH     BASE ADDRESS HIGH BYTE
612D- 99 42 62 3000         STA TBLYH,Y
6130- E6 0A    3010         INC INDX
6132- E6 09    3020         INC LINNUM   DOWN ONE LINE
6134- A5 09    3030         LDA LINNUM   VERTICAL POSITION
6136- C9 C0    3040         CMP #$C0     BOTTOM OF SCREEN?
6138- D0 E3    3050         BNE .4       IF NOT
```

```
613A- 60       3060          RTS           DONE; EXIT
               3070 MASKTBL
613B- 01 02 04
613E- 08 10 20
6141- 40       3080          .DA #$01,#$02,#$04,#$08,#$10,#$20,#$40
6142-          3090 OFFTBL  .BS $100
6242-          3100 TBLYH   .BS $C0
6302-          3110 TBLYL   .BS $C0
63C2- 8A 63 01
63C5- 02 00 00 3120 DATA0   .DA #$8A,#$63,#$01,#$02,#$00,#$00
63C8- 8A 62 FE
63CB- 01 00 00 3130 DATA1   .DA #$8A,#$62,#$FE,#$01,#$00,#$00
63CE- 8A 61 FE
63D1- 02 00 00 3140 DATA2   .DA #$8A,#$61,#$FE,#$02,#$00,#$00
63D4- 8A 60 02
63D7- 01 00 00 3150 DATA3   .DA #$8A,#$60,#$02,#$01,#$00,#$00
63DA- 8A 5F FF
63DD- 02 00 00 3160 DATA4   .DA #$8A,#$5F,#$FF,#$02,#$00,#$00
63E0- 8B 5E FF
63E3- 01 00 00 3170 DATA5   .DA #$8B,#$5E,#$FF,#$01,#$00,#$00
63E6- 8C 5D 02
63E9- 02 00 00 3180 DATA6   .DA #$8C,#$5D,#$02,#$02,#$00,#$00
63EC- 8D 5E 01
63EF- 01 00 00 3190 DATA7   .DA #$8D,#$5E,#$01,#$01,#$00,#$00
63F2- 8E 5F FF
63F5- FE 00 00 3200 DATA8   .DA #$8E,#$5F,#$FF,#$FE,#$00,#$00
63F8- 8E 60 02
63FB- FF 00 00 3210 DATA9   .DA #$8E,#$60,#$02,#$FF,#$00,#$00
63FE- 8E 61 FE
6401- FE 00 00 3220 DATA10  .DA #$8E,#$61,#$FE,#$FE,#$00,#$00
6404- 8E 62 FE
6407- FF 00 00 3230 DATA11  .DA #$8E,#$62,#$FE,#$FF,#$00,#$00
640A- 8E 63 01
640D- FE 00 00 3240 DATA12  .DA #$8E,#$63,#$01,#$FE,#$00,#$00
6410- 8B 61 FF
6413- FF 00 00 3250 DATA13  .DA #$8B,#$61,#$FF,#$FF,#$00,#$00
6416- 8C 61 02
6419- FE 00 00 3260 DATA14  .DA #$8C,#$61,#$02,#$FE,#$00,#$00
641C- 8D 61 01
641F- FF 00 00 3270 DATA15  .DA #$8D,#$61,#$01,#$FF,#$00,#$00
```

```
SYMBOL TABLE

0027- BASH
0026- BASL
60C8- BOOKKEEPING .01=60EA, .02=60FE
000E- CNTR
6041- COPY.DATA.IN .01=6043
604C- COPY.DATA.OUT .01=604E
000B- COUNTR
0001- DATA
63C2- DATA0
63C8- DATA1
63FE- DATA10
6404- DATA11
640A- DATA12
6410- DATA13
6416- DATA14
641C- DATA15
63CE- DATA2
63D4- DATA3
63DA- DATA4
63E0- DATA5
63E6- DATA6
63EC- DATA7
63F2- DATA8
63F8- DATA9
0003- DLX
0004- DLY
609C- DRAW
0007- ENDFLG
608C- ERASE .01=609B
602A- EXIT
60FF- FILL.TABLES .01=6104, .02=6106, .03=6113, .04=611D
0000- FLAG
F3D8- HGR2
FC58- HOME
00E6- HPAGE
F411- HPOSN
60A8- HPOSN1
6057- INC.POSITION .01=6068, .02=6071, .03=6082, .04=608B
000A- INDX
```

```
6034- INIT.PNTR
0009- LINNUM
613B- MASKTBL
000F- NDOTS
0010- OFFSET
6142- OFFTBL
0005- OLDX
0006- OLDY
C054- PAGE1
000C- PNTR
6011- REPT
6242- TBLYH
6302- TBLYL
0030- TEMP
C051- TEXT
0090- XHI
0020- XLO
0001- XPOS
0091- YHI
0021- YLO
0002- YPOS
```

NOTES AND SUGGESTIONS

1. Note the process through which the tables are filled. OFFTBL receives seven 0s, then seven 1s, then seven 2s, etc., until it contains 256 numbers. The entries for TBLYL and TBLYH can be calculated in several ways. Here we are taking advantage of the HPOSN subroutine to calculate the address of the leftmost byte of each high-resolution screen line. HPOSN stores the address in BASL, BASH ($26, $27), so after each call to HPOSN, the contents of BASL and BASH are copied into TBLYL and TBLYH, respectively.
2. More elaborate images can be animated. You can map out an image on graph paper, and assign initial values of DLY and DLY to each point. Then enlarge the data set (presently DATA0 through DATA15), and set NDOTS equal to the number of dots in the image.
3. What happens if the bit pattern is animated across an existing graphics image? Work through the bitmasking by hand, then check your answer by trying the program.

4. With access to the address tables TBLYL and TBLYH, the addressing structure of the graphics screen is not so cumbersome. Write an alternative to HCLR, a subroutine that clears the screen from top to bottam, or from left to right. Or, write a subroutine that copies an image from graphics page 1 to graphics page 2, filling page 2 from top to bottom.

CHAPTER 12

GAME DEVELOPMENT

In this chapter we will describe techniques of animating graphics images. We will use a video game as the context for this discussion, and will develop a working game as we progress. The development of a complete game would require an entire book by itself; so we will provide an elementary game, which can be adapted and expanded as you like.

Even this simplified game program will be rather long. It is, in fact, the longest example of this book. When approaching such a large task, we can minimize later frustration if we plan well at the outset. In this case that includes making decisions regarding the game activities to be included, and providing for expansion in case that is desired at a later date.

OUTLINE AND CONTROL LOOP

This will be a traditional "shoot-em-up" game. We will have a "gremlin" run across the top of the screen. A "defender" will be positioned at the bottom. By pressing the left- or right-arrow keys, the game player can move the defender in the corresponding direction. Pressing the "/" (slash) key will cause the defender to stop. If the space bar is pressed, a missile will be fired upwards. The program will note whether the missile hits the gremlin or not. To provide an incentive for accuracy, each miss will result in the partial construction of a barricade, or shield, which protects the gremlin. (The defender's missiles cannot penetrate this shield.) Each time the gremlin is hit the barricades will be partially removed. The game will end if the barricade reaches across the screen (if misses − hits = 7).

That's it. The program will not keep score nor display it. The gremlin will not fire on the defender. We provide no explosive sounds or displays if the gremlin is hit. Those, and other enhancements, are left to the reader. Suggestions will be made throughout the chapter.

```
CONTROLLER

JSR GREMLIN
JSR KEYBOARD
JSR DEFENDER
JSR MISSILES
JSR BARRICADES
JSR GREMLIN
JSR MISSILES
LDA #$60
JSR WAIT
BIT BRKD
BPL A
RTS
```

Above is the main control loop for the program, which follows the outline of the game as suggested. We have identified the main components of the program as subroutines, and call them in sequence. We will briefly outline the function of each of the subroutines here, then discuss them in detail.

GREMLIN. This subroutine will display the gremlin on the graphics screen. On each call, the subroutine will replace the previous image with one further to the right. When the gremlin reaches the far right of the screen, it will be restarted at the left.

DEFENDER. Draw the defender in an appropriate position: further left, further right, or in the same position as before. If the defender has reached the far left or far right screen positions, have it stop there.

KEYBOARD. Here we learn the wishes of the game player. The left-arrow key, the right-arrow key, the "/" key, and the space bar are recognized and used to control movement and firing activities.

MISSILE. Draw a missile along an upward path. If the missile bumps into anything (barricade, gremlin), take appropriate action. If missile is a miss, increase the size of the barricade.

BARRICADE. Draw the barricades on the screen. These will always be at the same vertical level. The width of the barricades will vary as the game progresses.

Miscellaneous. A pause (lines 1550,1560) is built into the main control loop. Without this pause, the action would be too fast to perceive. If more images were being drawn, the length of the pause could be decreased to maintain reasonable animation speed.

The GREMLIN subroutine is called twice by the control loop. This causes the gremlin to move twice as fast as the defender. It is easy to tamper with the relative speeds of the two by changing the frequency of the subroutine calls. In the same manner it is easy to control the speed of the missiles.

The control loop also provides for an exit from the game when the barricades extend across the screen. At this point the variable BRKD will have the value $80. BIT BRKD (line 1570) will result in the N-flag being set and the Z-flag being clear. The test BPL A (line 1580) will fail, and the program will end.

Note that additional subroutines can be called from this control loop. You might add more gremlins and other creatures, or a subroutine that causes the creatures to fire at the defender. A routine to keep score and to display the score would also be useful. With the control loop determined, we will now consider each of the subroutines.

You may notice that many of the variables were defined at page zero locations that are normally reserved for use by Applesoft. That does not present a problem here since the program is not intended to be called as a subroutine from an Applesoft program. Further, the program makes use of only one Applesoft subroutine (HGR2, to display and clear graphics page 2). While that subroutine does use page zero location $1C, it does so before the GREMLIN program assigns a value there.

Gremlin

If you have worked with Apple graphics before you know that there are several ways to generate graphic images. In BASIC the HPLOT, HPLOT TO, DRAW, and XDRAW commands provide for dots, lines, and shapes. We could access any of these from an assembly language program, but there is a better, faster way to generate the images we want.

Display Technique

The Apple graphics display is a bit-mapped raster screen. The display screen shows individual dots (pixels) turned ON or OFF, depending on whether corresponding bits are ON or OFF in the graphics page of memory. As a result, the screen display shows the data that is stored in the graphics page. To quickly display an image on the screen we will copy the corresponding data from a prepared data table to the graphics page. By controlling the destination addresses, we can have the image move around on the display screen.

Big Pattern

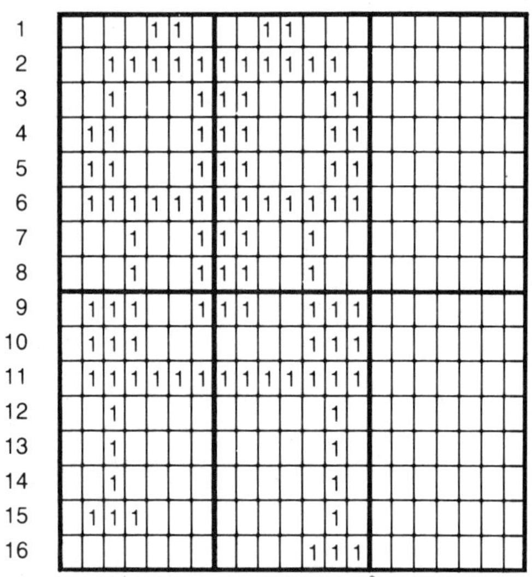

Row	Decimal			Hexadecimal		
1	48	12	0	$30	$0C	$00
2	124	63	0	$7C	$3F	$00
3	68	35	0	$44	$23	$00
4	70	99	0	$46	$63	$00
5	70	99	0	$46	$63	$00
6	126	127	0	$7E	$7F	$00
7	120	31	0	$78	$1F	$00
8	72	19	0	$48	$13	$00
9	78	115	0	$4E	$73	$00
10	14	112	0	$0E	$70	$00
11	126	127	0	$7E	$7F	$00
12	4	32	0	$04	$20	$00
13	4	32	0	$04	$20	$00
14	4	32	0	$04	$20	$00
15	14	32	0	$0E	$20	$00
16	0	112	0	$00	$70	$00

FIGURE 12.1

Figure 12.1 shows one of the bit patterns we will be using for the gremlin. At the right of the figure we show the corresponding data. Note that only seven bits of each byte are displayed. The eighth is a color bit. While we conventionally identify bit positions right-to-left, they are displayed left-to-right on the graphics screen.

You may note that three bytes are provided for the gremlin bit pattern, but only two are used. To see why, consider the movement of the gremlin. The leftmost edge of the bit pattern is shown in the second bit of the leftmost bytes. As the gremlin is moved to the right, this leftmost bit will progress through the third, fourth, fifth, sixth, and seventh bits of the left bytes, then to the first, second, . . . bit of the middle bytes, etc.

We will store data for seven complete gremlins and refer to each as a "frame." Each frame will be three bytes wide and will show the gremlin to be one bit further to the right than in the previous frame. These seven frames are shown in Figures 12.1 through 12.7. If the frames were copied successively into the same block (three bytes wide, sixteen bytes high) of the graphics screen, the gremlin would appear to walk to the right within this block. When the sequence of seven frames is completed, the cycle can be repeated with another block

Bit Pattern

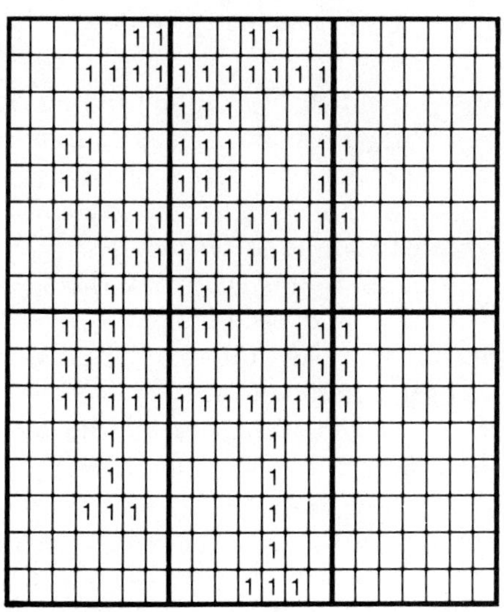

	Decimal			Hexadecimal		
1	96	24	0	$60	$18	$00
2	120	127	0	$78	$7F	$00
3	8	71	0	$08	$47	$00
4	12	71	1	$0C	$47	$01
5	12	71	1	$0C	$47	$01
6	124	127	1	$7C	$7F	$01
7	112	63	0	$70	$3F	$00
8	16	39	0	$10	$27	$00
9	28	103	1	$1C	$67	$01
10	28	96	1	$1C	$60	$01
11	124	127	1	$7C	$7F	$01
12	16	16	0	$10	$10	$00
13	16	16	0	$10	$10	$00
14	56	16	0	$38	$10	$00
15	0	16	0	$00	$10	$00
16	0	56	0	$00	$38	$00

FIGURE 12.2

Bit Pattern

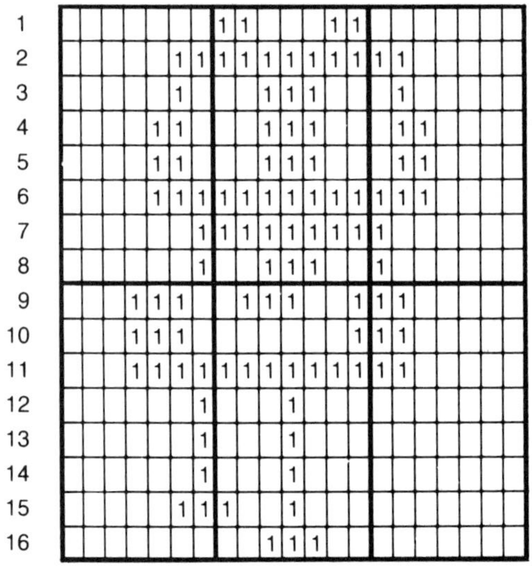

Row	Decimal			Hexadecimal		
1	64	49	0	$40	$31	$00
2	112	127	1	$70	$7F	$00
3	16	14	1	$10	$0E	$01
4	24	14	3	$18	$0E	$03
5	24	14	3	$18	$0E	$03
6	120	127	3	$78	$7F	$03
7	96	127	0	$60	$7F	$00
8	32	78	0	$20	$4E	$00
9	56	78	3	$38	$4E	$03
10	56	64	3	$38	$40	$03
11	120	127	3	$78	$7F	$03
12	64	8	0	$40	$08	$00
13	64	8	0	$40	$08	$00
14	64	8	0	$40	$08	$00
15	96	9	0	$60	$09	$00
16	0	28	0	$00	$1C	$00

FIGURE 12.3

(three bytes wide, sixteen bytes high) which begins one byte further to the right on the graphics screen.

Since five of the seven frames require three bytes to contain the image, it is simpler to make the other two frames three bytes wide than to handle them as special cases. Further, if each of the seven frames is consecutively copied into the same block of graphics memory, we do not have to take any action to erase an image when a new one is drawn; that is done automatically.

The seven frames (numbered 0–6) are stored in the data tables DATG1 and DATG2. DATG1 contains the data for the upper half of each frame while DATG2 contains the data for the lower half. The data is broken into two parts because of the inconvenient addressing structure of the graphics page.

The graphics screen is addressed in three segments (upper, middle, lower). Each segment has eight rows of forty blocks. Each block contains eight bytes. The addressing of bytes from left to right is easy: just add 1 to move one byte to the right. The addressing of bytes within an eight-byte block is also easy: add $400 (1024) to the address to move one byte down the screen. The addressing of vertically adjacent bytes in different blocks or in different segments is less convenient.

Bit Pattern

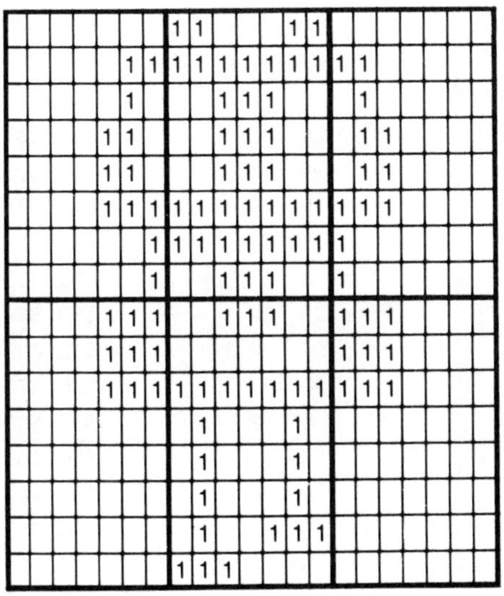

	Decimal			Hexadecimal		
1	0	99	0	$00	$63	$00
2	96	127	3	$60	$7F	$03
3	32	28	2	$20	$2C	$02
4	48	28	6	$30	$2C	$06
5	48	28	6	$30	$2C	$06
6	112	127	7	$70	$7F	$07
7	64	127	1	$40	$7F	$01
8	64	28	1	$40	$2C	$01
9	112	28	7	$70	$2C	$07
10	112	0	7	$70	$00	$07
11	112	127	7	$70	$7F	$07
12	0	34	0	$00	$22	$00
13	0	34	0	$00	$22	$00
14	0	34	0	$00	$22	$00
15	0	114	0	$00	$72	$00
16	0	7	0	$00	$07	$00

FIGURE 12.4

We will simplify addressing by storing the data for each frame of the gremlin in two parts. Each part will fit into a rectangular area that is three bytes wide and eight bytes high. When we wish to display a frame, we will do so by copying data into three adjacent (left-to-right) bytes, then move down one raster line (one byte lower on the screen) and copy three more bytes. If the first byte stored goes into the top of a screen block, we can copy twenty-four bytes very easily into three side-by-side screen blocks. With the top half of the image done we can turn to the bottom half, treating it in essentially the same way. (Actually it is easier to copy both halves concurrently, as you will soon see.)

Variables

The GREMLIN subroutine makes use of several variables. We will describe the function of each of them before discussing the operation of the subroutine.

BASG1 and BASG1 + 1 identify the base address of a raster line on the graphics screen. BASG1 contains the low-order byte of the address of the left-most byte of the raster line; BASG1 + 1 contains the high-order byte of the address.

Bit Pattern

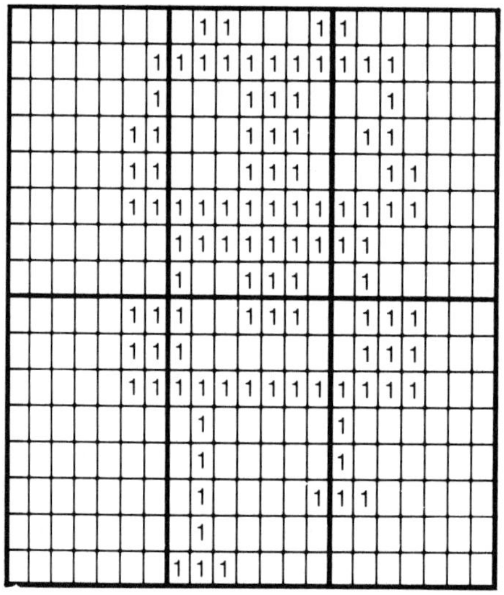

	Decimal			Hexadecimal		
1	0	70	1	$00	$46	$01
2	64	127	7	$40	$7F	$07
3	64	56	4	$40	$38	$04
4	96	56	12	$60	$38	$0C
5	96	56	12	$60	$38	$0C
6	96	127	15	$60	$7F	$0F
7	0	127	3	$00	$7F	$03
8	0	57	2	$00	$39	$02
9	96	57	14	$60	$39	$0E
10	96	0	14	$96	$00	$0E
11	96	127	15	$60	$7F	$0F
12	0	2	1	$00	$02	$01
13	0	2	1	$00	$02	$01
14	0	66	3	$00	$42	$03
15	0	2	0	$00	$02	$00
16	0	7	0	$00	$07	$00

FIGURE 12.5

We will use this address to position the upper half of the gremlin. BASG2, BASG2 + 1 serve the same purpose for the lower half of the gremlin.

As mentioned earlier, DATG1 and DATG2 are the addresses of the tables of data for the upper and lower halves of the gremlin. When we are ready to copy the data to the graphics screen we will arrange that the X-register will be an index to the data tables and the Y-register will index the raster line to identify which byte of memory is to receive the data. Then the commands

```
LDA DATG1,X
STA (BASG1),Y
LDA DATG2,X
STA (BASG2),Y
```

will copy the data.

We will be copying data into three consecutive eight-byte blocks in the graphics page. In doing so, we can increment the Y-register to indicate which block is being referenced. HORIZG will remember the index to the leftmost block. WIDTH identifies the width (three bytes) of the image, while HEIGHT

Bit Pattern

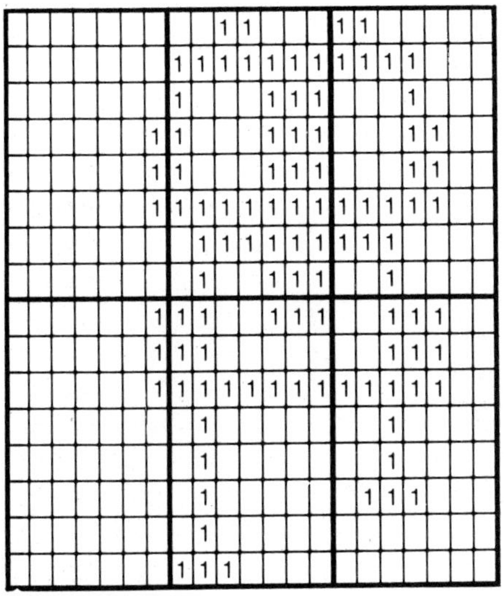

	Decimal	Hexadecimal
1	0 12 3	$00 $0C $03
2	0 127 15	$00 $7F $0F
3	0 113 8	$00 $71 $08
4	64 113 24	$40 $71 $18
5	64 113 24	$40 $71 $18
6	64 127 31	$40 $7F $1F
7	0 126 7	$00 $7E $07
8	0 114 4	$00 $72 $04
9	64 115 28	$40 $73 $1C
10	64 3 28	$40 $03 $1C
11	64 127 31	$40 $7F $1F
12	0 2 4	$00 $02 $04
13	0 2 4	$00 $02 $04
14	0 2 14	$00 $02 $0E
15	0 1 0	$00 $01 $00
16	0 7 0	$00 $07 $00

FIGURE 12.6

identifies the height (eight bytes) of each of the upper and lower halves of the gremlin.

The other variable that this subroutine uses is FRMNUMG, which is the number (0–6) of the frame that is being displayed. FRMNUMG is used to obtain the index to the data tables DATG1 and DATG2.

The Operation of the Subroutine

As the listing of Figure 12.7 shows, we first define the screen base addresses BASG1+1 and BASG2+1 (lines 2360–2380). These are changed by the subroutine and must be reset at each re-entry. BASG1 and BASG2 are never changed, and are set during initialization (lines 1320, 1390, 1400).

Next (lines 2390, 2400) we identify the height of each half of the gremlin to be eight bytes.

In copying the data from DATG1 and DATG2 to the graphics page we will copy twenty-four bytes from DATG1 and twenty-four bytes from DATG2 each time we draw one complete frame of the gremlin image. The X-register will

Bit Pattern

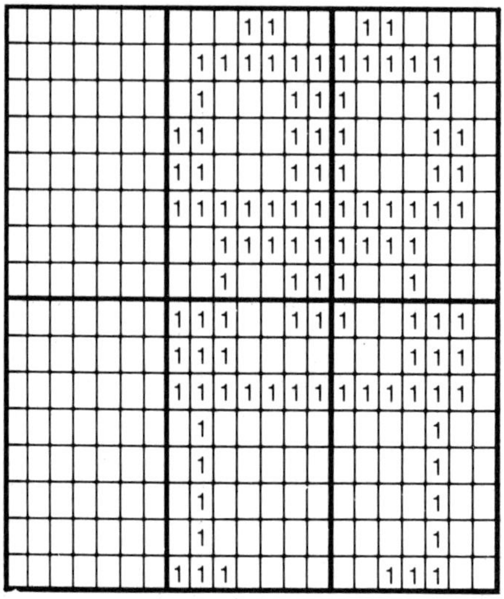

	Decimal	Hexadecimal
1	0 24 6	$00 $18 $06
2	0 126 31	$00 $7E $1F
3	0 98 17	$00 $62 $11
4	0 99 49	$00 $63 $31
5	0 99 49	$00 $63 $31
6	0 127 63	$00 $7F $3F
7	0 127 15	$00 $7C $0F
8	0 100 9	$00 $64 $09
9	0 103 57	$00 $67 $39
10	0 7 56	$00 $07 $38
11	0 127 63	$00 $7F $3F
12	0 2 16	$00 $02 $10
13	0 2 16	$00 $02 $10
14	0 2 16	$00 $02 $10
15	0 2 16	$00 $02 $10
16	0 7 56	$00 $07 $39

FIGURE 12.7

serve as the index to the data tables. We can increment the X-register (INX) through the twenty-four bytes as we are copying data, but each time we begin a new frame, we must calculate (or remember) the starting index.

While it is slightly faster (and certainly easier) to define an additional variable to remember this index, we will calculate it from our knowledge of the value of FRMNUMG. (Remember, our objective is to illustrate the methods discussed in previous chapters, even if they are occasionally not the best programming method.)

Since each frame requires twenty-four bytes from each of the two data tables DATG1 and DATG2, we can obtain the value of the starting index for a frame by multiplying FRMNUMG by 24 ($18). We accomplish this in lines 2430–2510. First we load the accumulator with the value of FRMNUMG. ASL will multiply this number by 2, so three consecutive ASLs will multiply FRMNUMG by 8. This result is stored in TEMP (line 2470) and the number in the accumulator receives one more ASL (line 2480). The accumulator now contains FRMNUMG times 16 and TEMP contains FRMNUMG times 8. Their sum (lines 2490, 2500) is the desired index, which is transferred to the X-register (line 2510).

The Copy Routine

The program now enters a pair of nested loops that will perform the actual copying of data. The outer loop (lines 2530–2720) is run eight times (each half of the gremlin is eight bytes high). On each pass the inner loop (lines 2560–2630) is executed three times (the gremlin is three bytes wide).

In lines 2530 and 2540 the width of the gremlin is stated. The Y-register receives the index to the leftmost screen position that will receive data (line 2550) and the data transfer begins (lines 2560–2590). One byte is copied from the data table for the upper half of the gremlin [LDA DATG1,X] and stored in the graphics page [STA (BASG1),Y] and one byte is copied from the data table for the lower half of the gremlin [LDA DATG2,X] and stored in the graphics page [STA (BASG2),Y]. With this transfer completed, the data table index is incremented (line 2600) and the graphics index is incremented (line 2610). The program is now ready to read the next data entry and store it one byte to the right of the last. This cycle is run three times due to the width of the image (lines 2620, 2630). This completes the inner loop.

It is necessary to reset the screen base addresses BASG1, BASG1 + 1 and BASG2, BASG2 + 1 and copy data into the raster line that is directly under the one just completed. To move down one raster line within a block, it is necessary to add $400 (1024) to the screen address. That affects only the high byte of the addresses (BASG1 + 1 and BASG2 + 1). Lines 2640–2700 perform this addition. Lines 2710, 2720 complete the outer loop of the copy subroutine.

A little bookkeeping must be done before returning from this subroutine. First, we must increment FRMNUMG in order that the next image is drawn further to the right (line 2730). Then we must check to see whether FRMNUMG moved past the last frame (FRMNUMG should vary from 0 through 6). If it has, we will increment HORIZG (to continue rightward movement) and reset FRMNUMG to 0 (lines 2770–2780). Finally the program determines whether the gremlin has reached the right side of the screen (lines 2810, 2820). If the gremlin has reached the right side of the screen, it is erased and restarted at the left (lines 2830–2850). Otherwise the subroutine is ended (lines 2820, 2860).

ERASE.G

Since arrival at the right side of the display screen requires the erasure of the gremlin image, we will refer you to ERASE.G at this time. This subroutine behaves very much like GREMLIN, and will not be discussed in as much detail. In fact we will point out only the differences.

Erasure is accomplished by copying zeros into graphics page memory locations. As a result, we do not need FRMNUMG, a data table, or an index to a data table. Further, there is no need to increment HORIZG (no rightward movement) or check to see if the image has reached the right screen boundary.

You may note that the image that is to be erased is only two bytes wide (the last frame drawn was number 6). The width of three is maintained, since this subroutine is called from elsewhere in the program where the width of the image to be erased is likely to be three.

NOTES AND SUGGESTIONS

This subroutine provided for only horizontal movement. If you would like to have vertical (or diagonal) movement as well, the screen addressing becomes a little more troublesome. It is then best to provide a complete screen base address table, as was done in Chapter 11. Then, with the vertical screen coordinate in the X-register, the base address can be read from a low-order address table LOBAS (192 bytes) and a high-order address table HIBAS (another 192 bytes) as follows:

```
LDA LOBAS,X
STA BASG1
LDA HIBAS,X
STA BASG1+1
```

This must be done every time a byte of data is transferred from a data table to the graphics page of memory.

DEFENDER

This subroutine is very similar to GREMLIN. It puts the "defender" on the bottom of the graphics display screen, arranging for movement to the left or right as instructed from the keyboard. It is the movement to the right or left that primarily distinguishes DEFENDER from GREMLIN.

Before considering the subroutine, note the design of the defender image. As in the case of the gremlin, there are seven frames, to provide for movement through seven positions before recycling. The seven frames, with corresponding data, are given in Figures 12.8–12.14. Note that the frames are still three bytes wide, but are shorter (six bytes high) than those for the gremlin. These seven frames of data are stored in the data table DATAD.

	Bit Pattern																					Decimal			Hexadecimal		
1								1														0	1	0	$00	$01	$00
2								1														0	1	0	$00	$01	$00
3								1														0	1	0	$00	$01	$00
4		1	1					1					1	1								6	97	0	$00	$61	$00
5		1	1	1	1	1	1	1	1	1	1	1	1	1								126	127	0	$7E	$7F	$00
6		1	1	1	1	1	1	1	1	1	1	1	1	1								126	127	0	$7E	$7F	$00

FIGURE 12.8

	Bit Pattern																					Decimal			Hexadecimal		
1									1													0	2	0	$00	$02	$00
2									1													0	2	0	$00	$02	$00
3									1													0	2	0	$00	$02	$00
4			1	1					1					1	1							12	66	1	$0C	$42	$01
5			1	1	1	1	1	1	1	1	1	1	1	1	1							124	127	1	$7C	$7F	$01
6			1	1	1	1	1	1	1	1	1	1	1	1	1							124	127	1	$7C	$7F	$01

FIGURE 12.9

	Bit Pattern																					Decimal			Hexadecimal		
1										1												0	4	0	$00	$04	$00
2										1												0	4	0	$00	$04	$00
3										1												0	4	0	$00	$04	$00
4				1	1					1					1	1						24	4	3	$18	$04	$03
5				1	1	1	1	1	1	1	1	1	1	1	1	1						120	127	3	$78	$7F	$03
6				1	1	1	1	1	1	1	1	1	1	1	1	1						120	127	3	$78	$7F	$03

FIGURE 12.10

Bit Pattern

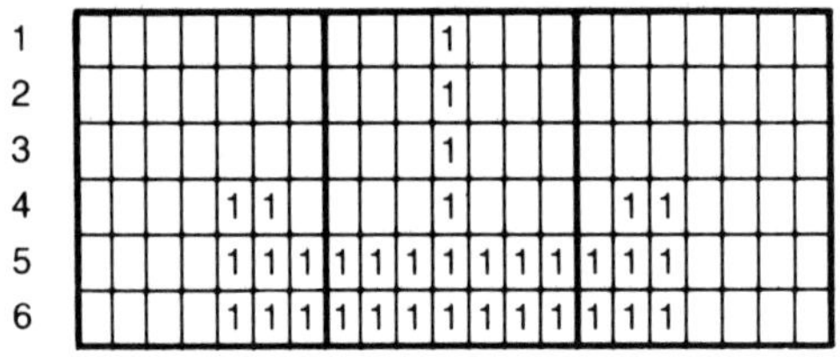

	Decimal			Hexadecimal		
1	0	8	0	$00	$08	$00
2	0	8	0	$00	$08	$00
3	0	8	0	$00	$08	$00
4	48	8	6	$30	$08	$06
5	112	127	7	$70	$7F	$07
6	112	127	7	$70	$7F	$07

FIGURE 12.11

Bit Pattern

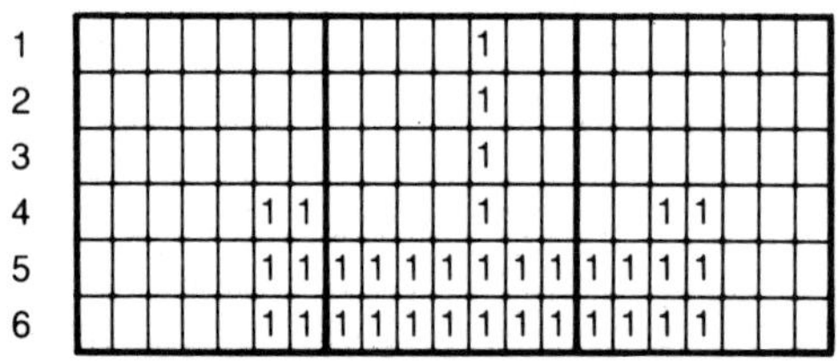

	Decimal			Hexadecimal		
1	0	16	0	$00	$10	$00
2	0	16	0	$00	$10	$00
3	0	16	0	$00	$10	$00
4	96	16	12	$60	$10	$0C
5	96	127	15	$60	$7F	$0F
6	96	127	15	$60	$7F	$0F

FIGURE 12.12

Bit Pattern

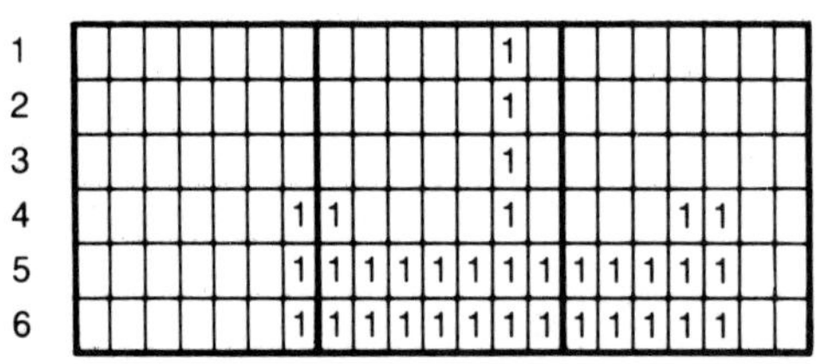

	Decimal			Hexadecimal		
1	0	64	0	$00	$40	$00
2	0	64	0	$00	$40	$00
3	0	64	0	$00	$40	$00
4	6	67	58	$00	$43	$30
5	0	127	63	$00	$7F	$3F
6	0	127	63	$00	$7F	$3F

FIGURE 12.13

Bit Pattern

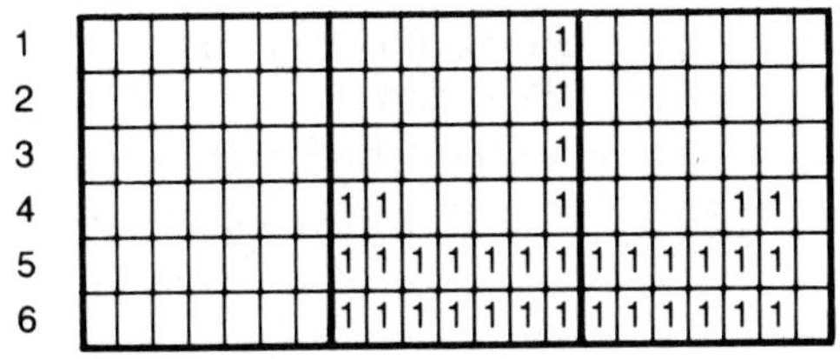

Row	Decimal	Hexadecimal
1	0 64 0	$00 $40 $00
2	0 64 0	$00 $40 $00
3	0 64 0	$00 $40 $00
4	6 67 58	$00 $43 $30
5	0 127 63	$00 $7F $3F
6	0 127 63	$00 $7F $3F

FIGURE 12.14

Direction of Movement

The variable DIR identifies the direction of movement of the defender. DIR is assigned a value of −1 ($FF) or 1 to direct movement to the left or to the right, and is given a value of 0 if the defender is to remain in one location without moving. The value of DIR is assigned in the KEYBOARD subroutine, which is discussed later.

The opening commands of DEFENDER (lines 1620–1660) use the value of DIR to branch to the DRAW component of the routine if the defender is stopped (DIR = 0) or to the LEFT component if the defender should be moving to the left (DIR = $FF). If DIR is positive, each of the branch tests will fail, and control of the program will fall through to line 1680, which is the start of the MOVE RIGHT component of the program.

The MOVE RIGHT part of the subroutine (lines 1680–1850) and the MOVE LEFT component (lines 1880–2000) are each preliminary to the DRAW component. These two movement routines are similar to one another, and serve as bookkeeping components. They check to see if the defender is at the screen boundary, and adjust the frame and byte index counters. Because of their similarities, we will discuss only the MOVE LEFT component, and will leave the details of MOVE RIGHT to the reader.

HORIZD serves the same function as HORIZG did in the GREMLIN subroutine. It remembers the byte index that identifies the horizontal position of the defender on the graphics screen. In line 1880 and 1890 the value of HORIZD is checked to see if the defender has reached the leftmost byte (HORIZD = 0). If it has not, further movement is permitted (line 1900).

If the defender has reached the leftmost byte, it can still continue to move left until FRMNUMD reaches 0. Lines 1910, 1920 test for this condition. If the defender has reached this leftmost position, DIR is set to 0 (to cause the defender to stop) and control is transferred to the DRAW routine.

If the defender is in fact moving to the left, lines 1960–2000 decrement FRMNUMD. If it has passed the last frame (FRMNUMD varies from 0–6) and is negative, then FRMNUMD is reset to 6 and HORIZD is decreased by 1 to continue the leftward movement. Program control then passes to DRAW.

DRAW

This routine is very similar to the heart of the GREMLIN subroutine. Its primary task is to copy the data that represents the defender from a data table (DATAD) to the graphics screen.

Lines 2020, 2030 set the screen base address to $4350. (BASD never changes, and was set at initialization.) Lines 2040, 2050 set the height of the image to 6.

Next, FRMNUMD is used to calculate the starting index to the data table. Since the defender is three bytes wide and six bytes high, each frame requires eighteen bytes of data. It follows that the starting index to each frame can be obtained by multiplying FRMNUMD by 18. That is accomplished in lines 2080–2160.

The nested loops of lines 2180–2320 are similar to those used in the GREMLIN subroutine. The only difference is that the defender's height (six bytes) requires only one base address (BASD, BASD+1), while the gremlin's height (sixteen bytes) required two base addresses (BASG1, BASG1+1 and BASG2, BASG2+1).

KEYBOARD

The KEYBOARD subroutine (lines 3150–3360) uses a sequence of branches to read and interpret keyboard input. Line 3150 reads the keyboard. If a key has been pressed the value obtained will have the high bit set, and thus will be a negative number. If this is not the case, there is no need to continue; line 3160 causes a branch out of the subroutine.

The left-arrow key causes the number $FF to be stored in the variable DIR. The right-arrow key stores the number 1 in DIR, and the "/" key stores a 0 in DIR. These three numbers are used to control the defender's movements, as described earlier.

The space bar controls the contents of MFLG, which is a flag used to identify missile status. If a missile has been fired and is moving upward on the screen, the MISSILE subroutine will have set MFLG to $FF. Lines 3310, 3320 use this information to prevent the launch of a second missile.

If there is no missile activity on the screen, MFLG will be set to 0. If the space bar is then pressed, lines 3330, 3340 set MFLG = 1 to initiate the launch of a missile.

Before leaving the subroutine, line 3350 toggles the keyboard strobe. This resets the high bit of KBD to 0. It will remain 0 until a key is pressed.

MISSILES

This subroutine controls missile activity. Before considering how it functions we will outline the function of each of its variables.

Variables

MFLG is a flag that signals the type of missile activity that is taking place. It will have one of the values −1 ($FF), 0, or 1. MFLG = −1 indicates that a missile has been launched, and should be continued on an upward course. MFLG = 0 indicates no missile activity, and MFLG = 1 signals the launch of a new missile.

The missile is displayed by drawing a short vertical line segment. This is done by storing one of the numbers 1, 2, 4, 8, 16, 32, 64 in a sequence of four vertically adjacent bytes on the graphics screen. These numbers are stored in the missile data table MISL and were chosen because each will turn on exactly one bit (see Figure 12.15). The number to be used is selected by the position of the defender's artillery. Thus FRMNUMD, which identifies the frame number and the bit position of the artillery, is copied to MSLNM (missile number), the index to the missile data table MISL.

1	0	0	0	0	0	0	1
0	1	0	0	0	0	0	2
0	0	1	0	0	0	0	4
0	0	0	1	0	0	0	8
0	0	0	0	1	0	0	16
0	0	0	0	0	1	0	32
0	0	0	0	0	0	1	64

FIGURE 12.15

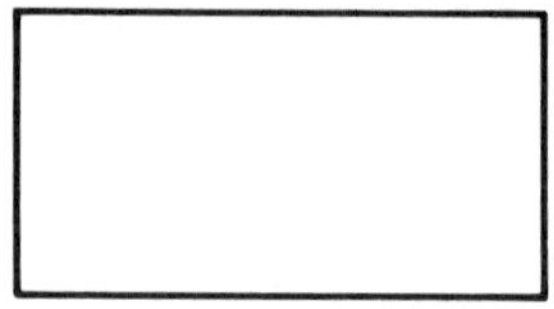

```
MISL     .DA  #1,#2,#4,#8,#16,#32,#64
```

FIGURE 12.16

As the missile moves upward, it is necessary to erase each old image as a new one is drawn. This requires different animation techniques than we have previously used, since the screen addressing structure makes the addressing of consecutive vertical bytes somewhat inconvenient. We adopt two strategies for handling this. First, the missile will be four bytes high and these bytes will be either the top four or the bottom four bytes of a graphics screen block. Second, we will use an address table to store the base addresses of the uppermost byte and the fifth byte of each row of screen blocks. Since there are twenty-four rows of screen blocks on the graphics page, we will need forty-eight addresses (two bytes each) or ninety-six bytes for the table, which we label ADDR.

As the missile moves upward, it will move from the top four bytes of one block to the lower four bytes of the next higher screen block; then to the top four bytes of that block, etc. MLEVL will remember the starting index to the ADDR table for each frame of the missile. We will use MLEVL to read two addresses from ADDR. The first will be BASMD, BASMD + 1, which is the beginning base address for the drawing of the missile in its new position. The second address will be BASME, BASME + 1, the beginning base address for the erasure of the missile from its old position.

HORIZM identifies the horizontal index that positions the missile along the raster line. As the missile moves upward, it may contact the barricades or the gremlin. If this happens, COLFLG is set to 1 to indicate that a collision has occurred. The variable HEIGHT is used again to indicate the height of the image (4 bytes).

The Operation of the Subroutine

MISSILE is the longest of the subroutines of this program. Fortunately, some of its components are very similar to parts of DEFENDER and GREMLIN. Other components perform routine bookkeeping chores.

Lines 3550–3370 read the value of MFLG and direct program control depending on its contents. If MFLG is positive lines 3580–3680 first reset MFLG to $FF to indicate that a missile is in motion, then zero the collision flag COLFLG. Next, the defender's frame number (FRMNUMD) is copied to MSLNM, which is an index to the missile table. The defender's horizontal byte counter (HORIZD) plus 1 provides the byte counter (HORIZM) for the missile. (The missile is launched from the defender's artillery, which is in the second byte of the defender's three byte width.) Finally, the initial missile level, MLEVL, is set at $50 (decimal 80). This identifies the point at which the missile is first drawn.

After lines 3580–3680 initialize the launch of a new missile, control passes to CONT, which is also used when a missile is continuing its upward path.

Lines 3700–3830 copy the base addresses for drawing and erasing the missile. These addresses are read from the ADDR table and stored in the base address pointers BASMD, BASMD+1 and BASME, BASME+1. The starting index is remembered by MLEVL. Note that after MLEVL is read, it can be decremented by 2 (each address uses two bytes) in preparation for the next call.

Lines 3850, 3860 read the missile table index and the missile screen byte index in preparation for drawing the missile. Before entering the drawing routine, MLEVL is tested. If the missile is not at the top of the screen the drawing can proceed (line 3890). If the gremlin reaches the top of the screen, it has missed the gremlin. Then the BRKD variable is adjusted, the missile flag is set to 0, and a branch is taken to erase the previously drawn missile.

BRKD

Consider the functioning of the barricade variable, BRKD. It will have one of the values 0, 1, 3, 7, 15, 31, 63, or 127, and will be copied by the BARRICADE subroutine into all forty bytes of a graphics screen raster line. If BRKD is equal to 127, the raster line will appear to be a solid line. If BRKD is 0, the raster line will be clear.

If we want to increase the width of the barricades, we will use the command sequence

```
SEC
ROL BRKD
```

This will shift all bits one position to the left, and move a 1 into the least significant bit. This is done when the missile misses the gremlin (lines 3900, 3910). If we want to decrease the width of the barricades, we will use the sequence

```
CLC
ROR BRKD
```

This will shift all bits one position to the right, discarding the least significant bit and moving a 0 into the most significant bit. This is done whenever the missile hits the gremlin (lines 4340, 4350).

DRAW

The DRAW component (lines 3960–4110) of this subroutine is very similar to the drawing components of the GREMLIN and DEFENDER subroutines. The names of the variables are slightly different, but the primary difference is the means of storing the image on the screen. Line 3980 puts the bit pattern in the accumulator. Before storing it in the graphics page of memory, line 3990 first tests to see if the corresponding bit in the graphics page is already turned on. If it is, the missile is about to collide with something (barricade or gremlin), the collision flag (COLFLG) is set (lines 4000, 4010), and a branch is taken to the ERASE routine. Otherwise lines 4030–4050 proceed to copy the missile bit pattern onto the graphics page. Lines 4060–4110 increment the screen base address and cycle back to copy the rest of the missile.

ERASE

Erasure (lines 4130–4250) is accomplished by a complementary draw (lines 4180, 4190). That is, the missile bit pattern (in the accumulator) is used to change corresponding bits from ON to OFF or from OFF to ON. Since the intent here is to turn a bit OFF, line 4160 first determines whether the bit is ON. A branch is taken around the complementary draw if the bit is already OFF (line 4170). The remainder of ERASE should look familiar to you by now.

EXIT

After the missile has been drawn in its new position and erased from its old position, control passes to the EXIT part of the MISSILE subroutine. Here the collision flag is checked (line 4280) to determine whether a collision has occurred. If so, the missile flag MFLG is set to zero so that the space bar will again be recognized by the KEYBOARD subroutine.

It is necessary to determine whether the missile has hit the gremlin or the barricades. The decision is based on the value of MLEVL. If MLEVL is less than

$30 (decimal 48) then the missile has passed by the barricades. Any collision must be with the gremlin. Control is passed to the HIT component (lines 4310–4410) which toggles the Apple speaker, erases the gremlin from its current location and restores it at the left of the screen, and removes one bit from each of the barricades.

BARRICADES

This subroutine (lines 3390–3480) is responsible for updating the barricades. This is done by copying a bit pattern into each of the bytes in one raster line on the graphics page. As described earlier, the bit pattern is stored as the variable BRKD. Its status is maintained in the MISSILE subroutine.

Since the graphics display screen is forty bytes wide, line 3390 loads the horizontal byte index (Y-register) with $28 (decimal 40). Line 3410 then stores the contents of the accumulator (BRKD) is each of the raster line pointed to by BASB, BASB + 1. The raster line base address was specified in the initialization to be $5228.

NOTES AND SUGGESTIONS

At the beginning of this chapter we noted that this game was rather primitive, but could be expanded. Try some of the following.

1. Arrange for a varied assortment of creatures instead of using the gremlin exclusively. This will require the use of an additional data set for each creature, and a means of cycling through the data sets.
2. Make the gremlin bidirectional, permitting right-to-left motion.
3. Have more than one creature on the screen at any one time. Place them at different screen levels.
4. Have the creatures fire at the defender.
5. Arrange for scorekeeping. Counting the number of hits will not be difficult. It will be more challenging to display the score on the graphics screen.

PROGRAM 12.1 Game

```
0006-           1000 HORIZD .EQ $06       SCREEN HORIZ BYTE LOCATION OF DEFENDER
0007-           1010 HORIZG .EQ $07       SCREEN HORIZ BYTE LOCATION OF GREMLIN
0008-           1020 HORIZM .EQ $08       SCREEN HORIZ BYTE LOCATION OF MISSILE
```

```
0009-           1030 FRMNUMD .EQ $09     FRAME NUMBER OF DEFENDER
000A-           1040 FRMNUMG .EQ $0A     FRAME NUMBER OF GREMLIN
000B-           1050 DIR     .EQ $0B     IDENTIFIES DIRECTION OF DEFENDER'S MOVEMENT
000C-           1060 HEIGHT  .EQ $0C     HEIGHT (# OF BYTES) OF IMAGE TO BE DRAWN
000D-           1070 WIDTH   .EQ $0D     WIDTH (# OF BYTES) OF IMAGE TO BE DRAWN
000E-           1080 TEMP    .EQ $0E     TEMPORARY STORAGE
000F-           1090 MFLG    .EQ $0F     IDENTIFIES WHETHER MISSILE IS TO BE DRAWN
0010-           1100 MSLNM   .EQ $10     MISSILE NUMBER (0 - 6)
0011-           1110 MLEVL   .EQ $11     INDEX TO BASE ADDRESS TABLE FOR MISSILES
0012-           1120 BASB    .EQ $12     BASE ADDRESS OF BARRICADES
0014-           1130 BASMD   .EQ $14     SCREEN BASE ADDRESS (UPPER) OF MISSILE
0016-           1140 BASME   .EQ $16     SCREEN BASE ADDRESS (LOWER) OF MISSILE
0018-           1150 COLFLG  .EQ $18     EXPLOSION FLAG
0019-           1160 BRKD    .EQ $19     BARRICADE BIT PATTERN
00FA-           1170 BASD    .EQ $FA     USES $FB ALSO
00FC-           1180 BASG1   .EQ $FC     USES $FD ALSO
00FE-           1190 BASG2   .EQ $FE     USES $FF ALSO
C000-           1200 KBD     .EQ $C000   READ KEYBOARD HERE
C010-           1210 STROBE  .EQ $C010   CLEARS KEYBOARD STROBE
FBDD-           1220 BELL    .EQ $FBDD   BEEP SPEAKER
FCA8-           1230 WAIT    .EQ $FCA8   MONITOR "PAUSE" ROUTINE
                1240         .OR $6000
                1250 *--------------------------------
6000- A9 00     1260 INIT    LDA #$00
6002- 85 19     1270         STA BRKD
6004- 85 07     1280         STA HORIZG
6006- 85 0F     1290         STA MFLG
6008- 85 0A     1300         STA FRMNUMG
600A- 85 09     1310         STA FRMNUMD
600C- 85 FC     1320         STA BASG1
600E- A9 01     1330         LDA #$01
6010- 85 0B     1340         STA DIR
6012- A9 52     1350         LDA #$52
6014- 85 13     1360         STA BASB+1
6016- A9 27     1370         LDA #$27
6018- 85 12     1380         STA BASB
601A- A9 80     1390         LDA #$80
601C- 85 FE     1400         STA BASG2
601E- A9 50     1410         LDA #$50
6020- 85 FA     1420         STA BASD
6022- A9 15     1430         LDA #$15
6024- 85 06     1440         STA HORIZD
```

```
6026- 20 D8 F3              JSR $F3D8    HGR2
                       *-------------------------------
                       * CONTROLLER
6029- 20 BB 60         A          JSR GREMLIN
602C- 20 41 61              JSR KEYBOARD
602F- 20 48 60              JSR DEFENDER
6032- 20 86 61              JSR MISSILES
6035- 20 6E 61              JSR BARRICADES
6038- 20 BB 60              JSR GREMLIN
603B- 20 86 61              JSR MISSILES
603E- A9 60                 LDA #$60
6040- 20 A8 FC              JSR WAIT
6043- 24 19                 BIT BRKD
6045- 10 E2                 BPL A
6047- 60                    RTS
                       *-------------------------------
                       DEFENDER
6048- A5 0B                 LDA DIR
                       * STATIONARY?
604A- F0 3E                 BEQ DRAW     IF STOPPED
                       * MOVE LEFT?
604C- 30 22                 BMI LEFT     IF MOVING LEFT
                       * MOVE RIGHT.
604E- A5 06                 LDA HORIZD   IF MOVING RIGHT
6050- C9 25                 CMP #$25     FAR RIGHT BYTE?
6052- D0 0C                 BNE MOVRT    IF NOT, THEN MOVE
6054- A5 09                 LDA FRMNUMD
6056- C9 06                 CMP #$06     LAST POSITION?
6058- D0 06                 BNE MOVRT
605A- A9 00                 LDA #$00     IF SO, STOP IT
605C- 85 0B                 STA DIR
605E- F0 2A                 BEQ DRAW     ALWAYS
                       *-------------------------------
6060- E6 09            MOVRT  INC FRMNUMD  KEEP MOVING RIGHT
6062- A5 09                 LDA FRMNUMD
6064- C9 07                 CMP #$07     PAST LAST FRAME?
6066- D0 22                 BNE DRAW       IF NOT, DRAW
6068- E6 06                 INC HORIZD   NEXT BYTE TO THE RIGHT
606A- A9 00                 LDA #$00     RESET FRMNUMD TO ZERO
606C- 85 09                 STA FRMNUMD
606E- F0 1A                 BEQ DRAW     ALWAYS
                       *-------------------------------
```

```
                1870 * MOVE LEFT
6070- A5 06     1880 LEFT   LDA HORIZD   MOVING LEFT
6072- C9 00     1890        CMP #$00     FAR LEFT BYTE?
6074- D0 0A     1900        BNE MOVLFT   IF NOT, THEN MOVE
6076- A5 09     1910        LDA FRMNUMD  LAST POSITION?
6078- D0 06     1920        BNE MOVLFT     IF NOT, THEN MOVE
607A- A9 00     1930        LDA #$00       IF LAST POSITION,
607C- 85 0B     1940        STA DIR          STOP MOVING
607E- F0 0A     1950        BEQ DRAW     ALWAYS
6080- C6 09     1960 MOVLFT DEC FRMNUMD  KEEP MOVING LEFT
6082- 10 06     1970        BPL DRAW
6084- A9 06     1980        LDA #$06     IF FRMNUMD IS NEG
6086- 85 09     1990        STA FRMNUMD    RESET IT TO 6
6088- C6 06     2000        DEC HORIZD     AND DECREMENT HORIZ INDEX
                2010 *--------------------------------
608A- A9 43     2020 DRAW   LDA #$43     SET DEFENDER BASE
608C- 85 FB     2030        STA BASD+1     ADDRESS TO $4350
608E- A9 06     2040        LDA #$06     DEFENDER IS
6090- 85 0C     2050        STA HEIGHT     6 BYTES HIGH
                2060 *--------------------------------
                2070 * CALCULATE INDEX FOR DEFENDER DATA TABLE
6092- A5 09     2080        LDA FRMNUMD  INDEX IS
6094- 0A        2090        ASL            FRMNUMD X 18
6095- 85 0E     2100        STA TEMP     TEMP HAS FRMNUMD X 2
6097- 0A        2110        ASL
6098- 0A        2120        ASL
6099- 0A        2130        ASL          ACC HAS FRMNUMD X 16
609A- 18        2140        CLC
609B- 65 0E     2150        ADC TEMP     ACC HAS FRMNUMD X 18
609D- AA        2160        TAX          X-REGISTER GETS INDEX
                2170 *--------------------------------
609E- A9 03     2180 .1     LDA #$03     DEFENDER IS
60A0- 85 0D     2190        STA WIDTH      3 BYTES WIDE
60A2- A4 06     2200        LDY HORIZD   SCREEN HORIZ POS
60A4- BD 79 63  2210 .2     LDA DATAD,X  COPY IMAGE
60A7- 91 FA     2220        STA (BASD),Y   TO SCREEN
60A9- E8        2230        INX          INCREMENT
60AA- C8        2240        INY            INDICES
60AB- C6 0D     2250        DEC WIDTH    DO THIS
60AD- D0 F5     2260        BNE .2         3 TIMES
60AF- 18        2270        CLC
60B0- A5 FB     2280        LDA BASD+1   ADD $400 (1024)
```

```
60B2- 69 04     2290          ADC #$04        TO DEFENDER'S SCREEN
60B4- 85 FB     2300          STA BASD+1      BASE ADDRESS
60B6- C6 0C     2310          DEC HEIGHT    DO THIS
60B8- D0 E4     2320          BNE .1          6 TIMES
60BA- 60        2330          RTS
                2340 *---------------------------------
                2350 GREMLIN
60BB- A9 42     2360          LDA #$42      SET GREMLIN SCREEN BASE
60BD- 85 FD     2370          STA BASG1+1     ADDRESSES TO
60BF- 85 FF     2380          STA BASG2+1     $4200 AND $4280
60C1- A9 08     2390          LDA #$08      GREMLIN IS TWO PARTS,
60C3- 85 0C     2400          STA HEIGHT      EACH 8 BYTES HIGH
                2410 *---------------------------------
                2420 * CALCULATE INDEX
60C5- A5 0A     2430          LDA FRMNUMG   INDEX IS
60C7- 0A        2440          ASL             FRMNUMG X 24
60C8- 0A        2450          ASL
60C9- 0A        2460          ASL
60CA- 85 0E     2470          STA TEMP      TEMP HAS FRMNUMG X 8
60CC- 0A        2480          ASL           ACC HAS FRMNUMG X 16
60CD- 18        2490          CLC
60CE- 65 0E     2500          ADC TEMP      ACC HAS FRMNUMG X 24
60D0- AA        2510          TAX           X-REGISTER GETS INDEX
                2520 *---------------------------------
60D1- A9 03     2530 .1       LDA #$03      GREMLIN IS
60D3- 85 0D     2540          STA WIDTH       3 BYTES WIDE
60D5- A4 07     2550          LDY HORIZG    INDEX TO GREMLIN SCREEN LOC.
60D7- BD 29 62  2560 .2       LDA DATG1,X   COPY TOP OF GREMLIN
60DA- 91 FC     2570          STA (BASG1),Y  TO SCREEN
60DC- BD D1 62  2580          LDA DATG2,X   COPY BOTTOM OF GREMLIN
60DF- 91 FE     2590          STA (BASG2),Y  TO SCREEN
60E1- E8        2600          INX           INCREMENT
60E2- C8        2610          INY             INDICES
60E3- C6 0D     2620          DEC WIDTH     DO THIS
60E5- D0 F0     2630          BNE .2          3 TIMES
60E7- 18        2640          CLC
60E8- A5 FD     2650          LDA BASG1+1   ADD $400 (1024)
60EA- 69 04     2660          ADC #$04
60EC- 85 FD     2670          STA BASG1+1    TO GREMLIN SCREEN BASE
60EE- A5 FF     2680          LDA BASG2+1     (MOVE DOWN
60F0- 69 04     2690          ADC #$04         ONE RASTER LINE)
60F2- 85 FF     2700          STA BASG2+1
```

```
60F4- C6 0C     2710          DEC HEIGHT   DO THIS
60F6- D0 D9     2720          BNE .1         8 TIMES
60F8- E6 0A     2730          INC FRMNUMG  MOVE RIGHT
60FA- A5 0A     2740          LDA FRMNUMG
60FC- C9 07     2750          CMP #$07     PAST LAST FRAME
60FE- D0 13     2760          BNE RET        IF NOT, CONTINUE
6100- A9 00     2770          LDA #$00     IF SO,
6102- 85 0A     2780          STA FRMNUMG    RESET FRMNUMG
6104- E6 07     2790          INC HORIZG     MOVE TO NEXT BYTE
6106- A5 07     2800          LDA HORIZG
6108- C9 24     2810          CMP #$24     AT FAR RIGHT OF SCREEN?
610A- D0 07     2820          BNE RET      IF NOT, CONTINUE
610C- 20 14 61  2830          JSR ERASE.G  IF SO, ERASE IMAGE
610F- A9 00     2840          LDA #$00     GO TO LEFT
6111- 85 07     2850          STA HORIZG     OF GRAPHICS SCREEN
6113- 60        2860 RET      RTS
                2870 *-------------------------------
                2880 ERASE.G
6114- A9 42     2890          LDA #$42     SET GREMLIN SCREEN BASE
6116- 85 FD     2900          STA BASG1+1    ADDRESSES TO
6118- 85 FF     2910          STA BASG2+1    $4200 AND $4280
611A- A9 08     2920          LDA #$08     GREMLIN IS
611C- 85 0C     2930          STA HEIGHT     8 BYTES HIGH
611E- A9 03     2940 .1       LDA #$03     GREMLIN IS
6120- 85 0D     2950          STA WIDTH      3 BYTES WIDE
6122- A4 07     2960          LDY HORIZG   INDEX TO GREMLIN SCREEN LOC.
6124- A9 00     2970          LDA #$00     STORE ZEROS IN
6126- 91 FC     2980 .2       STA (BASG1),Y  SCREEN LOCATIONS
6128- 91 FE     2990          STA (BASG2),Y  WHICH CONTAINED GREMLIN
612A- C8        3000          INY          INC INDEX
612B- C6 0D     3010          DEC WIDTH    DO THIS
612D- D0 F7     3020          BNE .2         3 TIMES
612F- 18        3030          CLC
6130- A5 FD     3040          LDA BASG1+1  ADD $400 (1024)
6132- 69 04     3050          ADC #$04       TO GREMLIN
6134- 85 FD     3060          STA BASG1+1    SCREEN BASE ADDRESSES
6136- A5 FF     3070          LDA BASG2+1
6138- 69 04     3080          ADC #$04        (MOVE DOWN ONE
613A- 85 FF     3090          STA BASG2+1       RASTER LINE)
613C- C6 0C     3100          DEC HEIGHT      DO THIS
613E- D0 DE     3110          BNE .1            8 TIMES
6140- 60        3120          RTS
```

```
               3130 *------------------------------
               3140 KEYBOARD
6141- AD 00 C0 3150        LDA KBD       READ KEYBOARD
6144- 10 27    3160        BPL RTN       IF NO KEYPRESS, RETURN
6146- C9 95    3170        CMP #$95      RIGHT ARROW
6148- D0 04    3180        BNE .1
614A- A9 01    3190        LDA #$01      SIGNAL TO
614C- 85 0B    3200        STA DIR         MOVE RIGHT
614E- C9 88    3210 .1     CMP #$88      LEFT ARROW
6150- D0 04    3220        BNE .2
6152- A9 FF    3230        LDA #$FF      SIGNAL TO
6154- 85 0B    3240        STA DIR         MOVE LEFT
6156- C9 AF    3250 .2     CMP #$AF      "/"  KEY
6158- D0 04    3260        BNE .3
615A- A9 00    3270        LDA #$00      SIGNAL FOR
615C- 85 0B    3280        STA DIR         NO MOVEMENT
615E- C9 A0    3290 .3     CMP #$A0      FIRE (SPACE BAR)
6160- D0 08    3300        BNE .4
6162- A5 0F    3310        LDA MFLG      IF MISSILE IS MOVING
6164- 30 04    3320        BMI .4          DON'T LAUNCH ANOTHER
6166- A9 01    3330        LDA #$01
6168- 85 0F    3340        STA MFLG      SET MISSILE FLAG
616A- AD 10 C0 3350 .4     LDA STROBE
616D- 60       3360 RTN    RTS
               3370 *------------------------------
               3380 BARRICADES
616E- A0 28    3390        LDY #$28      SCREEN INDEX
6170- A5 19    3400        LDA BRKD      GET BARRICADE CODE BYTE
6172- 91 12    3410 .1     STA (BASB),Y   AND STORE ON SCREEN
6174- 88       3420        DEY            RIGHT-TO-LEFT
6175- D0 FB    3430        BNE .1
6177- A5 19    3440        LDA BRKD
6179- C9 7F    3450        CMP #$7F      ACROSS SCREEN?
617B- D0 02    3460        BNE .2          IF NOT
617D- E6 19    3470        INC BRKD      SET EXIT SIGNAL
617F- 60       3480 .2     RTS
               3490 *------------------------------
6180- A9 10    3500 DELAY  LDA #$10
6182- 20 A8 FC 3510        JSR WAIT
6185- 60       3520        RTS
               3530 *------------------------------
               3540 MISSILES
```

```
6186- A5 0F     3550          LDA MFLG
6188- F0 F6     3560          BEQ DELAY     MFLG = 0 : NO MISSILE ACTIVITY
618A- 30 16     3570          BMI CONT      MFLG < 0 : CONTINUE A MISSILE
618C- A9 FF     3580          LDA #$FF      MFLG > 0 : LAUNCH A NEW MISSILE
618E- 85 0F     3590          STA MFLG      RESET MFLG
6190- A9 00     3600          LDA #$00
6192- 85 18     3610          STA COLFLG    ZERO EXPLODE FLAG
6194- A5 09     3620          LDA FRMNUMD
6196- 85 10     3630          STA MSLNM     IDENTIFY MISSILE NUMBER
6198- A5 06     3640          LDA HORIZD    MISSILE SCREEN BYTE LOCATION
619A- 85 08     3650          STA HORIZM      IS 1 LARGER
619C- E6 08     3660          INC HORIZM      THAN DEFENDER LOCATION
619E- A9 50     3670          LDA #$50      STARTING LEVEL
61A0- 85 11     3680          STA MLEVL       OF MISSILE
                3690 *-------------------------------
61A2- A6 11     3700 CONT     LDX MLEVL       SERVES AS INDEX
61A4- C6 11     3710          DEC MLEVL
61A6- C6 11     3720          DEC MLEVL
61A8- BD FE 63  3730          LDA ADDR,X
61AB- 85 14     3740          STA BASMD     ESTABLISH
61AD- E8        3750          INX             SCREEN BASE
61AE- BD FE 63  3760          LDA ADDR,X      ADDRESS FOR
61B1- 85 15     3770          STA BASMD+1     DRAWING MISSILE
61B3- E8        3780          INX
61B4- BD FE 63  3790          LDA ADDR,X
61B7- 85 16     3800          STA BASME     ESTABLISH
61B9- E8        3810          INX             SCREEN BASE
61BA- BD FE 63  3820          LDA ADDR,X      ADDRESS FOR
61BD- 85 17     3830          STA BASME+1   ERASING MISSILE
                3840 *-------------------------------
61BF- A6 10     3850          LDX MSLNM     MISSILE INDEX
61C1- A4 08     3860          LDY HORIZM    INDEX TO SCREEN BYTE LOCATION
61C3- A5 11     3870          LDA MLEVL     INDEX TO MISSILE ADDRESS TABLE
61C5- C9 06     3880          CMP #$06      TOP OF SCREEN
61C7- D0 09     3890          BNE DRW       IF NOT THERE YET
61C9- 38        3900          SEC           MISSED GREMLIN
61CA- 26 19     3910          ROL BRKD      ADD A BIT TO BARRICADES
61CC- A9 00     3920          LDA #$00      RESET MISSILE FLAG
61CE- 85 0F     3930          STA MFLG
61D0- F0 21     3940          BEQ ERASE     ALWAYS
                3950 *-------------------------------
61D2- A9 04     3960 DRW      LDA #$04      MISSILE IS
```

```
61D4- 85 0C    3970          STA HEIGHT     4 BYTES HIGH
61D6- BD F7 63 3980 .1       LDA MISL,X   GET MISSILE BIT PATTERN
61D9- 31 14    3990          AND (BASMD),Y  IS BIT ON ALREADY?
61DB- 05 18    4000          ORA COLFLG   IF SO, SET EXPLODE FLAG
61DD- 85 18    4010          STA COLFLG     TO NONZERO
61DF- D0 12    4020          BNE ERASE
61E1- BD F7 63 4030          LDA MISL,X   GET MISSILE BIT PATTERN
61E4- 11 14    4040          ORA (BASMD),Y  ADD IT TO THE
61E6- 91 14    4050          STA (BASMD),Y  CURRENT SCREEN CONTENTS
61E8- 18       4060          CLC
61E9- A5 15    4070          LDA BASMD+1  ADD $400 (1024)
61EB- 69 04    4080          ADC #$04       TO BASE ADDRESS
61ED- 85 15    4090          STA BASMD+1    (MOVE DOWN 1 RASTER LINE)
61EF- C6 0C    4100          DEC HEIGHT   DO THIS
61F1- D0 E3    4110          BNE .1         4 TIMES
               4120 *-------------------------------
61F3- A9 04    4130 ERASE    LDA #$04     MISSILE IS
61F5- 85 0C    4140          STA HEIGHT     4 BYTES HIGH
61F7- BD F7 63 4150 .3       LDA MISL,X   GET MISSILE BIT PATTERN
61FA- 31 16    4160          AND (BASME),Y  IS BIT ALREADY ON?
61FC- F0 04    4170          BEQ .4         IF NOT, DON'T ERASE IT
61FE- 51 16    4180          EOR (BASME),Y  COMPLEMENTARY DRAW
6200- 91 16    4190          STA (BASME),Y    TO ERASE BIT
6202- 18       4200 .4       CLC          ADD $400 (1024)
6203- A5 17    4210          LDA BASME+1    TO BASE ADDRESS
6205- 69 04    4220          ADC #$04       (MOVE DOWN
6207- 85 17    4230          STA BASME+1     1 RASTER LINE)
6209- C6 0C    4240          DEC HEIGHT   DO THIS
620B- D0 EA    4250          BNE .3         4 TIMES
               4260 *-------------------------------
               4270 * EXIT
620D- A5 18    4280          LDA COLFLG   HIT ANYTHING?
620F- F0 17    4290          BEQ RT1      IF NO
               4300 *-------------------------------
6211- A9 00    4310 HIT      LDA #$00     HIT SOMETHING!
6213- 85 0F    4320          STA MFLG     RESET MFLG
6215- A5 11    4330          LDA MLEVL    IF MLEVL IS
6217- C9 30    4340          CMP #$30       LESS THAN $30
6219- B0 0D    4350          BCS RT1      THEN HIT GREMLIN!
               4360 *-------------------------------
621B- 20 DD FB 4370          JSR BELL     HIT GREMLIN! RING BELL.
621E- 20 14 61 4380          JSR ERASE.G  ERASE GREMLIN
```

```
6221- A9 00              LDA #$00     START IT AT LEFT
6223- 85 07              STA HORIZG   OF SCREEN
6225- 18                 CLC          REMOVE 1 BIT
6226- 66 19              ROR BRKD       FROM BARRICADES
6228- 60          RT1    RTS
                  *--------------------------------
6229- 30 0C 00
622C- 7C 3F 00
622F- 44 23 00
6232- 46 63 00    DATG1  .DA #48,#12,#0,#124,#63,#0,#68,#35,#0,#70,#99,#0
6235- 46 63 00
6238- 7E 7F 00
623B- 78 1F 00
623E- 48 13 00           .DA #70,#99,#0,#126,#127,#0,#120,#31,#0,#72,#19,#0
                  * FRAME NUMBER 2
6241- 60 18 00
6244- 78 7F 00
6247- 08 47 00
624A- 0C 47 01           .DA #96,#24,#0,#120,#127,#0,#8,#71,#0,#12,#71,#1
624D- 0C 47 01
6250- 7C 7F 01
6253- 70 3F 00
6256- 10 27 00           .DA #12,#71,#1,#124,#127,#1,#112,#63,#0,#16,#39,#0
                  * FRAME NUMBER 3
6259- 40 31 00
625C- 70 7F 01
625F- 10 0E 01
6262- 18 0E 03           .DA #64,#49,#0,#112,#127,#1,#16,#14,#1,#24,#14,#3
6265- 18 0E 03
6268- 78 7F 03
626B- 60 7F 00
626E- 20 4E 00           .DA #24,#14,#3,#120,#127,#3,#96,#127,#0,#32,#78,#0
                  * FRAME NUMBER 4
6271- 00 63 00
6274- 60 7F 03
6277- 20 1C 02
627A- 30 1C 06           .DA #0,#99,#0,#96,#127,#3,#32,#28,#2,#48,#28,#6
627D- 30 1C 06
6280- 70 7F 07
6283- 40 7F 01
6286- 40 1C 01           .DA #48,#28,#6,#112,#127,#7,#64,#127,#1,#64,#28,#1
                  * FRAME NUMBER 5
```

```
6289- 00 46 01
628C- 40 7F 07
628F- 40 38 04
6292- 60 38 0C 4570        .DA #0,#70,#1,#64,#127,#7,#64,#56,#4,#96,#56,#12
6295- 60 38 0C
6298- 60 7F 0F
629B- 00 7F 03
629E- 00 39 02 4580        .DA #96,#56,#12,#96,#127,#15,#0,#127,#3,#0,#57,#2
               4590 * FRAME NUMBER 6
62A1- 00 0C 03
62A4- 00 7F 0F
62A7- 00 71 08
62AA- 40 71 18 4600        .DA #0,#12,#3,#0,#127,#15,#0,#113,#8,#64,#113,#24
62AD- 40 71 18
62B0- 40 7F 1F
62B3- 00 7E 07
62B6- 00 72 04 4610        .DA #64,#113,#24,#64,#127,#31,#0,#126,#7,#0,#114,#4
               4620 * FRAME NUMBER 7
62B9- 00 18 06
62BC- 00 7E 1F
62BF- 00 62 11
62C2- 00 63 31 4630        .DA #0,#24,#6,#0,#126,#31,#0,#98,#17,#0,#99,#49
62C5- 00 63 31
62C8- 00 7F 3F
62CB- 00 7C 0F
62CE- 00 64 09 4640        .DA #0,#99,#49,#0,#127,#63,#0,#124,#15,#0,#100,#9
62D1- 4E 73 00
62D4- 0E 70 00
62D7- 7E 7F 00
62DA- 04 20 00 4650 DATG2  .DA #78,#115,#0,#14,#112,#0,#126,#127,#0,#4,#32,#0
62DD- 04 20 00
62E0- 04 20 00
62E3- 0E 20 00
62E6- 00 70 00 4660        .DA #4,#32,#0,#4,#32,#0,#14,#32,#0,#0,#112,#0
               4670 * FRAME NUMBER 2
62E9- 1C 67 01
62EC- 1C 60 01
62EF- 7C 7F 01
62F2- 10 10 00 4680        .DA #28,#103,#1,#28,#96,#1,#124,#127,#1,#16,#16,#0
62F5- 10 10 00
62F8- 38 10 00
62FB- 00 10 00
```

```
62FE- 00 38 00 4690          .DA #16,#16,#0,#56,#16,#0,#0,#16,#0,#0,#56,#0
               4700 * FRAME NUMBER 3
6301- 38 4E 03
6304- 38 40 03
6307- 78 7F 03
630A- 40 08 00 4710          .DA #56,#78,#3,#56,#64,#3,#120,#127,#3,#64,#8,#0
630D- 40 08 00
6310- 40 08 00
6313- 60 08 00
6316- 00 1C 00 4720          .DA #64,#8,#0,#64,#8,#0,#96,#8,#0,#0,#28,#0
               4730 * FRAME NUMBER 4
6319- 70 1C 07
631C- 70 00 07
631F- 70 7F 07
6322- 00 22 00 4740          .DA #112,#28,#7,#112,#0,#7,#112,#127,#7,#0,#34,#0
6325- 00 22 00
6328- 00 22 00
632B- 00 72 00
632E- 00 07 00 4750          .DA #0,#34,#0,#0,#34,#0,#0,#114,#0,#0,#7,#0
               4760 * FRAME NUMBER 5
6331- 60 39 0E
6334- 60 01 0E
6337- 60 7F 0F
633A- 00 02 01 4770          .DA #96,#57,#14,#96,#1,#14,#96,#127,#15,#0,#2,#1
633D- 00 02 01
6340- 00 42 03
6343- 00 02 00
6346- 00 07 00 4780          .DA #0,#2,#1,#0,#66,#3,#0,#2,#0,#0,#7,#0
               4790 * FRAME NUMBER 6
6349- 40 73 1C
634C- 40 03 1C
634F- 40 7F 1F
6352- 00 02 04 4800          .DA #64,#115,#28,#64,#3,#28,#64,#127,#31,#0,#2,#4
6355- 00 02 04
6358- 00 02 0E
635B- 00 02 00
635E- 00 07 00 4810          .DA #0,#2,#4,#0,#2,#14,#0,#2,#0,#0,#7,#0
               4820 * FRAME NUMBER 7
6361- 00 67 39
6364- 00 07 38
6367- 00 7F 3F
636A- 00 02 10 4830          .DA #0,#103,#57,#0,#7,#56,#0,#127,#63,#0,#2,#16
```

```
636D- 00 02 10
6370- 00 02 10
6373- 00 02 10
6376- 00 07 38 4840        .DA #0,#2,#16,#0,#2,#16,#0,#2,#16,#0,#7,#56
               4850 DATAD
               4860 * FRAME NUMBER 2
6379- 00 01 00
637C- 00 01 00
637F- 00 01 00 4870        .DA #0,#1,#0,#0,#1,#0,#0,#1,#0
6382- 06 61 00
6385- 7E 7F 00
6388- 7E 7F 00 4880        .DA #6,#97,#0,#126,#127,#0,#126,#127,#0
               4890 * FRAME NUMBER 3
638B- 00 02 00
638E- 00 02 00
6391- 00 02 00 4900        .DA #0,#2,#0,#0,#2,#0,#0,#2,#0
6394- 0C 42 01
6397- 7C 7F 01
639A- 7C 7F 01 4910        .DA #12,#66,#1,#124,#127,#1,#124,#127,#1
               4920 * FRAME NUMBER 4
639D- 00 04 00
63A0- 00 04 00
63A3- 00 04 00 4930        .DA #0,#4,#0,#0,#4,#0,#0,#4,#0
63A6- 18 04 03
63A9- 78 7F 03
63AC- 78 7F 03 4940        .DA #24,#4,#3,#120,#127,#3,#120,#127,#3
               4950 * FRAME NUMBER 5
63AF- 00 08 00
63B2- 00 08 00
63B5- 00 08 00 4960        .DA #0,#8,#0,#0,#8,#0,#0,#8,#0
63B8- 30 08 06
63BB- 70 7F 07
63BE- 70 7F 07 4970        .DA #48,#8,#6,#112,#127,#7,#112,#127,#7
               4980 * FRAME NUMBER 6
63C1- 00 10 00
63C4- 00 10 00
63C7- 00 10 00 4990        .DA #0,#16,#0,#0,#16,#0,#0,#16,#0
63CA- 60 10 0C
63CD- 60 7F 0F
63D0- 60 7F 0F 5000        .DA #96,#16,#12,#96,#127,#15,#96,#127,#15
               5010 * FRAME NUMBER 7
63D3- 00 20 00
```

```
63D6- 00 20 00
63D9- 00 20 00 5020          .DA #0,#32,#0,#0,#32,#0,#0,#32,#0
63DC- 40 21 18
63DF- 40 7F 1F
63E2- 40 7F 1F 5030          .DA #64,#33,#24,#64,#127,#31,#64,#127,#31
63E5- 00 40 00
63E8- 00 40 00
63EB- 00 40 00 5040          .DA #0,#64,#0,#0,#64,#0,#0,#64,#0
63EE- 00 43 30
63F1- 00 7F 3F
63F4- 00 7F 3F 5050          .DA #0,#67,#48,#0,#127,#63,#0,#127,#63
63F7- 01 02 04
63FA- 08 10 20
63FD- 40       5060 MISL     .DA #1,#2,#4,#8,#16,#32,#64
63FE- 00 40 00
6401- 50 80 40
6404- 80 50    5070 ADDR     .HS 0040005080408050
6406- 00 41 00
6409- 51 80 41
640C- 80 51    5080          .HS 0041005180418051
640E- 00 42 00
6411- 52 80 42
6414- 80 52    5090          .HS 0042005280428052
6416- 00 43 00
6419- 53 80 43
641C- 80 53    5100          .HS 0043005380438053
641E- 28 40 28
6421- 50 A8 40
6424- A8 50    5110          .HS 28402850A840A850
6426- 28 41 28
6429- 51 A8 41
642C- A8 51    5120          .HS 28412851A841A851
642E- 28 42 28
6431- 52 A8 42
6434- A8 52    5130          .HS 28422852A842A852
6436- 28 43 28
6439- 53 A8 43
643C- A8 53    5140          .HS 28432853A843A853
643E- 50 40 50
6441- 50 D0 40
6444- D0 50    5150          .HS 50405050D040D050
6446- 50 41 50
```

```
6449- 51 D0 41
644C- D0 51     5160        .HS 50415051D041D051
644E- 50 42 80
6451- 52 D0 42
6454- D0 52     5170        .HS 50428052D042D052
6456- 50 43 50
6459- 53 D0 43
645C- D0 53     5180        .HS 50435053D043D053


SYMBOL TABLE

6029- A
63FE- ADDR
616E- BARRICADES
.01=6172, .02=617F
0012- BASB
00FA- BASD
00FC- BASG1
00FE- BASG2
0014- BASMD
0016- BASME
FBDD- BELL
0019- BRKD
0018- COLFLG
61A2- CONT
6379- DATAD
6229- DATG1
62D1- DATG2
6048- DEFENDER
6180- DELAY
000B- DIR
608A- DRAW
.01=609E, .02=60A4
61D2- DRW
.01=61D6
61F3- ERASE
.03=61F7, .04=6202
6114- ERASE.G
.01=611E, .02=6126
0009- FRMNUMD
000A- FRMNUMG
```

```
60BB- GREMLIN
.01=60D1, .02=6127
000C- HEIGHT
6211- HIT
0006- HORIZD
0007- HORIZG
0008- HORIZM
6000- INIT
C000- KBD
6141- KEYBOARD
.01=614E, .02=6156, .03=615E, .04=616A
6070- LEFT
000F- MFLG
63F7- MISL
6186- MISSILES
0011- MLEVL
6080- MOVLFT
6060- MOVRT
0010- MSLNM
6113- RET
6228- RT1
616D- RTN
C010- STROBE
000E- TEMP
FCA8- WAIT
000D- WIDTH
```

SECTION

V

Searching and Sorting

CHAPTER 13

SEARCHING AND SORTING

At some time you have probably wanted to sort a disk file. The data in this file will be either numeric or alphabetic. Writing an Applesoft Bubble Sort program to sort this list is a relatively simple task. However, as the number of elements on the list increases, the amount of time required to sort the list becomes irritatingly long. For example, to sort a list of 256 elements with an Applesoft program requires more than sixteen minutes. The sorting time can be reduced to approximately twenty-one seconds when the sorting routine is assembled in memory and called from Applesoft. That is a 97.8% reduction!

The purpose of this chapter is to show you how to write a sorting routine in assembly language that will sort 256 elements in less than twenty-five seconds. The more general problem of describing and comparing the efficiencies of different sorting techniques is beyond the purpose of this chapter. If you are interested in searching and sorting in the general sense, we suggest you begin by reading the article "A Comparison of Sorts, Revisited" by Howard Kaplan, published in *Creative Computing,* May 1983, page 217. If you wish a more definitive approach to searching and sorting, we suggest *The Art of Computer Programming,* Volume 3, by Donald Knuth, published by Addison-Wesley.

The sorting technique we use in the examples in this chapter is called a "bubble" sort, because the "lighter" elements "float" to the top of the list. We chose the bubble sort for three reasons: (1) It is the easiest to understand, and (2) it will sort 256 elements in less than twenty-five seconds. (3) It is also the "heart" of some very fast sort routines. This sorting technique is described the Kaplan article and is called "Quicksort." When Quicksort gets down to brass tacks it finally does a bubble sort on a much smaller sublist of the original list. If you need to sort lists in the thousands of elements, then it will benefit you to master the bubble sort given in this chapter and incorporate it into a Quicksort routine. The "last word" on searching and sorting has not yet been written.

The Applesoft program shown below will generate a list of random numbers and store them in the array F. Sorting disk files will be dealt with later.

```
10  REM GENERATE RANDOM NUMBERS
20  REM
30  PRINT "HOW MANY ELEMENTS?"
40  INPUT N
50  N = N - 1
60  DIM F(N)
70  PRINT "THE RANDOM NUMBERS WILL BE CALCULATED"
80  PRINT "ACCORDING TO:"
90  PRINT
100  PRINT "            X = R + S * RND(J)"
110  PRINT "            F(I)  = INT(X)"
120  PRINT
130  PRINT "INPUT J, R, S"
140  INPUT J,R,S
150  PRINT
160  PRINT "THE LIST"
170  FOR I = 0 TO N
180  X = R + S * RND(J)
190  F(I)  = INT (X)
200  PRINT I + 1;".   ";F(I)
210  NEXT I
220  REM
230  REM BUBBLE SORT
240  REM
```

```
250  LE = N - 1
260  FL = 0
270  FOR I = 0 TO LE
280  IF (F(I) < = F(I + 1)) GOTO 320
290  T = F(I)
300  F(I) = F(I + 1)
310  F(I + 1) = T
320  FL = 1
330  NEXT I
340  LE = LE - 1
350  IF (FL = 1) GOTO 250
360  PRINT
370  REM
380  REM PRINT THE SORTED LIST
390  REM
400  PRINT "THE SORTED LIST."
410  FOR I = 0 TO N
420  PRINT I + 1;".   ";F(I)
430  NEXT I
440  END
```

The generation of 256 integers is quick. The time-consuming part of the program is the bubble sort. Using only the second hand on a watch, this routine required sixteen minutes, eighteen seconds to sort 256 elements.

The time required for any bubble sort to run is proportional to the number of elements, N, squared. That is,

$$T = A * N^2$$

If the number of elements is doubled ($N \rightarrow 2N$), then the program takes four times as long to run ($T \rightarrow 4T$). This proportion holds true even if the bubble sort is assembled into machine language. How then is such a great time savings accomplished when using an assembled bubble sort routine? The A in the above equation is much smaller than it is for an Applesoft program. The assembled bubble sort will run approximately forty-five times faster. That is, 128 elements will be sorted in about five seconds; 256 elements in about twenty-one seconds.

The Applesoft bubble sort shown above compares F(I) with F(I+1); if F(I+1) is smaller the elements are swapped. Lines 290, 300, and 310 do the swapping. Line 290 moves F(I) into a Temporary location. Line 300 moves F(I+1) into F(I), and then T is moved into F(I+1). Line 320 sets a FLag. When the FLag is set another pass (line 350) through the list is required.

If you are uncertain on how this program sorts, try inserting these lines:

```
321  FOR I = 0 TO N
322  PRINT I+1;".   ";F(I)
323  NEXT I
324  INPUT A$
```

This modification will allow you to watch each "heavy" number "sink" to the bottom. The purpose of line 324 is to halt execution of the loop so that you can scan the list of numbers to see which number is "sinking." The variable A$ has no logical purpose in the program. When this modification is installed keep the number of elements small (less than ten).

If you insert this line into the program

```
331 PRINT "A PASS THROUGH THE LIST HAS BEEN COMPLETED."
```

along with the others you will see that one by one the heavy elements "sink" to the bottom. Notice that when this message first appears the "heaviest" element has "sunk" completely to the bottom. This element is now sorted; it need not be compared again. Therefore LE (Loop End) can be decremented by one (line 340).

The overall idea in this chapter is to write an Applesoft program to generate and print the the unsorted list, then call our assembled bubble sort. It will sort the list forty-five times faster than Applesoft could have. Finally return to the Applesoft program to print the sorted list. Our objective is to translate the Applesoft bubble sort into Assembly Language without changing the logic of the program. The program shown below is that translation.

PROGRAM 13.1

```
1000 *--------------------------------
1010 *    THIS EXAMPLE WILL SORT 256 OR LESS
1020 *    NUMBERS THAT WERE LOADED INTO AN
1030 *    ARRAY BY THE BASIC PROGRAM SHOWN ABOVE.
1040 *--------------------------------
1050         .OR $300      MUST STAY OUT OF $800
1060 *--------------------------------
1070 *                     BECAUSE THAT IS THE
1080 *                     STARTING LOCATION
1090 *                     OF APPLESOFT.
1100 *--------------------------------
```

```
0006-            ELEML  .EQ $06       LEFT-HAND ELEM
0008-            ELEMR  .EQ $08       RIGHT-HAND ELEM
0016-            MASK   .EQ $16       FOR THE COMPARISON
0019-            FLAG   .EQ $19       KEEP FLAG HERE
001E-            NUMB   .EQ $1E       THE NUMBER OF ELEM'S
001F-            COUNT  .EQ $1F       THE CURRENT NUMBER
0094-            FIRST  .EQ $94       ADDRESS OF FIRST NUMBER
009D-            MFAC   .EQ $9D
DF6A-            COMP   .EQ $DF6A
DFE3-            PTRGET .EQ $DFE3
E9E3-            MOVSI  .EQ $E9E3
EAF9-            MOVMI  .EQ $EAF9
EB2B-            MOVMO  .EQ $EB2B
EB53-            MOVSM  .EQ $EB53
                 *--------------------------------
                 *      BEGINNING OF PROGRAM
                 *--------------------------------
0300- 20 E3 DF   BEGIN  JSR PTRGET    PUT ADDR OF 1ST NUMBER INTO FIRST
0303- A5 94             LDA FIRST     GET LOCATION PART OF FIRST NUMBER
0305- 38                SEC           SET CARRY FOR SUBTRACTION
0306- E9 01             SBC #$01      BACKUP TO NUMBER TO SORT
0308- 85 1E             STA NUMB      LOCATION PART
030A- A5 95             LDA FIRST+1   GET PAGE PART OF FIRST NUMBER
030C- E9 00             SBC #$00      NEAT WAY TO TAKE CARE OF PG BNDRY
030E- 85 1F             STA NUMB+1    PAGE PART OF ADDRESS
0310- A0 00             LDY #$00      PREPARE FOR INDIRECT ADDRESSING
0312- B1 1E             LDA (NUMB),Y  LOAD NUMBER TO BE SORTED INTO A
0314- AA                TAX           MOVE IT TO X
0315- CA                DEX           TAKE OFF 1
0316- 86 1E             STX NUMB      STORE IT HERE
0318- A9 06             LDA #$06      SELECT COMPARISON      < = >
031A- 85 16             STA MASK      COMP WANTS IT HERE     4 2 1
                 *--------------------------------
                 * THIS IS THE TOP OF THE OUTER LOOP.
                 *--------------------------------
031C- A5 1E      PASS   LDA NUMB      RE-LOAD NUMBER OF ELEMENTS
031E- 85 1F             STA COUNT     SET THE COUNTER
0320- A9 00             LDA #$00      CLEAR THE FLAG
0322- 85 19             STA FLAG      IT IS CLEARED
0324- A4 95             LDY FIRST+1   GET PAGE PART OF FIRST NUMBER
0326- 84 07             STY ELEML+1   SAVE IT HERE
0328- A5 94             LDA FIRST     GET LOC PART OF ITS ADDRESS
```

```
032A- 85 06     1530        STA ELEML     LOC OF FIRST NUMBER ON LIST
                1540 *-------------------------------
                1550 * THIS IS THE TOP OF THE INNER LOOP.
                1560 *-------------------------------
032C- 20 E3 E9  1570 TOP    JSR MOVSI     MOVE IT INTO SFAC
032F- A4 07     1580        LDY ELEML+1   MUST RECOVER THESE
0331- A5 06     1590        LDA ELEML     AFTER THE JSR IN LINE 1570
0333- 18        1600        CLC           SET UP TO
0334- 69 05     1610        ADC #$05      RIGHT ELEM
0336- 85 08     1620        STA ELEMR     SAVE IT HERE
0338- 98        1630        TYA           PREPARE TO CHECK FOR PG BNDRY
0339- 69 00     1640        ADC #$00      FIX IF NECESSARY
033B- A8        1650        TAY           PUT IT BACK
033C- 85 09     1660        STA ELEMR+1   SAVE IT HERE
033E- A5 08     1670        LDA ELEMR     RIGHT ELEM IS READY
0340- 20 F9 EA  1680        JSR MOVMI     MOVE IT INTO MFAC
0343- 20 6A DF  1690        JSR COMP      DO THE COMPARISON
0346- A5 9D     1700        LDA MFAC      SET Z-FLAG; IS MFAC = 0?
0348- D0 13     1710        BNE NOSWP     NEED TO SWAP'EM?
                1720 *-------------------------------
                1730 * THIS SECTION SWAPS THE RIGHT AND THE LEFT ELEMENTS.
                1740 *-------------------------------
034A- A9 FF     1750        LDA #$FF      YES!
034C- 85 19     1760        STA FLAG      SO SET FLAG
034E- A0 04     1770        LDY #$04      MOVE ALL 5 PARTS
0350- B1 08     1780 SWAP   LDA (ELEMR),Y OF THE F-P NUMBER
0352- AA        1790        TAX             USE X AS TEMP STORAGE
0353- B1 06     1800        LDA (ELEML),Y MOVE LEFT PART
0355- 91 08     1810        STA (ELEMR),Y TO THE RIGHT
0357- 8A        1820        TXA             MOVE OLD RIGHT
0358- 91 06     1830        STA (ELEML),Y TO THE LEFT
035A- 88        1840        DEY             COUNT DOWN
035B- 10 F3     1850        BPL SWAP        MOVE THEM ALL YET?
                1860 *-------------------------------
035D- A4 09     1870 NOSWP  LDY ELEMR+1   DO NOT NEED TO SWAP'EM
035F- 84 07     1880        STY ELEML+1   OLD RIGHT BECOMES NEW LEFT
0361- A5 08     1890        LDA ELEMR     PREPARE TO MOVE UP RIGHT
0363- 85 06     1900        STA ELEML     THIS TAKES CARE OF PG PART
0365- C6 1F     1910        DEC COUNT     COUNT OFF ANOTHER 1
0367- D0 C3     1920        BNE TOP       DO'EM ALL YET?
                1930 *-------------------------------
                1940 * BOTTOM OF INNER LOOP.
```

```
                1950 *-------------------------------
0369- C6 1E     1960        DEC NUMB     DO NOT NEED TO RE-CHECK THE REST
036B- A5 19     1970        LDA FLAG     SET Z-FLAG; IS IT 0?
036D- D0 AD     1980        BNE PASS     DO ANY SWAPS?
                1990 *-------------------------------
                2000 * BOTTOM OF THE OUTER LOOP.
                2010 *-------------------------------
036F- 60        2020        RTS          HOW NICE IT IS!


SYMBOL TABLE

0300- BEGIN
DF6A- COMP
001F- COUNT
0006- ELEML
0008- ELEMR
0094- FIRST
0019- FLAG
0016- MASK
009D- MFAC
EAF9- MOVMI
EB2B- MOVMO
E9E3- MOVSI
EB53- MOVSM
035D- NOSWP
001E- NUMB
031C- PASS
DFE3- PTRGET
0350- SWAP
032C- TOP
```

& USAGE

The first executable line in the program (line 1280) indicates that the & command will be used to call the routine. PoinTeR GET will find the address of the first element in the numeric array and put it in FIRST (locations \$94, \$95). To understand the purpose of lines 1300 through 1390, you must realize that the last byte of the header contains the number of elements in the array. (Remember how Applesoft organizes numeric array storage. If you need refreshing on this see Chapter 8.)

PREPARATION FOR SORTING

Our plan is to sort 256 or fewer elements. Then we need only move the contents of the last header byte into NUMB. To accomplish this, one is subtracted from the location (low byte) part of the first element's address. The subtraction may cross a page boundary. For example ($94, $95) = 00 0B could be the contents of FIRST and FIRST + 1. When the subtraction is performed we want FF 0C not FF 0B! Lines 1330 and 1340 take care of this by using the C-flag. If a page boundary is crossed in the subtraction, the C-flag will be set and the page part (high byte, FIRST + 1), will be properly adjusted when the subtraction in line 1340 is executed.

The address of the number of elements is now formed in NUMB and NUMB + 1. Line 1370 loads the NUMBer of elements to be sorted into A, it is transferred to X, and one is subtracted. The number of elements is stored in NUMB. Next the type of comparison to be done is selected according to

```
< = >
4 2 1
```

Since $06 = $04 + $02, the type of comparison to be done is <=.

SORTING

We imagine going through the array a pair of elements (ELEML and ELEMR) at a time. The address of the left-hand element is contained in $06 and $07 (ELEML and ELEML + 1); the address of the right-hand element is contained in $08 and $09 (ELEMR and ELEMR + 1). We will use the COMParison routine, already in ROM, which was pointed out in Table 8.4. Its starting location is $DF6A and the kind of comparison that is done is stored in $16 (MASK). The number of elements to be sorted is contained in $1E (NUMB).

Each pass through the list begins by initializing COUNT to NUMB, setting the FLAG to zero and establishing the address of the first element in ELEML and ELEML + 1. The inner loop begins by loading the contents of ELEML into SFAC and then moving up by five bytes to ELEMR. A move of five bytes is required because each floating-point number is five bytes long (remember Chapter 8). Each move of five bytes requires a check to see if the Carry been set. If the Carry has been set that means a move across a page boundary has occurred. If a move across a page boundary occurred the page part of the address (ELEMR + 1) must be incremented by one. The floating-point number is then loaded into MFAC and the comparison is performed.

If the result of the comparison is false, the contents of MFAC are set equal to zero (00 00 00 00 00). If the result is true, the contents of MFAC are set equal to one (81 80 00 00 00). Next the contents of $9D (the first byte of MFAC) are loaded into A and the Z-flag is set according to the result. If Z=0 the branch to NOSWP is taken; if Z=1 the contents of ELEML and ELEMR are swapped.

On entry into the swap section of the program the flag is set indicating that a swap has occurred. The Y-register is initialized and used as an index register. Byte by byte the two floating-point numbers are swapped. First each byte is loaded into A (line 1780), then transferred into X. The X-register is used as the temporary storage location. Now a left byte is moved into a right byte. Finally the byte in X is moved to the left, Y is decremented, and the SWAP loop runs again (if necessary). In summary, the process goes (1) right byte into X, (2) left byte moved to the right, (3) X is moved to the left, (4) repeat four more times.

Now ELEMR becomes ELEML, and the COUNTer is decremented. A check for the end of the list is made and (if necessary) the inner loop is run one more time. If we are at the end of the list, check the FLAG to determine if another pass through the list is required. If a pass through the entire list is made and no swaps have occurred, then FLAG = 0, the list is sorted, and the RTS back to the Applesoft program is taken.

SEARCHING

Once the list of numbers has been sorted the construction of the frequency distribution is relatively easy. That is, the effort (time + thought) required to translate and debug the part of the Applesoft program that searches and counts identical elements does not seem justified. Who cares if you can trim a section of code that requires ten seconds or so to run in Applesoft down to less than one second? But it is the kind of exercise you should do as practice, or just for fun. The example shown below has the frequency distribution tacked onto the bottom the the earlier Applesoft program. This program has the bubble sort segment replaced by an & call (line 360) to the machine language bubble sort that is BLOADed into memory (line 70).

Finally, a sample run of the program is shown below. Do not forget to assemble and BSAVE the bubble sort to disk before running this example.

```
10  REM SORT RANDOM NUMBERS
20  REM BY LINKING TO MACHINE
30  REM LANGUAGE ROUTINE
40  REM LOADED AT $300
50  REM
```

```
60  D$ = CHR$ (4): REM CNTRL-D
70  PRINT D$;"BLOAD ML.BUBBLE"
80  PRINT "HOW MANY ELEMENTS?"
90  INPUT N
100  N = N - 1
110  DIM F(N)
120  PRINT "THE RANDOM NUMBERS WILL BE CALCULATED"
130  PRINT "ACCORDING TO:"
140  PRINT
150  PRINT "            X = R + S * RND(J)"
160  PRINT "            F(I) = INT(X)"
170  PRINT
180  PRINT "INPUT J, R, S"
190  INPUT J,R,S
200  PRINT
210  PRINT "THE LIST"
220  FOR I = 0 TO N
230  X = R + S * RND(J)
240  F(I) = INT (X)
250  PRINT I + 1;".  ";F(I)
260  NEXT I
270  REM
280  REM ESTABLISH THE & VECTOR
290  REM
300  POKE 1013,76
310  REM
320  REM ESTABLISH THE & LINK ADDRESS
330  POKE 1014,00
340  POKE 1015,03
350  REM LINK TO THE ROUTINE
360  & F(2)
370  REM
380  PRINT
390  REM
400  REM PRINT THE SORTED LIST
410  REM
420  PRINT "THE SORTED LIST."
430  FOR I = 0 TO N
440  PRINT I + 1;".  ";F(I)
450  NEXT I
460  REM
470  REM NOW CONSTRUCT THE
```

```
480  REM FREQUENCY DISTRIBUTION
490  REM
500  PRINT
510  PRINT "THE FREQUENCY DISTRIBUTION"
520  L = 0
530  C = 0
540  PC = 1
550  FOR R = 1 TO N
560  IF (F(L) <  > F(R)) GOTO 500
570  C = C + 1
580  GOTO 540
590  PRINT PC;".   ";F(L);".   ";C
600  L = R
610  C = 1
620  PC = PC + 1
630  NEXT R
640  PRINT PC;".   ";F(L);"   ";C
650  END

RUN
HOW MANY ELEMENTS?
?15
THE RANDOM NUMBERS WILL BE CALCULATED
ACCORDING TO:

          X = R + S * RND(J)
          F(I) = INT(X)

INPUT J, R, S
?4,10,-10

THE LIST
1.  2
2.  1
3.  6
4.  6
5.  7
6.  2
7.  3
8.  0
9.  3
10.  0
```

```
11.  6
12.  7
13.  3
14.  8
15.  6

THE SORTED LIST
1.  0
2.  0
3.  1
4.  2
5.  2
6.  3
7.  3
8.  3
9.  6
10.  6
11.  6
12.  6
13.  7
14.  7
15.  8

THE FREQUENCY DISTRIBUTION
1.  0  2
2.  1  1
3.  2  2
4.  3  3
5.  6  4
6.  7  2
7.  8  1
```

STRINGS

In this part of the chapter you need to know how strings are stored in memory. To make your results match those discussed in this part of the chapter you must enter the following list of names in the order they appear below.

```
1.  SANDY
2.  KELLY
```

3. MICHAEL
4. ANTHONY
5. BILL
6. LINDA
7. KAREN
8. ALICE
9. GLENN
10. NEAL
11. ROY
12. MOM
13. DAD
14. RICHARD
15. LINDA

Here is a short Applesoft program that will create the list on disk.

```
10  REM USE THIS PROGRAM
20  REM TO CREATE THE
30  REM LIST OF NAMES
40  D$ = CHR$ (4): REM CNTRL-D
50  PRINT "HOW MANY ELEMENTS?"
60  INPUT N
70  N = N - 1
80  DIM F$(N)
90  FOR I = 0 TO N
100  INPUT F$(I)
110  PRINT I + 1;".   ";F$(I)
120  NEXT I
130  PRINT
140  PRINT D$;"OPEN LIST"
150  PRINT D$;"WRITE LIST"
160  FOR I = 0 TO N
170  PRINT F$(I)
180  NEXT I
190  PRINT D$;"CLOSE LIST"
200  END
```

You will have to do this task only once, but get it done accurately. Once the list is created on disk you can read it as often as necessary with this program.

```
10  REM THIS PROGRAM WILL
20  REM READ IN THE LIST
```

```
30  REM OF NAMES
40  D$ = CHR$ (4): REM CNTRL-D
50  PRINT "HOW MANY NAMES DO YOU WISH TO READ IN?"
60  INPUT N
70  N = N - 1
80  DIM F$(N)
90  PRINT D$;"READ LIST"
100  FOR I = 0 TO N
110  INPUT F$(I)
120  NEXT I
130  PRINT D$;"CLOSE LIST"
140  PRINT
150  FOR I = 0 TO N
160  PRINT I + 1;".   ";F$(I)
170  NEXT I
180  CALL -151
190  END
```

The above program finishes with a CALL to the Monitor because we are interested in how Applesoft has stored the names in memory. Create this list on disk and run the program to read it into memory. Here is what you should see:

```
NEW
RUN
HOW MANY NAMES DO YOU WISH TO READ IN?
?15

(The list of names)
(When the monitor prompt appears)
(do the following memory listings.)

*6B.70

006B- 3B 09 6F 09 B6
0070- 95

*93B.96E                          This is the array space.
                                  Stored here are the string
093B- 46 80 34 00 01              descriptor blocks.
0940- 00 0F 05 FA 95 05 F5 95     Each descriptor block is
0948- 07 EE 95 07 E7 95 04 E3     three bytes long.  The first
0950- 95 05 DE 95 05 D9 95 05     byte contains the length
```

```
0958- D4 95 05 CF 95 04 CB 95    of the string.  The next two
0960- 03 C8 95 03 C5 95 03 C2    bytes point to the strings
0968- 95 07 BB 95 05 B6 95       themselves.

*95B6.95FF                       This is where the strings
                                 are stored:

95B6- 4C 49                      LI
95B8- 4E 44 41 52 49 43 48 41    NDARICHA
95C0- 52 44 44 41 44 4D 4F 4D    RDDADMOM
95C8- 52 4F 59 4E 45 41 4C 47    ROYNEALG
95D0- 4C 45 4E 4E 41 4C 49 43    LENNALIC
95D8- 45 4B 41 52 45 4E 4C 49    EKARENLI
95E0- 4E 44 41 42 49 4C 4C 41    NDABILLA
95E8- 4E 54 48 4F 4E 59 4D 49    NTHONYMI
95F0- 43 48 41 45 4C 4B 45 4C    CHAELKEL
95F8- 4C 59 53 41 4E 44 59 04    LYSANDY
```

Locations $6B through $70 contain the following information: (1) $6BB and $6C contain the starting address of the array space, (2) $6D and $6E contain the ending address of the array space, (3) $6F and $70 contain the starting address of the location in memory where the names are actually stored. Note that the string of names is not contained in the array space pointed to by $6B through $6E, as is the case for numeric arrays.

What is contained in the array space pointed to by $6B through $6E? The first seven bytes are the header. It is organized in the same fashion as it was in Chapter 8. The information you will see in the header after running the read list program is:

```
 Header -->    46     80     34    00     01     00     0F
Address -->  $93B   $93C   $93D  $93E   $93F   $940   $9401
             char1  char2  LENGTH of    # of   range of
              of     of    this block   DIMs   rightmost
             name   name                       index
              "F"    " "
```

The first bit in each byte of the name (char1 and char2) is used to identify the type of data contained in the array. In this case the ASCII Screen Character for a normal F is $C6 → 1100 0110, but the high bit has been turned off → 0100 0110, so a 46 appears as the first character of the array name. There is no second character in the name of our array, but the high bit is turned on → 1000 0000.

The pattern used by Applesoft to identify the type of information stored in memory is:

First bit of char1	First bit of chr2	Type of array
1	1	Integer
0	0	Real
0	1	String

For our array, the high bit of char1 is off, and the high bit of char2 is on, indicating the array contains information about strings, but not the strings themselves. The names are stored elsewhere in memory. The rest of the information in the array is organized in string descriptor blocks of three bytes. For example,

```
Array contents -->   05   FA   95
       Address --> $942 $943 $944
```

The first byte of the descriptor block is the length ($05) of the string starting at $95FA (SANDY). Looking at the $05 byte string at $95FA we see:

```
   ASCII -->     S     A     N     D     Y
Contents -->    53    41    4F    44    59
 Address --> $95FA $95FB $95FC $95FD $95FE
```

The rest of the information is organized in the same fashion. Looking at the last byte we see:

```
Array contents -->   05   B6   95
       Address --> $96C $96D $96E
```

Which points to

```
   ASCII -->     L     I     N     D     A
Contents -->    46    49    4E    44    41
 Address --> $95B6 $95B7 $95B8 $95B9 $95BA
```

In summary, the array contains the lengths of the strings and pointers to the strings. The strings themselves are stored at $95FE and grow downward.

There is an Applesoft routine in ROM that will compare two strings. The STRing CoMPare routine begins at $DF7D. To use this routine, the type of comparison to be done is stored in location $16 with the usual meaning. The low

TABLE 13.1 String Comparison Subroutine

Name	*Entry Point*	*Action Taken*
STRCMP	$DF7D	(SFAC) is compared to (MFAC)

MFAC is set to 1, if the result of the comparison is true. MFAC is set to 0 if the comparison is false. The contents of location $16 determine the type of comparison to be done according to:

Contents of $16	Comparison to be done	Mnemonic
1	[$A8,$A9]* > [$A0,$A1]	< = >
2	[$A8,$A9] = [$A0,$A1]	4 2 1
3	[$A8,$A9] >= [$A0,$A1]	
4	[$A8,$A9] < [$A0,$A1]	
5	[$A8,$A9] <> [$A0,$A1]	
6	[$A8,$A9] <= [$A0,$A1]	

*[$A8,$A9] means "pointed to by the contents of $A8,$A9."

byte of an address descriptor block must be loaded into $A8 (SFAC+3) and the high byte of the block loaded into $A9 (SFAC+4). The comparison string descriptor block is loaded into $A0 (MFAC+3) and $A1 (MFAC+4). Then JSR to $DF7D (STRCMP). When STRCMP returns, the result of the comparison is left in MFAC in floating-point form. MFAC is set to 1 (81 80 00 00 00) if the result of the comparison is true. MFAC is set to 0 (00 00 00 00 00) if the result of the comparison is false. The use of the string comparison is summarized in Table 13.1.

The assembly language routine shown below sorts strings. It is similar to the one that sorts numbers. It will sort 256 or less elements.

PROGRAM 13.2

```
1000 *-------------------------------
1010 *    THIS PROGRAM WILL SORT 256 OR FEWER STRING
1020 *    ELEMENTS WHICH WERE LOADED INTO AN ARRAY BY
1030 *    THE BASIC PROGRAM SHOWN ABOVE.
1040 *-------------------------------
1050           .OR $300            MUST STAY OUT OF $800
1060 *-------------------------------
```

```
                *                          BECAUSE THAT IS THE
                *                          STARTING LOCATION
                *                          OF APPLESOFT.
                *---------------------------------
0006-           ELEML  .EQ $06             LEFT-HAND ELEM
0008-           ELEMR  .EQ $08             RIGHT-HAND ELEM
0016-           MASK   .EQ $16             FOR THE COMPARISON
0019-           FLAG   .EQ $19             KEEP FLAG
001E-           NUMB   .EQ $1E             THE NUMBER OF ELEM'S
001F-           COUNT  .EQ $1F             THE CURRENT NUMB
0094-           FIRST  .EQ $94             ADDRESS OF FIRST ELEM
009D-           MFAC   .EQ $9D
00A5-           SFAC   .EQ $A5
DFE3-           PTRGET .EQ $DFE3
DF7D-           STRCMP .EQ $DF7D
                *---------------------------------
                *      BEGINNING OF PROGRAM
                *---------------------------------
0300- 20 E3 DF  BEGIN  JSR PTRGET          PUT ADDR OF 1ST ELEM INTO FIRST
0303- A5 94            LDA FIRST           GET LOCATION PART OF FIRST ELEM
0305- 38               SEC                 SET CARRY FOR SUBTRACTION
0306- E9 01            SBC #$01            BACKUP TO NUMBER OF ELEM'S
0308- 85 1E            STA NUMB            LOCATION PART
030A- A5 95            LDA FIRST+1         GET PAGE PART OF FIRST ELEM
030C- E9 00            SBC #$00            NEAT WAY TO TAKE CARE OF PG BNDRY
030E- 85 1F            STA NUMB+1          PAGE PART OF NUMB ADDRESS
0310- A0 00            LDY #$00            PREPARE FOR INDIRECT ADDRESSING
0312- B1 1E            LDA (NUMB),Y         LOAD NUMBER OF ELEM'S INTO A
0314- AA               TAX                 MOVE IT TO X
0315- CA               DEX                 TAKE OFF 1
0316- 86 1E            STX NUMB            STORE IT HERE
0318- A9 06            LDA #$06            SELECT COMPARISON     < = >
031A- 85 16            STA MASK            STRCMP WANTS IT HERE  4 2 1
                *---------------------------------
                * THIS IS THE TOP OF THE OUTER LOOP.
                *---------------------------------
031C- A5 1E     PASS   LDA NUMB            RESET THE
031E- 85 1F            STA COUNT           COUNTER
0320- A9 00            LDA #$00            CLEAR THE FLAG
0322- 85 19            STA FLAG            IT IS CLEARED
0324- A6 95            LDX FIRST+1         GET PG PART
0326- 86 07            STX ELEML+1         SAVE IT HERE
```

```
0328- A5 94     1490        LDA FIRST    GET LOC PART OF ADDRESS
032A- 85 06     1500        STA ELEML    SAVE IT HERE
                1510 *------------------------------
                1520 * THIS IS THE TOP OF THE INNER LOOP.
                1530 *------------------------------
032C- 18        1540 TOP    CLC          ESTABLISH ADDRESS OF
032D- 69 03     1550        ADC #$03     RIGHT HAND ELEM
032F- 85 A0     1560        STA MFAC+3   LOC IS READY TO GO
0331- 85 08     1570        STA ELEMR    SAVE IT HERE
0333- 8A        1580        TXA          PREPARE TO CHECK FOR PG BNDRY
0334- 69 00     1590        ADC #$00     FIX IT IF NECESSARY
0336- 85 A1     1600        STA MFAC+4   PG IS READY
0338- 85 09     1610        STA ELEMR+1  SAVE IT HERE
033A- A5 06     1620        LDA ELEML    ESTABLISH ADDRESS OF
033C- 85 A8     1630        STA SFAC+3   LEFT-HAND ELEM
033E- A5 07     1640        LDA ELEML+1  LOC IS READY
0340- 85 A9     1650        STA SFAC+4   PG IS READY
0342- 20 7D DF  1660        JSR STRCMP   DO THE COMPARISON
0345- A5 9D     1670        LDA MFAC     SET Z-FLAG; IS MFAC = 0?
0347- D0 13     1680        BNE NOSWP    NEED TO SWAP THEM?
                1690 *------------------------------
                1700 * THIS SECTION SWAPS THE RIGHT AND THE LEFT ELEMENTS.
                1710 *------------------------------
0349- A9 FF     1720        LDA #$FF     YES! SET FLAG
034B- 85 19     1730        STA FLAG     THE FLAG IS SET
034D- A0 02     1740        LDY #$02     MOVE ALL 3 PARTS
034F- B1 08     1750 SWAP   LDA (ELEMR),Y OF THE ADDRESS
0351- AA        1760        TAX            RIGHT ELEM TO TEMP
0352- B1 06     1770        LDA (ELEML),Y MOVE LEFT ELEM
0354- 91 08     1780        STA (ELEMR),Y TO RIGHT ELEM
0356- 8A        1790        TXA            MOVE THE RIGHT
0357- 91 06     1800        STA (ELEML),Y TO THE LEFT
0359- 88        1810        DEY            COUNT DOWN
035A- 10 F3     1820        BPL SWAP       DONE YET?
                1830 *------------------------------
035C- A6 09     1840 NOSWP  LDX ELEMR+1    DO NOT NEED TO SWAP'EM
035E- 86 07     1850        STX ELEML+1    OLD RIGHT BECOMES NEW LEFT
0360- A5 08     1860        LDA ELEMR      PREPARE TO MOVE UP RIGHT
0362- 85 06     1870        STA ELEML      THIS TAKES CARE OF PG PART
0364- 85 06     1880        STA ELEML      SAVE IT
0366- C6 1F     1890        DEC COUNT      COUNT DOWN
0368- D0 C2     1900        BNE TOP        DO'EM ALL YET?
```

```
                 1910 *--------------------------------
                 1920 * BOTTOM OF INNER LOOP.
                 1930 *--------------------------------
036A- C6 1E      1940        DEC NUMB      DO NOT NEED TO RE-CHECK THE REST
036C- A5 19      1950        LDA FLAG      SET Z-FLAG; IS IT 0?
036E- D0 AC      1960        BNE PASS      DO ANY SWAPS?
                 1970 *--------------------------------
                 1980 * BOTTOM OF OUTER LOOP.
                 1990 *--------------------------------
0370- 60         2000        RTS           HOW NICE IT IS!

SYMBOL TABLE

0300- BEGIN
001F- COUNT
0006- ELEML
0008- ELEMR
0094- FIRST
0019- FLAG
0016- MASK
009D- MFAC
035C- NOSWP
001E- NUMB
031C- PASS
DFE3- PTRGET
00A5- SFAC
DF7D- STRCMP
034F- SWAP
032C- TOP
```

& USAGE

The routine begins with a JSR PTRGET. When PTRGET returns, the address of the first string descriptor block is stored in FIRST ($94,$95). Lines 1260 through 1390 put the NUMBer of elements in NUMB (for this example this is 15 = $0F) and select the type of comparison to be done (<=).

SORTING

The top of the outer loop is very similar to the numeric sort routine. Reset the COUNTer, clear the FLAG, and re-establish the address of the first string. At the top of the inner loop the address of the right-hand string is established. The strings are compared; MFAC is loaded into A to set the Z-flag. If a swap is necessary the string descriptor blocks (not the strings themselves!) are swapped. Lines 1720 and 1730 set the FLAG. Line 1740 sets the counter in Y. The SWAP loop will run three times and all three bytes of the descriptor block are swapped.

At the bottom of the inner loop ELEMR becomes ELEML, and the COUNTer is decremented. A check for the end of the list is made and (if necessary) the inner loop is run again. When the end of the list is encountered, the FLAG is checked to determine if another pass through the list is required. When a pass through the entire list is made and no swaps have occurred (FLAG = 0) the list is sorted; the RTS back to the Applesoft program is taken.

The program shown below uses the & feature of Applesoft to call the string sorting routine.

```
10  REM SORT LIST BY LINKING
20  REM TO A ROUTINE BLOADED
30  REM AT 768 = $300
40  REM
50  D$ = CHR$ (4): REM CNTRL-D
60  PRINT D$;"BLOAD ML.STRING"
70  PRINT "HOW MANY NAMES TO BE SORTED?"
80  INPUT N
90  N = N - 1
100  DIM F$(N)
110  PRINT D$;"READ LIST"
120  FOR I = 0 TO N
130  INPUT F$(I)
140  NEXT I
150  PRINT D$;"CLOSE LIST"
160  PRINT
170  PRINT "THE LIST."
180  FOR I = 0 TO N
190  PRINT I + 1;".   ";F$(I)
200  NEXT I
210  REM
220  REM ESTABLISHED THE & VECTOR
230  REM
240  POKE 1013,76
250  REM
260  REM ESTABLISHED THE & ADDRESS
270  REM
280  POKE 1014,00
```

```
290  POKE 1015,03
300  REM
310  REM LINK TO THE ROUTINE
320  & F$(2)
330  REM
340  PRINT
350  PRINT "THE SORTED LIST."
360  FOR I = 0 TO N
370  PRINT I + 1;".   ";F$(I)
380  NEXTI
390  END
```

Before running the Applesoft program, assemble and BSAVE the sort routine to disk. An execution of the program is shown below.

```
]RUN
HOW MANY NAMES TO BE SORTED.
?15

THE LIST
1.  SANDY
2.  KELLY
3.  MICHAEL
4.  ANTHONY
5.  BILL
6.  LINDA
7.  KAREN
8.  ALICE
9.  GLENN
10.  NEAL
11.  ROY
12.  MOM
13.  DAD
14.  RICHARD
15.  LINDA

THE SORTED LIST
1.  ALICE
2.  ANTHONY
3.  BILL
4.  DAD
5.  GLENN
```

```
6.   KAREN
7.   KELLY
8.   LINDA
9.   LINDA
10.   MICHAEL
11.   MOM
12.   NEAL
13.   RICHARD
14.   ROY
15.   SANDY
```

NOTES AND SUGGESTIONS

1. If the string array F$ is dimensioned to hold N strings, the above subroutine will attempt to sort all of them, even if some have not been defined. Can you modify the subroutine so that null strings will not be sorted?
2. Modify the subroutine so that it can sort more than 256 entries.
3. Modify the program to count the number of swaps and passes that are required to sort a list.
4. Modify the Applesoft program to "do a sort on entry." That is, to assume that the list of names is being entered from the keyboard and sort each entry as it is entered.

APPENDIX A

MINIASSEMBLER

A number of good assemblers are available for the Apple II/IIe. Their prices and capabilities vary. However, even if you have not purchased one of these assemblers, you probably already own an assembler: the Miniassembler. It is included in Integer BASIC, so you get it for free with that language.

If you have an Apple IIe, or an Apple II Plus with a language card, you can have Integer BASIC available by booting the system with the DOS 3.3 System Master. Then type INT and press RETURN to have Integer BASIC active. With the Integer BASIC prompt (>) displayed, type CALL −2458 and press RETURN. The computer should "beep," and the Miniassembler prompt (!) should appear. The Miniassembler is active.

If you have an Apple II Plus with no language card, the Miniassembler is still available. It is part of INTBASIC, on the DOS 3.3 System Master disk. If you can't load Integer BASIC into a language card, you can still load INTBASIC into RAM and edit the Miniassembler so that it will be functional at a relocated address. The following Applesoft program does this, then stores the edited code back to disk under the name MINIASSEMBLER. Run the program. You can then use the Miniassembler if you BRUN MINIASSEMBLER. It will run at $2000 (8192).

The instructions for the use of the Miniassembler are given in the Apple II and IIe reference manuals. The Miniassembler is quite functional, and can be useful for entering and testing short program segments. It produces no source code, and does not provide the capability of using labels, so it is not at all convenient for assembling large programs. It is a good learning tool, and will work well for entering the short example programs in this book.

```
1  REM MINI MOVER
2  REM RELOCATES MINIASSEMBLER
3  REM TO RUN AT $2000
4  REM INTBASIC MUST BE ON THE
5  REM DISK IN THE DRIVE WHEN
6  REM THIS PROGRAM IS RUN
7  REM -------------------------
10  PRINT  CHR$  (4);"BLOAD INTBASIC,A$2000"
20  POKE 768, 160: POKE 769, 0: POKE 770, 76: POKE 771, 44:
    POKE 772, 254
30  REM MOVE TO LOCATION$2000
40  POKE 60,0: POKE 61,69: POKE 62,60: POKE 63,70: POKE 66,3:
    POKE 67,32: CALL 768
50  REM  FIX ENTRY
60  POKE 8192,76: POKE 8193,149: POKE 8194,32
70  REM  FIX JSR'S
80  POKE 8249,152: POKE 8250,32
90  POKE 8285,152: POKE 8286,32
100  POKE 8385,55: POKE 8386,33
110  POKE 8415,55: POKE 8416,33
115  POKE 8425,55: POKE 8426,33
120  POKE 8501,95: POKE 8502,32
130  INPUT "INSERT DISK ON WHICH MINIASSEMBLER IS TO BE
     SAVED, THEN PRESS 'RETURN'";A$
140  PRINT  CHR$  (4);"BSAVE MINIASSEMBLER,A$2000,L$140"
```

APPENDIX B

REPRESENTATIONS OF NUMBERS AND ARITHMETIC

There are three systems of numbers with which you must be familiar: base two, base ten and base sixteen. If we are working in base two, only two digits (0, 1) are needed. If we are working in the base ten system, ten digits (0, 1, 2, 3, 4, 5, 6, 7, 8, 9) are needed. And if we are working in the base sixteen system, sixteen digits (0, 1, 2, 3, 4, 5, 6, 7, 8, 9, A, B, C, D, E, F) are needed. No one who is reading this book needs to read anything about the base ten system; it is THE system that we use. No one needs any lessons on how it works. However, the base two system or the base sixteen system may be another matter.

Exactly what is a base? The idea of a base is intimately related to the idea of place value. Visualize any number in any base like this:

etc. – – – – . – – – etc.

The place values
go down here →

Each blank represents a place and each place has a value depending on the base. The point in the picture above points out the one's place. The one's place is always immediately to the left of the point. The one's place has the value of one. An important fact to keep in mind is that any number, N, except zero, raised to the zero power is one.

That is

$$N^0 = 1.$$

Hence in base two the one's place is represented as $2^0 = 1$.

In base ten, the one's place is represented as $10^0 = 1$. In base sixteen, the one's place is represented as $16^0 = 1$. So far, you know how to visualize the first place to the left of the point.

etc.	–	–	–	–	.	–	–	–	etc.
Base two →				2°					
Base ten →				10°					
Base sixteen →				16°					

The powers of the base go up one at a time to the left. That is

etc.	–	–	–	–	.	–	–	–	etc.
Base two →	2^3	2^2	2^1	2^0					
Base ten →	10^3	10^2	10^1	10^0					
Base sixteen →	16^3	16^2	16^1	16^0					

The powers of the base go down one at a time to the right. That is

etc.	–	–	–	–	.	–	–	–	etc.
Base two →						2^{-1}	2^{-2}	2^{-3}	
Base ten →						10^{-1}	10^{-2}	10^{-3}	
Base sixteen →						16s^{-1}	16^{-2}	16^{-3}	

All together the place values look like this:

etc.	–	–	–	–	.	–	–	–	etc.
Base two →	2^3	2^2	2^1	2^0		2^{-1}	2^{-2}	2^{-3}	
Base ten →	10^3	10^2	10^1	10^0		10^{-1}	10^{-2}	10^{-3}	
Base sixteen →	16^3	16^2	16^1	16^0		16^{-1}	16^{-2}	16^{-3}	

We shall not need the places to the right of the point for a while, so we shall no longer write them, nor the point.

Now consider a four-digit number, for example 1010. Until the base is known you do not know the value of the number. That is to say you do not know how many things—bytes, Apples, dollars, etc.—this picture, 1010, represents until you know the base so that the place values can be computed. If we consider the base ten, then the place values are well known, and the number means one thousand ten things. That is

1	0	1	0
10^3	10^2	10^1	10^0
1000	100	10	1

1*1000 + 1*10 = 1010 (one thousand ten)

However, if we consider the base two the place values are

1	0	1	0
2^3	2^2	2^1	2^0
8	4	2	1

and the same picture represents 1*8 + 1*2 = 10 (ten). That is to say 1010 base two is 10 base ten. In base sixteen the place values are

1	0	1	0
16^3	16^2	16^1	16^0
4096	256	16	1

1*4096 + 1*16 = 4112 (four thousand one hundred twelve). That is to say 1010 base-sixteen is 4112 base-ten.

In this book, when any misconception about bases is likely to occur, we will always put a $ sign in front of base sixteen numbers. Also, the name of the base sixteen place value system is the hexadecimal system, or hex for short. The name of the base two system is the binary system.

A word of caution: This picture, 10, has the name "ten" ONLY in the decimal system. In fact only the base ten pictures have names. It is improper, very misleading, and just wrong to write this picture, 10, think base two, and say "ten." This picture does not have a short name in base two, nor in base sixteen. You must say each digit place by place from left to right. That is you must say, "one zero," in either base two or base sixteen. You must never say "ten" when thinking base two or sixteen.

Remember: Only the base ten pictures have names.

The conversion between binary and hex is very easy, when groupings of four binary digits are done. Group any binary number in fours from the right; write down the place values under EACH group; convert each group to hex. As an example, take a rather long binary number, 111011010. Separate it into groups, 11 1101 1010; then write down the binary place values for EACH group.

The binary →	1	1	1	1	0	1	1	0	1	0
Place values →	2	1	8	4	2	1	8	4	2	1
Add each group →	2+1		8+4			+1	8		+2	
Base-ten sum →	3		13				10			
The hex →	3		D				A			

In summary, the binary representation 1111011010 has the hex representation 3DA. The process works equally well in the other direction. For example, what is the binary representation of F4D hex?

The hex →	F	4	D
The decimal → in binary	15	4	13
Place values →	8+4+2+1	4	8+4 +1
The binary →	1 1 1 1	0 1 0 0	1 1 0 1

In summary, hex F4D is 111101001101 in binary. From now on we shall write binary representations in groups of four digits.

The conversion from hex to base ten is reasonably quick; from the above examples you can see that it involves a knowledge of the hex place values and the mathematical operations multiplication and addition. The reverse conversion from base ten to hex is slightly slower because you must make a quantitative judgment to begin. A base ten to hex conversion involves knowledge of the hex system place values and the mathematical operations division and subtraction.

When a base ten number, 12,506, is to be converted to its hex representation, the quantitative judgement to be made is: What is the largest hex place value that will divide into the base ten number? In this example the answer is 4096 (which is 16^3). Do the division.

```
                                 3← The 4096's digit
Hex place value → 4096) 12506
                        12288
                          218← Proceed with the remainder
```

After this decision and division you know the leading digit in the hex representation.

$$\frac{3}{4096}\ \frac{\quad}{256}\ \frac{\quad}{16}\ \frac{\quad}{1}$$

Perform the same routine with the remainder, 218. What is the largest hex place value that will divide into the remainder? The answer is 16, but see that the place value, 256, has been skipped. Because it has been skipped a zero is put in its place. Now you know the first two digits of the hex representation.

$$\frac{3}{4096}\ \frac{0}{256}\ \frac{\quad}{16}\ \frac{\quad}{1}$$

Do the division.

```
                          13  → D ← the 16's digit
Hex place value → 16 ) 218
                         208
                          10  → A ← the 1's digit
```

Finally the entire hex representation is known

$$\frac{3}{4096}\ \frac{0}{256}\ \frac{D}{16}\ \frac{A}{1}$$

As a second example, suppose the base ten number, 51,376, is to be converted to its hex representation.

```
            12  → C ← the 4096's digit
4096 ) 51376
        49152
         2224
```

```
          8← the 256's digit
256 ) 2224
      2048
       176
```

```
       11← the 16's digit
16 ) 176
     176
       0← the 1's digit
```

In summary, the base-ten number 51,376 has the hex representation

C	8	B	0
4096	256	16	1

An understanding of the base two system is necessary because it is the easiest to use for describing the state (contents) of the smallest element of information in memory, the bit. More about how information is stored in memory is covered in Chapter 4. A bit is either on (1) or off (0). Hence only two symbols, digits, are required. The problem with binary representations is the length of the pictures. They are inconveniently long. The pictures are so long because the place values progress slowly upward in value. The binary representations are inconvenient to display on the screen, to write down, or even to see when they are so long. Hex representations relieve this problem.

Hex is used to display the information in memory for at least two important reasons. First, the length of the pictures in the hex system is much more compact, because the place values progress much more rapidly upward in value. So hex representations are more convenient to display on the screen, to write down, and even to see. Second, the interconversion between hex and binary is rapid and reasonably easy. In fact, the only reason for keeping the decimal system around is that, first, we have a great deal of prior training in its use. Second, we have ten fingers, which are handy memory storage devices in a pinch!

Since all of you have these years of training and practice invested in the base ten system, we will use it whenever possible for doing base sixteen arithmetic. The addition problem, 18 + 11, has the same picture for the result in base ten as in the base sixteen, 29. The difference is in the answer to the question, What does it, 29, mean? To answer that question you must apply the place values and do the conversion to base ten: 29 base-sixteen means 2*16 + 9*1 = 41 base ten.

When doing additions base sixteen the major difference occurs when the following addition is considered, 9 + 1. The result, 9 + 1 = A base sixteen. In base sixteen, two digits are not needed until sixteen is reached. That is, 9 + 1 = A, 9 + 2 = B, 9 + 3 = C, 9 + 4 = D, 9 + 5 = E, 9 + 6 = F, and then 9 + 7 = 10.

Most people have such an investment in the decimal system that it is the only one that "works" for them. Therefore, we propose to "cash in" on this investment as much as possible when hex arithmetic is required.

Remember the following convention table:

Base sixteen picture →	A	B	C	D	E	F
Base ten picture →	10	11	12	13	14	15

A short example, using the table, to begin. Consider the hex addition B + C

The hex →	B + C
Think base ten →	11 + 12 = 23 = 16 + 7 = 1(16) + 7 = \$17

And one more

The hex →	E + F
Think base ten →	14 + 15 = 29 = 16 + 13 = 1(16) + 13 = \$1D

When many-digit base sixteen arithmetic is required, as in this example

```
  3E9F
+ DA34
------
```

proceed as you would in base ten: do the addition column by column. That is

The hex →	F + 4 = 1 3 = 13
Think base ten →	15 + 4 = 19 = 16 + 3

Write down the 3, carry the one

```
     1
  3E9F
+ DA34
------
     3
```

then do

The hex →	1 + 9 + 3 = D
Think base ten →	1 + 9 + 3 = 13

Write down the D, but no carry this time.

```
  3E9F
+ DA34
------
    D3
```

Now do

The hex →	E + A = 1 8
Think base ten →	14 + 10 = 24 = 16 + 8

Write down the 8, carry the 1

```
   1
   3E9F
 + DA34
 ------
    8D3
```

Finally do

The hex →	1 + 3 + D =		1	1	= 11
Think base ten →	1 + 3 + 13 =	17 =	16	+ 1	

carry the 1, and the result is

```
   3E9F
 + DA34
 ------
  118D3
```

The bottom line is that hex arithmetic, done this way, is not as confusing as long as you "cash in" on all of your base ten training.

The same method "works" for subtraction. Consider this three-digit hex subtraction

```
   8A4
 - 7B5
 -----
```

and proceed as you would in base ten; do the subtraction column by column. This example begins by requiring a borrow from the A in the second column. Borrowing from the A means, A − 1 = 9. Put the 9 where the A was and move the 1 over to the 4.

```
    (1)
   894
 - 7B5
 -----
```

Do not forget that the borrowed one, (1), is worth sixteen. The arithmetic in the one's column is

The hex →	(1) + 4 − 5 =	F
Think base ten →	16 + 4 − 5 = 20 − 5 =	15

Write down the F

```
  894
- 7B5
-----
    F
```

then move to the next column; realize that another borrow is required, 8 − 1 = 7. Put the 7 where the 8 was and put the borrowed 1 above the 9

```
  (1)
  794
- 7B5
-----
    F
```

The sixteen's column subtraction is

The hex →	(1) + 9 − B = E
Think base ten →	16 + 9 − 11 = 14

Write down the E

```
  794
- 7B5
-----
   EF
```

and see that the last column is 7 − 7 = 0. Leading zeros are not written. The important point to remember in base sixteen subtraction is that borrows are worth sixteen.

Multiplication and division in base sixteen are not skills you need to develop to a high degree. Therefore, we shall not describe them here. You must, however, understand how negative numbers are represented in memory. The scheme is called 2's-complement notation. The binary system is the most convenient to use to see how the process works, because "taking the complement" means changing all the 1s to 0s AND changing all the 0s to 1s. For example,

The binary →	1011 0011
Its complement →	0100 1100

Understand why the usual notation, − (a negative sign), will not work. Everything in memory must be represented as strings of 1s and 0s! The convention is: If the leftmost binary digit is a 1, then the number is negative. When this convention for representing negative numbers is used the range of base ten numbers that can be represented (0 to 255) changes to (−127 to +127). The leftmost bit now designates the sign of the number, not its place value.

Remember: If the left most binary digit is a 1, then the number is negative!

In our examples of negative numbers in 2's-complement notation we shall always use eight-digit binary numbers. The reason eight-digit binary numbers are used will be even more obvious when you have read Chapter 8. Consider negative five base ten, −5. To find its 2's-complement representation, follow this procedure:

Positive base ten →		5
Eight-digit base two →	0 0 0	1 0 0 1
Base-two place values →	S 64 32 16	8 4 2 1
The complement →	1 1 1 1	1 0 1 0
Now add 1 →	+	1
The 2's-complement →	1 1 1 1	1 0 1 1
Conversion to hex →	8 4 2 1	8 4 2 1
In hex →	F	B

Note that the S under the leftmost digit means this is the Sign digit. Negative five base ten in 2's-complement notation is 1111 1011, which is FB in hex.

As a second example, find the 2's-complement notation of negative ninety-five, −95, base ten.

Positive base ten →		9 5
Eight-digit base two →	0 1 0 1	1 1 1 1
Base two place values →	S 64 32 16	8 4 2 1
The complement →	1 0 1 0	0 0 0 0
Now add 1 →	+	1
The 2's-complement →	1 0 1 0	0 0 0 1
Conversion to hex →	8 4 2 1	8 4 2 1
In hex →	A	1

Negative ninety-five, −95, base ten in 2's-complement notation is 1010 0001, which is A1 in hex.

The reverse conversion is just as quick. Suppose that a memory location contains DC, find the base ten picture.

The hex →					D					C
The 2's-complement →		1	1	0	1		1	1	0	0
Its complement →		0	0	1	0		0	0	1	1
Now add 1 →	+									1
Eight-digit base two →		0	0	1	0		0	1	0	0
Base two place values →		$\bar{S}$	$\overline{64}$	$\overline{32}$	$\overline{16}$		$\bar{8}$	$\bar{4}$	$\bar{2}$	$\bar{1}$
Convert to base ten →				32		+	4			
Positive base ten →										36
Put on the minus →										−36

In summary, there are two other place value systems, in addition to the base ten system, with which you must become familiar. Familiarity with the binary system is required because of the very nature of digital computers, and familiarity with the hexadecimal system is required because most of the binary information in the computer is displayed in this system because its representations are compact. A small amount of hex/base ten interconversion must be done by hand, but even this may be avoided if your assembler can do the interconversions. (Check the manual to see if it can do this.) Often additions and subtractions must be done in hex, but this task is not onerous providing you "cash in" on your base ten "investment."

In this book you will not need any more knowledge about the binary and hex systems than is presented here to fully understand their topics. By the time you finish these chapters, you will be in a position to "cash in" on your investment in your Apple II and have it do any arithmetic tasks for you.

APPENDIX C

FLOATING-POINT NOTATION

Appendix B discussed ways to represent numbers in binary and hexadecimal form. The methods presented there are intended to be used to represent integers. In this appendix, we will extend that discussion to include the representation of rational numbers (with fractional parts). We will also use the method to represent numbers (integer or rational) of arbitrary magnitude. The notation we use is generally referred to as the floating-point form of the numbers.

Let's begin by noting that the number 26.71875 can be written in binary form as

$$\begin{aligned} 11010.10111 = {} & 1(2)^4 + 1(2)^3 + 0(2)^2 + 1(2)^1 + 0(2)^0 + \\ & 1(2)^{-1} + 0(2)^{-2} + 1(2)^{-3} + 1(2)^{-4} + 1(2)^{-5} = \\ & 16 + 8 + 2 + .5 + .125 + .0625 + .03125 = \\ & 26.71875 \end{aligned}$$

or in hexadecimal form as

$$\$1A.B8 = 1(16)^1 + 10(16)^0 + 11(16)^{-1} + 8(16)^{-2} = 1(16) + 10 + 11(.0625) + 8(.00390625) = 26.71875$$

Note that multiplication by powers of 2 has the effect of shifting the location of the binary point in the binary form of the number. The number 26.71875 is represented by each of the following:

2^1 *(1101.01011100)
2^2 *(110.101011100)
2^3 *(11.0101011100)
2^4 *(1.10101011100)
2^5 *(.110101011100)

The last form listed (2^5 *(.110101011100)) is called the normalized form of the number. (If we were purists and insisted that everything be expressed in binary, we would write 10^{1001} * .1101010111. The base 2 → 10 and the exponent 5 → 0101 .) The 5 is called the exponent and the 1101010111 is called the mantissa of the number. If this normalized form is written with its mantissa in hexadecimal notation, it becomes 2^5 *.D5C. This is close to the form that Applesoft uses to store floating-point numbers.

In unpacked floating-point form, Applesoft uses one byte for the exponent of 2 (5), four bytes for the mantissa, and one byte for the sign of the number. Further, Applesoft uses "excess $80" notation when representing floating-point numbers ($80 is added to the exponent). The Applesoft model for floating point numbers is thus

```
_ _    _ _ _ _ _ _ _ _    _ _
EXP       Mantissa        SGN
```

When the above number (26.71875) is stored in this form, it becomes

```
8 5   D 5 C 0 0 0 0 0   0 0
```

In the SGN byte, only the highest bit is significant. If the number is negative, that bit is set to 1; if the number is positive, the bit is set to 0.

As a second example, let's represent the number 751.375 in excess $80 floating-point form. We first put it in binary form:

1011101111.011

then in normalized binary form

$2^{10}(.1011101111011)$

The exponent (decimal 10) in hex is \$A, and in excess \$80 form is \$8A. The mantissa (1011 1011 1101 1000) can be written in hexadecimal form as \$BBD8. The Applesoft excess \$80 floating-point form of the number is

8A	BB D8 00 00	00
EXP	Mantissa	SGN

NOTES

We can shorten the calculation of the floating-point form of a number N if we note that:

1. The EXP is the smallest integer which will cause $M = N/(2^{EXP})$ to be less than 1.
2. The first hex digit of the mantissa is obtained by dividing by .0625 (10). Successive digits are obtained by dividing the fractional part of the quotient by .0625.

Using the above procedure, we can obtain the following excess \$80 floating-point representations:

N = 1000	: 8A	FA	00	00	00	00
N = −1000	: 8A	FA	00	00	00	FA
N = .05	: 7C	CC	CC	CC	CD	00
N = −.05	: 7C	CC	CC	CC	CD	CC

Note that when N is negative, the sign byte agrees with the first byte of the mantissa. Since only the high-order bit of the sign byte is significant, other values could have been used. We used the first byte of the mantissa because that is what Applesoft does.

The above floating-point numbers are all in unpacked form. There is also a packed form of the numbers, which we turn to now.

Packed Form

You may feel it is wasteful to use a byte to designate the sign of a number when only one bit of that byte is important. That is true, and while the sign byte is necessary when numbers are being used for calculation purposes, the extra byte is inconvenient when a floating-point number is to be stored. Since only one bit of the sign byte is used, the byte could be dropped if the bit could be stored elsewhere.

Look back over the binary form of the mantissas calculated so far. You should find that the leading bit is always a 1. (This was a requirement for normalized form.) Since the bit is always a 1, we could do well without it (except at calculation time), or with that bit used as a sign bit. That is done in the packed form of the number. The high-order bit of the mantissa is set to 0 if the number is positive, and is set to 1 if the number is negative.

Note on Use of Packed Form

Packed form is used for storage of floating-point numbers, but unpacked form is required when the numbers are needed for calculation. Our earlier numbers can be written in packed form as:

```
N = 1000   : 8A  FA  00  00  00
N = -1000  : 8A  7A  00  00  00
N = .05    : 7F  4C  CC  CC  CD
N = -.05   : 7F  CC  CC  CC  CD
```

APPENDIX D

APPLESOFT ENTRY POINTS AND NOTES

Powers of 16

$16^2 = 256$	$16^3 = 4{,}096$	$16^4 = 65{,}536$	$16^5 = 1{,}048{,}576$	$16^6 = 16{,}777{,}216$

Reciprocal Powers of 16

$16^{-1} = 6.25 * 10^{-2}$	$16^{-2} = 3.90625 * 10^{-3}$	$16^{-3} = 2.44140625 * 10^{-4}$
$16^{-5} = 1.52587890625 * 10^{-5}$	$16^{-6} = 5.9604644775390025 * 10^{-8}$	

The MFAC and SFAC Layout

MFAC address →	9	D	9	E	9	F	A	0	A	1
SFAC address →	A	5	A	6	A	7	A	8	A	9
Contents →	8	4	A	D	0	0	0	0	0	0
	EXP		←			Mantissa				→
Place Value →	84-80									
	2		16^{-1}	16^{-2}	16^{-3}	16^{-4}	16^{-5}	16^{-6}	16^{-7}	16^{-8}

The Applesoft Array Header

Header →	41	00	1B	00	01	00	04
Address →	$8A4	$8A5	$8A6	$8A7	$8A8	$8A9	$8AA
	char1 of name "A"	char2 of name " "	LENGTH of this block		# of DIMs	Range of rightmost index	

TABLE 8.1 Two-Operand Subroutines

	Name	*Entry Point*	*Action Taken*
1.	ADD	$E7C1	(MFAC) ← (SFAC) + (MFAC)
	MFAC and SFAC already loaded; do the ADDition.		
2.	LADD	$E7BE	(MFAC) ← [Y,A] + (MFAC)
	MFAC is already loaded; (Y,A) points to the memory location of the packed number to be ADDed to (MFAC).		
3.	SUB	$E7AA	(MFAC) ← (SFAC) − (MFAC)
	MFAC and SFAC already loaded; (SFAC will have (MFAC) SUBtracted from it.		
4.	LSUB	$E7A7	(MFAC) ← [Y,A] − (MFAC)
	MFAC is already loaded; (Y,A) points to the memory location of the packed number that will have (MFAC) SUBtracted from it.		
5.	MULT	$E982	(MFAC) ← (SFAC) * (MFAC)
	MFAC and SFAC already loaded; do the MULTiplication.		
6.	LMULT	$E97F	(MFAC) ← [Y,A] * (MFAC)
	MFAC is already loaded; (Y,A) points to the memory location of the packed number to be MULTiplied by (MFAC).		
7.	DIV	$EA69	(MFAC) ← (SFAC) / (MFAC)
	MFAC and SFAC already loaded; DIVide (SFAC) by (MFAC)		
8.	LDIV	$EA66	(MFAC) ← [Y,A] / (MFAC)
	MFAC is already loaded; (Y,A) points to the memory location of the packed number that will be DIVided by (MFAC).		
9.	POWER	$EE97	(MFAC) ← (SFAC)
	MFAC and SFAC already loaded; (SFAC) is raised to the (MFAC) power.		

TABLE 8.2 One-Operand Subroutines

	Name	Entry Point	Action Taken
1.	LOG	$E941	(MFAC) ← LOG(MFAC)
2.	SGNA	$EB82	(A) ← SGN(MFAC)
3.	SGN	$EB90	(MFAC) ← SGN(MFAC)
4.	ABS	$EBAF	(MFAC) ← ABS(MFAC)
5.	INT	$EC23	(MFAC) ← INT(MFAC)
6.	SQR	$EE8D	(MFAC) ← SQR(MFAC)
7.	MMFAC	$EED0	(MFAC) ← (MFAC)
8.	EXP	$$EF09	(MFAC) ← EXP(MFAC)
9.	RND	$EFAE	($C9 – $CD) ← a random number
10.	COS	$EFEA	(MFAC) ← COS(MFAC)
11.	SIN	$EFF1	(MFAC) ← SIN(MFAC)
12.	TAN	$F03A	(MFAC) ← TAN(MFAC)
13.	ATN	$F09E	(MFAC) ← ATN(MFAC)

TABLE 8.3 Conversion Subroutines

<table>
<tr><th></th><th>Name</th><th>Entry Point</th><th>Action Taken</th></tr>
<tr><td>1.</td><td>CPMIL</td><td>$EBF2</td><td>(Ext→MFAC) → ($85,$86)</td></tr>
<tr><td></td><td colspan="3">The extension byte is rounded into MFAC and then MFAC is converted to a two-byte integer in $85,$86. See Table 8.4 for rounding only.</td></tr>
<tr><td>2.</td><td>CLIM</td><td>$DEE9</td><td>[$A0,$A1] → MFAC</td></tr>
<tr><td></td><td colspan="3">$A0,$A1 contain the starting address of a two-byte integer that is converted to excess $80 notation in MFAC.</td></tr>
<tr><td>3.</td><td>CPMI</td><td>$E108</td><td>(MFAC) → ($A0,$A1)</td></tr>
<tr><td></td><td colspan="3">MFAC must be positive and less than 32,768; the two-byte integer is formed in $A0,$A1.</td></tr>
<tr><td>4.</td><td>CMI</td><td>$E10C</td><td>(MFAC) → ($A0,$A1)</td></tr>
<tr><td></td><td colspan="3">MFAC must be between −32,768 and 32,768; the two-byte integer is formed in (A0,A1). If integer is negative, it is in 2's-complement notation.</td></tr>
<tr><td>5.</td><td>CIAYM</td><td>$E2F2</td><td>(A,Y) → (MFAC)</td></tr>
<tr><td></td><td colspan="3">The integer in A and Y is converted to excess $80 notation in MFAC.</td></tr>
<tr><td>6.</td><td>CIYM</td><td>$E301</td><td>(Y) → (MFAC)</td></tr>
<tr><td></td><td colspan="3">The integer in Y is converted to excess $80 notation in MFAC.</td></tr>
<tr><td>7.</td><td>CMIX</td><td>$E6FB</td><td>(MFAC) → (X)</td></tr>
<tr><td></td><td colspan="3">MFAC is converted to a one-byte integer in X.</td></tr>
<tr><td>8.</td><td>CMIL</td><td>$E752</td><td>(MFAC) → ($50,$51)</td></tr>
<tr><td></td><td colspan="3">MFAC is converted to a two-byte integer in locations $50,$51.</td></tr>
<tr><td>9.</td><td>CIAM</td><td>$EB93</td><td>(A) → (MFAC)</td></tr>
<tr><td></td><td colspan="3">The integer in A is converted to excess $80 notation in MFAC.</td></tr>
<tr><td>10.</td><td>CMIE</td><td>$EBF2</td><td>(MFAC) → ($9E,$9F,$A0,$A1)</td></tr>
<tr><td></td><td colspan="3">MFAC is converted to a four-byte integer in locations $9E through $A1.</td></tr>
</table>

Table 8.4 Odds and Ends

	Name	*Entry Point*	*Action Taken*
1.	NOT	$DE98	(MFAC) ← NOT(MFAC)
2.	OR	$DF4F	(MFAC) ← (SFAC) OR (MFAC)
3.	AND	$DF55	(MFAC) ← (SFAC) AND (MFAC)
4.	COMP	$DF6A	(SFAC) is compared to (MFAC)

MFAC is set to 1, if the result of the comparison is true. MFAC is set to 0 if the comparison is false. The contents of location $16 determines the type of comparison to be done according to:

Contents of $16	Comparison to be done
1	(SFAC) > (MFAC)
2	(SFAC) = (MFAC)
3	(SFAC) < (MFAC)
4	(SFAC) > or = (MFAC)
5	(SFAC) not = (MFAC)
6	(SFAC) < or = (MFAC)

	Name	*Entry Point*	*Action Taken*
5.	MULTI	$E2B6	(Y,X) ← ($AE,$AD) * (accum,$64) The hex integer in $AE,$AD is multiplied by the hex integer in A and $64.
6.	ADDH	$E7A0	(MFAC) ← (MFAC) + 1/2
7.	NORM	$E82E	(MFAC) ← normalized(MFAC)
8.	MULTT	$EA39	(MFAC) ← (MFAC) * 10
9.	DIVT	$EA55	(MFAC) ← (MFAC)/10
10.	ROUND	$EB72	(MFAC) ← (ext) The extension byte, $AC, is rounded into MFAC.
11.	COMPA	$EBB2	[Y,A] – (MFAC) (A) = $01, if the subtraction is negative; (A) = $00, if the subtraction is zero; (A) = $FF, if the subtraction is positive.

TABLE 8.5 Moves

	Name	Entry Point	Action Taken
1.	MOVSI	$E9E3	[Y,A] → (SFAC)
2.	MOV5S	$E9E7	[$5F,$5E] → (SFAC)
3.	MOVMI	$EAF9	[Y,A] → (MFAC)
4.	MOV5M	$EAFD	[$5F,$5E] → (MFAC)
5.	MOVM98	$EB1E	(MFAC) → ($98,$99,$9A,$9B,$9C)
6.	MOVM93	$EB21	(MFAC) → ($93,$94,$95,$96,$97)
7.	MOVMZ	$EB23	(MFAC) → [X]
	Move (MFAC) to the zero page location pointed to by X.		
8.	MOVM8	$EB27	(MFAC) → [$86,$85]
9.	MOVMO	$EB2B	(MFAC) → [Y,X]
10.	MOVSM	$EB53	(SFAC) → (MFAC)
11.	MOVMS	$EB63	(MFAC) → (SFAC)

TABLE 8.6 Stack Moves

	Names	Entry Point	Action Taken
1.	MSTAK	$DE10	(ext→MFAC) then PUSH (MFAC) onto the stack. This takes six bytes.
	This subroutine ends with a JMP instead of an RTS. The JMP address is stored in ($5E,$5F) by the subroutine itself. When used with STAKS, put the return address on the stack, page part first, before calling MSTAK.		
2.	STAKS	$DE47	PULL stack, six bytes, into SFAC.
	This subroutine must be called with a JMP and not with a JSR. (You do see why don't you? The stack is used to store the return address for a JSR.) It concludes with an RTS, so there must be a proper return address on the stack before STAKS is called.		

TABLE 8.7 Floating-Point Numbers in ROM

	Base Ten Value	Starting Address	Contents
1.	1/4	$F070	7F 00 00 00 00
2.	1/2	$EE64	81 00 00 00 00
3.	−1/2	$E937	80 80 00 00 00
4.	SQR(1/2)	$E920	80 35 04 F3 34
5.	SQR(2)	$E932	81 35 04 F3 34
6.	1	$E913	81 00 00 00 00
7.	10	$EA50	84 20 00 00 00
8.	2*PI	$F06B	83 49 0F DA A2
9.	PI/2	$F066	81 49 0F DA A2
10.	NAT. LOG(2)	$E93C	80 31 72 17 F8
11.	1 BILLION	$ED14	9E 6E 6B 28 00
12.	−32,768	$E0FE	90 80 00 00 20
13.	0.434255942	$E919	7F 5E 56 CB 79
14.	0.576584541	$E91E	80 13 9B 0B 64
15.	0.961800759	$E923	80 76 38 93 16
16.	1.442695041	$EEDB	81 38 AA 3B 29
17.	2.885390074	$E928	82 38 AA 3B 20
18.	−42.78203928	$EA46	86 AB 20 CE E7
19.	2.980232E−8	$EE84	9C 00 00 00 0A
20.	1.014753E−37	$EE69	FA 0A 1F 00 00

APPENDIX E

SUMMARY OF ASSEMBLY LANGUAGE MNEMONICS

6502 MICROPROCESSOR INSTRUCTIONS

ADC	Add Memory to Accumulator with Carry
AND	"AND" Memory with Accumulator
ASL	Shift Left One Bit (Memory or Accumulator)
BCC	Branch on Carry Clear
BCS	Branch on Carry Set
BEQ	Branch on Result Zero
BIT	Test Bits in Memory with Accumulator
BMI	Branch on Result Minus
BNE	Branch on Result not Zero
BPL	Branch on Result Plus
BRK	Force Break
BVC	Branch on Overflow Clear
BVS	Branch on Overflow Set
CLC	Clear Carry Flag
CLD	Clear Decimal Mode
CLI	Clear Interrupt Disable Bit
CLV	Clear Overflow Flag
CMP	Compare Memory and Accumulator
CPX	Compare Memory and Index X
CPY	Compare Memory and Index Y
DEC	Decrement Memory by One
DEX	Decrement Index X by One
DEY	Decrement Index Y by One
EOR	"Exclusive-Or" Memory with Accumulator
INC	Increment Memory by One
INX	Increment Index X by One
INY	Increment Index Y by One
JMP	Jump to New Location
JSR	Jump to New Location Saving Return Address
LDA	Load Accumulator with Memory
LDX	Load Index X with Memory
LDY	Load Index Y with Memory
LSR	Shift Right one Bit (Memory or Accumulator)
NOP	No Operation
ORA	"OR" Memory with Accumulator
PHA	Push Accumulator on Stack
PHP	Push Processor Status on Stack
PLA	Pull Accumulator from Stack
PLP	Pull Processor Status from Stack
ROL	Rotate One Bit Left (Memory or Accumulator)
ROR	Rotate One Bit Right (Memory or Accumulator)
RTI	Return from Interrupt
RTS	Return from Subroutine
SBC	Subtract Memory from Accumulator with Borrow
SEC	Set Carry Flag
SED	Set Decimal Mode
SEI	Set Interrupt Disable Status
STA	Store Accumulator in Memory
STX	Store Index X in Memory
STY	Store Index Y in Memory
TAX	Transfer Accumulator to Index X
TAY	Transfer Accumulator to Index Y
TSX	Transfer Stack Pointer to Index X
TXA	Transfer Index X to Accumulator
TXS	Transfer Index X to Stack Pointer
TYA	Transfer Index Y to Accumulator

THE FOLLOWING NOTATION APPLIES TO THIS SUMMARY:

A	Accumulator
X, Y	Index Registers
M	Memory
$\bar{C}$	Borrow
P	Processor Status Register
S	Stack Pointer
✓	Change
—	No Change
+	Add
$\wedge$	Logical AND
-	Subtract
$\veebar$	Logical Exclusive Or
↑	Transfer From Stack
↓	Transfer To Stack
→	Transfer To
←	Transfer To
V	Logical OR
PC	Program Counter
PCH	Program Counter High
PCL	Program Counter Low
OPER	Operand
#	Immediate Addressing Mode

FIGURE 1. ASL-SHIFT LEFT ONE BIT OPERATION

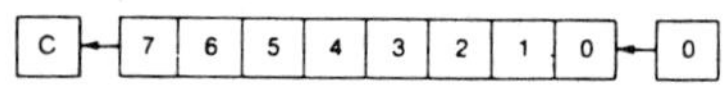

FIGURE 2. ROTATE ONE BIT LEFT (MEMORY OR ACCUMULATOR)

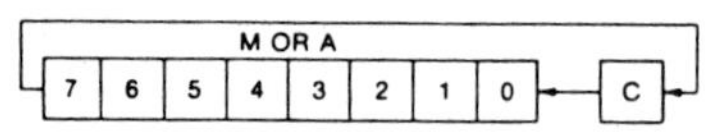

FIGURE 3.

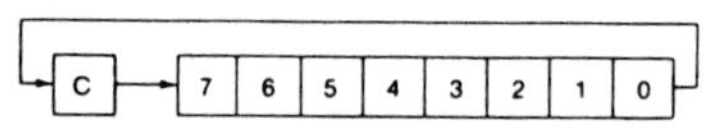

NOTE 1: BIT — TEST BITS

Bit 6 and 7 are transferred to the status register. If the result of A $\wedge$ M is zero then Z=1, otherwise Z=0.

PROGRAMMING MODEL

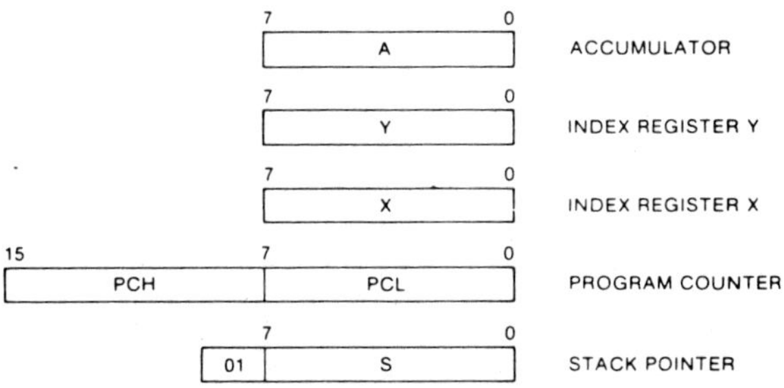

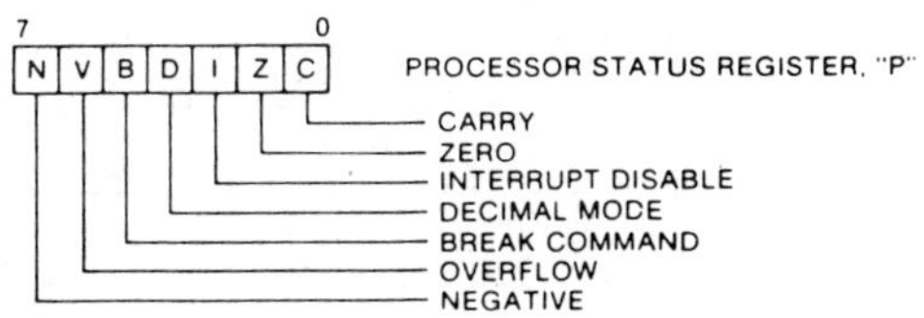

INSTRUCTION CODES

Name Description	Operation	Addressing Mode	Assembly Language Form	HEX OP Code	No. Bytes	"P" Status Reg. N Z C I D V
ADC Add memory to accumulator with carry	A·M·C → A.C	Immediate	ADC #Oper	69	2	√√√− −√
		Zero Page	ADC Oper	65	2	
		Zero Page.X	ADC Oper.X	75	2	
		Absolute	ADC Oper	6D	3	
		Absolute.X	ADC Oper.X	7D	3	
		Absolute.Y	ADC Oper.Y	79	3	
		(indirect.X)	ADC (Oper.X)	61	2	
		(Indirect).Y	ADC (Oper).Y	71	2	
AND "AND" memory with accumulator	A ∧ M → A	Immediate	AND #Oper	29	2	√√− − − −
		Zero Page	AND Oper	25	2	
		Zero Page.X	AND Oper.X	35	2	
		Absolute	AND Oper	2D	3	
		Absolute.X	AND Oper.X	3D	3	
		Absolute.Y	AND Oper.Y	39	3	
		(Indirect.X)	AND (Oper.X)	21	2	
		(Indirect).Y	AND (Oper).Y	31	2	
ASL Shift left one bit (Memory or Accumulator)	(See Figure 1)	Accumulator	ASL A	0A	1	√√√− − −
		Zero Page	ASL Oper	06	2	
		Zero Page.X	ASL Oper.X	16	2	
		Absolute	ASL Oper	0E	3	
		Absolute.X	ASL Oper.X	1E	3	
BCC Branch on carry clear	Branch on C=0	Relative	BCC Oper	90	2	− − − − − −

Note 1 Bits 6 and 7 are transferred to the status register if the result of A ∧ M is 0, Z = 1; otherwise Z = 0
Note 2 A BRK command cannot be masked by setting I

Name Description	Operation	Addressing Mode	Assembly Language Form	HEX OP Code	No. Bytes	"P" Status Reg. N Z C I D V
BCS Branch on carry set	Branch on C=1	Relative	BCS Oper	B0	2	------
BEQ Branch on result zero	Branch on Z=1	Relative	BEQ Oper	F0	2	------
BIT Test bits in memory with accumulator	A ∧ M, M_7 → N, M_6 → V	Zero Page Absolute	BIT* Oper BIT* Oper	24 2C	2 3	M_7√ M_6
BMI Branch on result minus	Branch on N=1	Relative	BMI Oper	30	2	------
BNE Branch on result not zero	Branch on Z=0	Relative	BNE Oper	D0	2	------
BPL Branch on result plus	Branch on N=0	Relative	BPL oper	10	2	------
BRK Force Break	Forced Interrupt PC+2 ↓ P ↓	Implied	BRK*	00	1	---1--
BVC Branch on overflow clear	Branch on V=0	Relative	BVC Oper	50	2	------
BVS Branch on overflow set	Branch on V=1	Relative	BVS Oper	70	2	------
CLC Clear carry flag	0 → C	Implied	CLC	18	1	--0---
CLD Clear decimal mode	0 → D	Implied	CLD	D8	1	----0-
CLI	0 → I	Implied	CLI	58	1	---0--
CLV Clear overflow flag	0 → V	Implied	CLV	B8	1	----- 0

CMP
Compare memory and
accumulator
	A — M	Immediate
		Zero Page
		Zero Page, X
		Absolute
		Absolute,X
		Absolute,Y
		(Indirect,X)
		(Indirect),Y
			CMP #Oper
			CMP Oper
			CMP Oper,X
			CMP Oper
			CMP Oper,X
			CMP Oper,Y
			CMP (Oper,X)
			CMP (Oper),Y
				C9
				C5
				D5
				CD
				DD
				D9
				C1
				D1
					2
					2
					2
					3
					3
					3
					2
					2
						√√√---

CPX Compare memory and index X	X — M	Immediate Zero Page Absolute	CPX #Oper CPX Oper CPX Oper	E0 E4 EC	2 2 3	√√√---
CPY Compare memory and index Y	Y — M	Immediate Zero Page Absolute	CPY #Oper CPY Oper CPY Oper	C0 C4 CC	2 2 3	√√√---
DEC Decrement memory by one	M — 1 → M	Zero Page Zero Page,X Absolute Absolute,X	DEC Oper DEC Oper,X DEC Oper DEC Oper,X	C6 D6 CE DE	2 2 3 3	√√----
DEX Decrement index X by one	X — 1 → X	Implied	DEX	CA	1	√√----
DEY Decrement index Y by one	Y — 1 → Y	Implied	DEY	88	1	√√----

Name Description	Operation	Addressing Mode	Assembly Language Form	HEX OP Code	No. Bytes	"P" Status Reg N Z C I D V
EOR "Exclusive-Or" memory with accumulator	A V M → A	Immediate	EOR #Oper	49	2	√√----
		Zero Page	EOR Oper	45	2	
		Zero Page,X	EOR Oper,X	55	2	
		Absolute	EOR Oper	4D	3	
		Absolute,X	EOR Oper,X	5D	3	
		Absolute,Y	EOR Oper,Y	59	3	
		(Indirect,X)	EOR (Oper,X)	41	2	
		(Indirect),Y	EOR (Oper),Y	51	2	
INC Increment memory by one	M + 1 → M	Zero Page	INC Oper	E6	2	√√----
		Zero Page,X	INC Oper,X	F6	2	
		Absolute	INC Oper	EE	3	
		Absolute,X	INC Oper,X	FE	3	
INX Increment index X by one	X + 1 → X	Implied	INX	E8	1	√√----
INY Increment index Y by one	Y + 1 → Y	Implied	INY	C8	1	√√----
JMP Jump to new location	(PC+1) → PCL (PC+2) → PCH	Absolute	JMP Oper	4C	3	------
		Indirect	JMP (Oper)	6C	3	
JSR Jump to new location saving return address	PC+2 ↓ (PC+1) → PCL (PC+2) → PCH	Absolute	JSR Oper	20	3	------
LDA Load accumulator with memory	M → A	Immediate	LDA #Oper	A9	2	√√----
		Zero Page	LDA Oper	A5	2	
		Zero Page,X	LDA Oper,X	B5	2	
		Absolute	LDA Oper	AD	3	
		Absolute,X	LDA Oper,X	BD	3	
		Absolute,Y	LDA Oper,Y	B9	3	
		(Indirect,X)	LDA (Oper,X)	A1	2	
		(Indirect),Y	LDA (Oper),Y	B1	2	
LDX Load index X with memory	M → X	Immediate	LDX #Oper	A2	2	√√----
		Zero Page	LDX Oper	A6	2	
		Zero Page,Y	LDX Oper,Y	B6	2	
		Absolute	LDX Oper	AE	3	
		Absolute,Y	LDX Oper,Y	BE	3	
LDY Load index Y with memory	M → Y	Immediate	LDY #Oper	A0	2	√√----
		Zero Page	LDY Oper	A4	2	
		Zero Page,X	LDY Oper,X	B4	2	
		Absolute	LDY Oper	AC	3	
		Absolute,X	LDY Oper,X	BC	3	
LSR Shift right one bit (memory or accumulator)	(See Figure 1)	Accumulator	LSR A	4A	1	0√√---
		Zero Page	LSR Oper	46	2	
		Zero Page,X	LSR Oper,X	56	2	
		Absolute	LSR Oper	4E	3	
		Absolute,X	LSR Oper,X	5E	3	
NOP No operation	No Operation	Implied	NOP	EA	1	------
ORA "OR" memory with accumulator	A V M → A	Immediate	ORA #Oper	09	2	√√----
		Zero Page	ORA Oper	05	2	
		Zero Page,X	ORA Oper,X	15	2	
		Absolute	ORA Oper	0D	3	
		Absolute,X	ORA Oper,X	1D	3	
		Absolute,Y	ORA Oper,Y	19	3	
		(Indirect,X)	ORA (Oper,X)	01	2	
		(Indirect),Y	ORA (Oper),Y	11	2	

Name Description	Operation	Addressing Mode	Assembly Language Form	HEX OP Code	No. Bytes	"P" Status Reg. N Z C I D V
PHA Push accumulator on stack	A↓	Implied	PHA	48	1	−−−−−−
PHP Push processor status on stack	P↓	Implied	PHP	08	1	−−−−−−
PLA Pull accumulator from stack	A↑	Implied	PLA	68	1	√√−−−−
PLP Pull processor status from stack	P↑	Implied	PLP	28	1	From Stack
ROL Rotate one bit left (memory or accumulator)	(See Figure 2)	Accumulator Zero Page Zero Page,X Absolute Absolute,X	ROL A ROL Oper ROL Oper,X ROL Oper ROL Oper,X	2A 26 36 2E 3E	1 2 2 3 3	√√√−−−
ROR Rotate one bit right (memory or accumulator)	(See Figure 3)	Accumulator Zero Page Zero Page,X Absolute Absolute,X	ROR A ROR Oper ROR Oper,X ROR Oper ROR Oper,X	6A 66 76 6E 7E	1 2 2 3 3	√√√−−−
RTI Return from interrupt	P↑PC↑	Implied	RTI	40	1	From Stack
RTS Return from subroutine	PC↑, PC+1 → PC	Implied	RTS	60	1	−−−−−−
SBC Subtract memory from accumulator with borrow	A − M − $\bar{C}$ → A	Immediate Zero Page Zero Page,X Absolute Absolute,X Absolute,Y (Indirect,X) (Indirect),Y	SBC #Oper SBC Oper SBC Oper,X SBC Oper SBC Oper,X SBC Oper,Y SBC (Oper,X) SBC (Oper),Y	E9 E5 F5 ED FD F9 E1 F1	2 2 2 3 3 3 2 2	√√√−−√
SEC Set carry flag	1 → C	Implied	SEC	38	1	−−1−−−
SED Set decimal mode	1 → D	Implied	SED	F8	1	−−−−1−
SEI Set interrupt disable status	1 → I	Implied	SEI	78	1	−−−1−−
STA Store accumulator in memory	A → M	Zero Page Zero Page,X Absolute Absolute,X Absolute,Y (Indirect,X) (Indirect),Y	STA Oper STA Oper,X STA Oper STA Oper,X STA Oper,Y STA (Oper,X) STA (Oper),Y	85 95 8D 9D 99 81 91	2 2 3 3 3 2 2	−−−−−−
STX Store index X in memory	X → M	Zero Page Zero Page,Y Absolute	STX Oper STX Oper,Y STX Oper	86 96 8E	2 2 3	−−−−−−
STY Store index Y in memory	Y → M	Zero Page Zero Page,X Absolute	STY Oper STY Oper,X STY Oper	84 94 8C	2 2 3	−−−−−−
TAX Transfer accumulator to index X	A → X	Implied	TAX	AA	1	√√−−−−

Name Description	Operation	Addressing Mode	Assembly Language Form	HEX OP Code	No. Bytes	"P" Status Reg. N Z C I D V
TAY Transfer accumulator to index Y	A → Y	Implied	TAY	A8	1	√√----
TSX Transfer stack pointer to index X	S → X	Implied	TSX	BA	1	√√----
TXA Transfer index X to accumulator	X → A	Implied	TXA	8A	1	√√----
TXS Transfer index X to stack pointer	X → S	Implied	TXS	9A	1	------
TYA Transfer index Y to accumulator	Y → A	Implied	TYA	98	1	√√----

HEX OPERATION CODES

00 — BRK
01 — ORA — (Indirect, X)
02 — NOP
03 — NOP
04 — NOP
05 — ORA — Zero Page
06 — ASL — Zero Page
07 — NOP
08 — PHP
09 — ORA — Immediate
0A — ASL — Accumulator
0B — NOP
0C — NOP
0D — ORA — Absolute
0E — ASL — Absolute
0F — NOP
10 — BPL
11 — ORA — (Indirect), Y
12 — NOP
13 — NOP
14 — NOP
15 — ORA — Zero Page, X
16 — ASL — Zero Page, X
17 — NOP
18 — CLC
19 — ORA — Absolute, Y
1A — NOP
1B — NOP
1C — NOP
1D — ORA — Absolute, X
1E — ASL — Absolute, X
1F — NOP
20 — JSR
21 — AND — (Indirect, X)
22 — NOP
23 — NOP
24 — BIT — Zero Page
25 — AND — Zero Page
26 — ROL — Zero Page
27 — NOP
28 — PLP
29 — AND — Immediate
2A — ROL — Accumulator
2B — NOP
2C — BIT — Absolute
2D — AND — Absolute
2E — ROL — Absolute
2F — NOP
30 — BMI
31 — AND — (Indirect), Y
32 — NOP
33 — NOP
34 — NOP
35 — AND — Zero Page, X
36 — ROL — Zero Page, X
37 — NOP
38 — SEC
39 — AND — Absolute, Y
3A — NOP
3B — NOP
3C — NOP
3D — AND — Absolute, X
3E — ROL — Absolute, X
3F — NOP
40 — RTI
41 — EOR — (Indirect, X)
42 — NOP
43 — NOP
44 — NOP
45 — EOR — Zero Page
46 — LSR — Zero Page
47 — NOP
48 — PHA
49 — EOR — Immediate
4A — LSR — Accumulator
4B — NOP
4C — JMP — Absolute
4D — EOR — Absolute
4E — LSR — Absolute
4F — NOP
50 — BVC
51 — EOR (Indirect), Y
52 — NOP
53 — NOP
54 — NOP
55 — EOR — Zero Page, X
56 — LSR — Zero Page, X
57 — NOP
58 — CLI
59 — EOR — Absolute, Y
5A — NOP
5B — NOP
5C — NOP
5D — EOR — Absolute, X
5E — LSR — Absolute, X
5F — NOP
60 — RTS
61 — ADC — (Indirect, X)
62 — NOP
63 — NOP
64 — NOP
65 — ADC — Zero Page
66 — ROR — Zero Page
67 — NOP
68 — PLA
69 — ADC — Immediate
6A — ROR — Accumulator
6B — NOP
6C — JMP — Indirect
6D — ADC — Absolute
6E — ROR — Absolute
6F — NOP
70 — BVS
71 — ADC — (Indirect), Y
72 — NOP
73 — NOP
74 — NOP
75 — ADC — Zero Page, X
76 — ROR — Zero Page, X
77 — NOP
78 — SEI
79 — ADC — Absolute, Y
7A — NOP
7B — NOP
7C — NOP
7D — ADC — Absolute, X NOP
7E — ROR — Absolute, X NOP
7F — NOP
80 — NOP
81 — STA — (Indirect, X)
82 — NOP
83 — NOP
84 —STY — Zero Page
85 — STA — Zero Page
86 — STX — Zero Page
87 — NOP
88 — DEY
89 — NOP
8A — TXA
8B — NOP
8C — STY — Absolute

8D — STA — Absolute
8E — STX — Absolute
8F — NOP
90 — BCC
91 — STA — (Indirect), Y
92 — NOP
93 — NOP
94 — STY — Zero Page, X
95 — STA — Zero Page, X
96 — STX — Zero Page, Y
97 — NOP
98 — TYA
99 — STA — Absolute, Y
9A — TXS
9B — NOP
9C — NOP
9D — STA — Absolute, X
9E — NOP
9F — NOP
A0 — LDY — Immediate
A1 — LDA — (Indirect, X)
A2 — LDX — Immediate
A3 — NOP
A4 — LDY — Zero Page
A5 — LDA — Zero Page
A6 — LDX — Zero Page
A7 — NOP
A8 — TAY
A9 — LDA — Immediate
AA — TAX
AB — NOP
AC — LDY — Absolute
AD — LDA — Absolute
AE — LDX — Absolute
AF — NOP
B0 — BCS
B1 — LDA — (Indirect), Y
B2 — NOP
B3 — NOP
B4 — LDY — Zero Page, X
B5 — LDA — Zero Page, X
B6 — LDX — Zero Page, Y
B7 — NOP
B8 — CLV
B9 — LDA — Absolute, Y
BA — TSX
BB — NOP
BC — LDY — Absolute, X
BD — LDA — Absolute, X
BE — LDX — Absolute, Y
BF — NOP
C0 — CPY — Immediate
C1 — CMP — (Indirect, X)
C2 — NOP
C3 — NOP
C4 — CPY — Zero Page
C5 — CMP — Zero Page
C6 — DEC — Zero Page
C7 — NOP
C8 — INY
C9 — CMP — Immediate
CA — DEX
CB — NOP
CC — CPY — Absolute
CD — CMP — Absolute
CE — DEC — Absolute
CF — NOP
D0 — BNE
D1 — CMP — (Indirect), Y
D2 — NOP
D3 — NOP
D4 — NOP
D5 — CMP — Zero Page, X
D6 — DEC — Zero Page, X
D7 — NOP
D8 — CLD
D9 — CMP — Absolute, Y
DA — NOP
DB — NOP
DC — NOP
DD — CMP — Absolute, X
DE — DEC — Absolute, X
DF — NOP
E0 — CPX — Immediate
E1 — SBC — (Indirect, X)
E2 — NOP
E3 — NOP
E4 — CPX — Zero Page
E5 — SBC — Zero Page
E6 — INC — Zero Page
E7 — NOP
E8 — INX
E9 — SBC — Immediate
EA — NOP
EB — NOP
EC — CPX — Absolute
ED — SBC — Absolute
EE — INC — Absolute
EF — NOP
F0 — BEQ
F1 — SBC — (Indirect), Y
F2 — NOP
F3 — NOP
F4 — NOP
F5 — SBC — Zero Page, X
F6 — INC — Zero Page, X
F7 — NOP
F8 — SED
F9 — SBC — Absolute, Y
FA — NOP
FB — NOP
FC — NOP
FD — SBC — Absolute, X
FE — INC — Absolute, X
FF — NOP

APPENDIX F

TEXT AND GRAPHICS NOTES

TABLE 7.2

Location	*Effect*
$C050	Display graphics
$C051	Display text
$C052	Full screen
$C053	Mixed screen
$C054	Page 1
$C055	Page 2
$C056	Lo-res graphics
$C057	Hi-res graphics

TABLE 10.1 Text-Page Addressing

L#	Pag1 Hex	Pag1 Dec	Pag2 Hex	Pag2 Dec	0 $00	1 $01	2 $02	3 $03	4 $04	5 $05	6 $06	7 $07	8 $08	9 $09	10 $0A	11 $0B	12 $0C	13 $0D	14 $0E	15 $0F	16 $10	17 $11	18 $12	19 $13	20 $14	21 $15	22 $16	23 $17	24 $18	25 $19	26 $1A	27 $1B	28 $1C	29 $1D	30 $1E	31 $1F	32 $20	33 $21	34 $22	35 $23	36 $24	37 $25	38 $26	39 $27
0	$400	1204	$800	2048																																								
1	$480	1152	$880	2176																																								
2	$500	1280	$900	2304																																								
3	$580	1408	$980	2432																																								
4	$600	1536	$A00	2560																																								
5	$680	1664	$A80	2688																																								
6	$700	1792	$B00	2816																																								
7	$780	1920	$B80	2944																																								
8	$428	1064	$828	2088																																								
9	$4A8	1192	$8A8	2216																																								
10	$528	1320	$928	2344																																								
11	$5A8	1448	$9A8	2472																																								
12	$628	1576	$A28	2600																																								
13	$6A8	1704	$AA8	2728																																								
14	$728	1832	$B28	2856																																								
15	$7A8	1960	$BA8	2984																																								
16	$450	1104	$850	2128																																								
17	$4D0	1232	$850	2128																																								
18	$550	1360	$950	2384																																								
19	$5D0	1488	$9D0	2512																																								
20	$650	1616	$A50	2640																																								
21	$6D0	1744	$AD0	2768																																								
22	$750	1872	$B50	2896																																								
23	$7D0	2000	$BD0	3024																																								

TABLE 10.2 Lo-Res Colors

Hex	*Dec*	*Color*	*Hex*	*Dec*	*Color*
\$0	0	Black	\$8	8	Brown
\$1	1	Magenta	\$9	9	Orange
\$2	2	Dark blue	\$A	10	Gray 2
\$3	3	Purple	\$B	11	Pink
\$4	4	Dark green	\$C	12	Light green
\$5	5	Gray 1	\$D	13	Yellow
\$6	6	Medium blue	\$E	14	Aquamarine
\$7	7	Light blue	\$F	15	White

TABLE 10.3 Lo-Res Subroutines

	Name	*Entry Point*	*Action Taken*
1.	CLRSCR	\$F832	Clears the entire (full screen) low-res screen.
2.	CLRTOP	\$F836	Clears the top (mixed screen) low-res screen.
3.	SETCOL	\$F864	Set color to use for plotting. Color number (\$0–\$F) is found in X.
4.	PLOT	\$F800	Plots a block whose vertical position is found in A and whose horizontal position is found in Y.
5.	HLINE	\$F819	Draws a horizontal line of blocks at vertical position given in A, from horizontal position given in Y rightward to horizontal position given in \$2C.
6.	VLINE	\$F828	Draws a vertical line of blocks at horizontal position given in Y, from vertical position given in A downward to vertical position given in \$2C.
7.	SCRN	\$F871	Reads the color of the block whose vertical position is given in A and whose horizontal position is given in Y. The color is returned in A.

TABLE 10.4 Hi-Res Page Addresses

L#	Pag1 Hex	Pag1 Dec	Pag2 Hex	Pag2 Dec	$00 0	$01 1	$02 2	$03 3	$04 4	$05 5	$06 6	$07 7	$08 8	$09 9	$0A 10	$0B 11	$0C 12	$0D 13	$0E 14	$0F 15	$10 16	$11 17	$12 18	$13 19	$14 20	$15 21	$16 22	$17 23	$18 24	$19 25	$1A 26	$1B 27	$1C 28	$1D 29	$1E 30	$1F 31	$20 32	$21 33	$22 34	$23 35	$24 36	$25 37	$26 38	$27 39
0	$2000	8192	$4000	16384																																								
8	$2080	8320	$4080	16512																																								
16	$2100	8448	$4100	16640																																								
24	$2180	8576	$4180	16767																																								
32	$2200	8704	$4200	16896																																								
40	$2280	8832	$4280	17024																																								
48	$2300	8960	$4300	17152																																								
56	$2380	9088	$4380	17280																																								
64	$2028	8232	$4028	16424																																								
72	$20A8	8360	$40A8	16552																																								
80	$2128	8488	$4128	16680																																								
88	$21A8	8616	$41A8	16808																																								
96	$2228	8744	$4228	16936																																								
104	$22A8	8872	$42A8	17064																																								
112	$2328	9000	$4328	17192																																								
120	$23A8	9128	$43A8	17320																																								
128	$2050	8272	$4050	16464																																								
136	$20D0	8400	$40D0	16592																																								
144	$2150	8528	$4150	16720																																								
152	$21D0	8656	$41D0	16848																																								
160	$2250	8784	$4250	16976																																								
168	$22D0	8912	$42D0	17104																																								
176	$2350	9040	$4350	17232																																								
184	$23D0	9168	$43D0	17360																																								

TABLE 10.5 Seeing the pixels

Byte address	→	< $ 4 2 3 C >	h			
Bit number	→	0 1 2 3 4 5 6	i			
Place value	→	1 2 4 8 1 2 4	b			
Color hi-bit = 0	→	V G V G V G V	i			
Color hi-bit = 1	→	B O B O B O B	t			What you see
Keypress		Contents			Hex	in color
1		1 0 0 0 0 0 0	0	→	01	Violet dot
2		0 1 0 0 0 0 0	0	→	02	Green dot
3		1 1 0 0 0 0 0	0	→	03	White fat dot
4		0 0 1 0 0 0 0	0	→	04	Violet dot
5		1 0 1 0 0 0 0	0	→	05	Violet bar
6		0 1 1 0 0 0 0	0	→	06	White fat dot
7		1 1 1 0 0 0 0	0	→	07	VWG smear
8		0 0 0 1 0 0 0	0	→	08	Green dot
9		1 0 0 1 0 0 0	0	→	09	V G dots
10		0 1 0 1 0 0 0	0	→	0A	Green bar
11		1 1 0 1 0 0 0	0	→	0B	WG bar
12		0 0 1 1 0 0 0	0	→	0C	White fat dot
13		1 0 1 1 0 0 0	0	→	0D	VW smear
14		0 1 1 1 0 0 0	0	→	0E	White bar
15		1 1 1 1 0 0 0	0	→	0F	White bar
16		0 0 0 0 1 0 0	0	→	10	Violet dot
17		1 0 0 0 1 0 0	0	→	11	V dot blk bar V dot
.		You can see the			.	
.		pattern now.			.	
.		The next			.	
.		interesting			.	
.		patterns occur			.	
.		when the hi-bit			.	
.		comes on and			.	
.		the colors			.	
.		change.			.	
.						
127		1 1 1 1 1 1 1	0	→	7F	V dot blk bar V dot
128		0 0 0 0 0 0 0	1	→	80	All black!
129		1 0 0 0 0 0 0	1	→	81	Blue dot
130		0 1 0 0 0 0 0	1	→	82	Orange dot
131		1 1 0 0 0 0 0	1	→	83	White fat dot
.					.	
.		Got the			.	
.		picture?			.	
.					.	

TABLE 10.6 Hi-Res Screen Line Numbers, and the Addresses of the Left Edge of the Screen

	Top Third				Middle Third				Bottom Third		
L#	Hex	Pag1	Pag2	L#	Hex	Pag1	Pag2	L#	Hex	Pag1	Pag2
0	$00	$2000	$4000	64	$40	$2028	$4028	128	$80	$2050	$4050
1	$01	$2400	$4400	65	$41	$2428	$4428	129	$81	$2450	$4450
2	$02	$2800	$4800	66	$42	$2828	$4828	130	$82	$2850	$4850
3	$03	$2C00	$4C00	67	$43	$2C28	$4C28	131	$83	$2C50	$4C50
4	$04	$3000	$5000	68	$44	$3028	$5028	132	$84	$3050	$5050
5	$05	$3400	$5400	69	$45	$3428	$5428	133	$85	$3450	$5450
6	$06	$3800	$5800	70	$46	$3828	$5828	134	$86	$3850	$5850
7	$07	$3C00	$5C00	71	$47	$3C28	$5C28	135	$87	$3C50	$5C50
8	$08	$2080	$4080	72	$48	$20A8	$40A8	136	$88	$20D0	$40D0
9	$09	$2480	$4480	73	$49	$24A8	$44A8	137	$89	$24D0	$44D0
10	$0A	$2880	$4880	74	$4A	$28A8	$48AB	138	$8A	$28D0	$48D0
11	$0B	$2C80	$4C80	75	$4B	$2CA8	$4CA8	139	$8B	$2CD0	$4CD0
12	$0C	$3080	$5080	76	$4C	$30A8	$50A8	140	$8C	$30D0	$50D0
13	$0D	$3480	$5480	77	$4D	$34A8	$54A8	141	$8D	$34D0	$54D0
14	$0E	$3880	$5800	78	$4E	$38A8	$58A8	142	$8E	$38D0	$58D0
15	$0F	$3C80	$5C80	79	$4F	$3CA8	$5CA8	143	$8F	$3CD0	$5CD0
16	$10	$2100	$4100	80	$50	$2128	$4128	144	$90	$2150	$4150
17	$11	$2500	$4500	81	$51	$2528	$4528	145	$91	$2550	$4550
18	$12	$2900	$4900	82	$52	$2928	$4928	146	$92	$2950	$4950
19	$13	$2D00	$4D00	83	$53	$2D28	$4D28	147	$93	$2D50	$4D50
20	$14	$3100	$5100	84	$54	$3128	$5128	148	$94	$3150	$5150
21	$15	$3500	$5500	85	$55	$3528	$5528	149	$95	$3550	$5550
22	$16	$3900	$5900	86	$56	$3928	$5928	150	$96	$3950	$5950
23	$17	$3D00	$5D00	87	$57	$3D28	$5D28	151	$97	$3D50	$5D50
24	$18	$2180	$4180	88	$58	$21A8	$41A8	152	$98	$21D0	$41D0
25	$19	$2580	$4580	89	$59	$25A8	$45A8	153	$99	$25D0	$45D0
26	$1A	$2980	$4980	90	$5A	$29A8	$49A8	154	$9A	$29D0	$49D0
27	$1B	$2D80	$4D80	91	$5B	$2DA8	$4DA8	155	$9B	$2DD0	$4DD0
28	$1C	$3180	$5180	92	$5C	$31A8	$51A8	156	$9C	$31D0	$51D0
29	$1D	$3580	$5580	93	$5D	$35A8	$55A8	157	$9D	$35D0	$55D0
30	$1E	$3980	$5980	94	$5E	$39A8	$59A8	158	$9E	$39D0	$59D0
31	$1F	$3D80	$5D80	95	$5F	$3DA8	$5DA8	159	$9F	$3DD0	$5DD0
32	$20	$2200	$4200	96	$60	$2228	$4228	160	$A0	$2250	$4250
33	$21	$2600	$4600	97	$61	$2628	$4628	161	$A1	$2650	$4650
34	$22	$2A00	$4A00	98	$62	$2A28	$4A28	162	$A2	$2A50	$4A50
35	$23	$2E00	$4E00	99	$63	$2E28	$4E28	163	$A3	$2E50	$4E50
26	$24	$3200	$5200	100	$64	$3228	$5228	164	$A4	$3250	$5250
37	$25	$3600	$5600	101	$65	$3628	$5628	165	$A5	$3650	$5650
38	$26	$3A00	$5A00	102	$66	$3A28	$5A28	166	$A6	$3A50	$5A50
39	$27	$3E00	$5E00	103	$67	$3E28	$5E28	167	$A7	$3E50	$5F.50
40	$28	$2280	$4280	104	$68	$22A8	$42A8	168	$A8	$22D0	$42D0
41	$29	$2680	$4680	105	$69	$26A8	$46A8	169	$A9	$26D0	$46D0
42	$2A	$2A80	$4A80	106	$6A	$2AA8	$4AA8	170	$AA	$2AD0	$4AD0
43	$2B	$2E80	$4E80	107	$6B	$2EA8	$4EA8	171	$AB	$2ED0	$4ED0
44	$2C	$3280	$5280	108	$6C	$32A8	$52A8	172	$AC	$32D0	$52D0
45	$2D	$3680	$5680	109	$6D	$36A8	$56A8	173	$AD	$36D0	$56D0
46	$2E	$3A80	$5A80	110	$6E	$3AA8	$5AA8	174	$AE	$3AD0	$5AD0
47	$2F	$3E80	$5E80	111	$6F	$3EA8	$5EA8	175	$AF	$3ED0	$5ED0
48	$30	$2300	$4300	112	$70	$2328	$4328	176	$B0	$2350	$4350
49	$31	$2700	$4700	113	$71	$2728	$4728	177	$B1	$2750	$4750
50	$32	$2B00	$4B00	114	$72	$2B28	$4B28	178	$B2	$2B50	$4B50
51	$33	$2F00	$4F00	115	$73	$2F28	$4F28	179	$B3	$2F50	$4F50
52	$34	$3300	$5300	116	$74	$3328	$5328	180	$B4	$3350	$5350
53	$35	$3700	$5700	117	$75	$3728	$5728	181	$B5	$3750	$5750
54	$36	$3B00	$5B00	118	$76	$3B28	$5B28	182	$B6	$3B50	$5B50
55	$37	$3F00	$5F00	119	$77	$3F28	$5F28	183	$B7	$3F50	$5F50
56	$38	$2380	$4380	120	$78	$23A8	$43A8	184	$B8	$23D0	$43D0
57	$39	$2780	$4780	121	$79	$27A8	$47A8	185	$B9	$27D0	$47D0
58	$3A	$2B80	$4B80	122	$7A	$2BA8	$4BA8	186	$BA	$2BD0	$4BD0
59	$3B	$2F80	$4F80	123	$7B	$2FA8	$4FA8	187	$BB	$2FD0	$4FD0
60	$3C	$3300	$5300	124	$7C	$33A8	$53A8	188	$BC	$33D0	$53D0
61	$3D	$3780	$5780	125	$7D	$37A8	$57A8	189	$BD	$37D0	$57D0
62	$3E	$3B80	$5B80	126	$7E	$3BA8	$5BA8	190	$BE	$3BD0	$5BD0
63	$3F	$3F80	$5F80	127	$7F	$3FA8	$5FA8	191	$BF	$3FD0	$5FD0

INDEX

— V —

— X —

— Y —

— Z —

13047 **1-2-3 Go!**
Julie Bingham

10924 **Starting With UNIX**
P.J. Brown

10355 **CP/M and the Personal Computer**
Thomas A. Dwyer and Margot Critchfield

05092 **Microcomputer Graphics for the Apple Computer**
Roy E. Myers

14775 **Applesoft BASIC Toolbox**
Larry G. Wintermeyer

10341 **Pascal: A Problem Solving Approach**
Elliot B. Koffman

10158 **Pascal from BASIC**
Peter Brown

06577 **Pascal for BASIC Programmers**
Charles Seiter and Robert Weiss

12080 **Looking at Lisp**
Tony Hasemer

00105 **Marketing Your Software**
William Nisen, Allan Schmidt, and Ira Alterman

14276 **The Integrated Software Book**
Jules Gilder

11507 **Dr. C. Wacko Presents Applesoft BASIC and the Whiz-Bang Miracle Machine**
David Heller and John Johnson